The Best of the Wine Country

A witty, opinionated and remarkably useful guide to California's vinelands

By Don W. Martin and Betty Woo Martin

Pine Cone Press • Columbia, California

OTHER BOOKS BY DON & BETTY MARTIN:

The Best of San Francisco • Chronicle Books © 1986, revised 1990

The Best of the Gold Country • Pine Cone Press © 1987, reprinted 1990, revised 1992

San Francisco's Ultimate Dining Guide • Pine Cone Press © 1988

The Best of Arizona • Pine Cone Press © 1990

Inside San Francisco • Pine Cone Press © 1991

Coming to Arizona • Pine Cone Press © 1991

Library of Congress Cataloging-in-Publication Data

Martin, Don and Betty—

The Best of the Wine Country.

Includes index.

1. California—Description & Travel (California Wine Country)—Guidebooks. 2. California—History (California wine industry).

TP557 641.2

Library of Congress card catalog number 91-90367

ISBN:0-942053-02-8

Cartography and icons • **Jil Weil**

Title page art & Illustrations • **Bob Shockley**

Photography • **Don W. Martin**

The Cover • Fall brings brilliant colors to a 110-year-old Petit Sirah vineyard in northern Sonoma County's Russian River Valley. The distinctive triple towers of Hop Kiln Winery rise in the background.

CONTENTS

MAPS

FOREWORD

Don Martin and I have been friends for many years, and we have seen many changes in the wine industry during those years. However, one thing remains unchanged: an interest in visiting the Wine Country.

There was a time when this interest was focused mostly on the Napa Valley, when the only food available was from a few old family restaurants. If you wanted to stay overnight, you had better have a friend with an extra room, or be willing to put up with a second-rate motel.

Well, those are from the not-so-good old days, as far as winery visitors are concerned. The number of places to eat and stay has multiplied and moved upscale dramatically. And the number of visitors has increased geometrically.

The Wine Country now offers everything from fancy resorts and convention facilities to some of the best restaurants in California. We now have our share of foreign ownership in the wine industry, which has brought wine and food flavors never dreamed of twenty years ago. And people have a choice of many wine-producing regions, which offer not only interesting wineries but some great wines.

There was a time when I could boast of having been in the door of the great majority of California's wineries. Today there are wineries that I may have heard of, but I'd have to check a phone book to find them—even some in Sonoma and Napa. There were about 240 wineries in California in 1970; today there are more than 800.

With all of these changes, how can winery visitors find their way around without some help? This book takes an honest approach to the problem, giving people direction and choices as they visit the state's many Wine Countries. I live here, and I plan to keep it within reach.

By the way, here's another important thing about ***The Best of the Wine Country.*** The authors have kept the tempo light, and they poke a little fun at people who take wine too seriously. Wine should add enjoyment to a meal, not complicate it.

Life is complicated enough. A glass of wine, as well as Don and Betty's guidebook, will help ease the pressure.

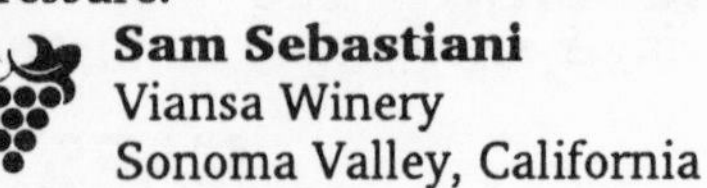

Sam Sebastiani
Viansa Winery
Sonoma Valley, California

This book is dedicated—with deep gratitude—to the authors of the Twenty-first Amendment to the Constitution of the United States of America.

WARNING: When used as directed, wine enhances food, reduces stress, encourages camaraderie, enlivens conversation and kindles romance. Used in moderation, it has been shown to aid digestion, promote good health and improve one's disposition. Recommended dosage is two glasses per meal. Excessive usage is unwise, potentially unhealthy and decidedly uncivilized.

"Quickly, bring me a beaker of wine, so that I may wet my brain and say something clever." —Aristophanes

INTRODUCTION

"Fine fruit flavors over a steely base. It's a serious wine that secretly just wants to have fun."

—Taster's description of a Domaine de la Bousquette Blanc de Noir

This book was written for people who want to explore California's wine country and learn more about wine. It was not written for wine writers. In fact, it might offend some of these Colombard commentators, since it has a little fun at their expense.

In flooding their tasting descriptions with silly adjectives, some of these Riesling reporters peddle more confusion than useful information.

Really. Can you imagine a Cabernet that is "heavy on the tongue with a leathery finish and a slight hint of basil?" Try to picture a Pinot Noir with a big nose. (A late harvest Jimmy Durante?)

Betty and I chuckle when these Riesling reporters try to bury us in a hailstorm of hyperbole. So, we begin each chapter of this book by quoting one of their more memorable tasting descriptions. Each is authentic, found in the rich repository of contemporary wine writing.

These Semillon scribes *do* have a lot to tell us. By reading their newspaper columns or reviews in ***The Wine Spectator***, we can learn what interesting wines have been released, which vintner is winning all the medals and what dynamite Zinfandel is priced under ten dollars. But many of these, writers, it seems, get paid by the adjective.

We **are** earnest about wine, incidentally. I've been a student of the California wine industry for thirty years, and I've sipped Sirah with serious intent since the age of consent. I was an active wine writer briefly, peddling my prose to Vintage Magazine and significant other publications. But I soon tired of searching for the ultimate adjective to properly portray the pedigree of a Pinot. To quote Carlo Rossi (or at least his ad agency):

"I'd rather drink my wines than talk about them."

And that's the subject of this book: discovering California wineries and drinking their wines—from Sonoma Sirah to Paso Robles Pinot.

There's no scarcity of books about the state's wine industry. However, some tell us more about the winemaker's relatives than we ever wanted to know; others offer encyclopedic listings of every winery in the state. Many focus on the Napa and Sonoma valleys, although California's winelands stretch from Mendocino to Temecula.

What you hold in your hand is a wine country *guidebook*, designed to steer you to more than 250 of California's more appealing wineries and tasting rooms. Like our other guides, it's selective. Instead of covering every corner of the state, we focus on areas with wineries in reasonable concentration. We won't send you to a remote corner of the San Joaquin Valley for a sip of generic sauterne.

Further, we include only wineries offering tasting and/or tours without prior arrangement. Thus, you can toss this book into the glove compartment of your Belchfire V-Six and head for the nearest vineyard. We also suggest nearby restaurants and lodgings, and other area attractions.

In researching this book, we solicited nothing but information. We visited tasting rooms as tourists, sipped the wine, took the tours, asked a few questions and left. We dined covertly, made our own sleeping arrangements and paid our admission at attractions and museums. Thus, ***The Best of the Wine Country*** is full of opinions—but they're all ours.

THE WINERIES

We select wineries which we feel will offer you an interesting tasting and/or touring experience. These range from fascinating to funky, from regal to rustic. Our judgments are personal and arbitrary; exclusion from this book should not be regarded as an affront or an oversight.

You'll note little symbols beside each winery listing. They mean just what you think they mean:

T • Tasting: the winery offers gratis sips of its product; a dollar sign following the symbol indicates a charge for wine samples.

GT • Guided tours are offered, generally on a specific schedule.

GTA • Appointment needed for guided tours.

ST • Self-guiding tours: signs, arrows and/or graphics will lead you through the winery.

CT • Casual tours, which can range from a peek into the aging cellars to an invitation to browse about on your own. Ask the tasting host or hostess for specifics.

• Picnic area is located near the winery. Most tasting rooms are licensed to sell and uncork a bottle for your lunch. It definitely *gauche* to bring your own bottle.

• A **gift shop** or good giftware and/or specialty food selection is located in or near the tasting room. Most tasting rooms sell a few winery-related logo items, but we don't use the symbol unless the assortment is reasonably extensive.

R • A **restaurant** is part of the winery or immediately adjacent.

At the end of each listing, under **Tasting notes,** we discuss the variety and general style of wines produced at the winery. We attempt no in-depth critiques, since quality will vary from one vintage to the next. And under **Vintners choice,** we let the winemakers have their say, asking them to select their favorite wine. When they insist on saying "All of our wines are great," or they decline to make a choice, we omit this listing.

Since we're talking about "the best" of the wine country, we have a little presumptuous fun by listing—at the end of each winery section—places that offer the most interesting tasting rooms, nicest picnic areas, best gift shops most informative tours and best wine values.

WINE COUNTRY DINING

Our intent here is to provide a selective dining sampler, not a complete list. We focus more on restaurants right in the wine country, rather than those in nearby cities.

We used several methods to select cafe candidates for possible inclusion: Inquiry among locals, suggestions from friends and from other guidebooks, and our own experiences. Comments are based more on overviews of food and service, not on the proper doneness of a specific pork chop.

Of course, one has to be careful about recommending restaurants. Obviously, people's tastes differ, and it's difficult to judge a cafe by a single meal. A chef might have a bad night, or a waitress might be recovering from one. Thus, your dining experience may be quite different from ours.

We graded the restaurants with one to four little wedges, for food quality, service and ambiance.

Δ **Adequate**—A clean cafe with basic but edible grub.

ΔΔ **Good**—A well-run establishment that offers a fine meal and good service.

ΔΔΔ **Very good**—Substantially above average; excellent fare, served with a smile in a fine dining atmosphere.

ΔΔΔΔ **Excellent**—We've found heaven, and it has a good wine list!

Price ranges are based on the tab for an average dinner, including soup or salad (but not wine or dessert). Obviously, places serving only breakfast and/or lunch are priced accordingly.

$—Average dinner for one is $9 or less

$S—$10 to $14

$$$—$15 to $24

$$$$—$25 to $34

$$$$$—Did you say you were buying?

Ø **Non-Smoking section** available in dining room. Double symbol means entire dining room is smoke-free.

Incidentally, many chefs go to bed with the chickens in the wine country, so dining hours are often earlier than in urban areas. Some in-vogue yuppie havens in Sonoma or the Napa Valley serve their souffles until suitable hours (and they charge San Francisco prices), but don't plan on pork chops much past 9 p.m. in Gilroy or Murphys.

VINELAND LODGINGS

We've checked most lodgings to insure that they're reasonably neat, clean and well run. We often rely on the judgment of the California State Automobile Association (AAA) because we respect its high standards. We also include some budget places that may fall short of Triple A ideals but still offer a clean room for a respite from wine sipping. Of course we can't anticipate changes in management or the maid's day off, but hopefully your surprises will be good ones.

Some of California's earliest bed and breakfast inns were established in the wine country, and their homey intimacy seems appropriate to the ambiance of the vinelands. We generally offer a good selection of them. We list only true B&Bs, not merely family homes with an extra room because the oldest son is out stomping grapes. With few exceptions, we've selected B&Bs only with four or more units.

Generally, we list lodgings that are in or near the vineyards, not those in neighboring cities. Again, we use our little wedges to rate them:

Δ **Adequate**—Clean and basic; don't expect anything fancy.

ΔΔ **Good**—A well-run establishment with comfortable beds and most essentials.

ΔΔΔ **Very good**—Substantially above average, with facilities such as a pool and spa.

ΔΔΔΔ **Excellent**—An exceptional lodging with beautifully-appointed rooms, often with a restaurant and resort facilities.

ΔΔΔΔΔ **Outstanding**—A world-class resort with full amenities.

Ø **Non-Smoking rooms** available. Double symbol means entire facility is smoke-free (common with bed & breakfast inns).

Price ranges are listed for rooms during high season—the most popular visitor months. Of course, many places reduce their rates during slower periods. Conversely, some hike their prices for peak holiday periods or local celebrations. Price codes below indicate the cost of a standard room for two during high season. All prices were furnished to us by the establishments.

$—a double for under $25
$$—$25 to $49
$$$—$50 to $74
$$$$—$75 to $99
$$$$$—$100 or more

It's always wise to make advance reservations. If you don't like the place and you're staying more than a day, you can always shop around after the first night and exchange lodgings.

MISCELLANY

Don't rely too much on times listed in this book because many places seem to change their hours more often than a dead-beat changes his address. Prices change, too—inevitably upward—so use those shown only as guidelines. Also, restaurants seem to suffer a rather high attrition rate, so don't be crushed if one that we recommended has become a laundromat by the time you get there.

We've cleverly edged this introduction section in a black border so you can thumb quickly back to it.

Enough talk. Let's go find a decent Zinfandel.

THANK YOU...

Nancy A. Light, director of communications for California's Wine Institute, and her predecessor **Sam Folsom** (now with Louis Martini Winery), for providing access to the institute's treasure trove of California wine and winery information. We add a special thanks to Nancy for catching some of our mistakes.

Norm Roby, former west coast editor of ***Vintage Magazine*** and now a ***Wine Spectator*** contributing editor, for publishing some of my first wine articles.

Lindy Lindquist, who hired me to help write winery newsletters, thus convincing me that I was not cut out for that sort of thing.

Kathleen Elizabeth Martin, former wine and gourmet foods specialist for Macy's California, for sharing her California wine knowledge.

Robert Mondavi for his efforts to convince America that wine should be regarded—not with awe or trepidation—but with simple respect. To quote Bob: "We view wine as an integral part of our culture, heritage and gracious way of life."

Justin Meyer, Napa Valley winemaker, for having the good sense to write a sensible book: ***Plain Talk about Fine Wine.***

David Darlington for authoring an eminently readable and informative book about our favorite wine: ***Angels' Visits: An Inquiry into the Mystery of Zinfandel***.

Millie Howie for steering us around northern Sonoma County in years past and helping us discover its fine wines and winemakers.

John and Jim Pedroncelli, northern Sonoma County winegrowers, and their former tasting room host **John Soule**, for introducing us to the simple honesty of Zinfandel.

Sam Sebastiani of Sonoma Valley for taking the time to sit with us on a ditch bank, bottle in hand, to talk about life, wine and the Sebastiani family legend.

The Ernie Fortino family, the "new immigrants" of Gilroy, for sharing their friendship, their enthusiasm and their honest wines.

A BIT ABOUT THE AUTHORS

This is the seventh guidebook by the husband and wife team of Don and Betty Martin. When not seeking the ultimate Zinfandel, Don devotes his waking hours to writing, photography and the operation of Pine Cone Press. He's been writing for a living since he was seventeen, starting with a weekly newspaper in Idaho. He served as a Marine correspondent in the Orient, worked for assorted California newspapers and functioned for several years as associate editor of the travel magazine of the San Francisco-based California State Automobile Association. He also contributes travel and wine articles and photos to assorted magazines and newspapers.

Wife Betty, equipped with the curious credentials of a doctorate in pharmacy and a California real estate broker's license, does much of the research for their travel books. She has sold travel articles and photos to various newspapers and magazines, and she has studied wines and food service at the hospitality management program of Columbia (California) College.

They make their home in Columbia State Historic Park, in the heart of the California gold country—and not far from some of the best of the wine country.

Nobody's perfect, but we try

This book is packed with thousands of facts, and a few of them are probably wrong. If you find an error in fact, or discover a great little place that deserves to be in the next edition, we'd like to know. We'd also like to learn your opinions of this book: What you liked and didn't like; what should have been included or ignored.

All who provide useful information will earn a free copy of the revised edition of ***The Best of the Wine Country*** or any other book on our list. (See the back of this book.)

Address your cards and letters to:
Pine Cone Press
P.O. Box 1494
Columbia, California 95310

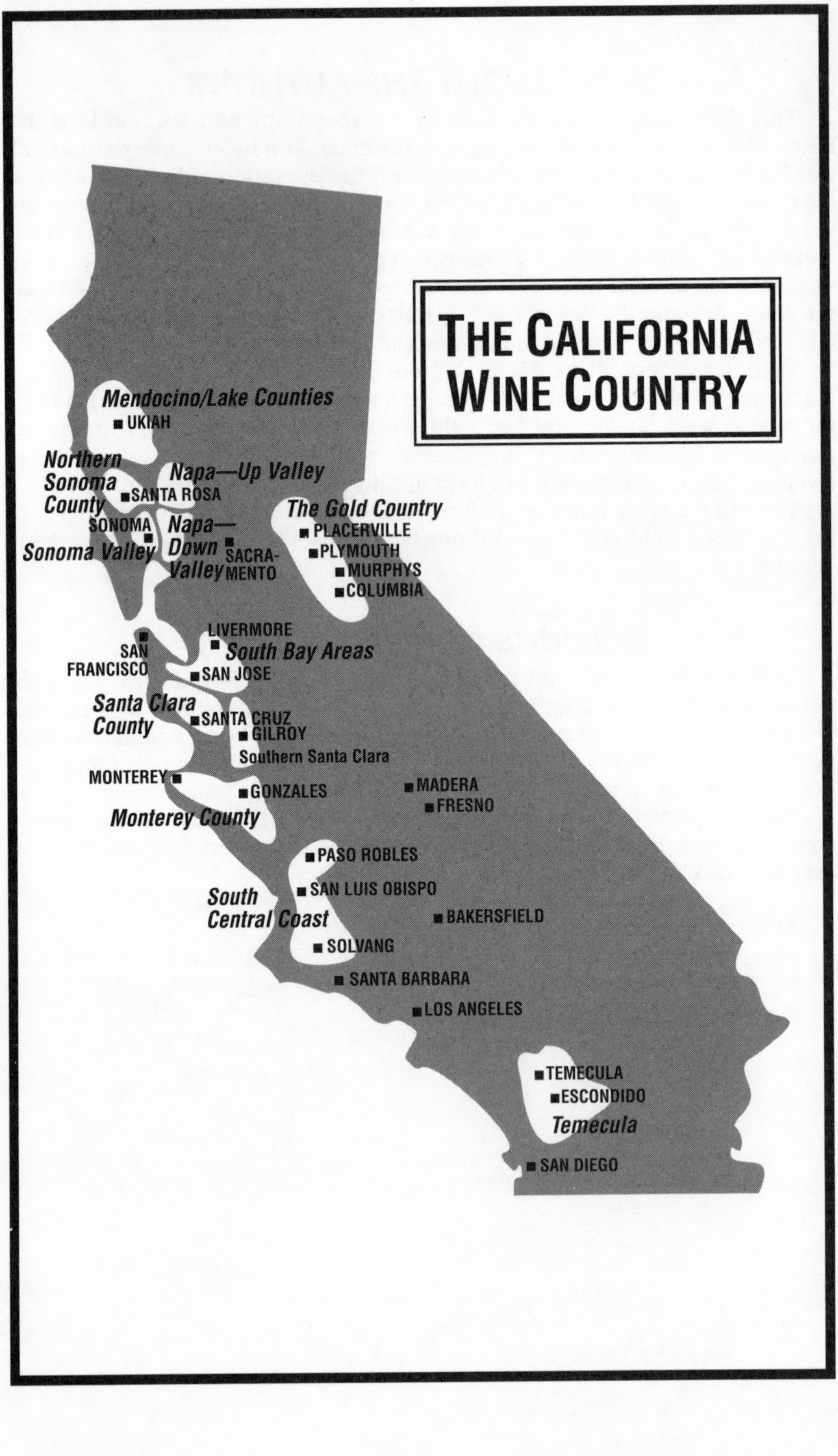
THE CALIFORNIA
WINE COUNTRY
Mendocino/Lake Counties
UKIAH
Northern
Sonoma
County
SANTA ROSA
Napa—Up Valley
SONOMA
Sonoma Valley
Napa—
Down
Valley
SACRA-
MENTO
The Gold Country
PLACERVILLE
PLYMOUTH
MURPHYS
COLUMBIA
SAN
FRANCISCO
LIVERMORE
South Bay Areas
SAN JOSE
Santa Clara
County
SANTA CRUZ
GILROY
Southern Santa Clara
MONTEREY
GONZALES
Monterey County
MADERA
FRESNO
PASO ROBLES
SAN LUIS OBISPO
South
Central Coast
BAKERSFIELD
SOLVANG
SANTA BARBARA
LOS ANGELES
TEMECULA
ESCONDIDO
Temecula
SAN DIEGO

"The wine is powerful but sleek; it expands across the palate like a fast car cruising a moonlit road, and disappears slowly, its tail-lights crimson in the pulsing summer night."

—Wine-taster's description of a Beringer Vineyards 1980 Reserve Cabernet Sauvignon.

Chapter One
CALIFORNIA: AMERICA'S WINELAND
It all started with *vitis vinifera*

This book was inspired not so much by a love for wineland geography as by an affection for the world's most civilized beverage.

My affair with wine began by accident, more than thirty years ago. While doing publicity for U.S. Marine Corps recruiting in San Francisco, I was invited along with other PR types to a tasting by California's Wine Institute. In my mind at the time, wine was just another beverage—something that occupied shelf space at the corner liquor store. My parents never drank alcohol, nor were they prohibitionists, so my attitude was neutral. I recall being a serious Scotch drinker at the time.

The wine tasting whetted both my appetite and my curiosity.

Although I couldn't tell a Chardonnay from a Charbono, I was intrigued by the almost reverent attitude that wine enthusiasts held for the stuff. With all that sipping and slurping and studied frowning, they seemed part of a mysterious cult. They used words like "nose", "finish" and "balance" in ways foreign to me. I wanted to learn more. Further, the idea of matching a particular beverage to food interested me, because I love good food.

My wife and I began visiting San Francisco Bay Area wineries, and we took wine study courses to learn more about this product. For a time, I was a freelance wine writer, but I ran out of adjectives long before I ran out of interesting wines.

The mystery is gone now, and we've learned to respect and appreciate this civilized beverage. And certainly, we've learned that the best place to become friends with wine is at the winery.

There, you can meet the winemaker, or at least a learned employee, who can discuss wine and unravel its mysteries. You can learn how they make the stuff, how and why they age it and how to best enjoy it with food. You'll also learn that most vintners are friendly, down-to-earth folk who don't worship their wine. They merely respect and enjoy it.

The greatest advantage of touring is obvious: you can try a variety of wines and decide which are easiest on your palate—and on your budget. For instance, you may prefer a lively Zinfandel or rich Gewürztraminer instead of the "noble wines" of Cabernet, Chardonnay, Pinot Noir and Riesling.

And where better to tour than in California? At last count, the state had nearly 800 wineries, producing 90 percent of America's wine. Wine grapes rank sixth among the state's agricultural products. Grapes of all types comprise California's second most valuable crop, exceeded only by dairy products. Wineries are a major tourist draw, as well. Some large Napa Valley establishments attract nearly 300,000 sippers a year.

Americans are wimps when it comes to drinking wine, however. U.S. per capita consumption is 3.73 gallons a year (1986 figures), compared with about 20 in France and Italy. However, wine drinking increased rapidly during the 1970s and 1980s as more Americans came to appreciate its value with food.

Where's the grapes?

And just where is California's wine country? As a matter of fact, wine grapes are grown in 45 of the state's 48 counties. However, premium grapes—those sensitive little fellows that require warm days, cool nights and well-drained soil—are much more limited.

Historically, most of California's premier wines have been produced in vineyards encircling the San Francisco Bay Area. North bay counties of Napa, Sonoma and Mendocino, and the Livermore and Santa Clara valleys to the south offer the proper conditions.

The northern counties are still major producers, but many south bay grapes have been squeezed out by the population crush, so vintners have sought new horizons. They're finding them in the Sierra Nevada foothills, in Monterey County, the central coast area between Paso Robles and Santa Barbara, and the Temecula Valley, north of San Diego.

These so-called premium growing areas produce only about 15 percent of California's total wine output. Most of the rest comes from the dry, hot and huge San Joaquin Valley. There, more hardy vines thrive to produce the huge—and generally drinkable—flood of jug wines.

Incidentally, when price supports were removed from wine a decade or so ago, some tasting rooms were faced with an awkward situation. Discount liquor stores sprang up quickly and tasters found they could get the stuff cheaper there.

That isn't necessarily so today. Many tasting rooms are meeting the challenge by offering their own discounts. In researching this book, we encountered numerous sales, with case markdowns ranging up to 30 percent.

Obviously, wineries like to sell their products at retail; thus the popularity of tasting rooms. Operators of larger wineries probably don't care where you buy their stuff, so long as you buy it. However, most of the smaller vintners' high quality wines aren't available at liquor outlets or supermarkets, so you'd best do your shopping at the source.

Besides, a tasting room nestled among the vines is a lot more interesting than a wine shelf nestled among the cabbages at Safeway.

In the beginning, somebody stepped on a grape

Historians debate which came first—wine or beer. Some scholars insist that beer was the first alcoholic beverage, since grain was cultivated before grapes. Others say wine came first because grapes are self-contained little alcohol factories. While beer has to be brewed from yeast and grain, grapes are coated with wild yeast and will ferment naturally when the skin is broken.

Stomp some grapes, step back, and you'll soon have wine. (Most winemakers, however, use cultured yeast to better control fermentation.)

"The wine industry certainly dates from at least 3000 B.C.," according to Maynard A. Amerine and Vernon L. Singleton's ***Wine: An Introduction*** (© 1977). "Some housewife probably left crushed grapes in a jar and found, a few days later, that an alcoholic product had been formed."

The discovery, in early 1991, of wine stains on the shards of a pre-Bronze Age Sumerian jar pushes the date back even further, to 3500 B.C.

The Tigris-Euphrates Valley in Iran, Iraq and Turkey is generally regarded as the cradle of agriculture and therefore of civilization. It's also the area where Noah supposedly parked his ark—on Turkey's Mount Ararat. According to Genesis 9:20-21, he "began to be a husbandman, and he planted a vineyard; and he drank of the wine and was drunken."

Thus, the Bible may have recorded history's first hangover.

Grapes grew wild in California, but early-day padres found them unsuitable for wine-making. They had to rely on unreliable shipments from New Spain (Mexico) for their essential altar wines.

Father Junipero Serra established the state's first mission at San Diego in 1769. However, some years passed before suitable grape vines—brought in from Mexico by way of Spain—were planted. The good padre wrote in 1781: "I hope that...the corn prospers and that the grape vines are living and thriving, for this lack of altar wine is becoming unbearable."

The vine in question, now called the mission grape, is a descendant of *vitis vinifera*. It's also the parent of Europe's great premium grapes, but these

ALL WINERIES OFFER CASE DISCOUNTS

had not yet found their way to California.

Although some regard Sonoma/Napa as the root of California viticulture, large-scale winemaking actually began in Los Angeles. Plantings were so common early in the 19th century that it was called "The City of Vineyards."

California's first full-time winemaker was Jean Louis Vignes, a Frenchman from Bordeaux. He arrived in Monterey by ship in 1831 and soon adjourned to Los Angeles, where he planted vineyards and established a major commercial operation. History records that he was the first to import European wine grapes. Equally important, he is credited with planting some of the first orange trees in California.

Vignes sold his orange and wine estate in 1855 to his nephews, Pierre and Jean Louis Sansevain. They became the state's leading wine merchants and established its first commercial sparkling wine operation. Then in 1862, the brothers quit their business and California's pioneer vineyards disappeared under spreading Los Angeles suburbs.

While not the first, Sonoma was the most important seat of the state's wine industry. The story involves an unlikely pair: an energetic young Mexican lieutenant and a flamboyant Hungarian count of questionable lineage.

In the years following Father Serra's arrival, the missions became vast agricultural empires. They were governed by the padres and worked by Indians who had been converted to Christianity—often unwillingly. Mexico won its independence from Spain in the 1820s and, some years later, it de-commissioned the missions. Their great landholdings were parceled out to favored soldiers and politicians.

Lieutenant Mariano Guadalupe Vallejo was sent to the most northern of the missions, San Francisco Solano in present-day Sonoma, to oversee its dissolution. The ambitious young officer established a military garrison and laid out a townsite. A good politician, he quickly attained the rank of military *commandante* of all northern California. And he picked up thousands of acres in Mexican land grants. The assertive Vallejo soon became a major producer of California wines.

The man from Hungary

Enter the visionary gentleman of dubious lineage. Agoston Haraszthy (*Har-RAS-they*) arrived in Sonoma in 1856, met General Vallejo and purchased land to start a vineyard. He had come to America in 1840 after fleeing his native Hungary, apparently for choosing the wrong side of a revolution. He was variously known as Colonel Haraszthy or Count Haraszthy, although the source of his military title is vague.

He certainly was an ambitious fellow, and a gad-about promoter. In the 16 years since touching American soil, he had founded the town of Sauk City, Wisconsin, crossed by wagon train to San Diego, dabbled in real estate, become a state assemblyman and later director of the U.S. Mint in San Francisco. He had attempted to raise wine grapes in Wisconsin, San Diego, San Francisco and San Mateo before finally finding the proper land and climate in Sonoma. The count and General Vallejo became fast friends. Two Haraszthy sons, in fact, married two Vallejo daughters.

Haraszthy's Buena Vista Farm became the most prosperous wine empire in America. He lived regally in a Pompeiian villa cresting a knoll above his vineyards. His greatest contribution to California viticulture was the impor-

HOW TO APPRECIATE A FINE WINE

All that sloshing and sniffing practiced by wine-tasters isn't supercilious foolishness. Many subtleties lurk in a bottle of fine wine. Only by following these steps can you discern all of the nuances of the essence of the grape.

See • Hold the glass up to the light and examine it for clarity. It should be—pardon the Nixon cliche—perfectly clear. Don't panic if you detect minute particles, however. They're probably harmless bits of cork or, in the case of aged reds, some tannin residue that was stirred up when the wine was poured.

Slosh • Coat the inside of the glass by swirling the wine vigorously (being careful, of course, that you don't slosh it all over the individual next to you).

Sniff • Hold the glass up to your nose and inhale deeply, drawing in all the wine's smells—referred to as the *nose* by the pros. The fresh, fruity fragrance of the grape is described as the *aroma*, while the more subtle dusky smell is the *bouquet*—the essence of fermentation and aging.

Sip and slurp • Your mother said this was bad manners, but it's the best way to taste wine: Take a sip, cradle it on your tongue, draw air over it, exhale through your nose, then swallow. This aeration—despite its odd sound—releases the wine's complex flavors. Your taste buds can detect only sweet, sour, salty and bitter. All the nuances of taste are in your nose, and mixing air with the wine helps bring out its subtleties.

A young white wine should taste fresh, crisp and fruity, while reds will be more complex and berry-like, perhaps with hints of wood from barrel-aging.

Some wine writers insist that they can detect cedar, cigar boxes, licorice, pencil shavings, pineapples, apricots, cassis, chocolate, pears, peaches, plums, eucalyptus and—good grief—even the suggestion of a sweaty saddle. We suspect, however, that they've just run short of adjectives. Or, perhaps they sampled too many wines.

tation of hundreds of thousands oif premium European grape cuttings. Many of these were made available to growers throughout the state.

The free-wheeling count's departure was appropriately bizarre. In 1868, restless for a new challenge, he went to Nicaragua to start a sugar cane plantation. Attempting to cross a stream, he fell into the water and vanished. Apparently, he was devoured by alligators.

Hard times for the grape

The wine industry which Haraszthy helped set into motion had to struggle during its formative years. Over-production and the depression of the 1870s dropped wine prices to ten cents a gallon. Then the industry was nearly ruined by the invasion of *phylloxera,* a louse that destroys grapevine roots. Toward the end of the century, an ironic solution was found: The roots of wild American grapes, which the European varieties had replaced, were resistant to the little bug. By grafting *vitis vinifera* cuttings onto *vitis californica* root stock, the wine industry was saved. For the moment, at least.

The 1906 San Francisco earthquake dealt the business a serious blow, both in and out of the wine country. Many Sonoma and Napa County wineries were ruined by the temblor, which in fact was centered north of San Francisco. Also, the city was the production and distribution center for much of California's wine, and the fire following the earthquake destroyed millions of gallons.

Then on January 16, 1920, the infamous Volstead Act further brutalized what was left of the industry. We know it as Prohibition, with a capital "P." Repeal, with a capital "R," came on December 5, 1933, when Utah became the 36th state to ratify the Twenty-First Amendment to the Constitution.

During that long dry spell, California wineries struggled mightily, and two-thirds of them closed. The rest survived by making sacramental wines and by selling grapes, since home winemaking was still legal. Particularly popular was a product with the wonderful name of Vine-Glo. It was a barrel of grape juice, complete with instructions for converting it to wine. Another product, a brick of compressed grape pomace, could be dissolved in water to create grape juice. A warning label stated:

"This beverage should be consumed within five days; otherwise it might ferment and become alcoholic."

The industry recovered slowly after Repeal. Thousands of acres of premium vines had been torn out and replaced with common grapes better suited to the production of Vine-Glo and wine bricks. Many Americans had gotten out of the wine-and-food habit. Further, the country was in the middle of the Depression. In 1934, several growers led by Napa's Louis Martini formed the Wine Institute to improve the quality of wine and promote its use. It's still the industry's leading voice.

World War II brought some financial respite to vintners. European wines were no longer available and the price of grapes went from $15 to $50 a ton. However a shortage of labor, containers and rail cars hampered growth. The industry didn't really get back on its feet until the Fifties. By the Seventies, it had become fashionable to serve wine with dinner and California's winemakers were off and running.

They haven't looked back, except to see if their competitor had somehow produced a better Chardonnay.

Winetalk: a quick study

A glossary in the back of this book contains a detailed listing of wine and winemaking terms. We present an abbreviated version here to guide you through the chapters ahead.

Acid — The tartaric and malic acid in a grape that give a wine its crisp after-taste.

Appellation — The term describes a legally defined grape-growing area, under the American Viticultural Area (AVA) system. For a label to bear an appellation designation, 85 percent of its grapes must come from that area, and the wine must be "fermented, manufactured and finished" there. Dry Creek, Carneros, Chalk Hill and Shenandoah Valley are typical California appellations. France's version—much older than ours—is *Appellation d'Origine Controlee* (AOC), which dictates the types of grapes that can be grown in each area. Typically, French wines are named for their appellation, while American premiums are named for the grape varietal.

Aroma — The smell of fruit in a wine. (See "bouquet" below.)

Balance — A catch-all term describing a wine in which nothing is out of balance: not too acidic, not too sweet, not too high in tannin.

Berry — To a vineyardist, grapes are berries; berry-like describes the flavor of the fruit in wine.

Big — No, it's not a large bottle. "Big" in winetalk refers to a wine with strong, complex flavor, full-bodied and often high in alcohol. Tasters use the expression "big nose" to describe a wine that yields a strong aroma and bouquet.

Body — The fullness of a wine, sometimes—but not always—referring to the viscosity or alcoholic content. A thin and watery wine lacks body.

Bouquet — The often complex smell of wine that comes from fermenting and aging, as opposed to aroma, which is the smell of the fruit.

Blush — A term describing a pink wine made from red grapes, usually Grenache, Zinfandel, Cabernet Sauvignon or Pinot Noir.

Breathing — The practice of letting a wine stand open so it absorbs oxygen, supposedly to enhance its aroma and taste. Experts disagree on its usefulness, but it's a harmless gesture to let your wine catch its breath.

Brilliant — Not a measure of the winemaker's cleverness, but the clarity of the wine. All good wines should be brilliant. So should a good winemaker, for that matter.

Bulk process — Cheap method of making sparkling wine by fermenting it in large sealed tanks to capture the bubbles.

Character — Term used to describe the good qualities of a wine. A poor wine, like a poor citizen, "lacks character."

Crush — It's often used as a noun in winetalk, referring to the harvest and subsequent crushing of wine grapes. "We had a good crush this year," a grower might say.

Dosage *(do-SAWJ)* — The bit of sugar syrup, brandy or aged wine added to champagne to make it less dry.

Dry — Crisp and not sweet or sour. In winetalk, it has nothing to do with lack of wetness.

Seven simple steps to winery touring success

1 • Plan your route in advance (which is why you bought this book) and set practical goals. Don't try to cover more than four or five wineries in a day. There is much to enjoy, to learn and to see in California's winelands. Why rush through them? Be selective. That's another reason you bought this book.

2 • If possible, hit the wine country on weekdays. This should be no great trick if you're on vacation. If you're limited to weekend visits, get an early start. It may go against your grain to start sipping at 10 a.m., but you're here to sample wines, not engage in social drinking. Most tasting rooms—even in busy Napa Valley—are virtually empty in the morning. The crowds hit after lunch and build until closing time.

3 • Plan for a picnic, since many wineries have picnic areas, often among the vines. Usually, you can find a deli in or near California's vinelands, and many tasting rooms also sell picnic fare. And don't be a plebeian; buy your picnic wine at the winery.

4 • Try to visit the wine country during the crush—again on weekdays. You can watch the proceedings and perhaps sample some of the grapes. At small wineries, you may even get to sip a little "must," the freshly crushed juice. The grape harvest ranges from late August through October, so call ahead to see what's being picked where. You'll find phone numbers with the listings in this book—still another good reason you bought it.

5 • Limit the number of samples you try at each winery. If you taste too many wines, their differences will begin to blur. So will your vision.

6 • Be sensible if you're the designated driver. Save the urge to party until you're safely back home, off the highway and close to the floor. Fortunately, only about two percent of people arrested for driving while intoxicated were drinking wine. Let's try to keep it that way.

Enology — The science of wine production, as opposed to viticulture, which is the science of grape growing and viniculture, the practice of growing *wine* grapes. (Classic spelling is *oenology*.)

Estate bottled — A wine in which all the grapes came from the vintner's "estate" or vineyards.

Finish — The aftertaste of a wine, created primarily by the acid. A crisp, properly balanced wine will have a "long, lingering finish"; a thin, watery one won't.

Flowery — The aroma and flavor of a wine that is more akin to blossoms than to the grapes.

Fresh — That rich, usually fruity taste of a young wine.

Fruity — The flavor of a wine that comes from the grape.

Horizontal tasting — No, it doesn't mean you've sampled too many wines. It's a comparative tasting of the same variety of wines from different vineyards. Vertical tasting is sampling the same variety of wines from different vintages.

Mèthode champenoise (*me-thoad sham-pen-WAH*) — The classic

French method of making sparkling wine, in which it is produced and aged in the same bottle.

Must — The liquid of freshly crushed grapes, on its way to becoming wine.

Noble grapes — The term—given somewhat arbitrarily—to Cabernet Sauvignon of Bordeaux, Pinot Noir and Chardonnay of Burgundy and Riesling of Germany.

Nose — The aroma and bouquet of a wine.

Oakey — Wine, usually red, with a strong flavor of the wood in which it was aged.

Off-dry — A winetaster's silly redundancy for slightly sweet.

Residual sugar — Sugar remaining in a wine to give it sweetness, usually measured by percentage. In table wines, fermentation can be stopped by lowering the temperature to kill the yeast cells, thus leaving residual sugar. In dessert wines, brandy is added, which pickles the yeast and stops fermentation.

Soft — A wine lacking harshness or rough edges.

Tannin — Organic acids found in plant matter. In wines, it comes primarily from the skins of grapes. Reds are higher in tannin because they're usually fermented with their skins. Tannin adds complexity—and an acidic harshness—to wine. Aging mellows these tannins while leaving the full, complex flavor. Don't be alarmed, but tannic acid also is used to treat leather, thus the word "tan."

U.C. Davis — You'll see this reference frequently on the pages that follow. The University of California at Davis, just west of Sacramento, pioneered the academic study of wine production in America. Many top winemakers and vineyardists are graduates. Fresno State University also offers major enology and viticultural programs.

Varietal — A word you'll encounter thousands of times. It simply means "variety," describing a wine made from a specific grape. Cabernet Sauvignon is a varietal; rosè is not. In most of Europe, wines are blended and named for the region in which they are produced. In America, wines are named for the primary grape therein. To be a "varietal," a wine must contain 75 percent of a particular variety of grape.

Viniculture — The science of growing grapes for wine production. Viticulture refers to grape-growing in general.

Vintage — The year in which grapes of a particular wine were harvested. A wine bottle can be "vintage dated" only if 95 percent of the grapes therein were harvested in that year. The harvest itself is sometimes called the "vintage."

Types of wine, premium and otherwise

The term "premium" refers to a wine made from one or more well-regarded grapes. It's often, but not always, made from a particular varietal.

Angelica — Sweet, ordinary dessert wine that originated in California, probably named for Los Angeles. It's sometimes made from the mission grape (see below).

Barbera (*bar-BEAR-ah*) — A red wine grape grown in northern Italy and to a lesser extent in California. Barbera is usually full-flavored but without the complexity of a Cabernet or Pinot Noir.

DECIPHERING A WINE LABEL

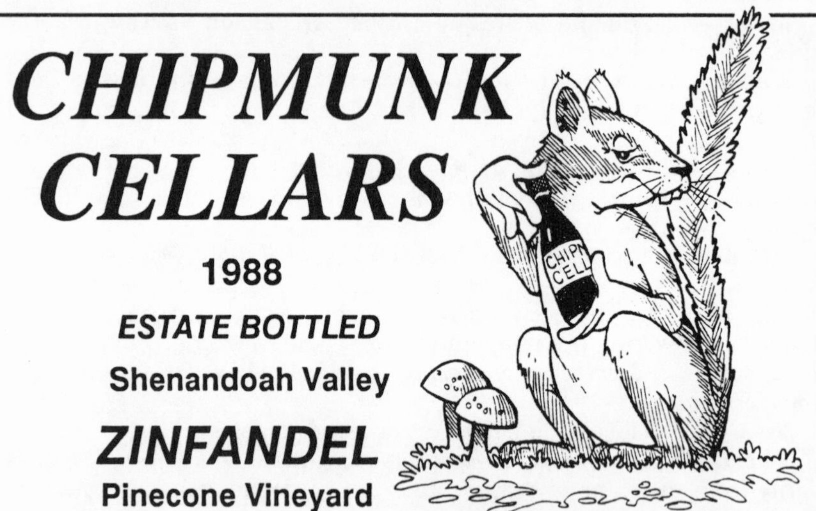

CHIPMUNK
CELLARS
1988
ESTATE BOTTLED
Shenandoah Valley
ZINFANDEL
Pinecone Vineyard

Produced & bottled by Chipmunk Cellars, Ltd.
Plymouth, California
Alcohol 13% by volume • contains sulfites

1988—A wine can be vintage dated only if 95% of the grapes were crushed in that year.

Estate Bottled means that all the grapes used in the wine came from vineyards owned or controlled by the winery.

Dry Creek Valley is an appellation or Approved Viticultural Area (AVA), an officially designated growing region; 85% of the grapes must be grown within that area.

Zinfandel: A varietal name can be used only if at least 75% of the wine came from that grape.

Pinecone Vineyard is a "designated vineyard." To be listed, at least 95% of the grapes must have come from that vineyard, which must be located in an AVA.

Produced and bottled indicates that at least 75% of the grapes were fermented by the bottling winery. "Made and bottled" requires that only 10% of the grapes be fermented by that winery. Such terms as "Vinted and bottled" or "Cellared and bottled" are non-specific. They don't require the bottler to have produced any of the wine.

Alcohol 13% by volume: This can vary 1.5% either way. To be sold as a table wine, the alcohol content must be between 7 and 14 percent.

Contains sulfites: This statement is required on American wine labels if sulfite content (naturally produced during fermentation and/or added to prevent spoilage) exceeds 10 parts per million. It does in most wines.

Beaujolais (*BO-sho-lay*) — In France, a wine from a specific district, near Burgundy. In California, the name refers to wine made from the Gamay grape, often labeled Gamay Beaujolais.

Blanc de blancs (*blawn-duh-blawn*) — The term describing white wine made from white grapes, usually applied to sparkling wine. And yes, it does seem redundant.

Blanc de noirs (*blawn-duh-nowar*) — White wine made from red (or black) grapes; literally "white from black," which makes more sense than "white from white."

Brut (*brute*) — One of the driest of champagnes.

Burgundy — In France, it refers to a specific wine producing region, famous for the Pinot Noir grape. In California, it means anything red.

Cabernet Sauvignon (*cab-air-nay sou-vin-YAWN*) — Considered the noblest of red wine grapes; the primary wine of a fine Bordeaux.

Carignan (*car-reen-YAN*) — Commonly planted red grape of medium quality; of southern French origin. Sometimes spelled "Carignane."

Chablis — A generic term in California, referring to any white wine. A specific growing region in France famous for its production of fine Chardonnay.

Champagne — A term describing sparkling wine in the United States. In the rest of the civilized world, it's applied only to effervescent wine produced in France's Champagne district. Some American winemakers honor this tradition and call their product sparkling wine.

Charbono — Red grape of Italian origin producing full-bodied, sometimes rough wine.

Chardonnay (*SHAR-doe-nay*) — One of the premiere white grapes. A good Chardonnay is dry, yet rich and full, sometimes spicy or nutty and with a hint of wood, since it's often barrel-aged. Sometimes called Pinot Chardonnay in California.

Chenin Blanc (*SHAY-nan blawn*) — White grape, producing a typically fruity wine.

Chianti (*kay-AN-tee*) — Italian red table wine, often from Tuscany, typified by full, berry-like flavor. Usually drunk young. In America, the term is loosely applied to any full-flavored, low-tannin wine. Spaghetti wine, if you will.

Colombard (*COL-lum-bahr*) — A French white grape, producing a full-bodied, usually high-acid wine. Often called French Colombard in California.

Fumè Blanc (*FU-may blawn*) — Literally "White Smoke," a name first used by Napa Valley's Robert Mondavi to describe a lush, subtly smoky-flavored white wine produced from the Sauvignon Blanc grape.

Generic — A wine of no particular pedigree, sometimes named for a wine-producing region of Europe, like Burgundy or Chablis.

Gewürztraminer (*Ge-WURZ-tra-mee-ner*) The world's most difficult-to-spell wine grape. Common in Germany, France's Alsace district and California. It's typically fruity, spicy and sometimes a bit sweet.

Green Hungarian — An ordinary white wine of unknown parentage, once common in California but now rare.

Grenache (*greh-NAHSH*) — Fruity southern French grape commonly used to make rosè wine in California. Sometimes labeled Grenache Rosè.

Gray Riesling — White wine grape of unknown parentage, since it isn't a riesling; first reference may have been at Wente Brothers Winery in the Livermore Valley.

Johannisberg Riesling — German white wine grape from the Rhine Valley. Typically fruity, usually fermented dry. It's a true Riesling, while many other grapes bearing that name are not.

Meritage — A term recently adopted by a group of California wineries to designate red or white premium wines blended from classic Bordeaux grape varieties. Red Meritage seems to be more common. A winery must join the Meritage Association to use the label, and must meet strict blending criteria. Fewer than 25 wineries qualify.

Merlot (*Mair-lo*) — Red grape producing a lush, full-flavored wine; often blended with Cabernet Sauvignon to ease its tannic edge, both in California and Bordeaux.

Petit Syrah or Sirah (*Puh-TEE see-RAW*) — Rather high-tannin red grape grown in California; of French origin.

Pinot Noir (*PEE-no nawahr*) — Classic French red grape; right up there with Cabernet; commonly grown in Burgundy. Thus in France, a great Burgundy is a great Pinot Noir.

Port — Sweet, fortified wine named for Orporto, the city in Portugal that is the center of the port trade.

Riesling (*REESE-ling*) — Noble white German grape predominately grown in the Rhine Valley. The name has come to be loosely associated with an assortment of white wines.

Rosè (*roe-ZAY*) — A pink wine made by drawing off a red grape's skins early in the fermenting process, since most of a wine's color comes from the skin. It is *never*—at least it should never be—a mixture of white and red wine.

Sauternes (*saw-TAIRN*) — French white wine, often sweet and usually golden. The term also is used to describe any number of generic sweet California wines; often spelled "Sauterne" here.

Sauvignon Blanc (*SO-veen-yawn blawn*) — It ranks with Chardonnay as one of the great French white wine grapes. Full bodied with a distinctive fruity bouquet.

Sec — French for dry (not sweet), yet it describes a sweeter style of champagne.

Sherry — Sweet or dry fortified wine whose name is derived from the Jerez district of Spain, where it originated.

Sylvaner — Premium white grape that originated in Germany or Austria.

Zinfandel — California's most widely planted premium red grape, sometimes called the mystery grape because of its uncertain origin. (See box in Chapter three.) The wine is typically fruity and can range from light and soft to complex and full-bodied; Zins usually are light in tannin, although those from older vines can be quite robust.

"Tannins in the background, flavors waiting to explode, a lady-like refinement poised to make a statement."

—Wine-taster's description of a 1985 Monogram Cabernet Sauvignon from Guenoc Winery, Middletown, Lake County

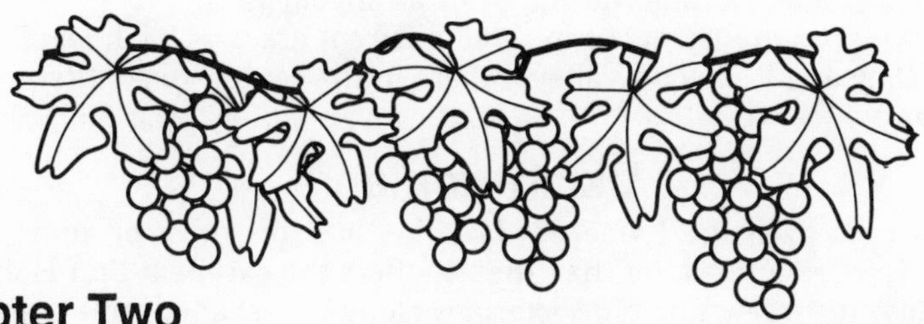

Chapter Two

MENDOCINO AND LAKE COUNTIES

The wine country's northern rim

Poised but not necessarily lady-like and certainly not ready to explode, we begin making our statement—about winery touring—at the top of the California Wine Country.

A few wineries are scattered farther north; one even resides in the redwoods around Arcata, north of Eureka. But that area is better known for clams and sawdust. For touring and tasting purposes, Mendocino and Lake counties offer California's northernmost grouping of vineyards and wineries.

The two areas are particularly appealing, for many of the wineries are in some of California's prettiest pastoral settings. Further, wines here have won more than their share of medals. In fact, Lake County boosters insist that their wineries have gleaned more awards per vineyard acre than any other region in the country.

MENDOCINO COUNTY

This area has been creating wines for more than a century, but until recently, most of it was bulk production. However, one Charles Wetmore sailed off to the Paris Exposition of 1899 with some of his Mendocino wines and sailed away with *le grand prix.*

Tryfon Lolonis and Adolph Parducci were two other Mendocino wine pioneers. Greek immigrant Lolonis planted vineyards in Redwood Valley in 1920; Italy's Parducci opened a Cloverdale winery in neighboring Sonoma County in 1916, then moved north to Mendocino's county seat of Ukiah in 1931. A Lolonis descendant is still making premium wines and the Parducci Winery thrives as the largest in the county.

Wine-making didn't become a serious growth industry until the early 1970s. Initially, most growers sold fruits of their labors to established Sonoma County wineries. Then, realizing that the Sonomans kept winning medals with Mendocino grapes, several producers began bottling their own wines. Weibel Vineyards provided a major incentive to winery growth in 1973 when it shifted much of its operation from crowded Alameda County to Mendocino and opened a sparkling new tasting room north of Ukiah.

Currently, about thirty Mendocino County wineries slap labels on their own bottles, and roughly half of these offer tasting to the passing public. Only Parducci offers a tour without prior arrangement .

Most wineries are clustered in three different areas—Ukiah-Hopland, Anderson Valley and Redwood Valley. All are in the central-to-southern reaches of the county.

Ukiah-Hopland

Ukiah calls itself the home of Masonite, but this town of about 13,000 residents is more interesting than that. It offers the excellent Sun House Historical Museum, a few fine old Victorians along tree-shaded streets and some serviceable restaurants. The county seat, Ukiah provides a good selection of shops and motels. Nearby Lake Mendocino is popular with boaters and campers.

Twelve miles south, tiny Hopland is turning its weathered storefronts into a charming tourist stop, offering several antique shops, boutiques and a couple of interesting cafes. The Hopland micro-brewery and Thatcher Hotel and Restaurant are particularly worth a visit. As you might imagine, hops were once the main crop here and one winery—Milano—occupies an old hop-drying shed.

A handful of wineries and several acres of vineyards are scattered in the green and golden contoured hills between Ukiah and Hopland. U.S. 101 loses its freeway status betwixt the towns and three wineries are just off the highway. Others have tasting rooms in Hopland. The assorted wineries offer a broad mix of reds and whites.

UKIAH-HOPLAND WINERY TOUR • Assuming you're driving north from the San Francisco Bay Area on U.S. 101, you'll encounter Hopland shortly after entering Mendocino County. Before you do, watch on your left for **Milano Winery,** just beyond the end of the freeway. From there, continue into **Hopland** for the tasting rooms of **Fetzer** and **Mendocino Vineyards** and the combined tasting facility for **McDowell, Jepson** and **Hidden Cellars.**

Continuing north from Hopland, you'll soon see **Jepson** on your left. Just beyond, turn west onto Henry Station Road and drive two miles to **Tijsseling Vineyards** on your left. Back on the highway, U.S. 101 regains freeway stature near **Ukiah**. Take the Talmage exit, go east to Ruddick-Cunningham Road and follow it to **Hidden Cellars,** which is in plain view, smack in the middle of a vineyard. Hop back on the freeway, follow it to Ukiah's northern edge, take Lake Mendocino Drive west and follow signs to **Parducci Wine Cellars.**

Milano Vineyards & Winery • T ⚔

14594 S. Highway 101, Hopland, CA 95449; (707) 744-1396. Daily 10 to 5; MC/VISA, AMEX. Most varieties tasted. A few wine-related gift items; no tours. Picnic area under arbor.

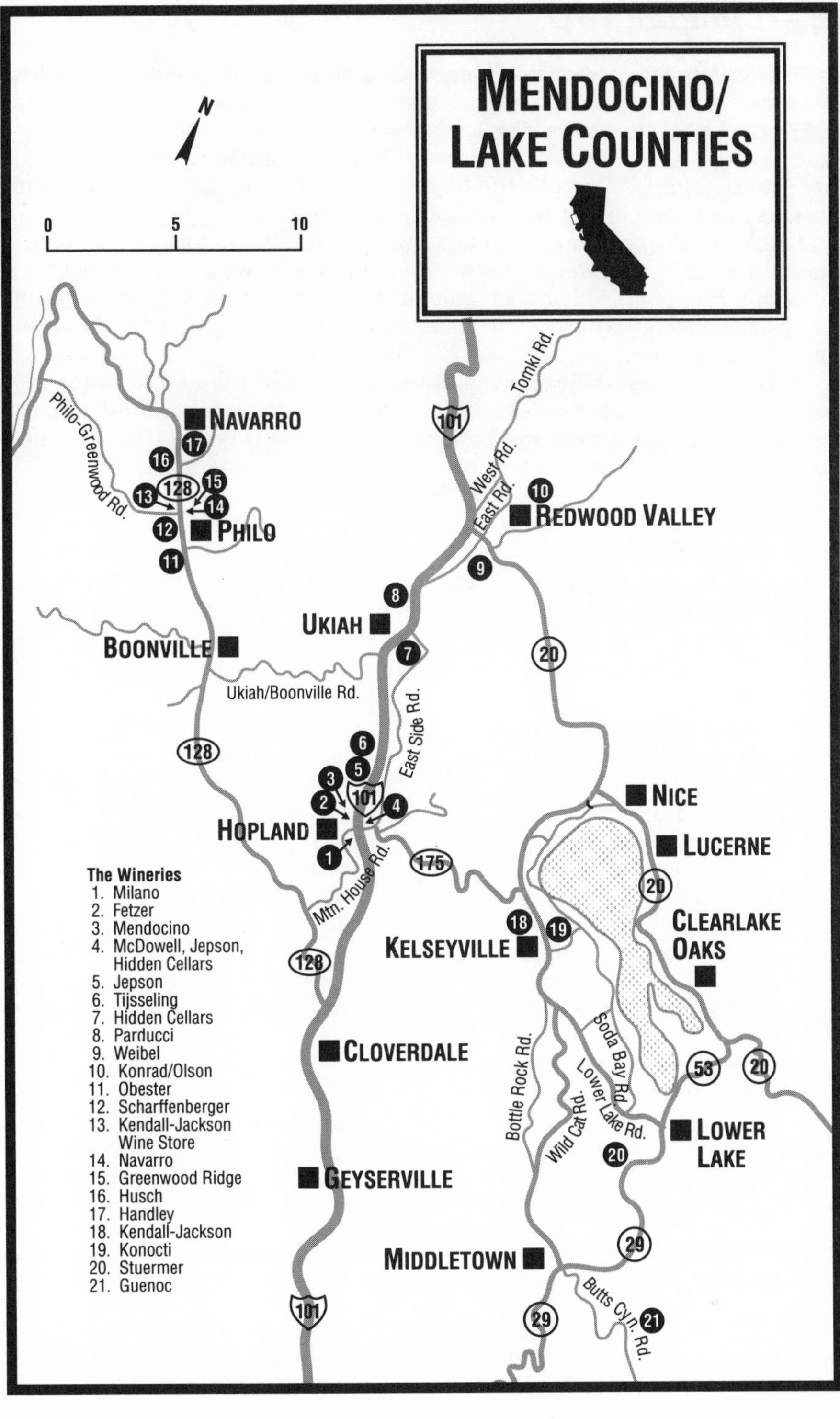

MENDOCINO/
LAKE COUNTIES
N
0
5
10
NAVARRO
PHILO
Philo-Greenwood Rd.
128
BOONVILLE
Ukiah/Boonville Rd.
UKIAH
101
West Rd.
East Rd.
Tomki Rd.
REDWOOD VALLEY
20
East Side Rd.
HOPLAND
Mtn. House Rd.
175
NICE
LUCERNE
CLEARLAKE
OAKS
KELSEYVILLE
CLOVERDALE
Bottle Rock Rd.
Soda Bay Rd.
Lower Lake Rd.
Wild Cat Rd.
53
LOWER
LAKE
GEYSERVILLE
MIDDLETOWN
29
Butts Cyn. Rd.
The Wineries
1. Milano
2. Fetzer
3. Mendocino
4. McDowell, Jepson, Hidden Cellars
5. Jepson
6. Tijsseling
7. Hidden Cellars
8. Parducci
9. Weibel
10. Konrad/Olson
11. Obester
12. Scharffenberger
13. Kendall-Jackson Wine Store
14. Navarro
15. Greenwood Ridge
16. Husch
17. Handley
18. Kendall-Jackson
19. Konocti
20. Stuermer
21. Guenoc

The Milone family's small winery is housed in one of the weathered hop kilns that once peppered this rural landscape. The winery dates only from 1977 but the Milones have long been a part of this land. Winemaker Frank's grandfather started farming here early in this century, raising hops, fruit and grapes. The family built the hop kiln in 1947. Through the years, emphasis shifted from hops and orchards to wine grapes.

Frank is an unpretentious, outgoing man and his wines are similar—honest and straightforward. The weathered hop kiln winery is dressed up a bit with a couple of leaded glass windows. The tasting room is in a cozy little upstairs shed attached to the main structure. There's room for about five folks at the counter.

Tasting notes: Milano wines were hearty and full-bodied, with pronounced varietal character. The list is simple: several vintage Chardonnays, a couple of fine Cabernets and Zinfandels and some rich late harvest wines. Prices are from the teens to mid-twenties. Red, white and blush table wines are drinkable and a good buy at $3.50.

Vintners choice: "Cabernet, Chardonnay, Zinfandel and late harvest wines, all reserves," says Frank with simple candor.

Fetzer Vineyards • T

13500 S. Highway 101, Hopland, CA 95449; (707) 744-1737. Daily 9 to 5; MC/VISA, DISC. Most varieties tasted. Large gift shop with extensive offerings of wine-related items, crystal and gourmet foods, plus a deli and picnic area.

One of the area's largest wineries with an annual output of 1.3 million cases, this family-owned operation has moved its public facilities into the old ivy-shrouded Hopland High School. The sturdy masonry structure has been fashioned into an impressive visitor complex with a tasting room and gift shops. It's cavernous but attractive, embellished with polished woods, brick columns and stacks upon stacks of wine cases.

The facility draws 50,000 visitors a year and comes close to being crowded on summer weekends. But we had no trouble finding a spot at the large tasting bar on an October Sunday. Unlike Parducci, this is a relatively new operation. The late Bernard Fetzer founded the winery in 1968 and quickly expanded it into a major producer. His nine children run the operation today.

Tasting notes: Fetzer offers an extensive list of reds and whites, from premium to jug, and virtually all are available for tasting. The overall style is light and fruity, although some of the Cabernets show good tannin strength. Many of the wines are remarkably good buys, ranging well below $5 for some very drinkable varietals. Fetzer markets some of the least-expensive wines in the county.

WINERY CODES • T = tasting with no fee; **T$** = fee for tasting; **GT** = guided tours; **GTA** = appointment required for tour; **ST** = self-guiding tours; **CT** = casual tours or a peek into the winery; = picnic area; = separate gift shop or good giftware selection. Price ranges listed in tasting notes are for varietals; jug wines often are available for less. **DINING & LODGINGS • ØØ** = smoke-free establishment; **Ø** = non-smoking tables or rooms.

McDowell and the Grapevine Tasting Group • T GTA ⌅

Downtown Hopland; (707) 744-1516. Daily in summer 10 to 5, weekends only the rest of the year; MC/VISA, AMEX. Most varieties tasted. A few wine-related gift items. (McDowell Valley Vineyards address: 3811 Highway 175, Hopland, CA 95449; 744-1503.)

This originally was the McDowell Valley Vineyards tasting room; it now offers sips of Jepson and Hidden Cellars wine as well. The structure looks a bit like a real estate office, with its offset pitched roof, but step inside and you're rewarded by a comfy chalet look with a cathedral ceiling and arched windows. A few picnic tables are placed about outside.

We visit Jepson and Hidden Cellars later, so we'll deal with McDowell wines here. The mid-sized winery, open only by appointment, is four miles east on Highway 175, toward Lake County. The facility is owned by Richard and Karen Keehn, who have earned scores of awards for their small list of varietals. The winery, a dramatic, flower-trimmed, energy-efficient affair built into an earthen berm, can be toured by prior appointment on weekdays. The Keehns' also host a variety of special events there.

Tasting notes: We liked the hearty, rich Cabernet and Zinfandel with a wonderful berry-like flavor. Wines are moderately priced, ranging from $4.50 for good table wines to the low teens for estate Zinfandels, Cabs and premium whites. Also on the list are Chardonnay, Fumè Blanc, Grenache, Cabernet Franc and Petite Syrah.

Vintners choice: "We are industry leaders in the Rhône variety category, and known for world-class Fumè Blanc, outstanding Zinfandel and great value Cabernet and Chardonnay," says PR director Pam Walker.

Mendocino Vineyards tasting room • T

Downtown Hopland; (707) 744-1728. Daily 10 to 5; MC/VISA. A few wine-related gift items. (Mendocino Vineyard address: 2399 N. State St., Ukiah, CA 95482; 462-2985.)

You may remember this winery as Cresta Blanca, part of the large Guild Winery co-op based in Lodi. Its Mendocino County operation was changed to Mendocino Vineyards in 1988. It focuses on more upscale varietals than Guild's Lodi area vineyards are capable of producing.

The large winery is in the north end of Ukiah, but the tasting room shifted recently to a rather handsome early American cottage in downtown Hopland.

Tasting notes: The style of the new wines is light and fruity with little wood. We found them quite refreshing, particularly a Fumè Blanc and Chardonnay. A non-vintage Cabernet and Zinfandel, also light but with a touch of oak, and a "Salmon Point Blush" complete the limited list. Price-wise, they're a steal: from $5.25 to $6.50.

Vintners choice: "Cabernets and red table wines," says a winery source. "These wines are blended with oak-aged vintages dating back six to eight years."

Jepson Vineyards • T CT ⌅

10400 S. Highway 101, Ukiah, CA 95482; (707) 468-8936. Daily 10 to 5; MC/VISA. Most varieties tasted. Wine-related gift items, picnic tables near tasting room. Winery tours given as time allows.

The first thing you notice, after spotting the Jepson Vineyards sign on U.S. 101, is an imposing century-old two-story farmhouse, once headquarters to Villa Baccala ranch. It now houses offices and meeting space for Jepson. The winery, in a sturdy white-painted stone and wooden structure, is a short distance away. The tasting room occupies a prim little bungalow fused to the main winery, looking something like a New England cottage built into the side of a warehouse.

Although small, the tasting room is spacious and light, accented by a gleaming brass chandelier hanging from a finished cedar-plank ceiling. A couple of umbrella tables out front extend a silent invitation to picnickers.

The winery complex and 100-plus acres of vineyards were purchased virtually intact a few years ago by Chicago investor Robert S. Jepson, Jr. This is no mom and pop operation. Jepson obviously has invested generously to create an upscale, state-of-the-art winery, which issues equally upscale premium wines.

Tasting notes: Jepson's limited list includes an excellent Chardonnay with a superb nutty finish, a crisp and fruit-filled Sauvignon Blanc, plus a Chenin Blanc and Colombard with the fruit evident in the nose and taste. Prices are modest, ranging from $8 to $10. The winery also produces brandy, distilled from French Colombard in the classic French pot-still method. It's not available for tasting, of course.

Tijsseling Vineyards • T CT ⛌

2200 McNab Ranch Rd. (west off U.S. 101); (707) 462-1810. Tasting room open weekends only in summer 11 to 5; other times by appointment. Selected wines tasted. Shaded picnic area; visitors can peek into the winery.

It's worth reserving a summer weekend for a visit to this pleasant ranch-style redwood winery complex, tucked into a peaceful vale two miles west of Highway 101. If it's not summer and you're in the neighborhood, give a call because a Tijsseling is generally about.

The complex, a merger of Tijsseling Winery and Tyland Vineyards, is operated by Alida Tijsseling, son Dick and his wife Judy. Established in 1977, the facility produces about 50,000 cases a year from its 250 acres of vines.

Tasting notes: The Tijsseling list is select and focused, and the recipient of a good number of medals. Varietals are lush and herbal barrel-aged Chardonnay and Sauvignon Blanc, a complex and peppery Cabernet Sauvignon and a full-bodied, rich Petite Sirah. The Tijsselings also produce white and red table wines, plus sparkling Brut and Blanc de Blanc, both by the classic *mèthode champenoise.* Prices range from $7 to the teens.

Vintners choice: "Superb Brut and Banc de Blancs champagnes, plus our estate-bottled Chardonnay and Cabernet," says Andrea Weira, exhibiting not a shred of modesty.

Hidden Cellars • T CT ⛌

1500 Ruddick-Cunningham Road (Box 448), Ukiah, CA 95482; (707) 462-0301. Weekdays 10 to 4; no credit cards. Most varieties tasted. Some wine logo items; small picnic area; informal tours.

A functional insulated redwood structure perched beneath a gnarled oak at the edge of a vineyard serves as the winery for small Hidden Cellars. An equally functional counter in a corner of the winery will handle about four tasters at a time. The tour consists of a glance around the room, taking in a collection of oak and redwood barrels, a single temperature-controlled stainless steel tank, a small crusher, the usual tangle of hoses and a couple of bicycles.

What all this suggests is that vintner-owner Dennis Patton focuses his energies on wine-making, not tasting room frills. Nearly all the wines on his limited list are regular award-winners.

The only thing hidden about the winery, which sits in full view on the historic Hildreth Ranch, is the origin of the name. Patton used that title when he began home winemaking in a sheltered valley of Mendocino's Mill Creek. He emerged into the open in 1981 and his annual output has increased from a few hundred gallons to about 10,000 cases.

Tasting notes: Winemaker Greg Gariano creates rich Chardonnay and Sauvignon Blanc and a remarkable Zinfandel that is pleasantly mellow and fruity, yet complex, with a crisp finish. Others on the list are Gewürztraminer, Johannisberg Riesling and some dessert wines. Prices start below $10 and range into the teens.

Vintners choice: "Chardonnay, Sauvignon Blanc and Zinfandel—due to our access to some small but excellent Mendocino vineyards," says the winery's Toni Klein.

Parducci Wine Cellars • T GT

501 Parducci Road, Ukiah, CA 95482; (707) 462-9463. Daily 9 to 6 in summer, 9 to 5 the rest of the year; MC/VISA, AMEX. All varieties except champagne are tasted. Gift shop with good selections of wine-related items and some specialty foods. Guided tours hourly from 10 to 4. Picnic tables near tasting room.

The forefather and largest of Mendocino's active wineries, this venerable facility was founded by Adolph Parducci in 1931. It is now operated by second and third generations, with son John Parducci in charge. A major interest was sold recently to a teachers' retirement investment group.

The large winery facility backs into low hills above the northern end of Ukiah, a sanctuary from tract homes that march threateningly in its direction. The tasting room is California Mission eclectic—white stucco with Spanish arches and a shake roof. The interior is richly adorned with dark walnut, terrazzo tile and leaded glass. A gift shop specializing in crystal and china glitters from a room opposite the large tasting area.

The hour-long tour through both vintage and modern facilities is quite thorough. We recommend it to those unfamiliar with the winemaking art.

Tasting notes: The extensive list covers most varietals, plus a range of jug and dessert wines; most are available for tasting. We favored a crisp and fruity Sauvignon Blanc; a nutty, lush Chardonnay; a full-bodied yet soft and rich Cellermaster Zinfandel and a Bordeaux-style Cellermaster Cab Merlot. Prices are moderate, with some fine varietals going for as little as $6, and ranging up to the mid-teens.

Redwood Valley

This is California's northernmost major wine producing area. For trivia fans, Konrad/Olson Vineyards has the state's most northern winery tasting room. The region is a rolling mix of oak-thatched hills, shallow valleys and ridge-like benchlands. Vineyards are scattered in the depressions and on the ridges, offering micro-climates where a surprising variety of premium wine grapes thrive. Among notable bottlings are Chardonnay, Sauvignon Blanc, Cabernet Sauvignon and Zinfandel. Much of the foothill area is chopped into country abodes that range from rustically elegant to scruffy. The higher reaches of the valley offer visions of tawny hills, moss-draped oaks and an occasional artistically rustic Earl Thollander barn.

Only two of Redwood Valley's several wineries are open to tasting without prior arrangement. Potter Valley, a spur of Redwood Valley, features a few vineyards, but at this writing, it had no wineries accessible without an appointment.

REDWOOD VALLEY WINERY TOUR • Following Highway 101 north past Ukiah, you'll see the impressive spired tasting room of **Weibel Vineyards** on your right, just beyond the Highway 20 (Calpella) interchange. However, recent freeway completion has isolated it somewhat. To get there, continue north to the West Road exit then double back on the frontage road, following directional signs.

From Weibel, go south to Highway 20, follow it about a mile and a half to Road A and take it uphill to Road B. It makes a sharp left within a short distance, but continue straight ahead onto the lane marked "Private road; use at your own risk." It's more inviting than it sounds and leads you—within a few hundred feet—to **Konrad/Olson Vineyards.**

Weibel Vineyards • T

7051 N. State Street, Redwood Valley, CA 95470; (707) 485-0321. Tasting daily 9 to 5; MC/VISA. All varieties tasted. Nice gift selection; landscaped picnic area; no tours.

Weibel's tasting room, with its upcurved laminated beams, supposedly forms an inverted champagne glass. Inside, a fountain bubbles appropriately as centerpiece to a dramatic sweep of open space. A curved tasting counter occupies one side. Gift items and wine displays are placed elsewhere about the roomy, circular tasting room.

It was built in 1973 at the point where U.S. 101 freeway construction ended, offering easy access. Although the new freeway breezes on by, it's worth backtracking along the frontage road to reach this inviting place. The grounds are equally attractive, featuring a picnic garden rimmed with grape vines and shaded by ancient oaks with white-painted trunks. A burst of petunias emerges from an old barrel-slat wine press. Beyond are foam-covered stainless steel tanks and utilitarian buildings of Weibel's crushing and fermenting facilities.

Tasting notes: Weibel's wines run the gamut from a few noteworthy varietals and serviceable sparkling wines to ordinary but honest jug wines, assorted sherries, ports and brandy. All but brandy are available for tasting. Overall, prices range from inexpensive to moderate. One sour note: samples are offered in ridiculous plastic mini-glasses, like restaurant salad dressing containers. Try to slosh wine in one of these things and you'll wind up wearing it.

Vintners choice: "Chardonnay, white Zinfandel, Green Hungarian, dry sherry and Chenin Blanc," says a winery spokesman.

Konrad/Olson Vineyards • T CT ⅏

3620 Road B, Redwood Valley, CA 95470; (707) 485-7523. Tasting daily 10 to 5 in summer, 11 to 4 the rest of the year; MC/VISA. Most varieties tasted. A few wine-related gift items; lake-view picnic area. Visitors can peek into the adjacent winery.

We use the double-jointed name because retired Rear Admiral E.G. Konrad and his wife Anne bought the winery in 1989 from founder Donald Olson. Both names now appear on wine labels, but winery signs may be converted to Konrad by the time you read this. The wood-sided winery sits atop a ridge, offering views of the Redwood Valley on one side and Lake Mendocino reservoir and the distant cloud-capped Coast Range on the other. The small tasting room is as comfortable as a family living room, with a fireplace and wicker chairs. A pleasant garden offers picnickers a lake-view lunch site.

Tasting notes: Konrad/Olson's produces full-flavored wines with strong varietal character—particularly the reds. Prices range from $9 for Sauvignon Blanc and Merlot to $12 for Chards and Cabs. A Chardonnay was balanced nicely between spice and fruit, with a subtle acid finish. A rather young Zinfandel was full-berried and drinkable, with gentle tannins and a Cabernet Sauvignon had a lively chili pepper nose and spicy-berry flavors, with soft hints of wood and tannin.

Vintners choice: "We're focusing on the higher end varietals, particularly Chardonnay and Cabernets," says winemaker Robinson.

Anderson Valley

This is exemplary rural northern California, a shallow valley rimmed by hills the color and shape of fresh-baked rolls. It's garnished by shady clusters of oaks, madrones and pines and accented by sloping vineyards and emerald pastures.

Grizzled old Boonville is the best known of the valley's hamlets. It gained fame a decade ago for its Boonville Hotel and Restaurant, recently reopened. It also offers an appealing beer pub and a couple of boutiques. Philo, with a population of 273, isn't much bigger than some of the winery complexes that surround it.

The valley is relatively new as a vineyard area. Although pioneers may have stomped a grape or two, current activity dates from 1971 when the Husch family established a winery near Philo. Most of the valley's vineyards and wineries line Highway 128 between Philo and Navarro. This is one of the colder and wetter of California's vinelands, so grapes from northern Europe such as Chardonnay, assorted Rieslings and Gewürztraminer do best. However, we did encounter some good Cabernet and Pinot Noir.

ANDERSON VALLEY WINERY TOUR • Take your pick of approaches. State Highway 253 from Ukiah, Highway 128 from Cloverdale or a combination of Mountain House Road and 128 from Hopland are equally twisty and scenic. None of the routes miss any wineries, which don't start cropping up until you pass Boonville.

Touring Anderson Valley winery tasting rooms is no great trick. Although some of the wineries are on side roads, all of their tasting rooms are neatly aligned along Highway 128 between Boonville and Navarro.

Driving northwest on Highway 128, you'll first find **Obester Winery,** on your left just short of **Philo**. Immediately beyond Philo is **Scharffenberger Cellars,** also on the left. A few miles farther along, just beyond the Greenwood Road junction is the new **Kendall-Jackson Wine Country Store**; it's on the left, at the site of the old Edmeades Winery. On the right are the side-by-side tasting rooms of **Navarro Vineyards** and **Greenwood Ridge Vineyards. Husch Vineyards** is a short distance beyond, on the left and **Handley Cellars** is on the right, near the hamlet of **Navarro**.

Obester Winery • T CT

9200 Highway 128, Philo, CA 95466; (707) 895-2328. Daily 10 to 5; MC/VISA, AMEX and DISC. Gift area with wine-related articles, books and Obester's line of mustards, dressings and other specialty food items. Picnic tables shaded by lath house. Informal tours when winemaker is free.

A clump of cheerful mustard-colored ranch structures mark the valley's newest tasting facility, just south of Philo. Paul and Sandy Obester began making wine in Half Moon Bay south of San Francisco. That area is better known for pumpkins, but they won their share of awards, using grapes brought in from various wine-producing areas. In 1989, they bought an old apple farm near Philo and began planting their own vineyards.

Tasting notes: The Obester list is small, leaning toward lush, full-fruited, medium-dry whites. Our favorites were a nutty and complex Chardonnay, an Alexander Valley Sauvignon Blanc and a Gewürztraminer with a nice floral aroma and fruity taste. The winery also produces a light-style Zinfandel and a rich, complex Pinot Noir. Prices are moderate, from $7 to $13.

Vintners choice: "Sauvignon Blanc, Johannisberg Riesling and Gewürztraminer. Whites are fruity and well-balanced," says Lynne Sawyer.

Scharffenberger Cellars • T GTA

P.O. Box 365, Philo, CA 95466; (707) 895-2957. Daily 11 a.m. to 5 p.m.; MC/VISA, AMEX. Four varieties of sparkling wine tasted. Picnic tables adjacent to tasting room. Tours of the new facility by appointment.

John Scharffenberger founded this complex in 1981 with a single-minded purpose—to produce wines similar to classic French Champagnes. And in deference to the French, he doesn't use the term "champagne."

You'll see the winery on your left, shortly after passing through tiny Philo. The tasting room is the most appealing in the Anderson Valley: an attractive sweep of space radiating out from a curved tasting bar. A cathedral ceiling accents the facility's openness.

Tasting notes: Scharffenberger employs Chardonnay and Pinot Noir—either singly or combined—to produce four sparkling wines. All are crisp, excellent examples of the *mèthode champenoise*, in which sparkling wines are produced, aged and marketed in the same bottle. If you don't like your champagne dusty dry, you should enjoy Scharffenberger's Brut, Brute Rosè, Blanc de Blancs and Cremant. Prices range from $18 to $20.

Kendall-Jackson Wine Country Store • T

5500 Highway 128, Philo, CA 95466; (707) 895-3232. Tuesday-Sunday 10 to 5; MC/VISA. A new tasting room and wine shop at the site of the former

Edmeades winery. See Kendall-Jackson Winery listing in the Lake County section below.

Navarro Vineyards • T GTA & CT ⌅

5601 Highway 128 (P.O. Box 47), Philo, CA 95466; (707) 895-3686. Daily 10 to 5; MC/VISA. Most varieties tasted. A few T-shirts and such; picnic tables on a deck overlooking vineyard. Ask to peek into the winery, or arrange for a tour by calling in advance.

Only a few vines separate Navarro and Greenwood Ridge tasting rooms; both are surrounded by vineyards that sweep toward forested hills. We'd recommend either for fine picnicking views.

A cozy tasting room that might accommodate half a dozen people (provided they're feeling friendly) occupies a corner of one of Navarro's modern, wood-faced structures. Visitors can adjourn to an outside deck to sip their wine while drinking in the vineland-mountain view. Upscale barn might be the proper architectural definition for this appealing complex.

Ted Bennett and Deborah Cahn established the winery in 1975 to focus on what Anderson Valley grows best—Gewürztraminer, Riesling and Chardonnay.

Tasting notes At the risk of repetition, we found the whites to be typically Anderson Valley: lush, high in fruit, with a nice acid finish. Navarro also produces a rather soft, well-balanced Pinot Noir. Prices range from $8 for a dry Semillon to $14 for Chardonnay and Pinot.

Vintners choice: Owner Ted Bennett leans toward his dry, late harvest Gewürztraminer, late harvest Riesling and Chardonnay.

Greenwood Ridge Vineyards • T ⌅

24555 Greenwood Rd., Philo, CA 95466; (707) 877-3262. Daily 10 to 6 in summer, 10 to 5 in the off-season; MC/VISA, AMEX. Most varieties tasted. Picnic tables on a deck overlooking vineyards and nearby hills.

Greenwood's tasting room is an intriguing hexagonal tepee, with a skylight to brighten the spacious interior. Decks with a few tables overlook the vineyards and a sign on a nearby pond advises visitors not to feed the alligators.

The main winery is a few miles away, perched on a ridge above Greenwood Road. It's just six miles inshore from the coastal hamlet of Elk. Owned by Allan Green, the winery focuses on Sauvignon Blanc, Pinot Noir, Riesling and Zinfandel, with a limited production of 4,000 cases a year. His small, select list of varietals has earned prestigious awards, including "Best of Class" for Cabernet at a recent California State Fair judging.

Green hosts the annual California Wine Tasting Championship the last weekend of July, with prizes for novice, amateur and professional sippers who can identify specific wines. If you feel you have a competitive palate, contact the winery for details.

Tasting notes: Five wines appeared on Greenwood's list when we visited the tasting room, comprising four varieties—Sauvignon Blanc, Riesling, Pinot Noir and Cabernet, with prices from $9 to $18. The whites were nicely balanced with good fruit flavor and a crisp acid finish. The Cabernet, mellowed by a hint of Merlot, tasted like a fine Bordeaux.

Husch Vineyards • T CT ⌅

4400 Highway 128, Philo, CA 95466; (707) 895-3216. Daily 10 to 6 in summer and 10 to 5 the rest of the year; MC/VISA. All varieties tasted. A few gift shop items; picnic area under a grape arbor. Informal peek into the winery, or tours by appointment.

Husch is the valley's only winery senior enough to offer a bit of funky charm. Established in 1971, it occupies an old farm complex that predates the winery itself. The tasting room is in a cute, weather-beaten granary that could pass for a miner's shack. Here, a remarkably amiable hostess named Margaret pours from a fair-sized list of ten wines.

The H.A. Oswald family bought the winery from the Husch clan in 1979. They produce only estate-bottled wines, drawing from the Husch vineyards and their La Ribera Vineyards near Ukiah.

Tasting notes: We found the wines to be pleasantly light: Dry and fruity for the Chardonnay, Sauvignon Blanc, Gewürztraminer and Chenin Blanc; soft and herbal for the Pinot Noir and Cabernet Sauvignon. Prices wander from $6.50 to $16.

Handley Cellars • T GTA ⌅

3151 Highway 128, (P.O. Box 66) Philo, CA 95466; 895-2190. Tasting 11 a.m. to 6 p.m. daily in summer and 11 to 5 the rest of the year; MC/VISA, AMEX. Most varieties tasted. Some wine-related gift objects; two picnic areas on a lawn and a garden courtyard. Tours by appointment only.

Step into the Handley's upscale tasting room and admire its international art, folkcraft and Persian carpets; note particularly the carved tasting bar from England. You might think this to be the haven of a long-established, much-traveled winery dynasty. Yet all of this—and a list of premium wines—was assembled within a few years by dynamic young Milla Handley and her husband Rex McClellan.

After graduating from the University of California at Davis in 1975, she worked for several other winemakers. Then she and Rex established this winery at an old ranch complex in 1987. Of course, Milla's heritage didn't hold her back. She's the great-great granddaughter of Oregon brewmaster Henry Weinhard.

Tasting notes: Eight wines appear on Milla Handley's small but eclectic list, ranging from varietal whites to Pinot Noir to a sparkling rosé. We found the dry whites to be the best of the lot, strong on the fruit, crisp and clean with a bit of acid at the end. Prices range from $7.50 to the mid-teens. A $5.75 semi-sweet Brightligher White would be a good hot weather quaffing wine.

Vintners choice: "Our barrel-fermented Chardonnays have won many gold medals; our Gewürztraminer is recognized as one of the best in California," boasted spokeswoman Gretchen O'Bergin.

LAKE COUNTY

Wrapped around California's largest natural freshwater lake, touched by no freeway or railroad, Lake County is for its serene rural setting. One of California's most thinly-populated counties, it has barely enough residents to fill an average ball park—less than 50,000. The county seat of Lakeport numbers only 5,000.

The county would be an island in time, ignored by the world outside, except that the pale blue rough-cut gem of Clear Lake draws thousands of summer visitors. They come to angle for bass, hurry across the lake's calm surface behind speedboat tow ropes or lie on its sandy shores. When summer ends, they leave the place to residents. They all seem to know one another as they go about their business in hamlets with ordinary names like Upper Lake and Kelseyville, or optimistic names like Lucerne and Glenhaven.

Viticulture here dates back to 1872 and more than thirty wineries once functioned. But the area's isolation made marketing difficult. Ironically, one of the county's early freight wagon roads led across the flanks of Mount St. Helena to the wine-rich Napa Valley. Lake County's wineries began to falter during a turn-of-the-century wine glut, then Prohibition closed the rest. Commercial crushing didn't resume until 1977. At last count, this rural enclave had only half a dozen wineries; four offer tastings without prior arrangements.

A visit to Lake County's vinelands is certainly worth the brief right-hand detour from neighboring Mendocino. For one thing, the rolling drive over the Mayacamas Mountains that divide the two counties is a remarkably scenic one. For another, the wineries are appealing and uncrowded. One, Kendall-Jackson, creates some of the most exceptional wines in America.

The remarkable record of Kendall-Jackson, winner of 129 medals including 36 golds in 1989, is the main source of the area's biggest boast. Lake County claims to win more awards per vineyard acre than any other wineland in the world. K-J's success may actually distort that record however, since many of its grapes are brought in from other areas.

LAKE COUNTY WINERY TOUR • Several wineries here are open only Thursday through Sunday, so bear that in mind in your scheduling.

Drive east from Hopland on State Highway 175 (Hopland Summit Road). It takes you through hillside vineyards, then up a corkscrew route to the crest of the Mayacamas Mountains. Enjoy views both east and west, then roller-coaster down to the Lake County floor. The scenery, a mix of wooded slopes, farmlands and vineyards, isn't as awesome as Mendocino County's vinelands, but it's pleasantly bucolic.

If you're pulling a trailer or driving a long-tailed motorhome, you may prefer a less twisting route by taking Highway 20 south from Redwood Valley above Ukiah. You'll even catch a bit of freeway—gawd knows why—between Upper Lake and Lakeport.

If you've taken the Highway 175 route, swing south onto Highway 29 and you'll shortly encounter Highlands Springs Road. Turn right, then make another quick right onto Matthews Road, which takes you to **Kendall-Jackson**. Return to Highway 29/175, continue south and you soon encounter **Konocti Winery** on your left. From there, drive about ten miles south on Highway 29 and you'll find **Stuermer Winery** on the right, just beyond the Highway 29/53 junction at the dinky hamlet of **Lower Lake**.

Continue south on Highway 29 and turn right on Butts Canyon Road in **Middletown**. After about six miles, you'll happen upon the fourth Lake County winery that keeps regular visiting hours, **Guenoc.**

Kendall-Jackson Winery • T

640 Matthews Rd., Lakeport, CA 95453; (707) 263-5299. Wednesday-Sunday 11 to 5; MC/VISA. Select varieties tasted. Wine-related gift items and specialty foods; picnic area in an oak grove and in a gazebo.

K-J's modern winery, established by Jess S. Jackson, is housed in a low-slung adobe brick structure on a green knoll surrounded by vineyards. Oaks and Japanese plums lend a bucolic aura, inviting picnickers and strollers. The tasting room, a simple brown cottage, is off to one side.

One of California's most-honored wine producers, it was named "Winery of the Year" by *Wine & Spirits Magazine* in 1989, by the American Wine Competition in 1987 and by the California State Fair in 1986. Wine blender Jed Steele was named winemaker of the year, as well.

Tasting notes: With all those accolades, one enters the tasting room like a kid in a candy store. Alas, only three or four wines from the rather extensive list are offered. We were given sips of a Dupratt Vineyard Chardonnay, Vintner's Reserve Chardonnay, Proprietor's Merlot and Durrell Vineyard Syrah. The first three were exceptional: The Chardonnays were spicy, full-flavored and lush and the Merlot was full of berries with a nippy tannic finish. The Syrah was complex and full of berries but not awesome. Prices are mostly in the mid-teens, ranging from $9 to $22.50.

Konocti Winery • T CT

Highway 29 at Thomas Drive (P.O. Box 890), Kelseyville, CA 95451; (707) 279-8861. Daily 10 to 5; MC/VISA. All varieties tasted. Wine-related gift items; picnic tables near tasting room. Casual tours; guided tours by prior arrangement.

Konocti, a winegrowers' co-op, is housed in a no-nonsense fabricated metal building fronted by a wooden bungalow tasting room. A fair selection of wine-focused gift items and picnic fare and specialty foods is offered.

The winery uses only Lake County grapes, drawing from vineyards of 25 member-growers. Active socially, Konocti Winery folk sponsor monthly wine and food pairings and an October harvest festival, open to the public.

Tasting notes: The list is brief but busy—Chardonnay, Fumè Blanc, Riesling, Cabernet Franc, Cabernet Sauvignon and Merlot, plus a blush Cabernet, jug white and red, and a sweet Muscat Canelli. We felt the Chardonnay and Cabernet were best—lush and complex with powerful varietal character. The red table wine is an excellent buy at $5, with strong Cabernet underpinnings.

Stuermer Winery • T CT

Highway 29 (P.O. Box 950), Lower Lake, CA 95457; (707) 994-4069. Tasting 10 to 5 daily in summer, Thursday-Sunday the rest of the year; MC/VISA. Casual winery tours; picnic tables nearby.

A small, brown bunker-like affair tucked up against a hill, Stuermer Winery produces only Cabernet under the family brand, plus a few varietals under the Arcadia label. It's the oldest of the present-day Lake County wineries, established in 1977 by the Harold Stuermer family.

Tasting notes: The list is short and tasty. The rich, complex and award-winning Stuermer Cabernet Sauvignon and a lush, fruity Arcadia

Sauvignon Blanc and Cabernet are worth the twisting trip over the Mayacamas Mountains.

Guenoc Winery • T CT ⌅

21000 Butts Canyon Road (P.O. Box 1146), Middletown, CA 95461; (707) 987-2385. Tasting Thursday-Sunday 10 to 4:30; MC/VISA. Most varieties tasted. Picnic area nearby; informal tours of the winery.

Lily Langtry made her mark in the entertainment world, but politics prevented the flamboyant British actress from scoring in the wine business. She bought this beautiful little valley and imported a winemaker from Bordeaux just after the turn of the century, then Prohibition put an end to the operation. She left behind a stately Victorian home, now occupied by present owners Orville Magoon and family. Her cameo graces the Guenoc label. The winery has the distinction of being the only single-vineyard appellation in America.

Visitors can look around the winery, housed in a straightforward rectangle perched atop a hill, and sample wines from a list embracing most of the classic varietals.

Tasting notes: The Chardonnay, Cabernet Sauvignon, Cabernet Franc, Merlot, Malbec, Petit Verdot, Sauvignon Blanc, Semillon, Zinfandel and Petite Sarah are all estate-produced. Our choices were the mellow Merlot, the spicy, medium-bodied Zin and the full-bodied Petit.

THE BEST OF THE BUNCH

The best wine buys • Fetzer Vineyards, Parducci Wine Cellars and Mendocino Vineyards.

The most attractive wineries • McDowell Valley Vineyards at 3811 Highway 175 (tasting room is in Hopland), Kendall-Jackson and Guenoc wineries in Lake County.

The most attractive tasting rooms • Weibel Vineyards in Redwood Valley, Scharffenberger Cellars and Handley Cellars in Anderson Valley.

The funkiest tasting room • Husch Vineyards in Anderson Valley.

The best gift shop • Parducci Wine Cellars in Ukiah and Fetzer Vineyards in Hopland.

The nicest picnic areas • Konrad/Olson Vineyards and Weibel Vineyards in Redwood Valley, Navarro and Greenwood Ridge in Anderson Valley, and Guenoc Winery in Lake County.

BEYOND THE VINEYARDS

Mendocino County

Escapees from the thickly populated San Francisco Bay Area flee to Mendocino to admire the bucolic landforms and play in the water. They fish in the **Russian River**, swim and boat in **Lake Mendocino** and scuff seaweed along the wild and handsomely rugged seacoast.

A particularly popular tourist drive is Highway 128 from Cloverdale to the sea. In **Boonville,** check out the old turn-of-the-century **Boonville Hotel**, the **Buckhorn Saloon** brewpub and the **Anderson Valley Historical Museum** in the Conn Creek School just beyond town.

The Boonville area is home to a curious language called *Boontling,* a rural slang developed by locals a century ago and still used by some. A tourist, for instance is called a *brightlighter* and good restaurant food is *bahl gorms.* Some Boonville shops sell *Boontling* dictionaries, should you wish to converse with the natives.

In addition to funny talk and wineries, Anderson Valley offers a couple of hushed redwood groves. Twisting Fish Rock Road above Yorkville takes you to the solemnly beautiful **Mailliard Redwood State Reserve**. Beyond Philo, follow Greenwood Road to **Hendy Woods State Park**, with hiking trails, picnic areas and campsites.

If you persist along Highway 128 or Greenwood Road, you'll encounter the Mendocino coast, on one of the prettiest stretches of seashore in America. Wind-graced meadows and redwood groves march down to a tumbled coastline of seastacks and hidden coves. Drive north to **Mendocino**, an old-style New England town that somehow wound up on the Pacific Coast. The picture-perfect village is busy with galleries, antique shops, boutiques, bed and breakfast inns and some remarkably good restaurants.

Meanwhile, back in **Ukiah,** visit the **Grace Hudson Museum and Sun House** with Indian lore and changing historic exhibits, at 431 S. Main Street. Ukiah also is noted for its collection of Victorian homes; a tour map is available at the chamber of commerce. A launch ramp, campground, picnic area and hiking trail at **Lake Mendocino** can be reached by driving north on Main Street, then going east on Lake Mendocino Drive.

From Ukiah, drive three miles east on Vichy Springs Road to **Vichy Springs Resort,** where Mark Twain, Ulysses S. Grant and ordinary folks have been soaking in mineral waters since 1854. You can rent a cozy cabin or ranch-style room or pay a $20 day use fee and have the run of the springs and the 700-acre grounds. (See listing under "Vineland lodgings.")

Hopland shelters several winery tasting rooms, as we noted before, along with a couple of interesting yesterday buildings. The nicely-restored **Thatcher Inn** offers rooms and a visually elegant dining room. The brick-front **Hopland Brewery** is a properly funky oldstyle brewpub with a tree-shaded beer garden. (See listings below.)

If you head north to **Willits**, you can ride the chuffing little **Skunk Train** through the redwoods to the old fishing village of **Fort Bragg,** home to a few decent seafood restaurants.

Lake County

Clear Lake is the largest freshwater pond entirely within California. Its shores are lined with marinas, fishing piers, swimming beaches and resorts. Some of these old resort towns, like **Lower Lake** and **Clearlake**, are a bit on the scruffy side. However, **Lakeport** is downright cute, with several restored Victorians, and false-front stores in its tidy downtown area.

Clear Lake State Park near Kelseyville offers hiking, swimming, a boat launch, camping and picnicking. **Anderson Marsh State Park** is an intriguing wetland on the lake's lower tip, encompassing a bird watching area and a pioneer farm complex.

In the pleasantly dusty town of **Lower Lake,** take a peek at the old **stone jail.** Measuring 12 by 17 feet, it's one of the smallest lockups in America. Lower Lake came to life during a brief quicksilver rush and the jail was built by brothers Theodore and John Copsey to house the town's rowdies. Apparently the Copsey brothers over-celebrated its completion and became its first occupants. They also became its first escapees, since they'd neglected to bolt down the roof.

Mendocino-Lake County activities & attractions

Boating, swimming • Lake Mendocino recreation area; 462-7581. Clear Lake recreation areas, 263-5092.

Boat rentals • Lake Mendocino Marina; 485-8644 or 485-0481.

Excursion train rides • California Western Railroad (Skunk Trains) through the redwoods from Willits to Fort Bragg; 964-6371 or 459-5248.

Museums •

Grace Hudson Museum and Sun House, 431 S. Main St., Ukiah; 462-3370. Wednesday-Saturday, 10 to 4:30 and Sunday noon to 4:30; donations requested. Indian artifacts and area history exhibits.

Anderson Valley Historical Museum, Highway 128, Boonville; 895-3207. Friday-Sunday 1 to 4 (longer summer hours). Historical exhibits of Anderson Valley and Boonville, including stuff on "Boontling" language; housed in old Conn Creek School.

Wineland events • Lake County Spring Wine Adventure, late April; 263-0911. California Wine Tasting Championships, late July at Greenwood Ridge Vineyards; 877-3262. Redwood Empire Fair and Wine Festival, August; 462-4705. Individual wineries also sponsor various events throughout the year.

Winery touring maps • ***Lake County Wineries***, available from Lake County Grape Growers Association, 65 Soda Bay Road, Lakeport, CA 95453; 263-0911. ***Mendocino Wine Country***, available at area wineries or from Mendocino County Vintner's Association, P.O. Box 1409, Ukiah, CA 95482; 463-1704.

WINE COUNTRY DINING

Mendocino County

Boonville Hotel Restaurant • ΔΔΔ $$$ ØØ

Highway 128 at Lambert Lane, Boonville; (707) 895-2210. California-American; ala carte meals $10 to $18; wine and beer. Wednesday-Sunday 6 p.m. to 9 p.m., lunch Sunday 11 to 2. Informal; reservations suggested. No credit cards; personal checks accepted. Oldstyle restaurant featuring light California *nouveau* fare such as sea scallop brochette with avocado and creative pizzas with leeks, grilled peppers and goat cheese. Locally done desserts are noteworthy. Dining room is non-smoking. (See hotel listing below.)

Broiler Steak House • ΔΔ $$$ Ø

8400 Uva Dr., Redwood Valley (just north of Ukiah; West Road exit west from U.S. 101, then north on Uva Road); 485-7301. Basic American; mostly steaks; dinners $12 to $20; full bar service. Sunday 3 to 10, Monday-Thursday 4 to 10, Friday-Saturday 4 to 11. Casual; reservations accepted; essential on weekends. MC/VISA, AMEX. Noisy, friendly family-style restaurant featuring steaks, accompanied by a huge salad and a melon-sized baked potato buried under a dollop of sour cream. The menu also lists chicken, chops and seafood; good local wine list. The decor consists of acoustical ceiling tile, potted plants and not much else.

Buckhorn Saloon (Anderson Valley Brewing Co.) • ΔΔΔ $ ØØ

14081 Highway 128, Boonville; (707) 895-BEER. Light pub grub; meals $5 to $10.50; beer and wine. Daily 11 a.m. to 10 p.m. Casual; no reservations. MC/VISA. Stylish Western saloon styled in natural wood and leaded glass, serving light fare such as sausages, piroshki, teriyaki chicken and fish and chips. Anderson Valley Brewing Company's hearty beers featured; try a pint of hearty, malt-rich High Rollers and you'll *know* you're drinking beer. Smoke-free dining.

El Sombrero • ΔΔΔ $$ Ø

131 E. Mill St. (Main Street), Ukiah; (707) 463-1818. Mexican; meals $9 to $12; full bar service. Tuesday-Friday 11:30 to 2 and 5 to 9, weekends 4 to 9, closed Monday. Casual; reservations accepted. MC/VISA. Appealing Mexican restaurant in a refurbished old farmhouse, with rough-hewn ceiling beams, high-back chairs and wrought iron lamps. Typical Mexican fare, plus specialties such as *camarones* (garlic prawns) and *pescado tampico* (fillet of sole with lemon, salsa and bay shrimp). Cozy attic cocktail lounge.

The Green Barn • ΔΔ $$ Ø

1109 S. State St. (Lewis Lane), Ukiah; (707) 462-5555. American; dinners $7 to $22; full bar service. Monday-Thursday 11 a.m. to 10 p.m., Friday-Saturday 11 to 11, Sunday 4 to 10. Casual; reservations accepted. MC/VISA, AMEX. Farm-style restaurant in a vintage two-story house. The menu also is typically down home: steaks, prime ribs, liver and onions and—good grief—even chicken fried steaks. Prices are quite modest, with mini-dinners from $6 to $7.

Hopland Brewery • ΔΔ $

13351 Highway 101 South, Hopland; (707) 744-1015. Light pub grub; meals $5 to $10; beer and wine. Sunday-Thursday 11 a.m. to 10 p.m., Friday 11 to midnight, Saturday 11 to 1:30 a.m. Casual; no reservations. MC/VISA. An oldstyle brewpub serving beer sausages, seafood, salads and other light snacks with its micro-brews; in a sturdy century-old red brick tavern with pressed tin walls and early American furnishings; beer garden shaded by a grape trellis.

Lotus Restaurant • ΔΔ $

403 S. State St. (Clay Street), Ukiah; (707) 463-2288. Chinese-Japanese; dinners $6 to $11; wine and beer. Monday-Thursday 11 a.m. to 9:30 p.m., Friday 11 to 10, Saturday noon to 10, closed Sunday. Casual; no reservations. MC/VISA. Storefront restaurant trimmed by an occasional paper lantern serves huge portions at modest prices. Both Chinese and Japanese fare; sushi bar.

The Maple Restaurant • Δ $

295 S. State St., Ukiah; (707) 462-5221. American; meals $5 to $10; wine and beer. Daily 7 a.m. to 7 p.m. Casual; no reservations. MC/VISA. Simple American diner with a basic Formica interior; inexpensive fare in generous portions. It's the kind of place where the waitress approaches your table with a smile and a coffee pot.

Thatcher Inn Restaurant • ΔΔΔΔ $$$ ØØ

13401 S. Highway 101 (Center Street), Hopland; (707) 744-1890. American-continental; dinners $12 to $16; full bar service. Breakfast Monday-Saturday 8 to 11, Sunday brunch 8 to 2; lunch Monday-Saturday 11:30 to 2, dinner daily 5:30 to 9:30. Informal; reservations accepted. Major credit cards. Housed in a restored stagecoach stop, with a changing menu ranging from Oriental pasta to *tournedos of beef Bèarnaise.* Handsomely restored with floral wallpaper, pressed-tin ceilings, burgundy nappery and marble-topped candle-lit tables. Stately, clubby bar with a mirrored back bar is adjacent.

Toll House Restaurant & Inn • ΔΔΔΔ $$$ ØØ

15301 Highway 253 (P.O. Box 268), Boonville; (707) 895-3630. American/continental nouveau; dinners $20 to $25; full bar service. Thursday-Sunday from 6 p.m. Informal; reservations advised. MC/VISA, DISC. Stylish extension of the turn-of-the-century Toll House Inn; eclectic, changing menu featuring fresh ingredients, including fruits and veggies from garden out back. Local wines; smoke-free dining room. (See inn listing below.)

Lake County

Anthony's Restaurant • ΔΔΔ $$ Y

2509 Lakeshore Blvd., Lakeport; (707) 263-4905. Italian-American; dinners $9 to $27; full bar service. Daily 5 to 10 p.m. Casual to informal; reservations accepted. Major credit cards. Attractive restaurant near the lake, dressed up in white lace tablecloths, black velvet drapes and red carpets. Varied menu with Italian specialties, a large seafood selection and typical steaks, chicken and chops.

Lakeside Restaurant & Bar • ΔΔ $$ Y

6330 Soda Bay Road, Kelsey Bay; (707) 279-9450. French-Continental; dinners $10 to $18; full bar service. Dinner nightly except Wednesday from 5:30. Informal; reservations suggested. MC/VISA. Attractive small restaurant operated by the former owners of La Petite Auberge in San Rafael. Menu features include escargot, rack of lamb Persille and fresh seafood. Good wine list.

Loon's Nest Restaurant • ΔΔΔ $$ Ø

5685 Main St., Kelseyville; (707) 279-1812. American-Continental; dinners $10.75 to $19; wine and beer. Dinner nightly 5:30 to 9. Informal; reservations suggested. MC/VISA, AMEX. Handsome dining room near the lake, with varied menu. Fare ranges from straightforward steak to chicken breast Florentine to marinated salmon in honey, sesame and ginger. Extensive Lake County wine list.

VINELAND LODGINGS

Mendocino County

Boonville Hotel • ΔΔΔ $$$$ ØØ

Highway 128 at Lambert Lane (P.O. Box 326), Boonville, CA 95415; (707) 895-2210. Rooms $65 to $145. MC/VISA. Refurbished historic hotel with Early American-style rooms featuring down comforters, fresh flowers and other amenities; free continental breakfast. All rooms are non-smoking. **Boonville Hotel Restaurant:** See listing above.

Garden Court Motor Inn • ΔΔ $$ Ø

1175 S. State St. (Talmage Road); 462-5646. Doubles $35, singles $32, suites $37. MC/VISA, DISC. Ten-unit motel with TV movies and room phones; some two-bedroom and kitchen units. Pool, shaded lawn area with picnic tables. Non-smoking rooms available.

Manor Inn • ΔΔ $$$

950 N. State Street (Low Gap Road), Ukiah, CA 95482; (707) 462-7584. Doubles $46 to $65, singles $42 to $48. Major credit cards. Room phones, TV, pool; some oldstyle refurbished rooms with high ceilings and polished woods. **Manor Inn Restaurant** serves from 7 a.m. to 10 a.m. American fare, dinners $8.95 to $14.95; full bar service. Non-smoking areas.

Super Eight Motel • ΔΔ $$$ Ø

1070 S. State St. (Talmage), Ukiah, CA 95482; (707) 462-1221. Doubles $48 to $62, singles $38 to $48. Major credit cards. Thirty-one room motel with TV movies, room phones and heated pool. Non-smoking rooms. **Sidera Kis Restaurant** serves Tuesday-Saturday 11 to 2 and 5 to 9, Sunday brunch 9:30 to 2; closed Monday. American-Greek; dinners $9 to $20; full bar service; non-smoking areas.

Vichy Springs Resort • ΔΔΔΔ $$$$$

2605 Vichy Springs Rd. (three miles east of U.S. 101), Ukiah, CA 95482; (707) 462-9515. Doubles $95 to $140, singles $75 to $105. All major credit cards. A refurbished 1854 hot springs resort with natural mineral baths, Swedish massage, therapy pool and other amenities. Modern furnished rooms in two guest cottages with fireplaces and in a ranch-style building. Rates include continental breakfast and the use of mineral baths and pool. Seven hundred acres for hiking, picnicking and mountain biking.

Lake County

Best Western El Grande Inn • ΔΔ $$$

15135 Lakeside Dr. (P.O. Box 4598), Clear Lake, CA 95422; (800) 528-1234 or (707) 994-2000. Doubles $65 to $70, singles $60 to $70, suites $70 to $95. Major credit cards. In-room phones, TV, refrigerators in suites; pool, hot tub. **Restaurant** serves Monday-Friday 6 a.m. to 10 p.m. and Sunday from 8 to 10. American fare; $10 to $20 for dinner; full bar service.

Harbor Inn • ΔΔΔ $$$$

8727 Soda Bay Rd., Kelseyville, CA 95451; (800) 862-4930 or (707) 279-4281. Doubles $70 to $90, singles $65 to $85, kitchen apartments $150 to $225. Major credit cards. Large lakeside resort with extensive landscaped grounds; marina, rental boats, two pools, playground, miniature golf, health spa, tennis; planned activities in summer. Rooms have TV, radios and phones. **Dining Room** and coffee shop serves 7 a.m. to 10 p.m.; American; meals $9 to $20; full bar service.

Skylark Motel • ΔΔ $$$

1120 N. Main St. (11th Street), Lakeport, CA 95453; (707) 263-6151. Doubles $58 to $90, singles $50 to $62, kitchenettes $80 to $95. All major *credit cards.* Forty-five room motel on the lake with boat launches and docks; TV, room phones, pool.

BED & BREAKFAST INNS

Mendocino County

Blackberry Inn Bed & Breakfast • ΔΔ $$$ Ø

7500 Highway 128 (P.O. Box 96), Philo, CA 95466; (707) 895-2961. Doubles $65 to $75. Three rooms, one with private bath; full breakfast. No credit cards. New England-style inn with contemporary furnishings in guest rooms; pool; fireplace in parlor. More than seven acres of grounds with access to nearby Hendy Woods State Park and the Navarro River.

Philo Pottery Inn • ΔΔ $$$$ Ø

8550 Highway 128 (P.O. Box 166), Philo, CA 95466; (707) 895-3069. Doubles $75 to $92, singles $70 to $87. Five rooms, two with private baths; full breakfast. MC/VISA. Restored 1888 redwood farmhouse that once served as a stage stop. Rooms furnished with American antiques, oldstyle beds with patchwork quilts and down comforters. Wood stove and library in living room; airy front porch with English garden; pottery gallery.

Sanford House • ΔΔΔ $$$$ Ø

306 South Pine St. (Stephenson Street), Ukiah, CA 95482; (707) 462-1653. Doubles $85 to $98, singles $75. Five rooms, private baths; full breakfast. Queen Anne Victorian built in 1904; once the home of State Senator John Bunyan Sanford. Nicely appointed rooms with antique armoires, four-poster beds and print wallpaper. Comfortable library and living room with fireplace; nicely landscaped grounds.

Toll House Restaurant & Inn • ΔΔΔΔ $$$$$ ØØ

15301 Highway 253 (P.O. Box 268), Boonville, CA 95415; (707) 895-3630. Doubles $115 to $150, kitchen unit for $190. Four rooms; private baths; full breakfast. MC/VISA, DISC. Elegantly restored 1912 toll house on 360-acre ranch; hiking, picnicking. Rooms furnished with an antique-modern mix; artworks adorn the walls. Some units with fireplaces and spa tubs. **Toll House Restaurant** serves Thursday through Sunday; see listing above. Inn and restaurant are smoke-free.

Thatcher Inn • ΔΔΔΔ $$$$ ØØ

13401 S. Highway 101 (Center Street), Hopland, CA 95449; (707) 744-1890. Doubles and singles $85 to $140. Twenty rooms with private baths; full breakfast and Sunday champagne brunch. MC/VISA, AMEX. Impeccably restored inn, housed in an 1890 stage stop hotel. Victorian and American antiques, floral print wallpaper, brass beds and armoires. Comfortable library with easy chairs and fireplace. Lounge and **restaurant** (see listing above).

Lake County

Forbestown Inn • ΔΔΔ $$$$ ØØ

825 Forbes St. (Ninth Street), Lakeport, CA 95453; (707) 263-7858. Doubles $75 to $95, singles $60 to $80. Four rooms, one with private bath; full country breakfast. MC/VISA, AMEX. Attractive 1869 Victorian in downtown

Lakeport. Rooms nicely furnished with American oak antiques, floral drapes, king and queen beds. Landscaped grounds; pool and spa.

Mendocino-Lake county information sources

The Greater Ukiah Chamber of Commerce, 495 E. Perkins St., Ukiah, CA 95482; (707) 462-4705.

Hopland Chamber of Commerce, P.O. Box 677, Hopland, CA 95449.

Lake County Chamber of Commerce, 875 Lakeport Blvd., Lakeport, CA 95453; (707) 263-5092.

WINE TASTING IS SERIOUS BUSINESS

"...Fresh, clean, elegant and lively, with a ripe black-current edge to the plum and cherry flavors. The tannins are firm, but rounded, and the flavors have amplitude, echoing fruit on and on."

—Description of a 1989 Guenoc Cabernet Sauvignon Lake County

Chapter Three

NORTHERN SONOMA COUNTY

From Zin vineyards to redwood forests

Mention Sonoma and some wine enthusiasts think of the Sonoma Valley and winery pioneers General Vallejo and Count Haraszthy. That's chronologically correct, since the California wine industry's roots go deep into Sonoma Valley soil.

Today, however, northern Sonoma County has more wineries, more vineyard acres and produces more wine than its better-known neighbor. In all of California, it's second only to the Napa Valley in total premium wine grape acreage, with more than 25,000 acres of vines.

A scenic southern extension of Mendocino County, northern Sonoma is a mix of tawny hills, redwood groves in hidden canyons and shady oak clusters bearded with Spanish moss. More than 1,400 miles of rural roads invite aimless wandering and spontaneous picnics beside trickling creeks. The Sonoma Coast, like the Mendocino Coast above it, is a spectacular sweep of sea stacks, velvety green headlands and charming yesterday towns weathered—like old men of the sea—by ocean breezes.

Let's not forget the main reason we came here. The north county's gravelly, loamy soils along the flanks of the Russian River and Dry Creek produce some of America's premier wines. The region offers a further advantage for the wine-tasting crowd: uncrowded wineries of an assortment ranging from tiny and rustic to historically musty to grandiloquently modern.

A few decades ago, this area was busy with hop yards and orchards. Some unused hop kilns survive, marked by their distinctive conical towers; a couple have been converted to wineries. Plums once were so profuse that the Healdsburg Chamber of Commerce sponsored annual tours to view the pretty pink-white blossoms. The area still blooms with springtime color, but it's wild mustard, California poppies and the tender green buds of awakening grapevines.

The first settlers in this area were not pious mission padres or grapestompers. They were Russian fur hunters, working down the coast from

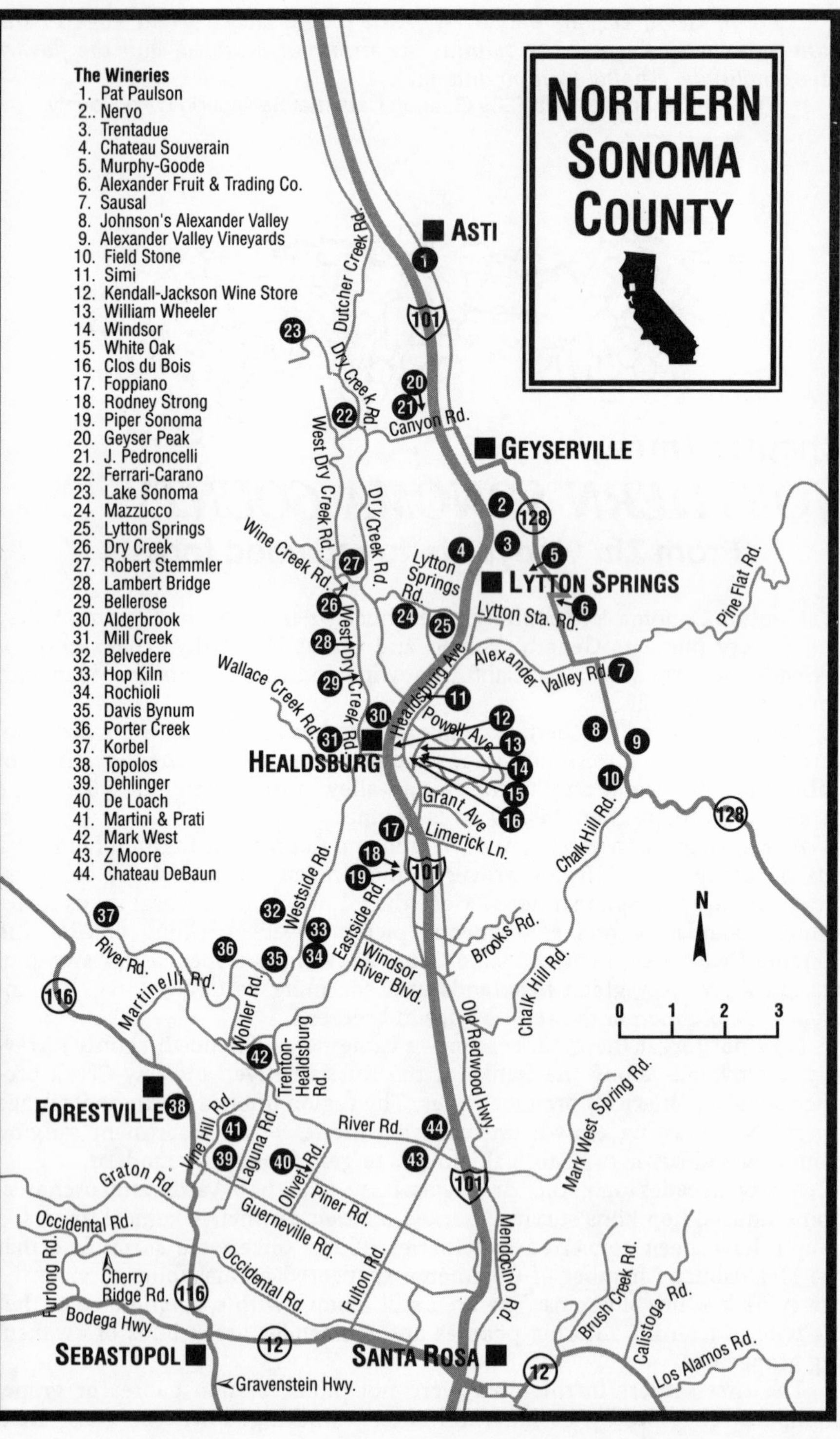

NORTHERN SONOMA COUNTY
The Wineries
1. Pat Paulson
2.. Nervo
3. Trentadue
4. Chateau Souverain
5. Murphy-Goode
6. Alexander Fruit & Trading Co.
7. Sausal
8. Johnson's Alexander Valley
9. Alexander Valley Vineyards
10. Field Stone
11. Simi
12. Kendall-Jackson Wine Store
13. William Wheeler
14. Windsor
15. White Oak
16. Clos du Bois
17. Foppiano
18. Rodney Strong
19. Piper Sonoma
20. Geyser Peak
21. J. Pedroncelli
22. Ferrari-Carano
23. Lake Sonoma
24. Mazzucco
25. Lytton Springs
26. Dry Creek
27. Robert Stemmler
28. Lambert Bridge
29. Bellerose
30. Alderbrook
31. Mill Creek
32. Belvedere
33. Hop Kiln
34. Rochioli
35. Davis Bynum
36. Porter Creek
37. Korbel
38. Topolos
39. Dehlinger
40. De Loach
41. Martini & Prati
42. Mark West
43. Z Moore
44. Chateau DeBaun
ASTI
GEYSERVILLE
LYTTON SPRINGS
HEALDSBURG
FORESTVILLE
SEBASTOPOL
SANTA ROSA
Dutcher Creek Rd.
Dry Creek Rd.
Canyon Rd.
West Dry Creek Rd.
Wine Creek Rd.
Lytton Springs Rd.
Lytton Sta. Rd.
Pine Flat Rd.
Alexander Valley Rd.
Healdsburg Ave
Wallace Creek Rd.
Powell Ave
Grant Ave
Limerick Ln.
Chalk Hill Rd.
Westside Rd.
Eastside Rd.
Brooks Rd.
Windsor River Blvd.
Old Redwood Hwy.
River Rd.
Martinelli Rd.
Wohler Rd.
Trenton-Healdsburg Rd.
Mark West Spring Rd.
Vine Hill Rd.
Laguna Rd.
Olivet Rd.
Graton Rd.
Piner Rd.
Guerneville Rd.
Occidental Rd.
Fulton Rd.
Mendocino Rd.
Brush Creek Rd.
Calistoga Rd.
Furlong Rd.
Cherry Ridge Rd.
Bodega Hwy.
Gravenstein Hwy.
Los Alamos Rd.
101
128
116
12
N
0 1 2 3

Alaska. Seeking the slippery sea otter, they established a colony called Romazov on the Sonoma Coast in 1809, followed three years later by the fortress of Rossiya—now Fort Ross State Historic Park.

Concerned by this intrusion, Mexican officials began moving north from San Francisco in the 1820s. They granted huge tracts of land to favored soldiers and politicians who had helped in their recent war for independence from Spain.

The Russians eventually withdrew and northern Sonoma County became the domain of contented *rancheros* who ran their cattle over the grassy hills. The first American to settle here was Cyrus Alexander. Arriving in the 1840s, he managed one of the Mexican land grants for several years in exchange for 9,000 acres of land. He never produced wine but he did plant some of the area's first grapes. The valley enclosing his ranch now bears his name.

The first vintners of significance were the brothers Korbel. Francis, Joseph and Anton settled along the Russian River in 1882, logged off the redwoods and began planting vineyards. Their winery survives to this day as the largest facility in the area.

More European vintners followed and hundreds of acres were soon graced by vines. Unhappily, Sonoma County was one of the first areas in the country to be hit by phylloxera. Even Luther Burbank, recently settled in Santa Rosa, joined the fight against the deadly scourge. Several wineries closed before root-grafting ended the crisis. Then many of the survivors were finished off by Prohibition.

One, however, was started right in the middle of Prohibition by an Italian optimist. John Pedroncelli bought a defunct winery in Dry Creek Valley in 1927, gambling that the foolish law soon would be repealed. His gamble paid off and his sons John, Jr., and Jim still run the place.

Generally warmer than Mendocino and the Sonoma Valley, northern Sonoma County produces excellent reds, particularly Zinfandel (see box). It's also noted for its award-winning Cabernet Sauvignon, Pinot Noir and Chardonnay.

We'll tour wineries in the area's three major viticultural regions. Alexander Valley lies alongside U.S. 101, extending from the Mendocino County border south to Geyserville, and east toward the Mayacamas Mountains. Dry Creek Valley is southwest and the Russian River Valley is below that, lying west of Santa Rosa.

Four towns along our routes offer restaurants and other respite. Burgeoning Santa Rosa, with 100,000 residents and growing, forms a suburban plug for the lower end of north county. Although it has ample cafes and motels and a good museum or two, we don't regard it as a wine country town. It is instead the northern outpost for San Francisco Bay Area sprawl, the seat of much of the county's recent population spurt. However, the area to the north becomes quickly rural.

Pleasantly rustic Healdsburg, which *is* a wine country town, is surrounded by vineyards and has a few downtown tasting rooms. Citizens of this burg of 10,000 are doing a fine job face-lifting their downtown area to preserve its oldstyle look. Its tree-shaded, landscaped plaza is rimmed by a bevy of boutiques, antique shops and a good restaurant or two. Several motels and inns permit wineland wanderers to bed down near the vineyards.

Geyserville and Cloverdale, also amidst the vines, offer fewer facilities. Tiny Geyserville is noted for a couple of good restaurants and two fine Victorian-era B&Bs, while Cloverdale has a handful of small motels and cafes.

Alexander Valley

Old Cyrus would be pleased to learn that the valley bearing his name still is essentially agricultural. No city disturbs its bucolic tranquility. Geyserville sits between Alexander and Dry Creek valleys. However, the closest thing to a community within the valley is the grizzled **Alexander Valley Store,** a general mercantile in the classic sense.

Less hilly than Dry Creek or Russian River valleys, Alexander is a patchwork of vineyards and pasturelands, flanking the upper reaches of the Russian River. The land climbs gently eastward toward low hills, giving way to clusters of oaks and groves of madrones.

ALEXANDER VALLEY WINERY TOUR • Begin at the top of the county, taking the Asti exit from Freeway 101 about four miles south of **Cloverdale**. Italian Swiss Colony—one of the area's earliest wineries—is no more, although the historic landmark sign survives. The facility was purchased by Wine World, Inc., (a division of Nestle's Chocolate, of all things) and the tasting room is closed. A short distance south on Asti Road is **Pat Paulsen Vineyards** tasting room, located in the former Asti village.

Continue south on Asti Road, paralleling the freeway for about five miles until you come to **Geyserville** (and the road becomes Geyserville Avenue). You could follow the freeway south, but we prefer smaller roads, free of freight trucks. You'll see Geyser Peak Winery west across the freeway, but ignore it for now. It marks the start of our Dry Creek Valley tour.

Pass through Geyserville, zig under the freeway a couple of times and you'll encounter **Nervo** and then **Trentadue** wineries on the east side of U.S. 101. Cross under the freeway on Independence Lane and follow it to architecturally striking **Chateau Souverain**.

Having played tag with the freeway, backtrack on Geyserville Avenue and turn right (east) onto Highway 128. You'll see **Murphy-Goode Estate Winery** on the right after a few miles. Staying on 128 (which does a couple of rural 90-degree turns), you find **Alexander Fruit and Trading Company** (yes, folks, it's a winery) and **Sausal Winery**, both on the left. Between them is the earlier-mentioned **Alexander Valley Store** at the junction of 128 and Alexander Valley Road. This century-old general store provides necessities and a small bar for locals, plus picnic fare and a selection of regional wines.

A bit farther along is **Johnson's Alexander Valley Winery** on the right and **Alexander Valley Winery** on the left. Finally, as the valley approaches Mount St. Helena and starts becoming attractively rumpled, you'll hit **Field Stone Winery** on the right. From there, retrace your route a bit, turn left onto Alexander Valley Road and follow it past the general store to Healdsburg.

Pat Paulsen Vineyards (Pat and Jane Paulsen Winery) • T ⌶

Asti Store Road, Asti, CA 95425; (707) 894-3197. Tasting daily 10 to 5 (closed Tuesday and Wednesday fall through spring); most major credit cards.

Most varieties tasted. Wine logo items and Pat Paulsen souvenirs.

Only the wines are serious here. The rest of this complex is an extension of the comedian's personality. The cottage-style tasting room markets campaign posters and buttons from his eternal quest for president, T-shirts that declare "Thou shalt not drink cheap wine" and other Paulson souvenirs. When we visited, "Pat Who? in '92!" campaign material was on sale. Pat's wife Jane runs the winery while he runs around the country, practicing his droll humor.

A sign stating "Art gallery; enter at your own risk" directs you to a battered farm shed. There, you'll find treasures such as the "original peppermill used at the Last Supper" and a plunger labeled as a magician's wand.

The pink stucco Paulson complex once was the tiny village of Asti, which served the nearby Italian Swiss Colony Winery. It is also—as you might guess—world headquarters for Pat Paulson for President. Plans were afoot for a deli and restaurant to be opened in the village in 1992, so you may be able to dine with the Paulson touch.

Tasting notes: The Paulson list is small and consistently good. We liked a crisply dry Sauvignon Blanc and a full-bodied, smoky-flavored Cabernet Sauvignon. Prices range from $7 to the early teens. Paulson's Refrigerator White jug wine is a good buy at $8.50 for a 1.5 liter. Unfortunately, tastings are served in dinky plastic glasses. That will never do at White House dinners, Mr. Paulson.

Vintners choice: "Cabernet Sauvignon and Sauvignon Blanc are our biggest award winners," says Jane. "And Refrigerator white, as an unusual table wine."

Nervo Winery • T ⨯

19550 Geyserville Ave. (P.O. Box 25), Geyserville, CA 95441. Tasting daily 10 to 5; MC/VISA. Most varieties tasted. A few wine-related gift items; picnic area beneath a grape arbor.

Although it's one of north county's oldest wineries and has the rustic look for proof, Nervo is part of an empire owned by the Trioni family and the Penfolds wine combine of Australia. Started as a family winery in 1908, it was sold by Frank Nervo to nearby Geyser Peak in 1974. Geyser, in turn, was purchased by Trioni-Penfolds.

The weathered old farm style complex is easy to spot. Just look for the ornamental red Santa Fe railway caboose sitting out front. The tasting room occupies a little cottage and the handsome stone winery is just beyond. The place is comfortably funky; decor consists of thousands of calling cards that have been tacked to walls and ceilings by generations of wine sippers.

Tasting notes: Nervo wines are remarkably inexpensive. We found a drinkable blush at $1.99 a bottle and a likable Farmers Table red wine with strong Zinfandel character for $2.64. Nervo bottles the usual white varietals

---

and some hearty reds that should be laid away for aging. The winery has no exterior marketing, so you'll have to journey to Geyserville to cash in on these prices.

Vintners choice: "Farmer's Table is the type of wine I like," says winemaker Raul Bandiera. "It's soft, yet full-flavored; a great spaghetti wine."

Trentadue Winery • T

19170 Geyserville Ave., Geyserville, CA 95441; (707) 433-3104. Daily 10 to 5 spring through fall and 10 to 4 in winter; MC/VISA, DISC. All wines sampled. Nice giftware selection and deli items; shaded picnic area.

You'll likely be greeted by a tail-wagging dog or two at this family-owned ranch complex amidst the vines. The combined tasting room and gift shop is upstairs in a masonry block winery building. A long list of wines and a good selection of glassware, wine-related items and other giftwares will tempt the visitor.

Leo Trentadue started the winery in 1969 and has expanded his operation considerably, with 170 acres now in vines. The family built the main winery in 1972.

Tasting notes: Trentadue's wines are uniformly excellent and moderately priced. The primary focus here is reds. The list includes some mature Zins and Cabs ready for drinking, yet with enough body to be put down for a few more years. Among our favorites were a full-flavored eight-year-old Zinfandel for $10, a hearty Old Patch Red blend for $8 and—from the list of whites—a crisply dry Semillon for $7.50. Prices range from $5 to the mid-teens. Trentadue also offers some fine ports, which can be sampled for a dollar a nip.

Vintners choice: "Merlot, Petit Sirah, Carignan and Old Patch Red," says Cindy Trentadue.

Chateau Souverain • T$ R

400 Souverain Rd., Geyserville, CA 95441; (707) 433-8281. Tasting in the cafe daily from noon to 10 p.m. Wednesday-Sunday; choice of four wines for $2.50; also wines by the glass; MC/VISA, AMEX. Most varieties tasted. A few wine-related gift items. See listing under "Wine country dining" for Chateau Souverain Restaurant.

One of the county's more striking winery structures, Chateau Souverain resembles a blend of hop kiln and manor house. A former tasting room has been converted into a stylish cafe trimmed with bright splashes of color and hanging tapestries. The adjoining restaurant is done in pink and beige, accented by chandeliers and embroidered panels. Wine is produced at this large complex, but there is no touring.

Ironically, it was designed for tours when it was built in 1972 by the Pillsbury Company; it was a popular stop on the wine trek. Its new owners, Wine World, Inc., are focusing instead on the restaurant operations.

Tasting notes: Tastings are conducted either at an attractive bar or at cafe tables. For a $2.50 fee, one selects four wines from a list of eight or nine. The list is small: Chardonnay, Sauvignon Blanc, Zinfandel, Cabernet Sauvignon and Merlot. If you find a particularly likable wine, you can order it by the glass—with lunch, since the cafe serves *hors d'oeuvres* and light entrees. We chose a Chardonnay, Zin, Merlot and Cab for our set-up and were quite pleased with all of them. Prices range from $7.50 to the mid-teens.

Vintners choice: "Our 1987 Sonoma County Chardonnay and 1987 Alexander Valley Cabernet," says spokeswoman Norma Cooper.

Murphy-Goode Estate Winery • T

4001 Highway 128 (P.O. Box 156), Geyserville, CA 95441; (707) 431-7644. Daily 10:30 to 4:30; MC/VISA. Select varieties tasted. A few wine-related gift items.

Tim Murphy and Dale Goode planted their first grapes in the Alexander Valley in the 1960s, then they joined with marketing specialist Dave Ready to establish the winery in 1985. The modern, medium-sized no-frills winery is fronted by an appealing cathedral-ceiling tasting room.

Tasting notes: Visitors choose from a small list: Fumè Blanc, Chardonnay, Cabernet and late-harvest Muscat. They tend to be light with pronounced fruit flavor, low in tannin and easy on the wood. A fruity Fumè Blanc and lush, soft Chardonnay were particularly tasty. Prices range from $9 to $12.50; higher for some aged "Library wines" that aren't tasted.

Vintners choice: "The reserve Fumè Blanc is our signature wine; much of our effort goes into it," said our tasting room hostess.

Alexander Valley Fruit and Trading Company • T

5110 Highway 128, Geyserville, CA 95441; (707) 433-1944. Daily 10 to 5; MC/VISA. Most varieties tasted. Interesting selection of gift items, focusing on wine and food gift packs. Picnic area on a knoll with a view of the vineyards.

Steve and Candy Sommer started their winery in 1984 with a sense of creativity. In addition to producing wines that win a fair share of medals, they assemble gift packs of wine and gourmet food items. Then Steve made *People Magazine* in 1990 when he came up with an unusual packing material: popcorn.

"It's organic, biodegradable, provides good packing protection and it isn't much heavier than styrofoam," Candy told us with honest enthusiasm.

You can buy it at the winery in 14-cubic-foot bags, should you decide to forsake styrofoam pebbles. One of their popular gift packs is wine, popping corn and gourmet seasoning. The name's great: "Hot to Pop."

All this creativity occurs in a tasting room with a country store theme, sitting amidst vineyards on an upslope from the highway. The winery, with a modest capacity of 15,000 cases, is out back.

Tasting notes: The Sommers are traditionalists when it comes to wines: crisp whites and hearty reds. The prices—inside or outside the gift packs—are moderate: $6 to $10; a bit more for some late harvest stuff. A two-year-old Zinfandel and a four-year-old Cabernet revealed the Sommer touch: big berry flavor and soft tannins. Carignan, Sauvignon Blanc, Chenin Blanc, Chardonnay and a couple of late harvest wines complete the list.

Vintners choice: "Our style of wine is light and fruity, as if it was just picked off the vines," says Candy.

Sausal Winery • T

7370 Highway 128, Healdsburg, CA 95448; (707) 433-2285. Daily 10 to 4; MC/VISA. Selected wines tasted. Few wine-related gift items; picnic area.

Prim landscaping and an arbor-shaded picnic area accent this small complex, perched on an upslope, half a mile off Highway 128. The small, simple tasting room is fused to the end of the handsome redwood winery.

The facility dates from 1973 although the Demostene family has been growing grapes in the Alexander Valley since 1925. Some of their vines are older still, dating back to the turn of the century. Four children of pioneer grape grower Leo Demostene operate the winery today.

Tasting notes: Sausal's repertoire is small—about six or eight wines and three of these are open for tasting on a given day. We sipped excellent Zinfandel and Cabernet which, typical of Sausal wines, were well-rounded with little hint of tannin or wood. Prices range from $5 for a white Zin to $14 for Zins and Cabs. One can purchase six-bottle packs of "verticals," with three vintages each of aged Zinfandel and Cabernet.

Vintners choice: "We are known for our traditional style Zinfandels," says the winery's Cindy Martin.

Johnson's Alexander Valley Winery • T CT ⛌

8333 Highway 128, Healdsburg, CA 95448; (707) 433-2319. Daily 10 to 5; MC/VISA, AMEX. Most varieties tasted. Some wine-related gift items; small picnic area. Visitors can peek into the winery.

A century-old barn on this family ranch complex holds a couple of surprises: modern wine-making equipment and a pair of grand theater organs. Ranks of pipes fill much of the winery, standing alongside stainless steel fermenters and aging casks. The tasting room itself is a simple affair: a wooden counter in a corner.

Johnson family members have been organ buffs for years and—at the time of our visit—were completing the assembly of an antique from Sacramento's old Capitol Theater. Which is all very strange, because no one in the family plays. However, they often host organ concerts with guest performers. The new addition will be computer-driven, so resonate tones can filter through the weather-worn old barn at the flip of a switch.

The small, century-old winery is presently owned by Tom and Gail Johnson; their daughter Ellen is the enologist.

Tasting notes: Wines are available only at the winery and a few local outlets. The list is small and the wines are uniformly tasty and fair priced, from $7 to the mid-teens. Our favorites were a wonderfully fruity non-barrel Chardonnay and a powerful, complex late harvest Zinfandel with 15.4 percent alcohol. Pinot Noir, Cabernet, white Zin and Johannisberg Riesling complete the selection.

Vintners choice: "Year in and year out, Pinot Noir is our best seller," says Tom. "We do well with our Cabs and Chardonnay, too."

Alexander Valley Vineyards • T GTA ⛌

8644 Highway 128, Healdsburg, CA 95448; (707) 888-7209. Daily 10 to 5; MC/VISA, AMEX. Most varieties tasted. Some wine-related gift items; picnic area. Tours by appointment.

This facility is as modern as neighboring Johnson's is rustic. The adobe brick winery is set in rumpled foothills above Highway 128, rimmed by landscaped grounds, sheltered by moss-bearded oaks. With vineyards in the foreground and a meadow rising beyond, it's one of the valley's most pleasing spots. It's also an historic spot, occupying lands settled by Cyrus Alexander a century and a half ago. His grave site is on a hill above the winery.

The Wetzel family purchased this land in 1963, planted vines and began producing premium varietals in 1975. All are estate-produced and vintage dated.

Tasting notes: Winemaker Hank Wetzel's reds are full-bodied yet light in tannin, with a touch of wood. We noted a pleasant spiciness in the Merlot and Zinfandel, and the Gewürztraminer was complex and dry with a strong acid finish. Cabernets were big wines, suitable for aging. Prices range from $7.50 to the mid-teens.

Vintners choice: "Cabernets," said Hank. "They're very stylistic, and older wines are available on request."

Field Stone Winery • T CT ⛱

10075 Highway 128, Healdsburg, CA 95448; (707) 433-7266 or (800) 54-GRAPE (California only). Daily 10 to 5. Most varieties tasted; MC/VISA. A few wine-related gift items; picnic area; casual winery tours.

Your casual tour begins the moment you step through the doorway of the distinctive bunker-style winery. The stroll to the small corner tasting room takes you past ranks of stainless steel fermenters and aging barrels. The winery is fashioned like a root cellar—dug into a hillside, then faced with local stone. Outside, properly gnarled old oaks and picnic tables made from wine barrels complete the earthy setting.

Producing only 8,000 cases a year, this family-owned winery focuses on Cabernets and Petit Sirahs, which have won an assortment of gold medals. Former Berkeley mayor Wallace Johnson established the firm in 1977. It's now operated by his daughter Katrina and her husband John Staten.

Tasting comments: The style is soft and fruity, with a subtly acidic finish in the whites and a touch of wood and tannin in the reds. Among our choices were a crisp, fruity Sauvignon Blanc, a gentle Chardonnay with a hint of oak, a complex Cabernet Sauvignon and a well-rounded Petit Sirah with enough tannin to keep it honest. Prices range from $9 to the low twenties.

Healdsburg & surrounds

Not only is Healdsburg in the heart of the wine country, some wine outlets are in the heart of Healdsburg. Several tasting rooms, orphaned from their wineries, are situated here.

We're not much drawn to storefront tasting rooms. Without the vineyards, picnic areas and embracing sights and smells of their wineries, they're rather sterile. The experience is akin to walking into a wine shop that carries only one brand. You're dealing with a clerk, not a winery employee. Of course, you do have the advantage of sampling before you buy.

As we mentioned earlier, this town of 10,000 is worth a stop for its old-style plaza, boutiques, antique stores, restaurants and bed and breakfast inns. Neighborhood streets are shaded by mature trees, some sheltering century-old Victorian homes.

HEALDSBURG AREA WINERY TOUR • Coming into town from your Alexander Valley trek, you'll blend onto Healdsburg Avenue and encounter the nicely landscaped **Simi Winery** complex, on your right.

Continue into Healdsburg to the **Swenson Building** with its domed clock tower on your right, opposite Healdsburg Plaza. It contains the recently-opened **Kendall-Jackson Wine Country Store** tasting room, plus an assortment of boutiques and cafes.

From here, follow Plaza Street (along the edge of the plaza) two blocks to the **William Wheeler Winery** tasting room at the corner of Plaza and East Street. Backtrack a block to Center Street, turn left and go two blocks south to **Windsor Vineyards** tasting room on Center just short of Mill Street. Then take three one-block turns: left onto Mill, right onto East and left onto Haydon. With luck, you'll wind up at **White Oak**, a downtown winery at Haydon and Fitch streets. Finally, go right onto Fitch Street one block to the large **Clos du Bois** complex.

That last paragraph can best be accomplished by walking. You can poke into the shops along the way.

Three other wineries, on the outer fringe of Russian River Valley, are near Healdsburg. It's logical, therefore, to return to Healdsburg Avenue and persist south (passing under Freeway 101) until your route becomes Old Redwood Highway. Just beyond town, you come to **Foppiano Wine Company** on your right, and then **Rodney Strong Vineyards** and **Piper Sonoma Cellars,** also on the right, sitting side by side among the vines.

Simi Winery • T GT

16275 Healdsburg Ave., Healdsburg, CA 95448; (707) 433-6981. Daily 10 to 4:30; MC/VISA, AMEX, DISC. Most varieties tasted free; small charge for some reserve wines. Good gift shop selection. Guided tours daily at 11, 1 and 3. Redwood-shaded picnic areas.

Venerable Simi is an island of yesterday, surrounded—but not altered—by the swelling city of Healdsburg. Its massive rough-cut stone winery with three-foot-thick walls was built by Chinese laborers in 1890. More practiced Italian stonemasons later added a smoother section. A modern octagonal tasting room stands nearby. The park-like complex—even the parking lot—is carefully landscaped and shaded by redwoods. (If we had a category for most attractive winery carpark, Simi would win.)

The one-hour tour provides a look at modern winemaking in an ancient, pleasantly musty yet spotlessly clean environment. Wine ferments in glossy stainless steel and sleeps in six thousand barrels in a time-worn loft. The sight would send a Dominican monk into ecstasy.

Established in 1876 by Giuseppe and Pietro Simi, the winery was inherited by Giuseppe's daughter in 1904. In an era when women were expected to tend to the stove and their knitting, the remarkable Isobel Simi Haigh took charge. She ran the operation for 66 years, surviving Prohibition, Depression and male chauvinism. She sold the winery in 1969. It has since gone through several owners, finally becoming a part of France's Moet-Hennessy/Louis Vuitton conglomerate.

Tasting notes: Although it's one of northern Sonoma's largest wineries with an output of 140,000 cases, Simi focuses on a few select varietals. The whites we tasted—Semillon, Sauvignon Blanc, Chenin Blanc and Chardonnay—were properly lush and fruity. The sole red is Cabernet Sauvignon, not a big wine but full-flavored with soft tannins. Prices are moderate, ranging from $6 to $16. Vertical offerings of Chardonnay and Cabernet may be purchased.

Vintners choice: "Chardonnay, Cabernet and Sauvignon Blanc," says visitor center manager Bill Wetmore, simply.

Kendall-Jackson Wine Country Store • T

337 Healdsburg Ave., Healdsburg, CA 95448; (707) 433-7102. Daily 10 to 5; MC/VISA. A new tasting room with gifts and wine logo items. See the Kendall-Jackson Winery listing under Lake County in the previous chapter.

William Wheeler Winery tasting room • T

130 Plaza St., Healdsburg, CA 95448; (707) 433-8786. Daily 11 to 4; MC/VISA. A few wine-related gift items.

The small Wheeler Winery offers Cabernet, a Rhône-style red, Chardonnay, Sauvignon Blanc, white Zinfandel and Merlot. Prices are mostly in the teens.

Vintners Choice: "Our R.S. Reserve, a unique Rhône-style blend, and our Chardonnay, for its finesse and elegance," says the winery's Susan Munger-Grande.

Windsor Vineyards tasting room • T

239 Center Street, Healdsburg, CA 95448; (707) 433-2822. Tasting Monday-Friday 10 to 5, weekends 10 to 6.

Although Windsor has won its share of medals, it's noted mostly for its marketing gimmickry. The firm specializes in mail order catalog sales and personalized labeling. If you want to serve Fumè Blanc labeled "Bottoms up to Beverly and Bill" at your next wedding reception, this is the place. The list includes the usual premium varietals. Prices are rather moderate, ranging from around $6 to the early teens.

White Oak Vineyards & Winery • T CT

208 Haydon St., Healdsburg, CA 95448; (707) 433-8429. Open Friday, Saturday and Sunday from 10 to 4; MC/VISA. Most varieties tasted.

White Oak functions in a warehouse in the Healdsburg industrial area. The small combined tasting room and office occupies a small cottage nearby. Founded in 1981 by former fisherman and building contractor Bill Meyers, the winery draws from local hillside vineyards.

Tasting notes: Meyers' Pinot Noir, Zinfandel, Cabernet Sauvignon, Chardonnay and Semillon are quite good, with strong varietal character. Prices range from around $7 to the mid-teens. Pinot Noir is the winemaker's favorite.

Clos du Bois • T GTA

Five Fitch St., Healdsburg, CA 95448; (707) 433-5576. Daily 10 to 5; MC/VISA, AMEX, DISC. Most varieties tasted. Tours by appointment.

The setting isn't glamorous, but the downtown Clos du Bois winery in leased warehouse space is state of the art. Some of the space-age equipment can be seen through viewing windows from the large, appealing tasting room and gift shop. On a slow weekday, your host may offer a vertical tasting from the extensive list.

Clos du Bois was founded by wine grower Frank Woods in 1974, then sold to Hiram Walker in 1986. With all that corporate money, a new facility

Ancient vines and an old farm house create a pastoral scene in Northern Sonoma County's Russian River Valley.

is being built beside the freeway north of Healdsburg. So you may find things moved from town by the time you read this.

Tasting notes: The wines were uniformly excellent (with numerous medals to prove it). The Sauvignon Blanc, early harvest Gewürztraminer and Chardonnay had exemplary varietal characteristics, fruity and dry with a hint of spice. A Cabernet was lush and berry-like with a gentle tannin finish. If you like a soft Bordeaux style, try the Marlstone, a blend of Cabernet Sauvignon, Cabernet Franc, Merlot and Malbec.

Vintners choice: "Sauvignon Blanc, Chardonnay, Gewürztraminer, Pinot Noir, Merlot, Marlstone and Cabernet Sauvignon," said spokeswoman Vanessa Oakes, shamelessly going through most of the list.

L. Foppiano Wine Co. • T CT ⌅

12707 Old Redwood Highway (P.O. Box 606), Healdsburg, CA 95448; (707) 433-7272. Daily 10 to 4:30; MC/VISA, AMEX, DISC. Most varieties tasted. Some wine-related gift items. Casual tours by appointment. Shaded picnic areas.

One of the county's pioneer wineries, the Foppiano facility looks its age, although modern equipment lurks beneath its weathered exterior. It was established by John Foppiano in 1896 and the family made jug wines for decades. Leaders of the third and fourth generations, both named Louis, have shifted the focus to premium varieties.

An unadorned, square-shouldered stucco building houses the century-old winery and a cottage-style hospitality center invites tasting. A few picnic tables are parked under shade trees around the farmyard.

Tasting notes: Although the winery is unpretentious, the wines are excellent. We encountered two outstanding reds: a lush, spicy Cabernet Sauvignon and a near-perfect Zinfandel. Other varieties offered under the family label are Sauvignon Blanc, Chardonnay and Petite Sirah, with prices from $7.50 to $10. Older vintages are available at predictably higher cost. Foppiano also markets honest, drinkable varietals under the Riverside Farm label; they're good buys at $5.75 to $6.75.

Vintners choice: The Foppianos have been making red wines for a century, explained our tasting room hostess, and they're particularly proud of the Petit Sirah and Zinfandel. "We're mostly a red wine winery."

Rodney Strong Vineyards • T CT ⌅

11455 Old Redwood Highway, Healdsburg, CA 95448; (707) 433-6511. Daily from 10 to 5; MC/VISA, AMEX, DISC. Most varieties tasted. Some wine-related gift items. Nice picnic area on "The Green," a lawn area near the vineyards. Informal tours.

This is one of the area's more interesting architectural creations—an earth-hugging structure of laminated beams and textured concrete. Before entering the tasting room, take a left or right just inside the winery door and stroll around the suspended walkway. You'll see assorted phases of the operation as various wedges of the winery come into view. The tasting room seems to hang above it all.

Rodney Strong started in the wine business 30 years ago, peddling mail-order wines out of a tasting room in Tiburon. The operation expanded to an old winery in Windsor and became Windsor Vineyards. Under that name, the present earthy structure was built. After assorted buy-outs and name changes that resulted in an identity crisis (at least for observers), Rodney Strong Vineyards now occupies the Windsor site. Now a separate firm, Windsor hawks its mail-order wines in Healdsburg.

Tasting notes: Rodney Strong's moderately long list offers an interesting mix, from slightly sweet Gewürztraminer (or off-dry, if you insist) to an excellent full-bodied River West Vineyard Zinfandel from 90-year-old vines. Overall, the style is soft and fruity with low tannins. Prices range from $7 to the high teens; more for some reserve selections.

Vintners choice: "Vineyard designated and estate bottled Sauvignon Blanc, Pinot noir, Cabernet Sauvignon and Chardonnay," says the winery's Bill Holland.

Piper Sonoma Cellars • T$ GTA

11447 Old Redwood Hwy., Healdsburg, CA 95448; (707) 433-8843. From 10 to 5, daily June through October and Friday through Monday the rest of the year. Three sparkling wines tasted for $3.50; also sold by the glass; MC/VISA, AMEX. Good selection of giftwares; picnic terrace. Guided tours by reservation.

Piper Sonoma speaks of European elegance and properly so, since it's owned by Piper Heidsiek, the champagne subsidiary of Remy Martin. The winery and high-style tasting room are in a textured concrete structure fronted by a terrace, formal gardens and a lily pond. Artworks and fancy furnishings grace a hospitality; a burgundy canopy accents the tasting bar.

Tours of the modern facility are conducted by prior arrangement at 11 and 2, followed by sparkling wine tasting. A glossy multi-media show details the mysterious process that puts those tiny bubbles in the bottle. The tour then shifts to the winery *moderne*, where computers and taste buds work together to produce the nose-tickling product.

Piper Sonoma of course follows the traditional *mèthode champenoise*, in which the champagne never leaves the original bottle until you drink it. (The slick brochure says "*mèthode champenoise* process" which, any first-year French student will tell you, is redundant.)

Tasting notes: Piper Sonoma produces three sparkling wines—brut, blanc de noirs and brut reserve. For $3.50, you get a generous sample of each, in properly slim glasses. They're cleverly set on an "educational placemat" that describes the wines' qualities, lists sparkling-wine terminology and coaches you in your sensory evaluation. All are fine examples of the sparkling art: crisp and dry with a clean finish, yet with strong hints of the Chardonnay, Pinot Blanc and/or Pinot Noir that went into their making.

Dry Creek Valley

Dry Creek Valley is one of our favorite wine-tasting haunts. We challenge any wineland to match this pastorale.

Vineyards carpet the narrow valley floor and ascend its benchlands. Live oak thickets crown rounded knolls and redwood groves are tucked into secret ravines. Ancient Zinfandel vines cover steep hillsides like knotted fists. Family farms with rusty pick-ups sitting out front share the valley with sleek new wineries built by urban millionaires who seek solace under a rural sun.

There's even a rustic Dry Creek country store to confirm the valley's rural heritage. Never mind that it sells *foi gras* and camembert in its deli.

The broad shoulders of Warm Springs Dam plug the upper end of the valley. Built in the mid-80s, the dam provides—ironically—a year-around trickle for the once-seasonal Dry Creek. Since it's an earthen dam covered with grass, its dominance of the upper valley is subtle. The reservoir, Lake Sonoma, provides water sports, fishing, shoreside hiking, camping and picnicking.

The valley is noted for producing big, perfectly-balanced Zinfandel from vines predating Prohibition. Zin is the valley's most widely planted grape.

The moderate ocean-tempered climate is ideal for Chardonnay, Pinot Noir and Cabernet Sauvignon as well.

DRY CREEK VALLEY WINERY TOUR • Start just north of **Geyserville**, taking the Canyon Road exit from U.S. 101 west to **Geyser Peak Winery,** within sight of the freeway. Continuing west, you soon encounter **J. Pedroncelli Winery** on the right. As Canyon Road T-bones into Dry Creek road, turn right and you'll see the impressive new **Ferrari-Carano** facility. Press northward on Dry Creek toward Warm Springs Dam to **Lake Sonoma Winery** on your right. Then re-trace your route south on Dry Creek Road.

As you drive, watch for **Timber Crest Farms** up a short road to your left. A small, busy retail room sells specialty foods such as dried fruits and vegetables, nuts, pasta sauces, preserves and apple butter. The stuff is pricey but it's tasty. You can sample many of the goodies. It's open weekdays 8 to 5 and Saturday 10 to 4.

At Lambert Bridge Road, you'll encounter **Dry Creek General Store.** It comprises the total "town" of Dry Creek, claiming a population of four. The inviting old store offers a deli, local wine selections and essentials such as food, clothing and fishing worms. Local boys sip their Coors at a tiny bar in a corner of the store. Picnic tables out front encourage visitors to linger. Since most people ask, that palatial mansion on the hill behind the store is not the residence of a wine baron. It was built by an area doctor.

Continue south a short distance to Lytton Springs Road, turn left and climb rolling hills to **Mazzucco Vineyards** and **Lytton Springs Winery**, both on the right. Now, backtrack a bit. Return on Lytton Springs to Dry Creek Road, go back to the general store and turn left onto Lambert Bridge Road. Drive the short distance to **Dry Creek Vineyard** on the left, then continue to **Robert Stemmler Winery** on the right. You soon hit West Dry Creek Road. Turn left (south) and drive over gently rumpled foothills to **Lambert Bridge Vineyards** and **Bellerose Vineyard,** both on the right. West Dry Creek is an exceptionally scenic route, lined with oak thickets, occasional redwoods, vineyards and small family farms. You may enjoy driving its full length as it parallels Dry Creek Road through the valley.

Just below Bellerose, West Dry Creek bumps into Westside Road near the bold arched gateway to **Madrona Manor.** Once the home of wealthy pioneer John Alexander Paxton, it's now an opulent inn and restaurant. Turn left onto Westside Road, heading east toward Healdsburg. Just short of the freeway, go right onto Kinley Drive then right again on Magnolia and follow it a short distance to **Alderbrook Winery.**

Geyser Peak Winery • T

22281 Chianti Rd., Geyserville, CA 95441; 433-6585. Daily 10 to 5; MC/VISA. Most varieties tasted. Small gift selection; covered patio picnic area.

The large Geyser Peak complex sits at the gateway to Dry Creek Valley although the winery itself is on the Alexander Valley side. It's a comely facility with landscaped grounds, terraced patios and a stone-faced ivy-covered winery built against a wooded hillside. Hiking trails wander about the grounds; one leads to a picnic area near the Russian River. It's difficult to believe that freeway traffic is but an exhaust belch away.

Geyser Peak traces its heritage loosely back more than a hundred years, when the Bagnani family sold jug wine and vinegar. Part of an old wooden structure still survives from those days. The winery closed and was resuscitate later in this century. It's now owned by the Trione-Penfolds combine.

Tasting comments: The list is long and busy and difficult to pinpoint. It runs the gamut from dry to less-than-dry whites to reds that lean toward the soft side. Among the interesting items we sipped were a "Semchard" (ugly name, but nice blend of Semillon and Chardonnay) and a soft, gentle Merlot. The wines are fair-priced, ranging from $5 to the mid-teens.

Vintners choice: "Our limited (estate-bottled) reserve Chardonnay and Cabernet Sauvignon and Meritage," says spokeswoman Shelly Steen.

J. Pedroncelli Winery • T GTA

1220 Canyon Road, Geyserville, CA 95441; (707) 857-3531. Daily 10 to 5; MC/VISA, AMEX. Most varieties tasted. Small deck with picnic tables. Guided tours by reservation.

Founded during Prohibition by John Pedroncelli, the winery has grown considerably under his sons' guidance. It now turns out about 100,000 cases annually. Jim handles much of the business and John is the primary winemaker.

We"ve watched the Pedroncelli complex grow for nearly a quarter of a century. The tasting room, once a counter in a cinderblock storage building, is now an attractive, airy space with high ceilings and a curving bar. Picnic tables near the vineyards encourage visitors to linger in this bucolic setting. It's all part of a pleasing, ranch-style complex of redwood buildings cradled among vine and oak-thatched hills between the Alexander and Dry Creek valleys.

Tasting notes: The Pedroncellis like their whites crisp and lean, and it was evident in their spicy Chardonnay and fruity Chenin Blanc. The Pinot Noir was soft and berry-like and a Cabernet Reserve was outstanding—big, powerful and complex. The Zinfandel was predictably excellent; *The Wine Spectator* rated the 1988 version as a best buy at $8 a bottle. Overall, prices range from $6 to $10; a few reserves go to the mid-teens.

Vintners Choice: "Zinfandel, which we've been making for 40 years," says third-generation Julie Pedroncelli. "We can draw from excellent Dry Creek Valley grapes."

Ferrari-Carano Vineyards and Winery • T GTA

8761 Dry Creek Rd., Healdsburg, CA 95448; (707) 433-6700. Daily 10 to 5; MC/VISA, AMEX. Selected wines tasted. Tasteful line of giftwares and clothing. Tours by appointment Tuesday-Saturday at 10 and 2.

From old family tradition we move to new monied opulence. Ferrari-Carano is a striking blend of manor house, castle and leading-edge winery. The large facility, fronted by a formal entryway and rimmed by billiard-green lawns, is the newest and certainly the most palatial of the Dry Creek operations. The tasting room-gift shop, with its window walls into the winery, is as stylish as a Rodeo Drive boutique.

All this largess comes from the coffers of Don and Rhonda Carano, owners of the El Dorado Hotel and Casino in Reno. The double-jointed winery

A ROSÉ BY ANY OTHER NAME?

Rosè is no longer the Rodney Dangerfield of American wines. For years, many wine enthusiasts, including this one, regarded pink wine as merely a compromise between red and white. Marketing strategies by some firms suggested that rosè "goes with anything," which didn't help its status. Diners intimidated by long wine lists would seek refuge in rosè.

Traditionally, most pink wine was made from Grenache, a sweet, high-yield grape from southern France. Rosè originated there and the word is French for "pink." You probably know that it's made from red grapes by withdrawing the skins early during fermentation. Since most of the color and body come from the skins, this produces a light, fruity wine. France has made some great rosès but most of that produced in California was considered rather ordinary.

Then in 1958, Sonoma County's Pedroncelli family bottled and marketed a rosè made from high-quality Zinfandel grapes, labeling it "Zin Rosè." The raspberry-like complexity of Zinfandel produced a much more pleasing pink wine, and it began winning awards. Others followed, with names like Rosè of Cabernet, Rouge Noir and the notorious "White Zinfandel" (which is actually pink). August Sebastiani produced a pink Gewürztraminer and called it Eye of the Swan.

In the 1980s, wine writer Jerry Meade coined the term "blush wine" to describe a premium rosè produced at northern Sonoma's Mill Creek Vineyards, and the floodgates were opened.

Soon, Zinfandel Blush, Cabernet Blush, Pinot Blush and White Zinfandel were among America's best-selling wines. Pink Zin led the pack, particularly after Sutter Home's Bob Trinchero got into the act. Buying up every loose grape he could find and mass-producing White Zin, he practically cornered that market. In 1987, he sold 2.5 million cases of his White Zinfandel, catapulting Sutter Home from one of Napa Valley's smallest wineries to one of its largest. Pink wine now comprises 38 percent of America's wine sales, and at least half of that is White Zin.

Pedroncelli's Zin Rosè is still an excellent wine, and it's still winning awards. It and other "blush" wines continue to be leading sellers. Finally, California's rosès are getting some respect.

name pays homage to Rhonda's grandmother, who inspired her interest in wine and food.

The facility, started with a vineyard purchase in 1981, may be even more opulent by the time you get there. A 14,500 square foot Italianate villa is on the drawing boards, to be linked to the present winery by a Bordeaux-style underground cellar.

Tasting notes: The Ferrari-Carano roster is brief but first rate. Fumè Blanc, Zinfandel and Cabernet Sauvignon, the wines selected for tasting on the day we visited, were outstanding. Others on the list are Chardonnay and a couple of inexpensive blends, Cuvee Blanc and Summer Blush (a Cabernet-

Merlot composite). Premium varietals start just under $10 and travel to the mid-teens; reserve selections go higher.

Lake Sonoma Winery • T CT

9990 Dry Creek Rd., Geyserville, CA 95441; (707) 431-1550. Most varieties tasted; MC/VISA. Wine-oriented collectibles and deli with picnic fare and specialty food items. Shaded picnic areas; informal winery tours.

A gravel road pitches steeply upward through hillside vineyards to Dry Creek Valley's newest member, completed in 1990. It's the closest winery to Warm Springs Dam. The view of the dam and the valley from the cheerful, airy tasting room and its wrap-around balcony is impressive. Winery founders Bob and Mary Lou Polson and their son Don chose this site for the view, hoping to lure folks headed for the Lake Sonoma Recreation Area.

It's a fine picnic spot, and the Polsons offer all the essentials from their tasting room deli. In summer, they host a Sunday afternoon potluck barbecue, by reservation.

Unlike some high rollers who've built glitzy wineries in the area, the Polsons are ordinary working folk. They struggled for two decades to make their hillside dream come true. Most of their output of about 3,000 cases a year is sold at the winery and through local outlets.

Tasting notes: Winemaker Don Polson's small list consists of Chenin Blanc, Sauvignon Blanc, Chardonnay, Zinfandel, Cabernet and Cinsault—a grape from France's Rhône Valley. His whites were clean, dry and crisp, as they should be. His Zinfandel—we tasted two vintages—were fruity and soft with a touch of tannin. Prices range from $6 to the mid-teens. In addition to tasting, one can buy most of their wines by the glass.

Vintners choice: "Dry Creek Valley Sauvignon Blanc from hillside vineyards; very fresh and crisp," says winemaker Don. "And our Dry Creek Valley Zinfandel; full, very berry-like."

Mazzucco Vineyards • T

1400 Lytton Springs Road, Healdsburg, CA 95448; (707) 431-8159. Daily 10 to 4; MC/VISA. Most varieties tasted. Small number of wine-related items. Tables on balcony overlooking airport.

Mazzucco's location on a vineyard slope overlooking the Healdsburg Airport is no accident. Its founder, Dr. Thomas Mazzucco of Van Nuys, Calif., is a private pilot. He selected this spot for a quick commute when he built the winery in 1985.

Visitors to the small facility can enjoy the view of vines and planes from a picnic deck outside the cottage-style tasting room.

Tasting notes: The hilly slopes along Lytton Springs Road are Zinfandel country. Thousands of vines—some a century old—line this pleasantly winding route. So it's no surprise that Mazzucco produces excellent full-bodied Zins. Two to three varieties are generally available, although the supply is sometimes exhausted. Two Alexander Valley Cabernets and three Chardonnays complete the selection. Merlot and Cabernet Franc from the Mazzucco vineyards give the Cab a Bordeaux style. We found them to be soft and lush yet full-flavored. The 1986 vintage was a major award winner. Prices range from $12 to $20.

Vintners choice: "We're famous for the big, hearty style of our Zinfandel," said a voice from the winery.

Lytton Springs Winery • T GTA ⌅

650 Lytton Springs Rd., Healdsburg, CA 95448; (707) 433-7721. Daily from 10 to 4; MC/VISA. Most varieties tasted. A few wine-related items; some picnic tables near the winery. Informal tours (as you approach the tasting counter); guided tours by appointment.

Lytton Springs is one of the more appealing of northern Sonoma County's small wineries. The hillside setting is impressive, amidst ancient Zinfandels with trunks the size of young oaks.

The tasting room, a counter at the rear of the winery, is at the same time funky and classy. It's set amidst barrels and tanks, with a Persian rug on the floor and stools at the counter. There is an implied invitation to relax and linger here.

Tasting notes: Established in 1977, Richard Sherwin's winery draws from the ancient vines surrounding it, producing some of the finest Zinfandels in California. These are *big* Zins—lush, complex, full of berries, with a good tannin finish. Reach for your checkbook or VISA if you're a Zin lover, for prices range from $15 to $20. Bear in mind that the yield from ancient vines is very low, and the wine is worth it. Also on the list are a private reserve Cabernet at $18 and a Cab-Merlot-Zin blend at $10.

Vintners choice: "We specialize in hearty red wines; big in style, forward, fruity and with jammy textures," says spokeswoman Stacy Smithson.

Dry Creek Vineyard • T ⌅

3770 Lambert Bridge Rd. (P.O. Box T), Healdsburg, CA 95448; (707) 433-1000. Daily 10:30 to 4:30; MC/VISA. Most varieties tasted. A few wine-related gift items; picnic area on a lawn near the tasting room.

David Stare, one of Dry Creek's first new-generation vintners, arriving here in 1972. For some reason, my clearest recollection of Dave—from an interview years ago—was that he was California's first vintner to get personalized license plate. Naturally, it read: WINERY. It's still on one of the pickups.

He's better known as a producer of consistent award-winning wines, notably Fumè Blanc and Zinfandel. Through the years, he has built his winery's capacity to 90,000 cases. The tasting room is in a nice setting—a sturdy structure suggestive of a manor house, climbing with ivy and rimmed by old trees and new lawns.

Tasting notes: Although we're red wine fans and this is red wine country, we were impressed with Dry Creek's crisp, fruity and perfectly balanced Chenin Blanc and Fumè Blanc. A nutty-flavored reserve Chardonnay was excellent as well; one of the valley's best. A classic Cabernet Sauvignon with a proper chili pepper nose, Cabernet Franc and red Meritage complete Dave's list. He makes fine Zins as well but alas, they were sold out when we visited. Prices range from $6.50 to the early twenties.

Vintners choice: "Our Fumè Blanc is considered the benchmark of this variety," says Mary Jo Chism. "We've developed a reputation for Dry Creek Valley appellation Zinfandel, reserve Chardonnay and Meritage, as well."

Robert Stemmler Winery • T ⌅

3805 Lambert Bridge Rd., Healdsburg, CA 95448; (707) 433-6334. Daily 10:30 to 4:30; MC/VISA. Most varieties tasted. A few wine-related gift items; picnic tables near tasting room.

Our first two impressions—both positive—were that Robert Stemmler's Pinot Noirs are outstanding, and that they bear one of California's most striking labels. Ancient Flemish tapestries depicting a wine harvest caught Stemmler's fancy when he was traveling in Europe. Prints from these tapestries now decorate his wine bottles and his tasting room, which might be described as an elegant lean-to.

The small winery, on a wooded knoll above the vineyards, was established in 1977 by the German-trained winemaker.

Tasting notes: Stemmler produces the ideal Pinot Noir: full, lush, well-rounded. Representing 85 percent of his production, it's one of the best in California. Also on the list are a couple of spicy, dry Chardonnays, Cabernet Sauvignon, and late harvest Johannisberg Riesling and Sauvignon Blanc, both rich with residual sugar. Prices start in the teens and approach the middle twenties.

Vintners choice: "We specialize in award-winning Pinot Noir," was spokeswoman Monique Boucher's understatement.

Lambert Bridge Vineyards • T GTA ⌆

4085 W. Dry Creek Rd., Healdsburg, CA 95448; (707) 433-5855 or (800) 634-2680. Daily 10 to 4:30; MC/VISA. Select varieties tasted. Gazebo and picnic area overlooking Dry Creek Valley. A few wine-related items; tours by appointment.

Perched in a wooden glen above scenic West Dry Creek Road, Lambert Bridge rivals Lytton Springs as one of the area's more attractive small wineries. The tasting room is in a shingle-sided redwood winery resembling a national park chalet. The simple counter is surrounded by tiered barrels; metal chandeliers hang from the winery rafters and a fireplace occupies one end of the structure. Vivaldi's spirited *Four Seasons* issues from hidden speakers.

Gerard Lambert started this small estate winery in 1975, focusing both on winery esthetics and a limited list of premium varieties. He appears to be succeeding at both.

Tasting notes: Lambert's list is short and first rate. Chardonnay was excellent, full and spicy with oak accents from extended barrel aging. A four-year-old reserve Cab, winner of three golds, was wonderfully complex and fruity, light on the wood. Others on the limited list, priced from $10 to the mid-twenties, are Fumè Blanc, Merlot and Amadeus, a late harvest Sauvignon Blanc dessert wine.

Vintners choice: "Our Chardonnay and Merlot are getting the most recognition at this time," quoth tasting room manager Maureen Kelly.

Bellerose Vineyard • T ⌆

435 W. Dry Creek Rd., Healdsburg, CA 95448; (707) 433-1637. Tuesday-Thursday 1 to 4:30, Friday-Sunday 11 to 4:30, closed Monday; MC/VISA, DISC. Most varieties tasted. Picnic area. Group tours only, by appointment.

We've found our second favorite wine label, and perhaps the valley's most elementary tasting room. Earthy, organic Bellerose more resembles an old farmyard than a modern winery. There's even a rusting piece of farm equipment or two, as if to prove the point. No Flemish tapestries here.

Charles and Nancy Richard, who started the winery on this ancient farm in 1978, practice organic agriculture. They even use a pair of draft horses named Rowdy and Curly. The critters, who contribute generously to the organic concept, are honored with their portraits on Bellerose' Workhorse Red Cabernet Sauvignon.

One sips Workhorse Red and some fine Bordeaux style wines in a tasting room that consists of a plank counter, not far from a cluttered office desk.

Tasting notes: Cuvee Bellerose, a Cabernet Sauvignon-Merlot blend done in the Bordeaux style, is an excellent, outspoken wine that will improve with age. Workhorse Red is a lighter Cab, ready for sipping now. Merlot and Sauvignon Blanc finish off the short list. Prices range from $8.95 for Rowdy and Curly through the teens and beyond for some of the reserves.

Alderbrook Winery • T GTA ⌅

2306 Magnolia Dr., Healdsburg, CA 95448; (707) 433-9154. Daily 10 to 5; MC/VISA. Most varieties tasted. A few wine-related gift items; picnic tables overlooking the vineyards. Guided tours by appointment.

Although freeway-close Alderbrook doesn't enjoy the secluded setting of other Dry Creek wineries, it's attractive within. Lots of windows and white-painted knotty pine accent the cheerful, open tasting room, housed in a primly attractive, gray and white-trimmed bungalow. The pleasant setting is popular for weddings, dinners and such.

The winery itself is housed in a refurbished 70-year-old redwood barn nearby. The facility was started in 1981 by a partnership of Mark Rafanelli, John Clark and Philip Staley.

Tasting notes: The Alderbook focus, unusual for Dry Creek but tasty in the result, is white wines. The Sauvignon Blanc and Semillon were lush and fruity, low in acid but with a pleasant finish. The Chardonnay also was gentle on the acid, while full-flavored and spicy. Prices are moderate, from $7.50 to $10.

Vintners choice: "We're best known for our Semillon and Chardonnay," says the winery's Kathleen Mooney.

Russian River Valley

The Russian River flows the length of northern Sonoma County, passing through Alexander Valley before reaching the so-called Russian River Valley. However, the Russian River appellation refers specifically to the lower part of the stream, from the point where it's joined by Dry Creek.

Initially, the terrain differences are subtle, and the lower Russian River Valley rivals Dry Creek in natural beauty. Farther west, the river swings away from the vineyards. It flows through an oldstyle riverbank resort area that has been popular since the 1920s.

Russian River vineyards occur in two distinct areas. The first group is clustered in rolling hills along Westside Road between Healdsburg and Rio Nido. The second gathering is south of the river, in a mix of farmlands and evergreen clusters. Both areas are accented here and there by redwoods.

As in Dry Creek Valley, gentle and forest-clad mountains are never far away and side roads invite wandering into concealed canyons.

One side trip is particularly inviting. From Westside Road near Hop Kiln Winery, turn right onto Sweetwater Springs Road. Follow its winding course past a cheerful creek, into darkened redwood groves, through the tiny old town of Sweetwater Springs and up to a high point offering views of half the county. Staying on its corkscrew course, you'll emerge below the redwood groves and hiking trails of Austin Creek State Recreation Area.

RUSSIAN RIVER WINERY TOUR • From Alderbrook Winery, where you've just finished a final sip of Semillon, retrace your route southwest along Westside Road. Or retire for the night in next-door **Healdsburg** and start afresh tomorrow.

Your first winery encounter will be **Mill Creek** on the right. It's technically in the Dry Creek Valley, but for tour purposes, we're including it with other Westside Road places. From there, you'll hit a string of wineries, beginning with **Belvedere** on the right, marking the technical start of the Russian River Valley. Then come **Hop Kiln** and next-door **Rochioli,** both on the left, **Davis Bynum** on the right and finally, tiny **Porter Creek,** a short distance up a side road on the right.

As Westside Road blends into River Road, continue west to the baronial wine estate of **Korbel.** Back-track onto River Road for about two and a half miles, then turn right onto Martinelli Road. Cross the Russian River, then go left onto the Gravenstein Highway (Highway 116). Follow it briefly to Forestville. Just beyond the tiny town, you'll see **Topolos at Russian River** on the right.

Pay attention from this point, because it gets complicated. Interesting wineries are scattered along a webwork of farm roads in this flatter part of the valley.

A short distance from Topolos on Highway 116, turn right into **Kozlowski Farms** at 5566 Gravenstein Highway. It's not a winery but a farm foods outlet specializing in organically produced jams, sauces, chutneys, relishes, homemade pies and other goodies. Dozens of items are available for tasting, and the place has a picnic area. Hours are 9 to 5 daily. Like Dry Creek's Timber Crest Farms, the stuff isn't cheap, but it's excellent.

Just beyond Kozlowski, turn left onto Guerneville Road and you'll find **Dehlinger Winery** at Guerneville and Vine Hill Road. Follow Guerneville to Olivet Road, turn left and drive a short distance to **De Loach Vineyards** which is on your left. Now, backtrack on Guerneville Road, turn right onto Laguna Road and follow it to **Martini & Prati,** cresting a hill on the left.

You lost yet? Continue on Laguna Road, drive straight across River Road (without turning) and your route becomes Trenton-Healdsburg Road. Soon, you happen upon **Mark West Vineyards** on your left.

Now, it gets easier. Return to River Road, turn left and follow it some miles to **Martinelli Ranch** on your right. Another farm products outlet, it specializes in apples and apple products, jams, dried fruits and nuts. Like the others, it offers samples. Hours are 10 to 6 daily.

Next door is **Z Moore Winery,** also on the right. Now you're approaching the freeway. Before surrendering to civilization's traffic, turn left onto Fulton Road and follow it to the glamorous **Chateau DeBaun,** one of the county's newest and most opulent wineries.

Mill Creek Vineyards • T

1401 Westside Rd. (P.O. Box 758), Healdsburg, CA 95448; (707) 433-5098. Daily noon to 4:30 in summer, Friday through Monday the rest of the year; MC/VISA. Select varieties tasted. A few wine-related items; picnic area in a grove above the tasting room.

The water wheel on Mill Creek's tasting room, useful only as an ornament, appears to have earned landmark status. It was featured on the 1991 cover of ***The Californias***, the state's tourist promotion magazine. The simple tasting room—with wheel attached—*does* look convincingly rustic, although it was built in the 1970s.

The small winery is owned by Charles and Vera Kreck and their offspring, who built much of the tasting room and winery by hand, using logs from their property. It sits among hillside vineyards above Westside Road.

Tasting notes: If you're attracted by the ornamental water wheel, you may stay for the wines, which we found to be very good, and fair-priced. The Chardonnay was complex and spicy with gentle acid. A Cabernet Sauvignon was soft and ready to drink, with a nice chili pepper nose and herbal flavor. The Krecks also produce an excellent Cabernet Blush (winner of a dozen medals in 1990) and a late harvest Sauvignon Blanc that's deliciously sweet without being cloying. Zinfandel, Merlot and other premiums also appear on their list. Prices range from $6.75 to $10.

Their Cabernet rosè, incidentally, is part of vineland history. It was this wine, according to Vera Kreck, upon which wine writer Jerry Meade first bestowed the term "blush. (See box on page 63.)

Vintners Choice: "Our Merlot was served in the White House and we've been famous for it ever since," Vera reported proudly.

Belvedere Winery • T

4035 Westside Rd., Healdsburg, CA 95448; (707) 433-8236. Daily 10 to 4:30; MC/VISA. All varieties available for tasting (limit of four samples). Nice selection of wine-related gift items and works by local artists; picnic area.

Belvedere is a comely winery in a nice locale, set amongst hillside vineyards. A short drive up a gravel lane takes you to a pair of neat wooden buildings, carefully set into the sloping landscape. Lawns and blooming flowers give the place a park-like quality. Honeysuckle droops from a porch overhanging the tasting room.

Winery founder Peter Friedman selects grapes from a variety of county vineyards to produce his reserve wines, which are sometimes issued with thematic labels. For instance, proceeds from his recent "Gifts of the Land Series," bearing wildlife labels done by noted artist Rod Frederick, went to conservation causes. Despite its prim, compact look, this is not a small operation. Belvedere produces half a million cases a year.

Tasting notes: Belvedere's reserve list carries four wines, all at $10.70: a fruity, crisp Chardonnay; a spicy, nicely acidic Merlot; a full-bodied Cabernet with a gentle tannin finish; and a rich, late harvest Muscat Canelli. The "Discovery" wines are excellent buys, ranging from $4 to $6.50. That series includes Chardonnay, Sauvignon Blanc, Cabernet Sauvignon, white Zinfandel and a jug white and red.

Vintners choice: "Reserve Russian River Valley Chardonnay and Robert Young Alexander Valley Merlot," says the winery's La Vonne Holmes.

Hop Kiln Winery at Griffin Vineyards • T CT

6050 Westside Rd., Healdsburg, CA 95448; (707) 433-6491. Daily 10 to 5; MC/VISA, AMEX. Most varieties tasted. Some wine-related gift items; art exhibits. Picnic tables under sheltering fig tree, others near a pond.

After visiting a pretend water wheel, we go to a real hop kiln—at least a former one. Dr. L. Martin Griffin succeeded in preserving the esthetics of a century-old hop dryer when he converted it into a winery in the 1970s. Some of the original equipment is intact and the tasting room is fashioned of aged wood, in keeping with the antiquity of the place. Adorned with the works of local artists, it occupies a mezzanine above the winery. A tour thus consists of walking to a railing and peering down at stainless steel vats and wooden barrels.

The triple towers of Hop Kiln, a registered historical landmark, made the cover of this book. Alas, those century-old Petit Sirah vines—whose brilliant fall colors we captured in the foreground—have been replaced by a younger vineyard.

Tasting notes: The list is surprisingly long for a winery that issues only 10,000 cases a year, but Marty Griffin likes to work with small lots. His Gewürztraminer was the best we tasted in the county, and the Zinfandel was full, complex and acidic, yet comfortably soft. A 1989 Petite Sirah, from our vines on the cover, was lush, wonderfully busy and with a nice berry-acid finish. Others on the list are white Zinfandel, Chardonnay, Johannisberg Riesling, Napa Gamay, a fruity white called A Thousand Flowers, Cabernet Sauvignon and a good jug red. Prices are moderate, ranging from $7.50 to the mid-teens.

Vintners Choice: "Zinfandel, Marty Griffin's Big Red, Gewürztraminer," said Jo Anne Strobl. "Our red wines are known for being robust and fruity."

J. Rochioli Vineyard and Winery • T GTA ⌅

6192 Westside Rd., Healdsburg, CA 95448; (707) 433-2305. Daily 10 to 5; MC/VISA, AMEX. Selected wines tasted. Shaded picnic area overlooking the vineyards. Tours for small groups by appointment.

Next door to Hop Kiln, Rochioli has the look of comfortable rural prosperity. Passing through a stone gate, you enter a tidy farm complex shaded by ancient trees and accented by gardens. A trim little tasting room, in a cottage overlooking the vineyards, is brightened by art and photo exhibits. Picnic tables occupy a vineyard-view patio.

This small estate winery, producing about 60,000 case a year, has been owned by the Rochioli family since the end of Prohibition.

Tasting notes: Curiously, we felt Rochioli's least expensive wine was their best—a $9 Sauvignon Blanc. Others on the list are noteworthy, particularly a state-of-the-art Chardonnay and a soft, full estate Pinot Noir. The Gewürztraminer was well-crafted and slightly sweet. Powerful Cabernets, not usually available for tasting, have won several medals. Prices range into the mid-teens.

Vintners choice: "We're known for our Chardonnay and Pinot Noir," said Theresa Rochioli. "We have fine soils and micro-climates that bring out the best flavors in these grapes."

Davis Bynum Winery • T GTA ⌅

8075 Westside Rd., Healdsburg, CA 95448; (707) 433-5852. Daily 10 to 5; MC/VISA. Most varieties tasted free; small fee for some limited release wines. A few wine-related gift items; picnic patio beside winery. Guided tours by reservation.

Straightforward masonry block structures cluttered with equipment are trademarks of the Davis Bynum Winery, sitting just above a farmyard off Westside Road. The wine price list is written on a chalkboard above the plain, tiled counter in the small tasting room.

Former newspaperman Davis Bynum started his winery in 1968 in a store front in Albany, a town near Oakland far from the nearest serious grapevine. He moved to this former hop ranch in 1974. Wine grapes are drawn from several premium vineyard areas.

Tasting notes: Bynum's list is weighted toward whites, which are moderately priced, from $7 to $12.50. The overall style is rather soft, light and crisp. Of those whites, we tilted toward a Semillon and Chardonnay. Reds include light, peppery Cabernet and gentle, spicy and subtly acidic Pinot Noir. This is always a nice feature: palate-clearing bits of bread are available between tastes.

Porter Creek Vineyards • T

8735 Westside Rd., Healdsburg, CA 95448; (707) 433-6321. Daily 10:30 to 4:30 in summer, weekends only the rest of the year; MC/VISA. Selected wines tasted.

You've heard of home winemakers operating out of their garage. Soft-spoken George R. Davis is a *professional* winemaker doing that. Actually, only the tasting room is garaged, and it's a rustic classic: a plank laid over wine barrels. The small winery is up a dusty lane in Porter Creek Valley, just beyond a 1920s-style cottage. The setting hearkens back to the wine country's earlier days, when one stopped by the local vintner with an empty jar to have it filled.

George's operation is hardly archaic, however, and his wines have won several awards. He's been doing business here since 1978, drawing grapes mostly from his own hillside vineyards of Pinot Noir and Chardonnay.

Tasting notes: From George's small list, we discovered an excellent Chardonnay, full and complex, crisp and perfectly balanced; a light yet full-flavored Estate Pinot Noir and a lush, berry-like Hillside Pinot. Prices range from $10.50 to $18; a tasty Pinot Blanc goes for $6.50.

Vintners choice: "Pinot Noir from our own hillside vines produces a flavorful, nicely concentrated wine," said George.

Korbel Champagne Cellars • T GT

13250 River Rd., Guerneville, CA 95446; (707) 887-2294. Daily 9 to 5; MC/VISA, AMEX. All varieties except brandy tasted. Extensive gift selection; landscaped picnic areas. Winery tours daily every 45 minutes in summer, and hourly from 10 to 3 the rest of the year; garden tours daily at 11 and 2.

This isn't just a winery; it's an institution. From a visitor standpoint, it's one of the most interesting such institutions in California. Started in 1882, it evolved into a baronial estate with great stone, vine-covered buildings, a tower right out of medieval Germany and oldstyle European gardens. The setting is equally impressive, in a narrowing of the Russian River Valley, rimmed by wooded hills on one side and a vineyard tilting toward the redwood-bordered river on the other.

The setting so resembles central Europe that television's *Combat* series was filmed here for two years. During the shooting, the obliging special ef-

ZINFANDEL: A GRAPE WITHOUT A COUNTRY?

Picture this: California wine pioneer Agoston Haraszthy eagerly sorts through the latest batch of grape cuttings he'd shipped from Europe. He picks up a bundle of slips and squints at them curiously.

"Hmmm, can't read the label...all smudged. Must've gotten wet in the hold of the ship." He ponders for a moment, then says: "I think I'll call it 'Zinfandel.' That's a nice European-sounding name."

Some historians say Haraszthy introduced our most widely planted premium red. They claim that it arrived, fuzzy label and all, with thousands of cuttings he shipped from Europe during the 1860s.

New research has defrocked that theory. Author David Darlington has devoted an entire book, ***Angels' Visits***, to Zinfandel and its origins. He points out that it was being grown as a table grape in New England in the 1830s, before Haraszthy ever touched American soil.

What, then, *is* the source of the so-called mystery grape? Like the best of mysteries, this one may never be solved. Researchers find no reference to the word "zinfandel" in European documents. However a clonal copy, *Primitivo*, was discovered in southern Italy in 1967 by plant pathologist Austin Goheen of the U.S. Department of Agriculture. Lab tests proved that the Primitivo is indeed a twin to our Zin.

And where did *that* come from? Possibly from the Mideast, according to wine historian Charles Sullivan. Italy was a crossroads of the earliest civilizations, and Greeks or Albanians fleeing the Ottoman Turks might have introduced the vine. However, with 2,000 grapes growing in Italy today, it's impossible to trace their sources.

American Zinfandel *has* been traced—to those 19th century New England nurserymen. Long Island's Robert Prince listed a black "Zinfardel" of Hungary in his 1850 botanical catalog. Other sources mention "Zinfindel," obviously having trouble agreeing on the spelling. Captain F. W. Macondray of Massachusetts may have introduced Zinfandel to California when he came to San Francisco in 1848.

We like to regard Zinfandel as "America's grape," since it came to California during the Gold Rush, by way of New England. Unlike its noble European ancestors, it's sassy and lively on the palate. It's versatile, suitable for everything from light, fruity blush wines to rich, heavy ports. Young plants produce soft Beaujolais-style reds; old vines yield huge, complex wines rivaling venerable Cabernets.

As author Darlington suggests, Zin is a slightly flawed beauty, like Meryl Streep. It's more intriguing and approachable than some paragon of perfection. Those who venerate Cabernet and Chardonnay are considered aficionados. We Zinfandel enthusiasts are more of a cult.

Dry Creek Valley, the Sierra Nevada foothills and Paso Robles are the state's best Zin areas. Among vintners specializing in "America's wine" are Pedroncelli, Lytton Springs, Rafanelli, Swan and Ravenswood in Sonoma County; Storybook Mountain and Mayacamus in Napa Valley; Ridge in the Santa Cruz Mountains; Mastantuono, Saucelito Canyon and Pesenti in the Paso Robles area; and Amador Foothill, Story Vineyard, Stevenot and Santino in the Sierra foothills.

fects people blew up old redwood stumps that had been cluttering up the vineyards for decades.

The Korbel tour is one of the most complete in the business. Guests gather at a tiny railway station that once served the valley, visit a formal garden, then stroll into the ancient, wonderfully musty stone cellar. There, a well-done mini-museum recalls the Korbel story with old photos, documents and artifacts. Visitors move from the museum to a theater for a nicely photographed slide show, then they're led through the champagne cellars where the complex process is explained. Finally, eager to sample what they've been studying, they're escorted to the plush, carpeted hospitality center for a tasting conducted by their guide.

One learns a remarkable statistic on this tour: Korbel produces seventy percent of all the *mèthode champenoise* made in this country—more than one million cases annually.

Assorted Korbels operated the winery until 1954, when it was purchased by the present owners, Gary B. and Richie C.Heck.

Tasting notes: The sparkling wines, ranging from semi-dry to dry, are clean, crisp and a good buy for under $10. Although it has been producing primarily sparkling wine and brandy for several years, the firm is expanding to include a line of still wines.

Topolos at Russian River Vineyard • T GTA R

5700 Gravenstein Highway N., Forestville, CA 95436; (707) 887-1575. Daily 11 to 5; MC/VISA, AMEX. Most varieties tasted. Good giftware selection; guided tours by appointment. Restaurant; see listing under "Wine country dining" below.

This pleasantly funky winery complex looks like it was designed by 1960s flower children. The tasting room is small and cozy, fashioned of old wood; its giftwares lean toward folk crafts. Weather-darkened buildings hold assorted wine-making gear. A nearby garden is planted with native flowers and grasses. Above all this, the soft clink of glassware announces the presence of a restaurant, which features a *nouveau*-tilted menu.

The earthy operation is the work of Michael, Jerry and Christine Topolos. They produce fewer than 10,000 cases a year, in small, carefully nurtured lots. Not surprisingly, the grape picking, winemaking and even labeling are done by hand. They use, whenever possible, pesticide-free grapes.

Tasting notes: From this funky setting emerge some excellent wine buys—if you like big, assertive reds. For the price, a powerful, peppery Zinfandel ($7.50) was one of the best wines we've tasted. A big Zinfandel Rossi from 80-year-old vines ($10) is another good buy. Also on the list is a full-flavored Grand Noir, spicy Petit Sirah, a soft and herbal Sauvignon Blanc and Alicante Bouschet. Rarely bottled in California, Alicante is a French cross breed of Grenache, Tenturier du Cher and Aramond grapes, producing an inky dark, full-bodied red.

Vintners choice: "Our Zinfandel from old vines, Petite Sirah, Grand Noir and Alicante Bouschet," reports a voice from Topolos.

Dehlinger Winery • T CT

6300 Guerneville Rd., Sebastopol, CA 95472; (707) 823-2378. Daily 10 to 5; MC/VISA. Most varieties tasted. A few wine logo gift items; picnic area.

We like tasting rooms located inside the winery, surrounded by the feel, sight and good earthy smells of the wine-making process. When you step through the double doors of the small Dehlinger Winery, arrows direct you past vats and barrels to a simple counter. The arrows are redundant, since the place is cozily small. Tasting room decor consists mostly of ribbons that virtually cover a wall behind the counter.

Outside, an old house crouches on a hill above the vineyards, ominously suggestive of the set for *Psycho*. Its role isn't sinister all; it's used by the winery owner for entertaining, according to our tasting room host. Tom Dehlinger established this small winery in 1975, and bottles about 8,000 cases a year.

Tasting notes: The list is short and, fortunately, not sweet. The Chardonnay was crisp, dry and wonderfully nutty; one of the better we've sampled. Cabernet Franc and Cabernet Sauvignon were both light with soft acids, yet spicy with excellent bouquets. Prices range from $12 to $14.

De Loach Vineyards • T GT ⌆

1791 Olivet Rd., Santa Rosa, CA 95401; (707) 526-9111. Daily 10 to 4:30; MC/VISA, AMEX. All current releases tasted. Lawn picnic area; guided tours weekdays at 2 p.m. and weekends at 11 a.m. and 2 p.m.

A Japanese courtyard marks the entry to this modern redwood ranch-style winery, offering an interesting architecural mix. Art decorates the walls of the tasting room and glossy ceramic tile covers the floor and tasting bar. After sipping, visitors can adjourn to a lawn picnic area near the vineyards and—something unique for wineries—pitch a game of horseshoes.

Located on a plain between the Russian River Valley and Santa Rosa, the winery was established by the De Loach family in 1979. All of its wines are estate-bottled.

Tasting notes: "Uniformly excellent" reads the note I'd scratched on my steno pad. The Chardonnay was fruity and well balanced; the Sauvignon Blanc soft and rich. Both the Zinfandel and white Zin displayed pleasant, peppery noses; flavors were rich and properly berry-like. Pinot Noir and Fumè Blanc complete the list, whose prices range from $7.36 into the mid-twenties. Some limited selection wines go higher.

Vintners choice: "We're especially proud of our Chardonnays and Zinfandels," wrote Kristin Thigpen, the firm's communications director.

Martini & Prati Winery • T

2191 Laguna Rd., Santa Rosa, CA 95401; (707) 575-8064. Daily 11 to 4; MC/VISA. Most varieties tasted. A few wine-related gift items.

Amidst operations ranging from upscale to deliberately funky, we've found an old fashion winery making old fashioned wines. As if to prove the point, the tasting room hostess serves it in a traditional thick little Italian drinking glass.

A water tower crowns this complex, which looks more like an industrialized farmyard than a winery, with its cluster of pitched-roof warehouses and scatter of equipment. It's obviously been "added-to" as the winery grew since its founding in the 1880s. Present owners Elmo Martini and Edward Prati have run the place since 1951, although assorted Martinis go back to 1902. This is a big operation, producing two million gallons of wine sold in bulk, plus 15,000 or so cases for Martini & Prati labels.

Tasting notes: The list is long and the wines are—well—not bad for the price, which starts around $5 and doesn't go too much higher. The best thing we tasted was an inexpensive port, a blend of Zinfandel, Petit Sirah and Carignan. The "Ravioli Red" (great name) was rich and just short of sweet, which some will like. Assorted varietals, sherries and even a vermouth fill out the directory.

Vintners Choice: "We're known for our dessert wines," reports Jeani Martini.

Mark West Vineyards • T CT

7000 Trenton-Healdsburg Rd., Forestville, CA 95436; (707) 544-4813. Daily 10 to 5; MC/VISA. Most varieties tasted. Gift area with selection of wine country items, specialty foods and picnic fare. Two picnic area; informal winery tours by request.

Mark West accords one of the valley's more hospitable winery settings. The shingle-sided tasting room and winery occupy a landscaped yard rimmed on three sides by vineyards. Wooded hills of the Coast Range offer a scenic backdrop. Two lawn areas beckon picnickers, who can assemble lunch at the tasting room deli. The place is popular for weddings and other functions encouraged by the sociable owners, Joan and Robert Ellis.

The Ellis family created Mark West in the early 1970s, planting three classic varietals—Pinot Noir, Chardonnay and Gewürztraminer—for their estate-bottled wines.

Tasting notes: Mark West produces big, full-flavored wines suitable for immediate sipping or laying away. The three estate wines are rich with varietal character. A Zinfandel from a 90-year-old vineyard was powerful and complex, finished in oak; a three-year-old Pinot Noir was soft with good berry flavor; and a barrel-fermented Chardonnay Reserve was properly toasty and buttery. Gewürztraminer, Johannesburg Riesling and a hand-riddled Blanc de Noir sparkling wine completes the list. Wines are moderately priced for their quality, ranging from $8.50 to the high teens.

Vintners choice: Joan Ellis favors her three estate wines, "Chardonnay, Pinot Noir and Gewürztraminer, handcrafted in traditional style."

Z Moore Winery • T

3364 River Road, Windsor, CA 95492; (707) 544-3555. Daily 10 to 5. Most varieties tasted. Some wine-related gift items. Picnic area under a huge, gnarled oak.

Housed in a triple-towered hop kiln, Z Moore Winery (without the period) offers sanctuary from busy River Road traffic hurrying toward Freeway 101. The weathered farm buildings seem miles removed from encroaching Santa Rosa suburbs.

"We'd have more visitors," our host said, glancing out the window at the teeming highway, "but they whiz by so fast, they miss the place."

The place shouldn't be missed. The distinctive tasting room occupies one of the drying towers of the hop kilns, affording views of vineyards, ancient apple orchards and distant peaks—as well as the highway. Started in 1986 by Daniel Moore and wife Natalie Zuccarelli-Moore (now we find the Z), it specializes in small lots of carefully crafted wines. Output is about 5,000 cases.

Tasting notes: Those hurried motorists are missing some excellent whites, particularly Z Moore Chardonnay, barrel-fermented Gewürztraminer and flower petal rich late harvest Gewürztraminer. Two everyday wines are better than ordinary and we love their names: Quaff Gamay Beaujolais and Quaff Gewürztraminer. Prices range from $6.25 for quaffing to the early teens for premiums; limited Chardonnays are $18.

Vintners choice: "Gewürztraminer," says Deborah Womack. "We offer three different styles, from trend-setting barrel fermented dry to the Quaff label to a late-harvest dessert style."

Chateau DeBaun • T CT ⌅

5007 Fulton Rd., Fulton, CA 95439; (707) 571-7500. Daily 10 to 5; major credit cards. Most varieties tasted. Wine-related gift items; landscaped picnic area; vineyard tours by appointment.

Chateau indeed. This opulent wine estate begs to be nestled on a high slope above the Rhine or alongside a meandering stream in Burgundy. It sits instead near busy Freeway 101, loftily trying to dismiss the constant growl of traffic.

Inside, one can wrap oneself in old world opulence, surrounded by brass chandeliers, etched glass and carefully-select artworks. We're tempted to call this a tasting *salon*, with its curved brass-trimmed counter and other posh touches. A banquet hall is next door; the winery is elsewhere. The grounds, appropriate to a chateau, feature formal gardens, a fountain and a gazebo, of course.

It all comes within an inch of being overdone, particularly when the wines are labeled "Overture" and "Prelude" and the garden is described as the *jardin symphonė*. Music-lovers and successful entrepreneurs Ken and Grace DeBaun finished this symphonic facility in 1989. Here, they seek to compose sparkling wine from the U.C. Davis-developed Symphony grape. They weave that melodic theme throughout the operation. So of course, the wine presses are called Gilbert and Sullivan.

Tasting notes: Considering the obvious investment, wines are moderately priced. The Symphony series of sparkling wines, quite crisp and fruity, start at $6. For Romance and Rhapsody, the price goes to $11. Two varietal still wines are $10 each; surprisingly, they're merely called Pinot Noir and Chardonnay.

Vintners choice: In a word, from DeBaun's Tim Hayes: "Symphony."

THE BEST OF THE BUNCH

The best wine buys • Nervo and Trentadue wineries in Alexander Valley; J. Pedroncelli Winery in Dry Creek Valley; Simi Winery and Foppiano Wine Company in Healdsburg; Topolos in Russian River Valley.

The most attractive wineries • Simi Winery in Healdsburg; Ferrari-Carano Winery and Lambert Bridge Vineyards in Dry Creek Valley; Chateau Souverain in Alexander Valley; Hop Kiln Winery, Korbel Champagne Cellars, Mark West Vineyard and Chateau DeBaun, all in Russian River Valley.

The most interesting tasting rooms • Alexander Valley Fruit and Trading Company, Johnson's Alexander Valley Winery and Field Stone Winery in the Alexander Valley; Ferrari-Carano Winery in Dry Creek Valley, Clos du Bois in Healdsburg; Mill Creek Vineyards, Hop Kiln Winery, Korbel

Champagne Cellars, Z Moore Winery and Chateau Debaun, all in the Russian River Valley.

The funkiest tasting rooms • Pat Paulsen Vineyards and Nervo Winery in Alexander Valley; Porter Creek Vineyards and Topolos in the Russian River Valley.

The best gift shops • Alexander Valley Fruit and Trading Company in Alexander Valley; Ferrari-Carano Winery and Lake Sonoma Winery in Dry Creek Valley; and Korbel Champagne Cellars in the Russian River Valley.

The best picnic areas • Field Stone Winery in Alexander Valley; Simi Winery, Rodney Strong Vineyards and Piper Sonoma Cellars in Healdsburg area; Lake Sonoma Winery and Lambert Bridge Vineyards in Dry Creek Valley; Hop Kiln Winery and Korbel Champagne Cellars in the Russian River Valley.

The best tour • Korbel Champagne Cellars (guided), in the Russian River Valley.

BEYOND THE VINEYARDS

Lake Sonoma, created by the construction of Warm Springs Dam in the mid-1980s, out-draws the wineries. Hundreds of thousands of the beer and boating set flock here each summer. Facilities include a visitor center, fish hatchery, boat launches, marina, hiking trails, picnicking and camping on a knoll with a view of the lake and surrounding countryside.

In Healdsburg, you can visit the new **Edwin Langhart Historical Museum** in the 1911 Andrew Carnegie Library building at 221 Matheson Street. Books and documents relating to the California wine industry and a few early-day wine artifacts are featured in the **Sonoma County Wine Library Collection** in the city's new library at 139 Piper Street.

Earlier in this century, the lower **Russian River Valley** was home to posh and glitzy riverside resorts. At lantern-lit dance pavilions, revelers swayed under the stars to the swinging sounds of Harry James and Jimmy Dorsey. Those days are gone, but many resorts survive in a scaled down and sometimes funky fashion. Canoeing and swimming are popular; be advised that you're likely to encounter a nudie beach or two.

A winding drive north from Guerneville on Armstrong Woods Road takes you to the hushed redwood groves of **Armstrong Redwoods State Reserve** and **Austin Creek State Recreation Area**, with hiking, picnicking and such. If you head downstream on State Highway 116, you can explore the stunning sea stack vistas of the **Sonoma Coast**. Prowl about New England-style **Jenner**, then go south south to **Bodega**, forever marked as the bucolic setting for Alfred Hitchcock's *The Birds*. Much of the oceanfront is part of **Sonoma Coast State Beach** with hiking, picnicking, camping, swimming (on rare warm days) and beach-bundling.

If you head north from Jenner, your route will twist along the splendid coastline to **Fort Ross State Historic Park,** a faithful reconstruction of an early Russian fortress and fur trading post. Beyond is **Salt Point State Park,** a classic ecological wedge of coastal environment, stair-stepping from rough-hewn surf to evergreen highlands. **Kruse Rhododendron State Reserve** is just above that, a stunning study in color when the flowers bloom in spring.

Northern Sonoma County activities & attractions

Bicycle rentals • Spoke Folk Cyclery, 249 Center St., Healdsburg; 433-7171.

Canoeing • Bob Trowbridge Canoe trips, one to four days with return shuttle; 433-7247.

Farm products • For a map and guide to direct-outlet farms selling fresh and prepared fruits, vegetables, meats, dairy products and wines, contact ***Sonoma County Farm Trails,*** P.O. Box 6674, Santa Rosa, CA 95406; 544-4728 or pick up free map at most member outlets.

Guided winery tours • "Surrey & Sip" horse-drawn wine tour with picnic lunch, $55 or antique car wine tour with picnic lunch, $60; 894-5956. Five Oaks Farm Horse-Drawn Vineyard Tours with lunch or early dinner, $45; 433-2422.

Hot-air ballooning • Air Flamboyant, 575-1989; Airborn of Sonoma County, 433-3210; Once in a Lifetime, 578-0580.

Museums •

Edwin Langhart Historical Museum, 221 Matheson Street, Healdsburg; 431-3325. Tuesday-Sunday noon to 5; local history exhibits in a classic Carnegie library building.

Sonoma County Wine Library Collection, City Library, 139 Piper St., Healdsburg; 433-3772. A few early winery artifacts and extensive collection of wine-oriented books and documents; hours vary.

Water sports • Healdsburg Veterans Memorial Beach Park, 433-1625; Lake Sonoma, 433-9483; Russian River resorts, 869-2584.

Wineland events • Russian River Wine Road Barrel Tasting, early March; 433-6782. Passport to Dry Creek, food and tastings at several wineries, late April, $30; books up *very* early; 433-3031. Russian River Wine Festival, mid-May, $10; (800) 648-9922. Polo, Wine and All That Jazz, early June, Sonoma County Wine Library Association, P.O. Box 15225, Santa Rosa, CA 95402; 571-1926. Sonoma County Showcase and Wine Auction, mid-August; 579-0577. Sonoma County Harvest Fair, early October; 545-4203. Individual wineries also sponsor various events throughout the year.

Winery tour maps • Free ***Russian River Wine Road*** map of wineries, restaurants and lodgings, available throughout the area, or contact Russian River Wine Road, P.O. Box 46, Healdsburg, CA 95448; 433-6782 or (800) 648-9922 (California only). Mattioli's ***In Your Pocket Guide*** to wineries, lodging, shops, restaurants and recreation, one dollar; available in many gift shops and tasting rooms, or call 965-2006.

WINE COUNTRY DINING

Catelli's The Rex • ∆∆ $$ Y T

21047 Geyserville Ave., Geyserville; (707) 857-9904. Italian-American; dinner $9 to $17; full bar service. Lunch Monday-Friday 11:30 to 2, dinner nightly 5 to 9. Casual; reservations for six or more. MC/VISA. The local hangout; expect to see a couple of vintners and their spouses seriously discussing the Zinfandel crop. A plain front shields an ordinary interior with ceiling fans, tables and a few booths. The menu, heavily Italian, is busy with pastas, parmigiana, steaks, seafoods and chops. Outdoor patio.

Chateau Souverain Restaurant • ΔΔΔ $$$$ T ØØ

400 Souverain Rd., Geyserville; (707) 433-8281. American-continental; dinner $25 to $35; full bar service. Lunch in the cafe Wednesday-Sunday noon to 10; lunch in the restaurant Wednesday-Saturday 11:30 to 3 and dinner Wednesday-Sunday 5:30 to 9, Sunday brunch 10:30 to 2:30; restaurant and cafe closed Monday and Tuesday. Informal to casual; reservations recommended. MC/VISA, AMEX. Elegant restaurant done in pinks and beiges, decorated with embroidered panels. Changing eclectic menu, offering such fare as roast salmon with celery root crust, and macadamia nut crusted Hawaiian sea bass. Smaller **Souverain Cafe** leans toward *hors d'oeuvres* and light fare. Both are smoke-free.

Healdsburg Coffee Company • Δ $ ØØ

312 Center St., Healdsburg; (707) 431-7941. American; light fare; meals $4 to $6; wine and beer. Monday-Friday 8 to 6, Saturday Sunday 9 to 6. Casual; no reservations. MC/VISA. A cheerful place offering soup, salad, sandwiches, quiche, espresso and local wine. On Healdsburg Plaza, with homey oak-antique decor; smoke-free.

Jacob Horner • ΔΔΔ $$$ Y ØØ

106 Matheson St. (on the Plaza), Healdsburg; (707) 433-3939. California nouveau; dinners $14 to $22; full bar service. Lunch Monday-Saturday 11:30 to 2, dinner Tuesday-Saturday 5:30 to 9 (to 9:30 Friday-Saturday). Informal; reservations advised. MC/VISA, AMEX. Locally popular place with stylish Victorian decor; changing menu with items such as Sonoma *cassoulet*, Petaluma

VINEYARD DINING

duck and Sonoma County chicken *paillard*, along with some vegetarian dishes. Smoke-free dining room.

John Ash & Company • ΔΔΔΔ $$$ Ø

4330 Barnes Road (River Road), Santa Rosa; (707) 527-7687. American nouveau; dinners $15 to $25; full bar service. Lunch and dinner daily except Monday. Informal; reservations advised. MC/VISA. Award-winning restaurant with creative fare assembled by chef-owner John Ash. The menu features such innovative savories as sea bass with herbs and eggplant, boned quail stuffed with veal and walnuts and creative pastas. On the edge of the wine country with a vineyard view, near River Road and U.S. 101.

Madrona Manor Restaurant • ΔΔΔΔ $$$$ ØØ

1001 Westside Rd., Healdsburg; (800) 258-4003. California nouveau; dinners $30 to $35; wine and beer. Dinner nightly 6 to 9, Sunday brunch 11 to 2. Informal to dressy. Reservations advised; required on Saturdays. Major credit cards. A Victorian mansion with three elegant little dining rooms. North County's most opulent restaurant, featuring entrèes such as Peking duck with almond coconut rice, stuffed mild chilies, and salmon steak with mixed herbs. Multi-course prix fixe dinners for $50. Smoke-free dining room.

Russian River Vineyards Restaurant • ΔΔ $$$ Ø

5700 Gravenstein Highway N., Forestville; (707) 887-1562. Continental with a Greek tilt; dinners $14 to $21; wine only. Lunch 11:30 to 2:30, dinner 5:30 to 9:30, Sunday brunch 10:30 to 2:30. Casual to informal; reservations advised. Major credit cards. Cheerful place with eclectic decor and menu, perched atop funky tasting room of Topolos winery. Fare includes Mediterranean dishes such as *Souvlaki* (spicy lamb brochette), prawns Santorini, roast duckling in Madeira and black current sauce, and essential American New York peppercorn steak. Patio dining; live music nightly.

Western Boot Steakhouse • ΔΔ $$ Ø

Nine Mitchell Lane, Healdsburg; (707) 433-6362. Steak and Italian; dinners $7 to $18; wine and beer. Lunch 11:30 to 2, dinner 5 to 9. Casual; reservations accepted. MC/VISA. Family style cafe with pleasant decorative scatter, including items donated by customers. Busy menu wanders from thick steaks to ribs to fish to pastas.

VINELAND LODGINGS

The list below represents lodgings near north Sonoma County's vinelands. There's a considerably larger selection of motels, bed and breakfast inns and few hotels in Santa Rosa. Small resorts line the Russian River and more are in communities along the Sonoma Coast. For information on these places, contact chambers of commerce listed at the end of this chapter.

Hotels and motels

Best Western Dry Creek Inn • ΔΔ $$$ Ø

198 Dry Creek Rd. (at U.S. 101), Healdsburg, CA 95448; (800) 222-5784 or (707) 433-0300. Doubles and singles $50 to $75. Major credit cards. A 104-room motel with TV movies, room phones and in-room coffee service. Pool, spa; gift bottle of wine and free continental breakfast.

Fairview Motel • Δ $$ Ø

74 Healdsburg Ave. (at U.S. 101), Healdsburg, CA 95448; (707) 433-5548. Doubles $44 to $46, singles $38. Major credit cards. Eighteen rooms with TV movies and phones; pool, spa and playground.

Hotel La Rose • ΔΔ $$$ ØØ

308 Wilson St. (just off freeway between Fourth and Fifth), Santa Rosa, CA 95401; (707) 579-3200. Doubles and singles $55 to $75. MC/VISA, AMEX. Nicely restored Art Deco hotel with rooms done in a mix of antique and modern. On northern edge of Santa Rosa near the wine country. All rooms non-smoking. **Hotel La Rose Restaurant** serves lunch Tuesday-Friday 11:30 to 2 and dinner Tuesday-Saturday 5:30 to 9:30. California nouveau featuring fresh fish and pastas; dinners $13 to $21. Full bar service; non-smoking areas.

Huckleberry Springs • ΔΔΔ $$$$$

8105 Old Beedle Rd. (end of Tyrone Road; P.O. Box 400), Monte Rio, CA 95462; (707) 865-2683. Cottages $175 including dinner and breakfast. Five units with private baths. MC/VISA, AMEX. Rustic, luxurious country lodge on 56 acres. Contemporary furnishings in cottages; oldstyle lodge with antiques, folk art and graphics collection. Landscaped Japanese-style spa.

Madrona Manor • ΔΔΔΔ $$$$$ Ø

1001 Westside Rd. (P.O. Box 818), Healdsburg, CA 95448; (707) 433-4231. Rooms $110 to $200. Major credit cards. Beautifully restored 1881 Victorian mansion. Twenty-one rooms with antique and modern furnishings, fireplaces in many. Nine rooms in the mansion, others in cottages about the grounds. Music room lounge with fireplace, books, piano and light food service. Located on eight wooded, landscaped acres. **Madrona Manor Restaurant**—see listing above.

Bed & breakfast inns

Belle de Jour Inn • ΔΔΔ $$$$$ ØØ

16276 Healdsburg Ave. (opposite Simi Winery), Healdsburg, CA 95448; (707) 433-7892. Doubles $115 to $165, singles $110 to $160. Four cottages with private baths; full breakfast. MC/VISA, DISC. Posh accommodations in ranch-style complex near downtown Healdsburg. Antique and contemporary furnishings; fireplaces, spas, refrigerators in rooms. Breakfast served in cottages or in dining room of an 1869 Italianate ranch home.

Camellia Inn • ΔΔ $$$$ Ø

211 North St., Healdsburg, CA 95448; (707) 433-8182. Doubles $65 to $115, singles $55 to $105. Nine rooms, seven with private baths; full breakfast. MC/VISA, DISC. Nicely appointed rooms in 1869 Italianate Victorian that served as Healdsburg's first hospital. Furnished with Victorian and American antiques. Spas and fireplaces in some rooms. Heated pool, gardens.

Campbell Ranch Inn • ΔΔΔ $$$$ Ø

1475 Canyon Rd. (1.6 miles west of 101), Geyserville, CA 95411; (707) 857-3496. Doubles $90 to $125, singles $80 to $115. Five rooms with private baths; full breakfast selected from menu. MC/VISA, DISC. Modern ranch style

B&B on a wooded knoll with vineyard views. Spa, tennis courts, pool and gardens. Four rooms in main house, one cottage; modern furnishings, king beds. Living room and family room with TV and fireplace.

Country Meadow Inn • ΔΔΔ $$$$ ØØ

11360 Old Redwood Hwy. (south of Eastside Road), Windsor, CA 95492; (707) 431-1276. Doubles $75 to $145, singles $70 to $140. Five rooms with private baths; full breakfast featuring home-grown ingredients. MC/VISA, DISC. Handsome shingle-sided 1890 ranch home among gardens and trees. Rooms furnished with Victorian and American country antiques. Some rooms with fireplaces, whirlpool tub. Decks, pool, extensive grounds.

The Estate Inn • ΔΔΔ $$$$$ ØØ

13555 Highway 116 (Mayes Canyon Road), Guerneville, CA 95446; (707) 869-9093. Rooms $100 to $175. Ten rooms with TV, room phones and private baths; full breakfast. MC/VISA, AMEX. Opulent Mission revival mansion surrounded by lush landscaping, built in 1922 during the salad days of the Russian River resorts. European and American antiques, original art. Pool, spa, formal gardens. **Restaurant** serves prix fixe American-continental dinners for guests only, from $20 to $25.

Frampton House • ΔΔΔ $$$$ ØØ

489 Powell Ave. (one mile north of the Plaza), Healdsburg, CA 95448; (707) 433-5084. Doubles $70 to $90, singles $60 to $80. Three rooms with private baths; full breakfast, MC/VISA. Restored early American home sheltered by mature trees; American antique furnishings with accent on oak. Pool, spa, sauna, bicycles; fireplace in sitting room. Breakfast served in solarium above pool.

Grape Leaf Inn • ΔΔΔ $$$$ ØØ

539 Johnson St. (Grant Street), Healdsburg, CA 95448; (707) 433-8140. Doubles $80 to $125, singles $60 to $105. Seven rooms with private baths; full breakfast. MC/VISA. Refurbished 1900 Queen Anne Victorian. Nicely appointed rooms with whirlpool tubs, skylight roofs, air conditioning. Wraparound porch and landscaped, tree-shaded yard.

Haydon House • ΔΔΔ $$$$ ØØ

321 Haydon St. (Fitch Street), Healdsburg, CA 95448; (707) 433-5228. Doubles $75 to $135, singles $65 to $125. Eight rooms, four with private baths; full breakfast. MC/VISA. Queen Anne Victorian with lawn, gardens, picnic area and sun porch. Rooms with Victorian and European antiques, featuring wicker furniture, down comforters, four-poster canopied beds.

Healdsburg Inn on the Plaza • ΔΔΔ $$$$ ØØ

116 Matheson St. (Healdsburg Avenue), Healdsburg, CA 95448; (707) 433-6991. Doubles and singles $65 to $150. Nine rooms, all with TV, phones and private baths; full breakfast; free champagne brunch on weekends. MC/VISA. Oldstyle inn with Victorian furnishings and original artworks. Bright, cheerful rooms; some overlooking Healdsburg Plaza. Solarium and roof garden, gift shop and gallery with works of California artists. Former Wells Fargo Express office.

Hope-Bosworth & Hope-Merrill houses • ΔΔΔ $$$$ ØØ

21238 and 21253 Geyserville Ave. (P.O. Box 42), Geyserville, CA 95441; (707) 857-3356. Bosworth—$65 to $90, five rooms, two private and three shared baths; Merrill—$95 to $125, seven rooms with private baths; full breakfast. MC/VISA. Two turn of the century Victorians across the street from one another in downtown Geyserville. Completely refurbished, furnished with antiques. The 1904 Hope-Bosworth is American country style; 1870s Hope-Merrill is Victorian with European antiques. Some rooms with fireplaces and spas. Library, gardens, grape arbor. Wine country picnic lunches prepared; $30 for two including wine and gift wicker basket.

Ridenhour Ranch House Inn • ΔΔ $$$$ ØØ

12850 River Rd. (next to Korbel), Guerneville, CA 95446; (707) 887-1033. Doubles and singles $65 to $115. Eight rooms, five with private baths, full breakfast. MC/VISA. Ranch style redwood home furnished with American and English antiques and Oriental rugs. Seven rooms in ranch house, one cottage; some with TV. Hot tubs, gardens and meadows on more than two acres.

Santa Nella House • ΔΔ $$$$ ØØ

12130 Highway 116 (Odd Fellows Park Road), Guerneville, CA 95446; (707) 869-9488. Doubles and singles $85 to $90. Four rooms with private baths; champagne brunch. MC/VISA. An attractively refurbished Victorian-Italianate farm house. Hot tub, spa; near Russian River beaches. Rooms furnished with English antiques.

Ye Olde Shelford House • ΔΔ $$$$ ØØ

29955 River Rd. (a mile east of U.S. 101), Cloverdale, CA 95245; (707) 894-5956. Doubles and singles $85 to $110. Six rooms, four with private baths; full breakfast. MC/VISA. Imposing 1885 Victorian country home overlooking the vineyards and wooded hills. Victorian and American antiques; hot tub, pool, bicycles. Sitting room; front porch with old-fashioned swing.

Northern Sonoma County information sources

Cloverdale Chamber of Commerce, 471 S. Cloverdale Blvd. (P.O. Box 476), Cloverdale, CA 95425; (707) 894-2862.

Forestville Chamber of Commerce, P.O. Box 546, Forestville, CA 95436; (707) 887-2266.

Geyserville Chamber of Commerce, P.O. Box 276, Geyserville, CA 95441; (707) 433-6585.

Healdsburg Chamber of Commerce, 217 Healdsburg Ave., Healdsburg, CA 95448; (707) 433-6935.

Lake Sonoma Recreation Area, 3333 Skaggs Springs Rd., Geyserville, CA 95441-9644; (707) 433-9483.

Russian River Chamber of Commerce, 14034 Armstrong Woods Rd. (P.O. Box 331), Guerneville, CA 95446; (707) 869-2584.

Santa Rosa Chamber of Commerce, 637 First St., Santa Rosa, CA 95404; (707) 547-1414.

Windsor Chamber of Commerce, P.O. Box 367, Windsor, CA 95492; (707) 838-4323.

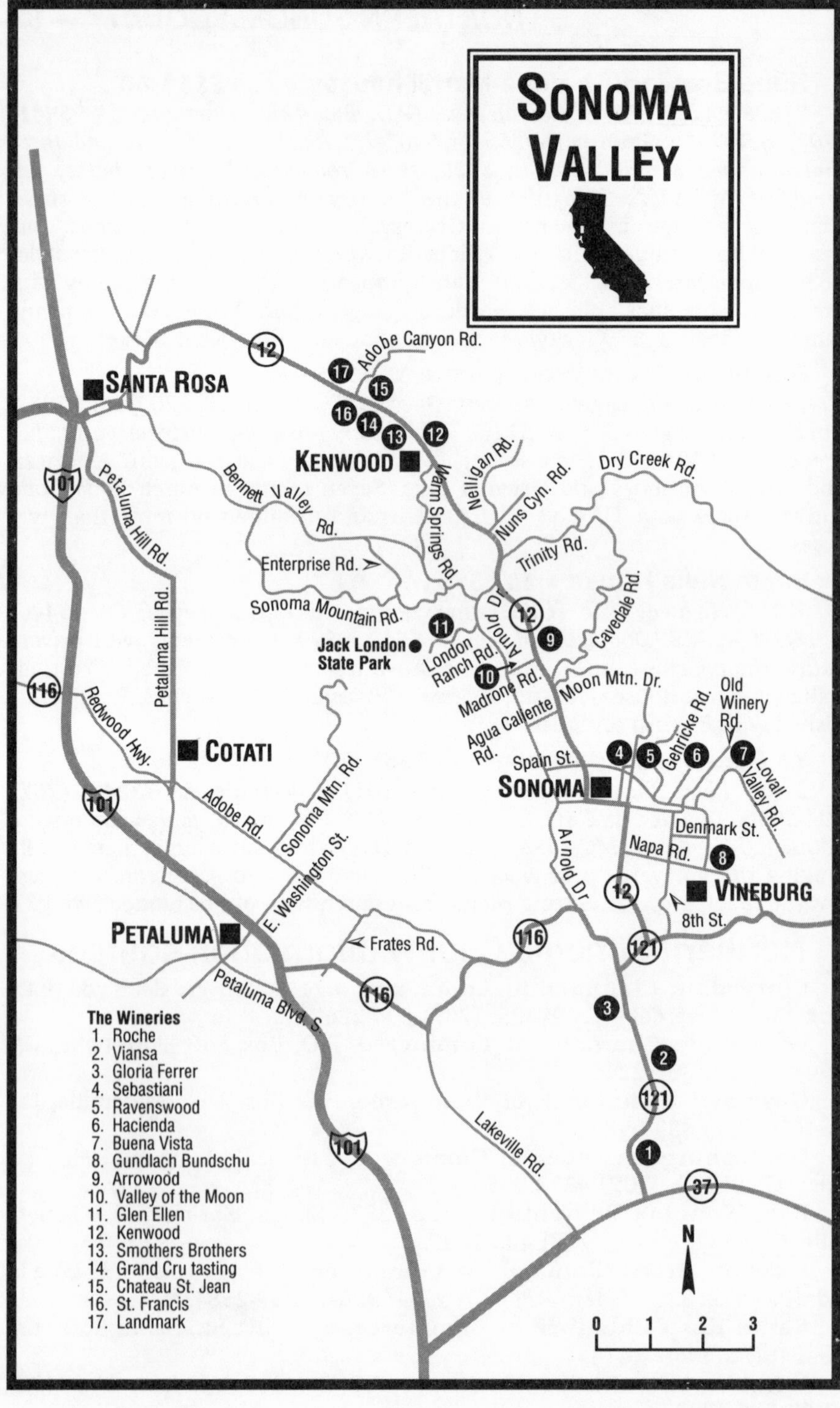

SONOMA VALLEY
SANTA ROSA
KENWOOD
COTATI
SONOMA
VINEBURG
PETALUMA
Jack London State Park
Adobe Canyon Rd.
Bennett Valley Rd.
Enterprise Rd.
Sonoma Mountain Rd.
Warm Springs Rd.
Nelligan Rd.
Nuns Cyn. Rd.
Dry Creek Rd.
Trinity Rd.
Cavedale Rd.
Arnold Dr.
London Ranch Rd.
Madrone Rd.
Moon Mtn. Dr.
Agua Caliente Rd.
Spain St.
Gehricke Rd.
Old Winery Rd.
Lovall Valley Rd.
Denmark St.
Napa Rd.
8th St.
Petaluma Hill Rd.
Redwood Hwy.
Adobe Rd.
Sonoma Mtn. Rd.
E. Washington St.
Frates Rd.
Petaluma Blvd. S.
Lakeville Rd.
12
101
116
121
37
The Wineries
1. Roche
2. Viansa
3. Gloria Ferrer
4. Sebastiani
5. Ravenswood
6. Hacienda
7. Buena Vista
8. Gundlach Bundschu
9. Arrowood
10. Valley of the Moon
11. Glen Ellen
12. Kenwood
13. Smothers Brothers
14. Grand Cru tasting
15. Chateau St. Jean
16. St. Francis
17. Landmark
N
0 1 2 3

"Lean and silky, with nice, toasty orange peel shades to the plum and tomato aromas and flavors, echoing spice notes on the finish."

—Wine-taster's description of a 1989 Buena Vista Carneros Pinot Noir

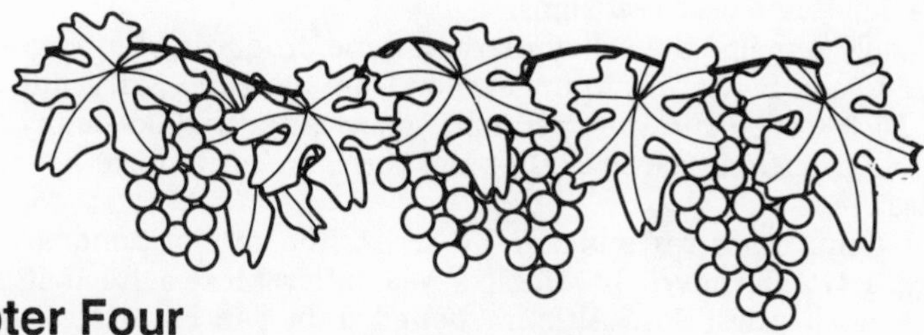

Chapter Four
THE SONOMA VALLEY
Where California wine and history blend

About twenty years ago, as I was wrapping up an interview with vintner Sam Sebastiani, his father August poked his head through the doorway.

"You got any plans tonight?" he asked.

I shook my head.

"The hell you don't. You and I are going to dinner."

"Sure." I welcomed the prospect of an evening with this Sonoma Valley wine legend. "But, why the sudden invitation?"

August frowned. "I've got one of those fancy New York wine writers in my office and I need an excuse to get rid of him."

We adjourned to the Sonoma Grove Restaurant, where Gus addressed the waitress with his usual gentle gruffness: "Bring my friend here the second best steak in the house. I'll take the best one and bring us a bottle of Zinfandel."

"Of course, Mister Sebastiani." The waitress grinned wickedly. "What brand?"

August's death in 1980 closed a significant chapter in the Sonoma Valley wine history book. Friendly but incisive, folksy yet astute, he turned a bulk winery into Sonoma's largest producer of varietals. When a wine glut hit in the 1970s, he introduced "jug varietals," marketing premium wines in oversized bottles at affordable prices. He was the first American winemaker to produce *nouveau* style Gamay Beaujolais and release it within weeks of bottling, in the French tradition.

At home in bib overalls, ill at ease in suit and tie, he hosted elegant harvest dinners in San Francisco to exhibit Sonoma Valley wines to the press and to the world. Not to be overshadowed, wife Sylvia earned a reputation as an outstanding chef and authored a best-selling cookbook, ***Mangiamo.***

Although Sonoma Valley is famous for its wine legends of Haraszthy and Vallejo, the Sebastiani family has written much of its current history. The saga began in 1904 when Italian immigrant Samuele Sebastiani began producing bulk wines. His son August joined him in the business in 1934. When Samuele died in 1946, August changed the focus to varietals and built the winery into one of the largest in America. Sebastiani and Sonoma are almost synonymous. The name reaches beyond the winery to appear on a theater, a depot and on street signs.

The family remains the valley's largest wine producer, shipping four million cases a year. Sylvia, her youngest son Don, daughter Maryanne and her husband Dick Cuneo run the operation today. After a 1986 family feud resembling a script from *Falcon Crest*, older son Sam left to form his own winery, Viansa.

If that family spat resembles a TV script, the rest of Sonoma's history reads like a Gothic novel. In 1823, a year after Mexico freed itself from Spain, maverick priest Jose Altimira bolted from San Francisco's cold and damp Mission Dolores to form a new branch north of the bay. Although the church condemned his action, he was supported by the Mexican California governor and the mission survived. Altimira named it San Francisco Solano, in honor of a missionary to the Peruvian Indians.

In the 1830s, when the Mexican government stripped the missions of their vast landholdings, Mariano Guadalupe Vallejo was given the task of dissolving Mission Solano. In doing so, he laid out a town with a classic Spanish plaza as its focal point. He called it Sonoma, a name local Indians had given the valley. The plaza remains as its historic centerpiece.

As more Americans arrived, Mexico began losing its grip on its northern outpost of California. On June 14, 1846, a rag-tag bunch of Sacramento Valley gringos marched on Sonoma, imprisoned an angry, sputtering Vallejo in his own barracks and proclaimed California as an independent republic. The group fashioned a crude flag with the outline of a bear (which looked more like a pig), and raised it over the plaza. These "Bear-Flaggers" were later described by Vallejo's sister as a "group of rough-looking desperados."

It was the shortest republic on record. On July 9, a U.S. Naval force led by Commondore John Sloat captured Monterey and annexed California to the United States.

From that point forward, Sonoma's history is concerned mostly with wine. Vallejo, an American supporter even before his imprisonment, became the town's leading citizen and its first major grape grower. Wayfaring Hungarian Count Agoston Haraszthy arrived in 1856. A year later, he established Buena Vista, which ultimately became the largest winery in America.

Traveling to Europe under state legislative sanction in the early 1860s, he imported hundreds of thousands of varietal grape cuttings. They formed the foundation for today's premium California wines. It's not an exaggeration to call Haraszthy the father of California viniculture and Sonoma the cradle of the state's premium wine industry.

Like other California winelands, the valley suffered from a wine glut, then phylloxera and finally Prohibition. Haraszthy's failing Buena Vista Winery was shut down when the 1906 earthquake caved in its cellars.

Three wineries preserve shards of Sonoma Valley's vineland history. Buena Vista was re-opened in 1943 by newsman Frank Bartholomew and it continues to thrive. Sebastiani owns many of the original mission and Vallejo vineyards. Owners of Hacienda Wine Cellars have some of Haraszthy's old vineyards and they built a replica of his Pompeiian style villa.

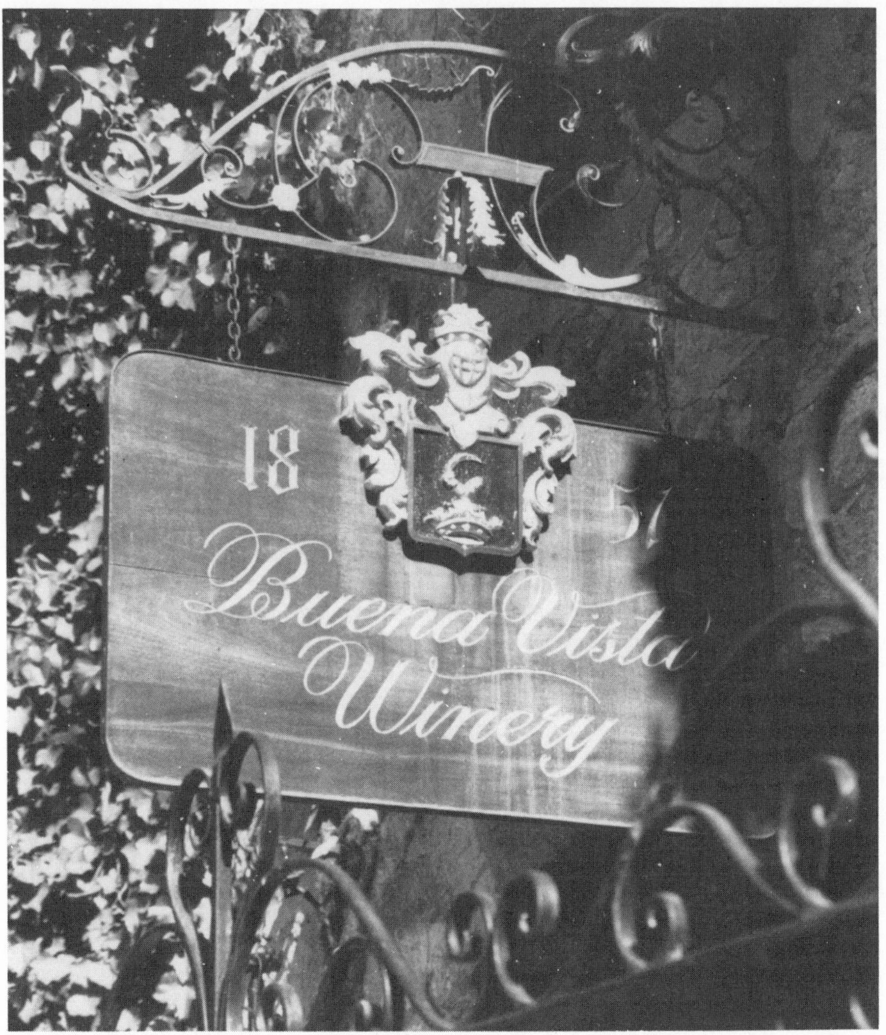

Decades of ivy lace the rough stone walls of Sonoma Valley's Buena Vista Winery, founded in 1857 by flamboyant Agoston Haraszthy.

Another historical figure left his mark on the Sonoma Valley, but he blended words, not wine. Jack London, fresh from his literary triumphs, bought land above Glen Ellen in 1905 and devoted the last eleven years of his life to building his "Beauty Ranch." The Valley of the Moon, an Indian description of this scenic land, was popularized in London's book by that name.

Sonoma Valley's wineries are grouped in two areas, in and about Sonoma itself and farther up the valley around Glen Ellen and Kenwood.

SONOMA AREA WINERY TOUR • Signposts on street and highway intersections help direct you to the valley's assorted tasting rooms.

To approach Sonoma from the San Francisco Bay Area, go east on State Highway 37 from U.S. 101, then turn north onto State Highway 121 at

Sears Point International Raceway. You'll encounter three modern wineries along Highway 121, all perched on upslopes and surrounded by vineyards, spaced a couple of miles apart: **Roche Carneros Estate Winery** and **Viansa**, both on the right, and **Gloria Ferrer Champagne Caves** on the left. This gently hilly area is the Carneros, an appellation shared by the Napa and Sonoma valleys.

Near the Gloria Ferrer entrance, you'll note the **Schellville Airport,** where you can admire some interesting old planes and perhaps book a flight in an open-cockpit biplane (see activities, below).

Continue on Highway 121, then swing left onto Highway 12, which becomes Broadway and bumps into **Sonoma Plaza**. Take a right at the stop sign, drive to Fourth Street, turn left and follow it to **Sebastiani Vineyards.** Its extensive facilities border the corner of Fourth and Spain Street. Go east on Spain a few blocks, then turn north (left) onto Gehricke Road and follow it uphill to **Ravenswood,** tucked among the trees.

Return to Spain Street and continue east until it becomes Lovall Valley Road. At a kink in Lovall Valley, head northeast on Castle Road to **Hacienda Wine Cellars**. Note the reconstructed Haraszthy villa on a low hill as you approach. Retreat to Lovall Valley Road, stay with it a short distance and turn left onto Old Winery Road, lined with giant eucalyptus trees. This takes you to **Buena Vista Winery** at the end of the road.

Backtrack on Old Winery, jog right onto Napa Street, then left onto Eighth Street and turn left onto Denmark Street. All this joggling brings you to **Gundlach-Bundschu Winery**. Signs will help guide the way.

Roche Carneros Estate Winery • T GTA ⌶

28700 Arnold Dr. (Hwy. 121), Sonoma, CA 95476; (707) 935-7115. Daily 10 to 5 (to 6 in summer); MC/VISA, AMEX. Most wines tasted free, fee for some reserves. Giftwares and specialty foods.Picnic area; tours by appointment.

Housed in a hilltop double-pitched roof winery suggestive of an urban barn, Roche offers a pleasing view of the Carneros region, San Pablo Bay, and Sonoma Valley. Picnickers can enjoy the view from tables near the winery. The tasting room is spacious and inviting, like an oversized living room. Samples of Sonoma Valley specialty foods are featured in the gift area.

Joseph and Genevieve Roche planted their vineyards in 1983, intending to concentrate on Chardonnay and Pinot Noir, which do well in the Carneros Appellation. They're still the best of Roche's wines. The small, stylish family winery produces about 4,500 cases a year.

Tasting notes: Roche wines come in two price ranges. Sauvignon Blanc, a couple of Chardonnays and Pinot Noir Blanc are from \$5.95 to \$12.95. Both premium whites exhibited good varietal character, rich and long on fruit. The higher end Pinot Noir and Merlot, priced from \$15.95 to \$18.85, also were outstanding, complex and full flavored. The unfiltered Pinot Noir was excellent.

WINERY CODES • T = tasting with no fee; **T$** = fee for tasting; **GT** = guided tours; **GTA** = appointment required for tour; **ST** = self-guiding tours; **CT** = casual tours or a peek into the winery; ⌶ = picnic area; 🎁 = separate gift shop or good giftware selection. Price ranges listed in tasting notes are for varietals; jug wines often are available for less. **DINING & LODGINGS • ØØ** = smoke-free establishment; Ø = non-smoking tables or rooms.

Viansa Winery • T GTA

25200 Arnold Dr. (Highway 121), Sonoma, CA 95476; (707) 935-4700. Daily 10 to 5; MC/VISA. Most varieties tasted. Large gift selection; complete kitchen with deli, picnic and gourmet food items. Valley-view picnic area; informal peek into the winery, or guided tours by appointment.

When Sam J. Sebastiani started left the family business in 1986, he bottled wines under his own name, but they often were confused with the long-established family labels. So he and his wife Vicki combined their names and came up with "Viansa." Their new $7 million winery reflects Sam's touch of elegance and Vicki's flair for wine and food.

Fashioned as a tile-roofed Tuscan villa, it's tucked into the brow of a hill high above Carneros. A nearby picnic area offers a 360-degree view. The tasting room, aptly described by Sam and Vicki as their "Italian marketplace," is one of the valley's most appealing. Murals embellish the walls, and a century old Italian wine cart is the focal point of an extensive giftware and specialty food shop. The Viansa Kitchen issues pastas, *foccacia* bread sandwiches, salads, desserts and other "California-Italian" fare.

It may be our imagination, but a figure in one of the murals—a reclining Roman aristocrat immersed in the good life—bears a passing resemblance to Sam.

Tasting notes: Viansa produces a Sauvignon Blanc, a couple of Chardonnays, three Cabernets, a sweet Barbera Blanc and two Muscat Canelli dessert wines. The Sauvignon Blanc was properly crisp and fruity and a barrel-fermented Reserve Chardonnay was state of the art: nutty, silky and rich, with a touch of oak. A Reserve Cabernet exhibited good balance between the grape and the oak, drinkable now but with enough tannin to suggest putting it away for a few years. Prices range from $9 to the mid-teens, and beyond for some limited reserves.

Vintners choice: "Our Cabernet Sauvignon is currently the highlight because of the blend of vineyards from Napa and Sonoma, with a touch of Cabernet Franc to add more fruit to the taste," according to Sam.

Gloria Ferrer Champagne Caves • T$ GT

23555 Highway 121, Sonoma, CA 95476; (707) 996-7256. Daily 10:30 to 5:30; MC/VISA. Sparkling wines by the glass from $3.50 to $7.50. Some wine-related gift items. Guided tours hourly from 11 to 4.

From Tuscany, we're ferried to the hills of Spain, where the Jose and Gloria Ferrer family has produced sparkling wine for five centuries. In 1986, they transported the essence of rural Barcelona to this hillside niche in the Carneros. The tile-roofed winery with its graceful Spanish arches shields an underground *cava*, where sparkling wines are coaxed into graceful maturity.

Plan to arrive at tour time to take the full measure of this elegant facility. You'll view fermenting tanks and a bottling line from a gallery, then descend into gunnited caves under 20 feet of earth. Here, great tiers of champagne glisten dully in the subdued light. Along the way, you absorb a quick course in *mèthode champenoise* as practiced by the Ferrer family. The tour adjourns to the stylish *Sala de Catadores* (Hall of the Tasters) for a bit of the bubbly, accompanied by *tapas*—Spanish *hors d'oeuvres.*

Tasting notes: Three sparkling wines are sold by the glass—Gloria Ferrer Brut, Royal Cuvee and Carneros Cuvee. Our Ferrer Brut was crisp and faultlessly clean, with subtle aromas and tastes of the fruit. The wines have won numerous awards, including a best in show at a recent San Francisco Wine Expo. Bottle prices are in the mid-teens.

Sebastiani Vineyards • T GT

389 E. Fourth St., Sonoma, CA 95476; (707) 938-5532. Daily 10 to 5. Most varieties tasted. Good giftware selection. Picnic areas near the winery and along the vineyards on Spain Street. Tours every half hour from 10:30 to 4.

Sebastiani Vineyards, whose history we've already covered, forms a transition between town and country. The ancient cut-stone winery is on the edge of a tidy old residential area, while vineyards stretch toward low hills. Nearly 150,000 people a year throng through the winery. The tours are quick and efficient, spilling their happy cargo into the large, earthy tasting room.

The place is permeated with old wine and family history. Ancient beams hold up the ceiling; the arc of a huge wine cask anchors one corner of the room. A stained glass window glitters with the family logo. Faded photos adorn cut-stone walls, Samuele's original basket press and vintage winemaking equipment fills odd niches.

A remarkable gentleman named Earle Brown took up woodcarving when most men retire, and spent the next decade or so inscribing images on every door, barrel top, cask and other exposed wood surface he could find in the winery. The resulting display is perhaps one of the largest wood carving exhibits in America.

Tasting notes: The Sebastiani list is broad-based, ranging from premium varietals to jug wines, including varietal jugs introduced by August. The premium whites are fruity and crisp, not overly filtered and fined—a fate often suffered by high-volume wines. Most of the reds are soft and lush, ready to drink, although some Merlots, Cabernets and Zinfandels are suitable for cellaring. Zinfandel, to my mind, is their best product. A spicy, soft and fruity version recently won a gold, and it's priced at only $8. The long list covers nearly every varietal produced in California, with prices ranging from $6 to the early teens.

Vintners choice: "Chardonnays, Gewürztraminer, Merlot and Cabernets, using local grapes with which we've worked for many years," says hospitality manager Ed Loudon.

Ravenswood • T GTA

18701 Gehricke Rd., Sonoma, CA 95476; (707) 938-1960. Daily 10 to 4:30; MC/VISA. Selected wines tasted. A few wine logo gift items. Picnic area with hillside and vineyard views; guided tours by appointment.

This is where you go for a little Zin. Or perhaps a lot, if you love the "mystery grape" as we do. This winery, tucked into a wooded slope and besiege by vineyards, specializes in Zinfandel. And most are BIG Zins. We came away with a mixed case.

The rustic, stone fronted tasting room looks properly ancient, yet it was opened in early 1991. A picnic terrace offers fine views of vines, pines, giant eucalyptus, wooded slopes and the edges of Sonoma below.

Ravenswood began life in the mid-70s in a prefab warehouse in Sonoma and moved recently to this more enticing spot. Winemaker Joel E. Peterson is obsessed with the notion of bringing out all the earthy, powerful character of Zinfandel, and he usually succeeds. Tasters who like big red wines give his Zin high marks.

"No wimpy wines allowed," reads a sign in the small tasting room.

Tasting notes: Intelligently conducted tastings will carry you through a couple or three Zins and perhaps a Cabernet and Chardonnay, the only other wines on the chalkboard list. The Vintners Blend Zin was the softest of the lot, yet still big and complex, with a nice tannic nip. A Canard Vineyards Zinfandel was heavy with fruit and spicy with a hint of wood, suitable for aging. The Sonoma County Zin had a spicy Zinfandel nose, complex and tannic, offering great aging potential. Prices range from $9 to the high teens.

Hacienda Wine Cellars • T GTA

1000 Vineyard Lane (P.O. Box 416), Sonoma, CA 95476; (707) 938-3220. Daily 10 to 5; MC/VISA. Most varieties tasted. Some wine logo gift items. Oak-shaded picnic area overlooking the vineyards; guided tours by appointment.

The "villa" catches your eye before you see the winery. "This building is a reconstruction of the Pompeiian villa erected on this site in 1857 by Count Haraszthy," reads a sign.

It's not generally open to the public, but the winery tasting room just up the road certainly is. And it's attractive in its own right, housed in a century-old, oak-shaded Spanish-California structure that once served as a community hospital. Vineyards spill away from this wooded setting, and picnic areas occupy a park-like shaded slope.

Frank Bartholomew, who recycled Buena Vista Winery in 1943, established Hacienda as well—three decades later. It is now owned by A. Crawford Cooley and his son Robert.

Tasting notes: The Clair de Lune Chardonnay was excellent, buttery, spicy and lush with a hint of wood. A Dry Chenin Blanc was soft, flowery in nose and taste, also with a touch of oak. The reds, Pinot Noir and Cabernet Sauvignon, exhibited a slightly grassy nose and flavor that was not unpleasant. Both were rich in berries, with soft finishes. A rich, velvety and nutty Vintage Port, served with a Hershey's Kiss, was outstanding.

Vintners choice: "Chardonnay, dry Chenin Blanc, Cabernet Sauvignon, Pinot Noir, Vintage Port and Antares (Bordeaux blend)," said son Robert, shamelessly covering most of the list.

Buena Vista Winery • T GT ST

18000 Old Winery Rd. (P.O. Box 1842), Sonoma, CA 95476; (707) 938-1266. Daily 10 to 5; major credit cards. Most varieties tasted; some free, others for a $2.50 fee. Extensive gift selection; specialty foods; art gallery. Self-guiding tours; historical presentations at 11:30 and 2 in summer, 2 p.m. only the rest of the year. Picnic areas in the winery courtyard, and terraced on a steep slope.

If any winery in America is steeped in antiquity, it is Buena Vista. Shaped of rough blocks quarried from its own tunnels, bunkered into a steep slope, shaded by giant eucalyptus, it exudes the mystique of a viticultural Mayan ruin. Prowling the tunnels of the ancient winery or its next-door Press House, you can see the pick marks where Chinese laborers dug the tunnels. Stone blocks from the digging were then used to create the facades.

Self-guiding tours take you into the ancient recesses of the original wine cellars. Historical tours follow the trail of Agoston Haraszthy, which began in strife-torn Hungary and ended at this place.

The tasting room, in the Press House, is rimmed by a balconied art gallery, where works of San Francisco Bay Area artists are on exhibit. The cultural-conscious Moller-Racke family of Europe, present winery owners, sponsors midsummer Mozart concerts and a fall Shakespeare fest in the courtyard.

Tasting notes: Four gratis tastings are offered from a list that covers most varietals. Older reserve wines can be sampled for a fee. We liked the complex, buttery spiciness of the Summerfest Chardonnay and the lush, herbal flavor of a Fumè Blanc. Of the reds, a Barricia Vineyard Zinfandel displayed a proper peppery nose; it was soft for early drinkability. The Carneros Estate Cabernet Sauvignon also was herbal, with a soft finish. Buena Vista makes one of society's better cream sherries: velvety, nutty and lush. Prices range from $8 to the high teens.

Vintners choice: "We're known for our Chardonnay, Pinot Noir and Cabernet," said tasting room manager Jeri Wilson.

Gundlach-Bundschu Winery • T ⩙

2000 Denmark St., Sonoma, CA 95476; (707) 938-5277. Daily 11 to 4:30; MC/VISA. Selected wines tasted. Some wine-related gift items. Picnic area up a slope with a valley view.

Gundlach-Bundschu combines antiquity, a modern wine facility and humor. The weather-worn stone winery, etched with a patina of lichen, was built by Jim Bundschu's ancestors in the 1860s. Inside, a contemporary winery functions. The inviting, funky tasting room in a corner of the winery is decorated with off-beat Gundlach-Bundschu advertising posters. One shows a patrolman telling a motorist in an old Kaiser: "If you can't say 'Gundlach-Bundschu Gewürztraminer,' you shouldn't be driving!" In a more serious vein is a rather striking 1930s style mural honoring Mexican vineyard workers.

Jacob Gundlach started the winery in 1858 and was joined by Charles Bundschu, who married his daughter, in 1862. The 1906 earthquake destroyed their San Francisco warehouse and Prohibition closed the winery. However, the Bundschus continued growing grapes in the Sonoma Valley. Jim, great-great-great grandson of Charles, decided to re-open the ancient winery in the early 1970s.

Tasting notes: The focus here is intense varietal character. "We don't try to follow market trends; we find people who like our wines," says Jim. The whites are unusually lush and complex, in a rich German style. A Chardonnay was nutty, spicy and crisp and a Gewürztraminer had an excellent crushed flower petal nose and taste. Gamay Beaujolais and Cabernet were fruity and ready to drink. The Cab has nicely herbal with a soft touch of wood. Prices range from $7 to the mid-teens.

Vintners choice: "Reds, because," Jim said, flatly.

GLEN ELLEN-KENWOOD WINERY TOUR • From **Sonoma Plaza**, take Spain street west and go right onto State Highway 12 (the Sonoma Highway), headed northwest toward Santa Rosa. You'll pass the strung out, unplanned scatter of three communities—Boyes Hot Springs, Fetters Hot Springs and Agua Caliente. This is the least appealing area of the Sonoma Valley. As the names suggest, it was once a hot springs resort area. Boyes was spring training grounds for the old San Francisco Seals and Oakland Oaks. However, with the lone exception of beautifully refurbished Sonoma Mission Inn, the once glossy resort area is rather tarnished.

Once you clear Fetters, you enter open countryside and the prettiest part of the Sonoma Valley. Vineyards climb gentle slopes, nudging foothills of the Mayacamas Mountains to the east. Looking west, you see more vines scattered across the level valley floor; the Sonoma Mountains fill that horizon. Continue on the Sonoma Highway past Madrone Road, then watch for a sign to **Arrowood Winery,** up a vineyard slope to your right.

Now, backtrack to Madrone Road, turn right (west) and you soon encounter **Valley of the Moon Winery** on your right. Continue on Madrone to Arnold Drive, turn right and follow it through the park-like grounds of **Sonoma State Hospital**. Its lush canopy of trees provides a serene setting for the institution. Beyond the hospital, you approach the oldstyle hamlet of **Glen Ellen.**

Jack London Village, which has no ties to the noted author, is a themed shopping complex on the edge of town, built into an aged winery and brandy distillery. It was rather dog-eared when we visited. Continue into Glen Ellen, with its picturesque brick and wooden stores. Turn left onto London Ranch Road, toward **Jack London State Historic Park.** This takes you to **Glen Ellen Winery** on your right. You'll likely want to continue on to the park, which preserves London's ranch, the ruins of his Wolf House stone mansion and the home of his wife, Charmian.

Return to Glen Ellen and continue along Arnold Drive, which swings right and connects with Sonoma Highway (Route 12). Follow the highway northwest toward **Kenwood**, where many of the valley's wineries are clustered. You first see **Kenwood Vineyards,** uphill on your right, and the **Smothers Brothers Wine Store** a bit farther along on the left. Beyond Smothers is **Grand Cru's** cottage tasting room, also on the left.

You next encounter **Chateau St. Jean**, up a vineyard lane to the right. **St. Francis Winery** is on the left, directly across the highway. A bit farther along, at Sonoma Highway and Adobe Canyon Road, is the new **Landmark Vineyards.**

Arrowood Vineyards and Winery • GTA

14347 Sonoma Hwy. (P.O. Box 987), Glen Ellen, CA 95442; (707) 938-5170. Daily 10 to 4:30; MC/VISA. Small sales room; tasting sometimes available. A few wine-related items. Guided tours by appointment.

Arrowood, housed in an appealing rural New England style structure, is tucked into a hillside vineyard. Wicker chairs on an oldstyle porch invite visitors to linger over the view. Arrowood doesn't always offer tasting, but if a bottle happens to be open, visitors are welcome to sample some of the valley's finest wines. They can be purchased in a cheery combination kitchen/sales room. It's presided over by co-owner Alis Demers Arrowood, whose eyes sparkle with enthusiasm for her husband's wines. She suggests that visitors call ahead for a tour of the small, well-appointed winery.

Richard Arrowood made wine—and won medals—for several other vintners before he and Alis opened this facility in 1987. He buys grapes from several vineyards, produces and barrel-ages each batch separately, then skillfully blends them to create award-winning results.

Tasting notes: From Arrowood's short list, we tasted two exceptional wines. A Chardonnay Reserve was among the best we've sampled in the state—perfectly balanced, lush, spicy and silky with a crisp acid finish. A Cabernet Sauvignon, blended with Merlot, Cabernet Franc and Malbec, had a peppery, rich nose and a soft, spicy, berry-like flavor with a subtle touch of wood. Merlot also is available, but only when Dick can find exceptional grapes. Prices range from $18.75 to $25.

Valley of the Moon Winery • T

777 Madrone Rd., Glen Ellen, CA 95442; (707) 996-6941. Daily 10 to 5; all major credit cards. Selected wines tasted. Good selection of wine logo items and giftwares. Tree-shaded picnic area.

You first notice a no-nonsense collection of ranch buildings typical of pioneer family wineries. Then a giant bay laurel catches your eye; it's at least 400 years old. Crouched behind it, a mere century old, is a ruggedly handsome stone tasting room. In the wood-paneled interior, a family member likely will pour samples from the extensive list.

The winery was established in the 1800s and was operated at one time by Senator George Hearst. Closed by Prohibition, it came back to life in 1942 when Enrico Parducci, founder of the San Francisco Sausage Company, purchased the site. His son Harry, grandson Harry Jr., and assorted other family members operate the facility today.

Tasting notes: Valley of the Moon has long been noted for solid everyday wines, which still represent good, drinkable buys. The new generation has added premium varietals, and they've been winning their share of medals. The flavors of Chardonnay and Sauvignon Blanc are straight from the grape—fruity and full with nice acid finishes. A Cabernet Sauvignon offered a complex nose and taste, spicy with a hint of wood. Zinfandel, one of their best wines, was full of berries and peppery with a hint of oak. Premium varietal prices range from $6.50 to $12.

Vintners choice: "Cabernet and Zinfandel are the best of our reserves," quoth Harry, Jr., "and I really like the Chardonnay."

Glen Ellen Winery • T ST

1883 London Ranch Rd., Glen Ellen, CA 95442; (707) 935-3047. Daily 10 to 4:30; MC/VISA, DISC. Most varieties tasted. Good selection of wine logo and gift items. Informal self-guiding tours; picnic area in a redwood grove.

Glen Ellen is one of the wine industry's more startling success stories. Started in 1980 by New York wine merchant Bruno Benziger, it now ships 3.7 million cases of wine worldwide. It's second only to Sebastiani in the Sonoma Valley in production and claims to sell more wine in California, France and Japan than any other single firm. More than 250 growers statewide are kept busy feeding the hungry Glen Ellen machine.

The facilities are located in a wooded vale surrounded by vineyards. It appears to be an old, well-maintained farmyard with its random scatter of neat white clapboard buildings, shaded by mature oaks. However, all except the original house are of recent vintage. The tasting room is in a cheery knotty pine cottage.

Tasting notes: Wines are issued under three labels—the more upscale Benziger series and the less expensive Glen Ellen Proprietor's Reserve and M.G. Vallejo lines. Since the Glen Ellen label wines were so inexpensive,

MEDAL, MEDAL, WHO'S GOTTA MEDAL?

As you visit assorted wineries, you'll note that many have walls full of ribbons. Does that mean all their wines are wonderful? How can so many wineries win so many prizes? Doesn't anyone ever lose?

A gold medal doesn't mean that a wine won first place, only that it scored high in a tasting. Several wines entered in a particular competition—or none—might be worthy of a gold.

To further cloud the issue, some smaller wineries don't enter many competitions because they can't afford the gratis bottles that they're expected to provide.

Are we suggesting that medals aren't important; that just about any wine can win? What does all this mean?

It means that California produces a lot of remarkably good wines; that there's a treasure trove of tasting out there. It also means that a gold medal wine doesn't stand alone. However, like a member of a great university's graduating class, it does stand in good company.

For the real jewels, look for wines with sweepstakes or best of show awards, which *are* one-of-a-kind.

What we seek, when we snatch up our VISA and go afield to replenish our wine cellar, are award-winning wines at modest prices. And yes, you can find them.

The best buys in wines are often those from long-established vineyards such as Sebastiani, Pedroncelli, Fortino and Fetzer. For example, Mendocino County's Parducci was the industry's winningest winery in 1988, yet its premium wines are among the cheapest in the state. Newer boutique wineries may produce some great stuff with their smart young winemakers, but they may have big mortgages, reflected in the price you pay.

When all else fails, we fall back on the wisdom often uttered by our longtime acquaintance, wine writer Fred Cherry:

"The best wine is the wine in your glass."

Of course, ole Fred *really* likes his wine.

$4.99 to $6.49, we decided to challenge them to a taste test. The Chardonnay was properly crisp and fruity, a Sauvignon Blanc lush and full-flavored and both Zinfandel and Merlot had youthful, berry-like character. Our conclusion: they're good buys.

Vintners choice: "Our Chardonnay," said assistant tasting room manager Robert Grove. "It's the world's top selling Chard," he added, displaying his affinity for Glen Ellen statistics.

Kenwood Vineyards • T

9592 Sonoma Hwy., Kenwood, CA 95452; (707) 833-5891. Daily 10 to 4; MC/VISA. Most varieties tasted. Good selection of wine items and giftwares.

Kenwood is located in a wood-sided ranch style structure amidst the vineyards, upslope from the highway. The grounds are carefully kept, with terraced gardens and fieldstone borders. The large, airy tasting room suggests an oversized chalet, with wood paneled walls and open beams. It's a nice example of rustic taste and style.

The facility came to being in 1970 when the Martin Lee family bought the old turn-of-the-century Pagani Brothers Winery, with an eye toward premium varietals. They've kept their focus, and Kenwood wines win a generous share of medals.

Tasting notes: Wines available for tasting are posted, and they represent a liberal portion of the list. Our favorite was a Beltane Ranch Chardonnay, barrel fermented with good fruit, spiciness and crisp acid. Jack London Pinot Noir was full flavored and berry-like with a soft drink-it-now finish. The Sonoma Valley Zinfandel had an herbal nose and taste and a crisp nip of tannin. Prices range from $7 to the mid-teens, and go a bit higher for select reserves.

Vintners choice: "Sauvignon Blanc and Jack London Cabernet Sauvignon," spoke a voice from the winery.

Smothers Brothers Wine Store • T$

9575 Sonoma Hwy. (P.O. Box 789), Kenwood, CA 95452; (707) 833-1010. Daily 10 to 4:30; MC/VISA, AMEX. All wines tasted for a fee. Extensive wine logo, giftware and curio selection.

This facility is a blend of tasting room, wine store and curio shop. The musical-comedy brothers' winery is elsewhere. However, their presence is evident here, with the Tom Smothers yo-yo collection, assorted other S-B souvenirs and a couple of their gold records adorning a wall. It's more of a souvenir shop with a tasting counter, yet it lacks the rustic whimsy of Pat Paulsen's place in Asti.

Tasting notes: The tasting counter also offers sips from other wineries—Coturri, Van Der Kamp and fellow comic Paulsen. Samples range from 25 cents to a dollar. We focused on the Smothers wines: Chardonnay, Cabernet Sauvignon, white Riesling and—you guessed—Mom's Favorite White.

The Chards and Cabs were quite pleasing; with good, spicy fruit in the former and big, full body in the latter. Prices range from $12 to the high teens, and you might catch some sale items. Mom's is yours for $5.

Vintners choice: "Chardonnay and Cabernet," said the winery's Ann Bertram.

Grand Cru Vineyards • T GTA

8860 Sonoma Hwy.(P.O. Box 789), Kenwood, CA 95452; (707) 833-2325. Daily 10 to 4:30; most major credit cards. Most varieties tasted. Lawn picnic area. Guided tours by appointment at the winery, at #1 Vintage Lane, off Henno Road. Or one can peek in from the tasting room.

This downtown tasting facility in a tiny cottage was opened by Grand Cru in mid-1991. The original A-frame tasting room at the winery is open daily from 10 to 5 (although it was closed during open hours when we visited). A fair number of gift items are available in the cottage, and picnic tables are set up on a lawn out front, alongside Sonoma Highway.

Grand Cru was launched in 1970 on the grounds of the venerable 1886 Lemoine Winery. Walt and Tiny Dreyer purchased the facility ten years later. Walt's German grandfather emigrated to San Diego in 1910 and went into the orchard business, and his father was a major Tulare county farmer, so the transition to vintner was not surprising.

Tasting notes: Sauvignon Blanc, Chardonnay, Chenin Blanc, Gewürztraminer and Cabernet Sauvignon comprise the list. We particularly liked the Sauvignon Blanc, soft, fruity and spicy, with an almost-Chardonnay character. Chenin Blanc had a not unpleasant spritzy finish and the Cabernets were soft, peppery and full-flavored, with a gentle tannic finish. Prices range from $6.50 to $13.50; higher for some reserves.

Vintners choice: "Chenin Blanc, Gewürztraminer, white Zinfandel and Saugivnon Blanc are consistent award winners," says the winery's Bettina Dreyer.

Chateau St. Jean • T ST

8555 Sonoma Hwy., Kenwood, CA 95452; (707) 833-4134. Daily 10 to 4:30; MC/VISA, AMEX. Selected wines tasted. Some wine logo and giftware items; shaded picnic areas. Self-guided tours daily from 10:30 to 4.

St. Jean (pronounced as in denims) is a chateau in every sense of the word; it may be the valley's most attractive winery. Tasting room and offices are in the Spanish style manor house of a former country estate. The winery occupies a beige stucco creation with a distinctive witch's hat tower. The hat serves no purpose other than providing an awesome view of the countryside. The grounds, busy with lawns, fountains, patios and mature trees, are as carefully groomed as a proper English garden.

Self-guided tours take you through the towered structure too comely to be a winery. From carpeted hallways, you look down upon rows of stainless steel and tiers of French oak. Graphics along the wall offer a flash course in winemaking. A winding stairway leads to the medieval-style tower for a view of russet tile rooftops and the greater Sonoma Valley.

Established in 1974, the winery was purchased in 1983 by Suntory International. It's corporate backing is evident in the careful grooming of this stylish facility.

Tasting notes: Selected wines are opened for tasting; only whites were available the day we visited. Fumè Blanc was flowery, soft and smooth with good acid; an Estate Chardonnay was buttery, complex and delicious; Gewürztraminer had the delectable nose and taste of crushed flower petals, with a crisp acid finish. A sparkling Brut was dry and fruity, with a bit of a grassy taste. The winery also produces Pinot Noir and Cabernet. Prices range from $6.50 to $19; higher for some late harvest wines.

St. Francis Winery • T GTA

8450 Sonoma Hwy., Kenwood, CA 95452; (707) 833-4666. Daily 10 to 4:30. Most varieties tasted; choice of four from the list. Good giftware selection; sheltered picnic garden; tours by appointment.

Smaller than St. Jean but also well-groomed, neighbor St. Francis has an affluent rural European look, in a tree-shaded garden setting. The matched winery buildings have shingled roofs and cupolas, with burgundy awnings accenting the handsome oak tasting room.

The winery was started in 1972 by Joseph and Emma Martin. They have built a following for their Merlot and other ribbon-winning varietals, as they gradually built up their winery to its present good-looking state.

Tasting notes: The Sonoma County Cabernet was our favorite, big and peppery, with nice oak tones; it was very drinkable, yet tannic enough for aging. A Zinfandel, from old vines and aged in American oak, was excellent as well, lushly berry-like and gently spicy. A Sonoma County Gewürztraminer had the proper flower petal aroma and flavor, and the Barrel Select

Chardonnay was buttery and spicy. Prices range from $7.50 to the mid-teens.

Vintners choice: "We're known for our Merlot," said tasting room manager Penny Cassina. "We also produce outstanding Cabernet Sauvignon and Chardonnay."

Landmark Vineyards • T GTA

101 Adobe Canyon Rd., Kenwood, CA 95452; (707) 833-0053. Daily 10 to 4:30; MC/VISA. Selected wines tasted. Good selection of wine-related items and specialty foods. Picnic tables near the tasting room. Guides tours by appointment.

This pleasing new facility of beige stucco with shake roofs forms a large Spanish-style semi-courtyard. A tile-floored, vaulted-ceiling tasting room and a stylish gift and gourmet food shop occupy one wing. An imposing mural of the winery's premiere product, Chardonnay, dominates the wall behind the tasting counter.

Established in 1974 by William Mabry III, Landmark began operations northern Sonoma County near Windsor, then moved to this site in mid-1990. It's now a partnership between Mabry and Damaris Deere Ethridge, great granddaughter of farm implement pioneer John Deere.

Tasting notes: Chardonnays dominate the short list and they're excellent. A Damaris Alexander Valley Reserve was rich and complex, and a Proprietor's Reserve Chard had a wonderfully nutty taste with a crisp yet silky finish. Landmark also produces a Brut sparkling wine and an Alexander Valley Cabernet Sauvignon. Prices range from $7.99 to the mid-teens.

Vintners choice: "Our premium Chardonnays," says hospitality manager Kathleen Heintz, not surprisingly. "They will cellar and age for a good amount of time."

THE BEST OF THE BUNCH

The best wine buys • Sebastiani Vineyards, Glen Ellen Winery and Valley of the Moon Winery.

The most attractive wineries • Viansa, Gloria Ferrer Champagne Caves, Buena Vista Winery, Kenwood Vineyards, Chateau St. Jean and Landmark Vineyards.

The most interesting tasting rooms • Viansa, Sebastiani Vineyards, Buena Vista Winery and Landmark Vineyards.

The funkiest tasting room • Gundlach-Bundschu Winery.

The best gift shops • Viansa, Sebastiani Vineyards, Buena Vista Winery and Landmark Vineyards.

The nicest picnic areas • Viansa, Ravenswood, Hacienda Wine Cellars, Buena Vista Winery, Gundlach-Bundschu Winery, Glen Ellen Winery and Chateau St. Jean.

The best tours • Gloria Ferrer Champagne Caves (guided), Sebastiani Vineyards (guided), Buena Vista (historic; also self-guiding), Chateau St. Jean (self-guiding).

BEYOND THE VINEYARDS

Sonoma is the historic focal point of the valley and you'll want to spend considerable time here. Start at the eight-acre **Sonoma Plaza** with its

1906 mission revival **City Hall.** It was built with four matching "front entries" so none of the surrounding merchants would feel slighted. The **Bear Flag Monument** honoring California's brief tenure as a republic stands at the plaza's northeast corner.

The Sonoma Chamber of Commerce **Visitors Information Center** occupies an old Carnegie library building on the Plaza's east side. It faces the Italianate **Sebastiani Theatre,** a classic old movie house with a 72-foot tower. Various elements of **Sonoma State Historic Park** line Spain Street: **Mission San Francisco Solano,** the reconstructed **Sonoma Barracks, Toscano Hotel** and site of **Casa Grande,** once General Vallejo's home and headquarters.

A few blocks south on Spain Street, you'll encounter Vallejo's final home, a striking gingerbready Victorian called **Lachryma Montis,** Latin for "mountain tear." There's a small admission fee to some of the elements of the historic park. One same-day ticket is good for all, including Jack London State Historic Park and—over the mountains—Petaluma Adobe State Historic Park.

Dozens of other yesteryear buildings occupy the streets of old Sonoma. To spot them, you can purchase a copy of the Sonoma League for Historic Preservation's ***Sonoma Walking Tour*** at the visitor's center.

The plaza is rimmed with a good assortment of restaurants, boutiques, specialty shops and wine shops. A group of them are tucked into the Spanish-style **El Paseo de Sonoma,** an arcade on the east side of the plaza.

In addition to wine, history and shopping, a fourth element draws nearly a million annual visitors to Sonoma: food. Since wining and dining are closely allied, the town has a reputation as a specialty food center. These places are worthy of a your attention:

Sonoma French Bakery, on the plaza at 470 First St. East, makes the best sourdough bread north of San Francisco, along with other baked goodies. Get there early, since the bread supply often runs out. Hours are Wednesday-Saturday 8 to 6 and Sunday 7 to noon; phone 996-2691.

Sonoma Cheese Factory, on the north side of the plaza at #2 Spain St., is a large deli and cafe specializing in local and international cheeses. You can watch soft "jack" style cheese, a local specialty, being made through a window. (See listing under "Wine country dining" below.) Hours are 8:30 to 5:30 weekdays and 8:30 to 6 weekends; phone 996-1931.

Sonoma Sausage Company, on the west side of the plaza at 453 First St., makes every kind of sausage from British bangers to bratwurst, along with potato salad and excellent patès. It's open Monday-Saturday 9:30 to 5:30 and Sunday noon to 5; phone 938-8200.

Vella Cheese Company, a block east of the mission, then a block north at 315 Second St., is Sonoma's other pioneer cheese-making firm, offering cheeses, picnic fare and specialty foods. It's housed in a 1905 rough-cut stone brewery building. It's open Monday-Saturday 9 to 6 and Sunday 10 to 5; phone (800) 848-0505 or locally 938-3232.

The Cherry Tree specializes in cherry juice, cider and other fruit juices and food items. Its main store is at 1901 Fremont Drive (Highways 12-121), just east of Broadway on the route to Napa. The smaller, original cherry tree stand is south on Highway 121, as you come in from the Bay Area. Hours are 6:30 a.m. to 8 p.m. at the Fremont Drive store and 9 to dusk at the stand; phone 938-3480.

SOUTHERN SONOMA COUNTY DRIVING TOUR • The following loop tour touches other points of interest in the southern half of the county. Assuming you visited Jack London State Historic Park during your winery prowling, we'll head you off in another direction.

From the Sonoma Plaza, drive south on Broadway, perhaps stopping for a choo-choo ride at **Train Town** on your left (see activities, below). About a mile beyond Train Town, turn right onto Watmaugh Road, which crosses Arnold Drive, then swings left and blends onto Stage Gulch Road (Highway 116). This takes you into rolling hill country, thatched here and there with oak clusters and madrone groves.

Follow Stage Gulch two and a half miles, turn left onto Adobe Road and follow it to **Petaluma Adobe State Historic Park,** a reconstruction of Vallejo's ranch headquarters. Continue on Adobe Road about a mile and a half, turn left onto Washington Street and follow it into **Petaluma.** You'll cross U.S. 101 freeway and wind up in the heart of this old town with the funny name. It's noted for false front and rare iron front stores downtown, and for some attractive Victorian homes on its tree-lined residential streets.

Petaluma has a couple of curious claims to fame. It's home to the World's Wristwrestling Championships and an annual ugly dog contest.

Once you've explored Petaluma, follow D Street (lined with some fine old homes) until it becomes Red Hill Road. Drive nine miles to **Marin French Cheese Factory,** where you can watch camembert and other smelly cheeses being made, and picnic beside a duck pond. You're now in Marin County, but never mind that. This route takes through some of the prettiest hilly landscape in all of northern California.

Stay on Red Hill (which changes its name to Petaluma-Point Reyes Road) until it intersects with Highway 1 at **Tomales Bay**, about ten miles from the cheese place. Tomales is a narrow inlet formed by the famous San Andreas Fault—infamous if you're a fidgety California resident.

From here, you could stray completely off course by heading south to **Point Reyes National Seashore** on the Point Reyes Peninsula. Or bear with us and bear north on State Highway 1 along the skinny bay's eastern shore, passing funky little **Marshall,** a town that seems transported from the New England seacoast. Continue to the equally rustic town of **Tomales**, seven miles north, then turn seaward and prowl the hideaway coastal hamlet of **Dillon Beach**. Press on north to **Bodega Bay,** a bucolic harbor town made famous by Alfred Hitchcock's film, *The Birds*.

To complete a loop, head inland on the Bodega Highway through more bucolic countryside to the former Russian settlement of **Sebastopol** (which doesn't look Russian). Pick up Highway 12 and follow it to **Santa Rosa,** a town of nearly 100,000. It offers **Luther Burbank Gardens, Robert L. Ripley Museum, Sonoma County Museum** and other amusements. (Write to the chamber of commerce listed below for specifics.)

Tracking Highway 12's snaking route through Santa Rosa will return you to the Valley of the Moon, ready to move on to our next chapter, Napa

County. A scenic approach to the valley is north along Calistoga Road, which branches off Highway 12 about five miles from Santa Rosa.

Sonoma Valley activities & Attractions

Auto racing • Sears Point International Raceway, auto and cycle races most weekends, Highway 37 at 121, Sonoma, CA 95476; 938-8448.

Farm products • For a map and guide to direct-outlet farms selling fresh and prepared fruits, vegetables, meats, dairy products and wines, contact ***Sonoma County Farm Trails,*** P.O. Box 6674, Santa Rosa, CA 95406; 544-4728 or pick up free map at most member outlets.

Horseback riding • Guided trail rides through Jack London State Park and Sugarloaf Ridge State Park by Sonoma Cattle Company, 996-8566.

Hot air ballooning • Air Flamboyant, 4714 Woodview Dr., Santa Rosa, CA 95407; 456-4711. Sonoma Thunder, P.O. Box 641, El Verano, CA 95433; 538-7359.

Museums & historical exhibits •

Sonoma State Historic Park, P.O. Box 167, Sonoma; 938-1578. Daily 10 to 5; modest admission charge (one ticket good for all units of the park). Includes Mission San Francisco Solano, Sonoma Barracks, La Casa Grande and Toscano Hotel all on Sonoma Plaza and General Vallejo's Home, south of the plaza off Spain Street.

Jack London State Historic Park, London Ranch Road, Glen Ellen; 938-5216. Daily 10 to 5; modest admission charge. Author's ranch, Wolf House ruins and wife's home.

Scenic flights • Aero-Schellville (open-cockpit biplane), 23982 Arnold Dr., Sonoma; 938-2444. Helicopter Network c/o the Cherry Tree; 252-7874. Sonoma Flight Academy, Sonoma Sky Park, 21840 Eighth St. East, Sonoma; 935-9745.

Spas, mineral springs • Agua Caliente Mineral Springs, 17350 Vailetti Dr., Agua Caliente, CA 95416; 996-6822. Morton's Warm Springs, 1651 Warm Springs Rd., Kenwood, CA 95452; 833-5511. The Spa at Sonoma Mission Inn, P.O. Box 1447, Sonoma, CA 95476; 938-9000.

Train rides • Train Town, 20264 Broadway, Sonoma; 938-3912.

Wineland events • Heart of the Valley barrel tasting at eight Kenwood area wineries, mid-March; 833-4666. Polo, Wine and All That Jazz, early June, contact Sonoma County Wine Library Association, P.O. Box 15225, Santa Rosa, CA 95402; 571-1926. Sonoma Valley Wine Festival, mid-July; 938-6791.

Sonoma County Wine Auction, early August; 527-7701. Midsummer Mozart and autumn Shakespeare festivals at Buena Vista Winery; 938-1266. Sonoma Vintage Festival, oldest in California with parade, grape stomps, wine tasting, late September; 996-2109. Individual wineries also sponsor various events throughout the year.

Wine country tours • Sonoma Charter & Tours, P.O. Box 1972, Sonoma, CA 95476; 938-4248. Linda Viviandi Touring Company, 500 Michael Dr., Sonoma, CA 95476; 938-2100. Wine Country Wagons, P.O. Box 1069, Kenwood, CA 95452; 833-2724.

Winery maps • Free ***Sonoma Valley Viticultural Area*** map, at many wineries and Sonoma Valley Visitors Bureau, or write Sonoma Valley

Vintner's Association, P.O. Box 238, Sonoma, CA 95476. ***Official Sonoma Valley Visitors Guide***, $1, available at Sonoma Valley Visitors Bureau and at many wineries and shops.

WINE COUNTRY DINING

Big Three Cafe • ΔΔΔ $$$ ØØ

In Sonoma Mission Inn, 18140 Sonoma Highway, Boyes Hot Springs; (707) 938-9000. California-Italian; dinners $12 to $20; full bar service. Weekdays 7 to 3 and 5:30 to 9:30, weekends 7 to 9:30. Informal to casual; reservations accepted, essential for dinner. Major credit cards. Bright, airy and informal restaurant, featuring the California *nouveau* or pizza specialties. Open kitchen, wood burning pizza oven and wine tasting bar. Smoke free.

Depot 1870 Restaurant • ΔΔΔΔ $$ Ø

241 First St. West (Spain Street), Sonoma; (707) 938-2980. Northern Italian; dinners $9 to $16; wine and beer. Lunch Wednesday-Friday 11:30 to 2, dinner Wednesday-Sunday from 5. Informal to casual; reservations accepted. Major credit cards. Chef-owned restaurant with dining at poolside in a landscaped garden, or in an early American setting indoors. Northern Italian specialties such as *petto al paillard* (grilled chicken breast marinated in Italian herbs) and *gamberoni saltati* (prawns sauteed with garlic, shallots, white wine and lemon).

Kenwood Restaurant • ΔΔΔΔ $$$ ØØ

9900 Sonoma Highway, Kenwood; (707) 833-6326. French country cuisine; dinners $10 to $20; full bar service. Daily except Monday from 11:30 to 9. Informal to casual; reservations advised. MC/VISA. An open, cheerful place among the vineyards, with an outdoor dining patio if you want to get closer to the grapes. Changing menu with a strong *nouveau* tilt, featuring local fare such as roast Petaluma duck with wild rice and orange sauce and braised Sonoma rabbit with mushrooms, tomatoes and polenta.

La Casa • ΔΔ $ Ø

121 E. Spain St. (opposite the mission), Sonoma; (707) 996-3406. Mexican; dinners $4.50 to $10; full bar service. Daily from 11:30 a.m. Casual; reservations accepted. Major credit cards. Cheery little Latin place, locally popular. Extensive menu features the usual Mexican specialties, singly or in *combinaciòns*.

Magliulo's Restaurant • ΔΔΔ $$$ Ø

691 Broadway, Sonoma; (707) 996-1031. Italian-American; dinners $10 to $20; full bar service. Open daily, lunch 11 to 3 and dinner 5 to 9. Informal to casual; reservations on Saturdays only. MC/VISA, DISC. Attractive restaurant in an early American home with warm woods, ironwork, cut glass and potted plants. Busy menu ranges from New York steak and rack of lamb to a full spectrum of Italian dishes. Lantern-lit dining garden.

Oreste's Golden Bear • ΔΔ $$$ Ø

1717 Adobe Canyon Rd., Kenwood; (707) 833-2327. Northern Italian; dinners $13.50 to $20.75; wine and beer. Monday-Saturday 11:30 to 9:30, Sunday 11 to 2 and 4:30 to 9:30. Informal to casual; reservations suggested on weekends. MC/VISA, AMEX. Rustically casual in a rural wooded setting, spanning a creek; a popular local hangout for decades. Menu is essentially Italian, but touches on American chicken, chops and seafood.

Restaurant Pasta Nostra • ΔΔ $$ Ø

139 E. Napa St. (just east of the plaza), Sonoma; (707) 938-4166. Italian; dinners $11 to $18; wine and beer. Lunch Thursday-Monday 11:30 to 2:30, dinner Monday-Thursday 5 to 9, Friday-Saturday 5 to 10 and Sunday 4:30 to 9. Casual; reservations accepted. MC/VISA. Cheerful new restaurant in a restored Victorian home. Pasta-focused menu, plus interesting items such as chicken with lemon, rosemary and garlic and a combined veal parmesana-scalloppini. Attractive dining patio.

Ristorante Piatti • ΔΔΔ $$$ Ø

405 First St. West (in the El Dorado Hotel), Sonoma; (707) 996-2351. Regional Italian; dinners $12 to $25; full bar service. Daily from 11:30, various closing hours. Informal to casual; reservations advised. MC/VISA. Lively *trattoria*, popular as a business lunch hangout. Open kitchen with wood-burning rotissiere; specialties include angel hair pasta, spaghetti with duck *ragout*, black and white pasta with fresh mussels and grilled seafoods. Tree-shaded dining patio.

Sonoma Cheese Factory • ΔΔ $ Ø

#2 Spain St. (north side of plaza), Sonoma; 996-1931. Delicatessen; meals $3 and up; wine and beer. Weekdays 8:30 to 5:30, weekends 8:30 to 6. Casual; MC/VISA, AMEX. Large deli, handy for a quickie lunch or picnic fare, including box lunches. Sandwiches, salads, 200 varieties of cheese, local wines and assorted specialty foods. Tables indoors and on a shaded patio.

Vineyards Inn • ΔΔ $$ Ø

8445 Sonoma Highway (Adobe Canyon Road), Kenwood; (707) 833-4500. Mexican-American; dinners $7 to $14; full bar service. Daily except Tuesday from 11:30, various closing times. Casual; reservations for groups only. MC/VISA. Mexican fare served in an early American-style inn. Large menu also strays north of the border, offering gringo fare such as Waikiki Chicken, Enchiladas San Francisco with dungeness crab meat, and even lamb chops.

VINELAND LODGING

Even with the Sonoma Valley's popularity, motels are rather scarce. The area offers an assortment of bed & breakfast inns, historic hotels and—for those with a taste and budget for luxury—the Sonoma Mission Inn and Spa. Nearby Santa Rosa has scores of lodgings.

Best Western Sonoma Valley Inn • ΔΔΔ $$$$$ Ø

550 Second St. West (a block west of plaza), Sonoma, CA 95476; (800) 528-1234 or (707) 938-9200. Doubles and singles $105 to $125; off-season $75 to $95. Major credit cards. Nicely-appointed 72-unit motel with pool, spa, coin laundry. Rooms have TV movies, phones, refrigerators; some with fireplaces.

El Dorado Hotel • ΔΔΔ $$$$ Ø

405 First St. West (west side of plaza), Sonoma, CA 95476; (800) 289-3031 or (707) 996-3030. Doubles $85 weekdays, $120 to $130 weekends (with continental breakfast). MC/VISA. Refurbished 27-room mission-style hotel. Attractive rooms with terraces overlooking courtyard or plaza; continental furnishings with Spanish accents; swimming pool. **Ristorante Piatti** listed above.

Sonoma Hotel • ΔΔ $$$

110 W. Spain St. (northwest corner of plaza), Sonoma, CA 95476; (707) 996-2996. Doubles $62 to $105 (includes continental breakfast and nightly bottle of wine). MC/VISA, AMEX. Restored 1874 hotel; 17 rooms furnished with Victorian and early California antiques. Five rooms with private baths; others share. **Sonoma Hotel Bar & Grill** serves daily 11:30 to 8; American, mostly light fare and sandwiches; dinners $10 to $13; full bar service.

Sonoma Mission Inn and Spa • ΔΔΔΔ $$$$$ Ø

18140 Sonoma Highway, Boyes Hot Springs; mailing address P.O. Box 1447, Sonoma, CA 95476; (800) 862-4945 in California or (800) 358-9022 elsewhere, locally (707) 938-9000. Doubles and singles $155 to $290. Major credit cards. Elegantly restored Mediterranean style resort on seven acres with a complete health spa, tennis courts and two pools. The 170 beautifully appointed rooms have TV movies, room phones and typical resort amenities. **The Grille** serves daily 11:30 to 2:30 and 6 to 9; California *nouveau*; dinners $25 to $40; overlooking pool and gardens; full bar service; smoke-free dining room. Also see **Big Three Cafe** above.

Westerbeke Ranch • ΔΔΔ $$$ Ø

2300 Grove St. Carringer, (off Arnold Drive), Sonoma, CA 95476; (707) 996-7546. Rooms $60 to $80. MC/VISA. Fifteen cabins and rooms, some with shared baths, in a wooded ranch retreat" used both for conferences and individuals. Pool, sauna, hot tub, racquetball court. **Dining Room** serves California *nouveau* and vegetarian dishes, for guests only; Mexican decor.

Bed & breakfast inns

Beltane Ranch Bed & Breakfast • ΔΔΔ $$$$ Ø

11775 Sonoma Highway (P.O. Box 395), Glen Ellen, CA 95442; (707) 996-6501. Doubles $95 to $120, singles $80 to $100. Four rooms, all with private baths; full breakfast. No credit cards. An 1892 Colonial style ranch house in a pleasant country setting. Tennis court, pleasant gardens, hammocks and hiking trails. Rooms are furnished in American and European antiques.

Gaige House • ΔΔΔ $$$$ Ø

13540 Arnold Dr. (north of Warm Springs Road), Glen Ellen, CA 95442; (707) 935-0237. Doubles $85 to $150, singles $85 to $145. Eight rooms, all with private baths; full breakfast. MC/VISA, DISC. An Italianate Victorian dating from 1890, furnished with English and American antiques. Spacious yard, pool; some rooms with radio-TV and fireplaces; one with tub spa.

Gee-Gee's Bed & Breakfast • ΔΔ $$$$ ØØ

7810 Highway 12 (between Oakmont and Kenwood), Santa Rosa, CA 95409; (707) 833-6667. Doubles $75 to $90, singles $70. Four rooms, two private baths, two shared; full breakfast. MC/VISA, AMEX. A cheerful turn-of-the-century ranch house with antique and modern furnishings. Pool, decks, gardens, outdoor breakfast if weather permits, gratis bicycles, fireplace in common room.

Glenelly Inn • ΔΔ $$$$ ØØ

5131 Warm Springs Rd. (off Arnold Drive), Glen Ellen, CA 95442; (707) 996-6720. Doubles and singles $75 to $120. Eight rooms, all with private baths; full breakfast. MC/VISA. A refurbished 1916 country resort in the French Colonial style. Rooms done in American and European antiques. One-acre landscaped grounds with spa and rose garden. Common room with stone fireplace.

Kenwood Inn • ΔΔΔ $$$$$ ØØ

10400 Sonoma Hwy. (downtown), Kenwood, CA 95452; (707) 833-1293. Doubles and singles $125 to $225. Four rooms, all with private baths; full breakfast. MC/VISA, AMEX. An opulent Italian style villa converted from a turn-of-the-century store; Mediterranean furnishings. All rooms with fireplaces, down comforters, gratis chocolates and wines. Swimming pool; extensive landscaped grounds among the vineyards.

Sonoma Chalet • ΔΔ $$$$ Ø

18935 Fifth St. West (Verano Avenue), Sonoma, CA 95476; (707) 938-3129. Doubles $75 to $110. Seven rooms, four with private baths; continental breakfast. MC/VISA, AMEX. Country-style farm house; rooms furnished with early American antiques; fireplaces, wood-burning stoves. Spa, bicycles, complimentary sherry.

Thistle Dew Inn • ΔΔΔ $$$$ Ø

171 W. Spain St. (a block west of plaza), Sonoma, CA 95476; (707) 938-2909. Doubles and singles $80 to $100. Six rooms, all with private baths; full breakfast. MC/VISA. Lodgings in an 1869 Victorian and a 1905 early American home; modern furnishings, decorated with arts and crafts. Spa, bicycles, afternoon *hors d'oeuvres*.

Victorian Garden Inn • ΔΔΔ $$$$ Ø

316 E. Napa St. (block and a half east of plaza), Sonoma, CA 95476; (707) 996-5339. Doubles $79 to $135. Four rooms, all with private baths, one cottage with fireplace; full breakfast. MC/VISA, AMEX. An 1880 Greek Revival style home furnished with country antiques. Pool, landscaped grounds and patio; complimentary evening wine.

Trojan Horse Inn • ΔΔΔ $$$$$ Ø

19455 Sonoma Hwy. (between West Napa and Spain), Sonoma, CA 95476; (707) 996-2430. Doubles $110 to $130 ($20 less mid-week). Six rooms, all with private baths; full breakfast. MC/VISA, AMEX. Victorian style farmhouse with extensive landscaped grounds on banks of Sonoma Creek. Rooms furnished with English and American antiques; armoires, brass beds. One room with fireplace, one with spa. Complimentary bicycles, evening cocktails.

Sonoma Valley information sources

Santa Rosa Chamber of Commerce, 637 First St., Santa Rosa, CA 95404; (707) 547-1414.

Sonoma State Historic Park, P.O. Box 167, Sonoma, CA 95476; (707) 938-1519.

Sonoma Valley Visitors Bureau, 453 First St. East, Sonoma, CA 95476; (707) 996-1090 or 966-1033.

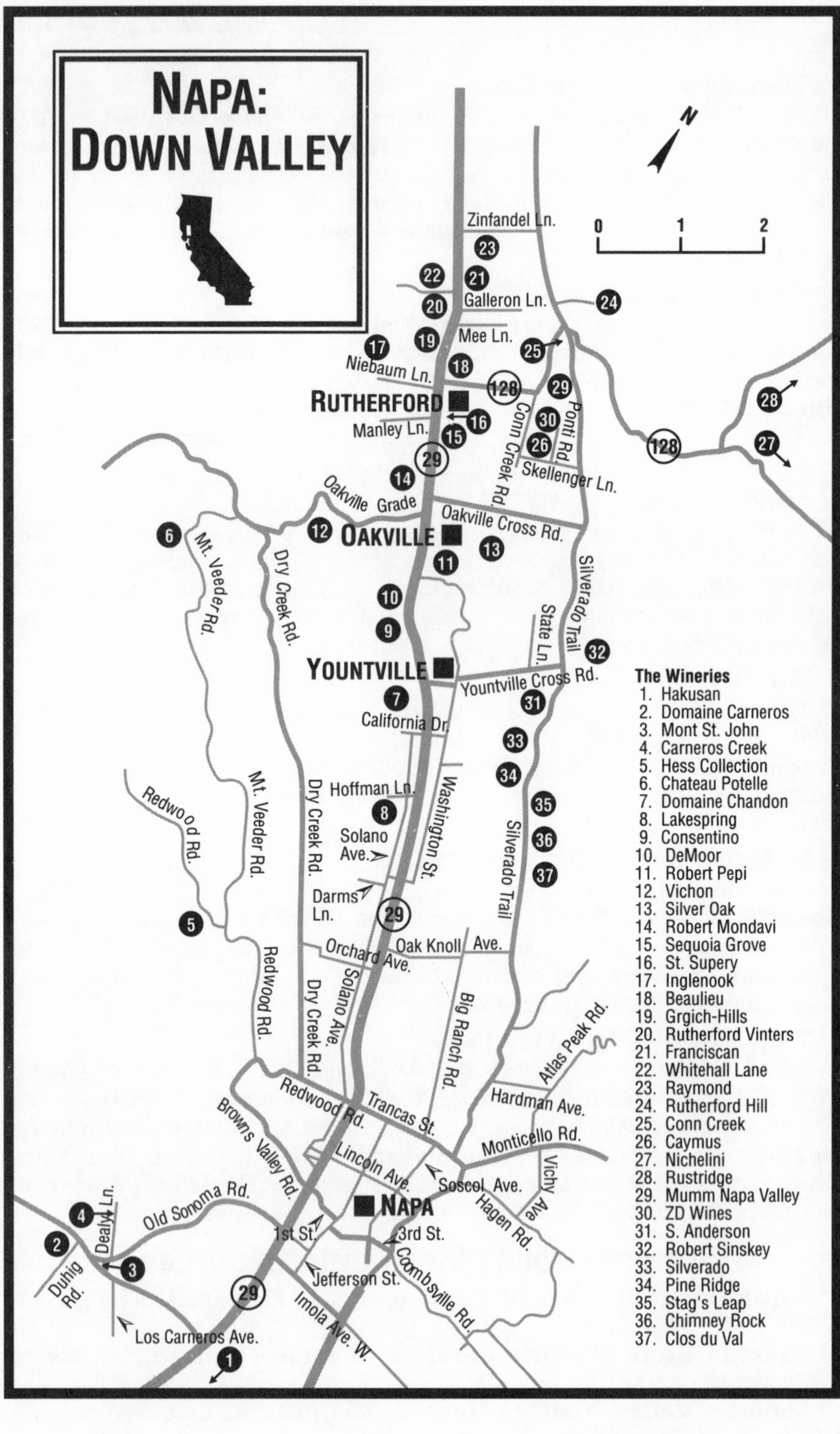

NAPA:
DOWN VALLEY
N
0 1 2
Zinfandel Ln.
Galleron Ln.
Mee Ln.
Niebaum Ln.
RUTHERFORD
Manley Ln.
Conn Creek Rd.
Ponti Rd.
Skellenger Ln.
Oakville Grade
OAKVILLE
Oakville Cross Rd.
Mt. Veeder Rd.
Dry Creek Rd.
Silverado Trail
State Ln.
YOUNTVILLE
Yountville Cross Rd.
California Dr.
Hoffman Ln.
Washington St.
Redwood Rd.
Solano Ave.
Darms Ln.
Orchard Ave.
Oak Knoll Ave.
Big Ranch Rd.
Atlas Peak Rd.
Hardman Ave.
Trancas St.
Browns Valley Rd.
Monticello Rd.
Lincoln Ave.
Soscol Ave.
Vichy Ave.
Hagen Rd.
NAPA
Old Sonoma Rd.
Dealy Ln.
1st St.
3rd St.
Duhig Rd.
Jefferson St.
Coombsville Rd.
Imola Ave. W.
Los Carneros Ave.
29
128
The Wineries
1. Hakusan
2. Domaine Carneros
3. Mont St. John
4. Carneros Creek
5. Hess Collection
6. Chateau Potelle
7. Domaine Chandon
8. Lakespring
9. Consentino
10. DeMoor
11. Robert Pepi
12. Vichon
13. Silver Oak
14. Robert Mondavi
15. Sequoia Grove
16. St. Supery
17. Inglenook
18. Beaulieu
19. Grgich-Hills
20. Rutherford Vinters
21. Franciscan
22. Whitehall Lane
23. Raymond
24. Rutherford Hill
25. Conn Creek
26. Caymus
27. Nichelini
28. Rustridge
29. Mumm Napa Valley
30. ZD Wines
31. S. Anderson
32. Robert Sinskey
33. Silverado
34. Pine Ridge
35. Stag's Leap
36. Chimney Rock
37. Clos du Val

"The amazing violet-spice complexity wrapped around a carload of berrylike, cherry-ish fruit plays tag with nuances of vanilla, toasted oak and faint cigar-box scents..."

—Description of a Caymus Special Selection Cabernet Sauvignon

Chapter Five

NAPA: DOWN VALLEY

Southern area, from Napa to Rutherford

Approached from the south, California's most famous wine valley appears to be more of a plain. The landscape, too gentle here to be called hilly, cradles the Napa River as it wanders aimlessly toward the San Pablo arm of San Francisco Bay.

From its outskirts, Napa—the valley's foundation city—seems little different from any other mid-sized American community. It could as well be Cedar Rapids, Iowa, or Boise, Idaho. Driving along the freeway portion of Highway 29, you see no clue to a fabled wineland, other than a purple grape cluster decorating the free-standing sign of the Napa Valley Center shopping complex.

Yet vineyards are all about you, crouching behind the subtly rolling terrain. The Carneros region is to the southwest, where the Napa and Sonoma valley flood plains merge at the edge of the bay. More vines garnish foothills of the Vaca Range to the northeast, hidden now by spreading Napa suburbs. Other vineyards stride up the flanks of the Mayacamas Mountains to the northwest. Directly north, just beyond the final city stoplight at Redwood Road, grapes cover the valley floor like green shag carpeting.

As you drive north, the two low mountain ranges draw near to create a *Falcon Crest* vision of the Napa Valley so familiar to Americans. Ranks of vines march away from the highway like a retreating army in green camouflage. Ivy-walled wineries stand at roadside; mansions built by yesterday's wine barons sulk behind protective cloaks of trees. The great bulk of Mount St. Helena commands the northern horizon. Two main routes, Highway 29 and the Silverado Trail, run roughly parallel along the valley's edges, linked by crossroads to form a crooked ladder.

The Napa Valley is everything everyone says it is—and less. Nearly 250 wineries dot the basin; some of the larger ones draw 300,000 visitors a year. Tour buses may inundate tasting rooms without warning; insurance widows from Indiana will giggle nervously and ask for a sip of something sweet.

Highway 29 can become traffic-tangled on summer weekends. Gimmicks such as the Napa Valley Wine Train, the "authentic" *City of Napa* sternwheeler and themed shopping centers lure visitor hoards.

Yet you can find picturesque, tucked-away wineries with tasting rooms that are rarely crowded, winding country lanes bereft of cars, and lonely ramparts with valley vistas to draw your breath away.

To avoid the mob, visit the Napa Valley on a weekday, when even the major wineries are uncrowded. If that's not practical (most of us work for a living), focus on wineries off Highway 29. The Silverado Trail, running through more attractive terrain in the Vaca foothills, entices only a fraction of the valley's visitors. Finally, get an early start. Most tasting rooms open at 10 a.m., yet crowds rarely peak until after lunch. Consider retreating to your motel pool in the late afternoon—the busiest time of day for tasting rooms.

Many valley wineries charge for tasting, a practice which we applaud, since it discourages those out for a free drinking spree. Tasting room folks scornfully refer to them as "recreational drinkers."

Fees are quite nominal—two or three dollars to sample a variety of wines. Generally, you can keep the glass, which bears the winery's logo, or you can apply the charge toward a bottle purchase. Glasses come in assorted sizes, so one winds up with a rather eclectic collection. (When we mentioned this to one tasting room host, he grinned and quipped: "Just come back here eight times, and you'll have a uniform set.")

We were impressed by the overall excellence of the wines as we visited the valley's tasting rooms. Despite its touristy reputation—deserved or not—the Napa Valley is home to serious vintners who produce some of America's finest wines. Not surprisingly, they're generally more expensive that similar varieties from other areas. Even unprocessed grapes command a higher price. They may be no better than comparable Sonoma fruit, but these are *Napa* grapes, thank you!

At last count, the valley contained 239 wineries, yet only ten of them control a third of the grape crop and produce 40 percent of the wine. The largest is Christian Brothers, followed by Charles Krug, Robert Mondavi, Beringer and Beaulieu—all household names. Yet with all this vinicultural largess, this fabled Eden produces only two percent of California's wines.

California's most famous wine valley isn't its first. By the time Napa wine production began in earnest in the 1860s, the Los Angeles vineyards had passed their peak and Sonoma was regarded as the cradle of commercial viniculture.

A hunter-gatherer Indian tribe variously called Wappo or Nappa inhabited the valley for nearly 4,000 years. "Nappa" may mean "bountiful place" or salmon or spear point or grizzly bear. We will never know, for the gentle Stone Age Wappo—victims of servitude, disease and bullets dealt by the Spanish and later American settlers—exist no more.

When Mission San Francisco Solano was established in Sonoma in 1823, the Napa Valley was seen suitable only for grazing land. Huge chunks of it were granted to citizens of the newly-freed Mexico who had helped in its fight for independence from Spain. But for the most part it remained undeveloped—the domain of deer, grizzlies and wild oats.

The first outside settler was American frontiersman George Calvert Yount. After working for Sonoma's Mariano Vallejo, he was granted Rancho

Caymus in the Napa Valley in the 1830s. The first American citizen to obtain a Mexican land grant, he planted vineyards and orchards near the town named in his honor. It's likely that he made a bit of wine from Mission grapes for his table and thus became one of the valley's earliest vintners.

Napa's first commercial wine production is attributed to John Patchett in 1858. Then came families whose names still ring in Napa Valley history books: Charles Krug in 1860, Jacob Schram of Schramsberg in 1862, the Beringer brothers in the 1870s, Gustave Neibaum of Inglenook in 1899 and Georges de Latour, who established Beaulieu at the turn of the century.

Others left their marks on the valley, as well. Flamboyant Mormon Sam Brannan, who had shouted out California's 1848 gold discovery in the streets of San Francisco, built the valley's first mineral springs resort in 1868. Styled after the grand Saratoga spa of New York, it was called by Brannan—perhaps in drunken jest—"the Calistoga of Sarifornia." During the summer of 1880, impoverished, ailing Scottish writer Robert Louis Stevenson and his bride Fanny spent their honeymoon in an old mining shack high in the flanks of Mount St. Helena. (See box in Chapter 6.)

Napa Valley's history pursued the typical pattern—the 1870s wine price crash, phylloxera, Prohibition, Repeal and a gradual rebuilding during this century's first half. The Christian Brothers came to the valley in 1930, Louis M. Martini established his winery in 1933 and Cesare Mondavi bought the Charles Krug facility ten years later. When Cesare died in 1959, it was passed to sons Peter and Robert. World War II slowed vineyard and winery growth. Life moved slowly in the idyllic valley for many quiet years.

Then, after a family spat said to be one of the seeds for TV's *Falcon Crest,* Robert Mondavi left Krug. In 1966, he opened the first "new" winery in the valley in several years. Indeed, it was a new concept—one of the first wineries designed for public tours, vineyard concerts and other special events. The energetic, outspoken Mondavi has become a leading defender of wine's public image and a foe of what he calls "neo-prohibitionists." Not surprisingly, he is one of the chief subjects in James Conaway's recent and rather revealing book, ***Napa: The Story of an American Eden***.

America's sudden "discovery" of wines in the late 1960s was both a boon and a menace to the Napa Valley. Vineyard acreage tripled and wineries multiplied; the valley became the target of every tour bus route. Many visitors put down roots and Napa's suburbs swelled northward, threatening prime vine land. A four-lane expressway bulled its way through the vineyards, seeking to alleviate Highway 29 congestion.

Vintners and other concerned citizens rushed to rescue their enchanted land. An agricultural preserve was established in 1968 to protect prime vineyards. The new highway was stopped at Yountville, so the rest of Highway 29 remains congested. Residents wisely decided that the cure would have been more painful than the illness.

Despite its growing popularity, the area still has its quiet moments and its quiet places. Early on a weekday morning, you can discover a Napa Valley much like that observed by Robert Louis Stevenson in 1880:

"The stirring sunlight and the growing vines, and the vats and bottles in the caverns, made a pleasant music for the mind."

Since the valley has more wineries than any other area in America, we've divided it into two chapters. We use the local reference, "down valley" for the southern end and "up valley" for the north. In touring down valley, we'll divide it again, first visiting the Carneros and Mount Veeder areas near Napa, then the heart of the valley along Highway 29 and the Silverado Trail.

CARNEROS-MOUNT VEEDER WINERY TOUR • As we mentioned earlier, the Sonoma and Napa valleys share the Carneros. Cooled by bay breezes, this gentle terrain is ideal for Chardonnay and Pinot Noir; much of it goes into sparkling wines. The tilted, rocky soils of nearby Mount Veeder in the Mayacamus range nurture exceptional Cabernets.

Napa's Carneros can be reached by two approaches from the Bay Area. From U.S. 101, turn east onto State Highway 37 north of Novato, then swing north onto Highway 29 in Vallejo. If you're following Interstate 80 north, take Highway 37 west through Vallejo, then turn north onto Route 29.

From Vallejo, take Highway 29 north. At its intersection with Highway 12, you'll see **Hakusan Sakè Gardens** on the right; it makes wine not from grapes but from rice. To reach it, turn right onto Highway 12, then left onto North Kelly Road. Continue north on Kelly from Hakusan, since it merges into Route 12. After a short distance, fork left onto Highway 29, then go west on Highway 121 (following the Sonora sign) into the **Carneros.**

This is subtly rolling terrain, as softly contoured as a slender woman. Many vineyards but few winery tasting rooms occupy this area. Your first encounter will be the palatial **Domaine Carneros** on the left at the Duhig Road junction. From here, you may want to follow Duhig into the Carneros terrain, enjoying vineyard vistas and distant blue slices of San Pablo Bay.

Return to Highway 121 from Domaine Carneros, fork left onto Old Sonoma Road and you'll soon see **Mont St. John Cellars** on your right. Now, continue on Old Sonoma a short distance to Dealy Lane and follow it to **Carneros Creek Winery.**

Next, return to Old Sonoma Road and follow it into **Napa**. Just short of the freeway, turn left and drive a mile along a frontage road, past Napa Valley Center. Turn right onto First Street, cross the freeway and take a right-hand cloverleaf down to it. You're now headed north into the Napa Valley.

The freeway ends at a stoplight at the intersection of Redwood Road; go left onto Redwood and follow it west into the foothills of wooded Mount Veeder. After about six miles, turn left at the junction of Redwood and Mount Veeder roads (staying on Redwood). The impressive **Hess Collection** winery is about a mile beyond, on your left.

Return to Redwood Road and turn left onto Mount Veeder Road, continuing west. It winds steeply into the Mayacamas, passing bearded oaks, pines and occasional redwoods. After ten miles, you'll see a small sign to **Chateau Potelle,** reached by a winding dirt road. It was rough and rain-gutted when we visited, but folks at this tucked-away mountain winery promised that it would be improved. (Also, note in the listing below that hours are limited; call ahead before making the climb.)

WINERY CODES • **T** = tasting with no fee; **T$** = fee for tasting; **GT** = guided tours; **GTA** = appointment required for tour; **ST** = self-guiding tours; **CT** = casual tours or a peek into the winery; ⚔ = picnic area; 🎁 = separate gift shop or good giftware selection. Price ranges listed in tasting notes are for varietals; jug wines often are available for less. **DINING & LODGINGS** • ØØ = smoke-free establishment; Ø = non-smoking tables or rooms.

From Chateau Potelle, continue a mile or so downhill on Mount Veeder until it ends at Dry Creek Road. Go right, then right again after a mile, staying on Dry Creek. This takes you back to Redwood Road in the Napa suburbs.

You'll note that this route is more scenery than winery. We think the drive into the thickly wooded Mayacamas Mountains is worth the effort. If you don't care for excessive twisting and turning, you could skip Chateau Potelle and return to Napa.

Hakusan Sakè Gardens • T ST

Highway 12 at Highway 29 (#1 Executive Way), Napa, CA 94558; (707) 258-6160. Daily 9 to 6 in summer, 9 to 5 the rest of the year; MC/VISA. Sakè samples tasted free, with a bit of sushi. Some gift items. Self-guiding tours; formal Japanese garden adjacent to tasting room.

Why not start your tour with the wine of another nation? Hakusan is the only sakè distillery in America producing Japanese rice wine from local rice—grown in California's central valley. Sips of cold and warm sakè and a sweet dessert wine are served in a large, airy tasting room done in Tokyo-modern style, furnished like a spacious Japanese restaurant. A hostess serves the sakè and a sushi roll at a table, and invites you to watch a video about the history of sakè and the establishment of Hakusan.

From here, you can walk past windows of the modern, warehouse-like distillery, whose stainless steel and ranks of pipes are suggestive of a present-day winery. Signs tell you what you're seeing. Your path then leads you through a tranquil (except for adjacent Highway 29 traffic) Japanese garden, back to the hospitality center. *Hakusan,* incidentally, means "white mountain."

Sakè has been traced to 700 B.C., when it was called *kuchikami no sakè,* which describes how it was made. Rice and chestnuts or millet were chewed into a wad, then spat into a wooden tub to ferment. Fortunately, today's production methods are a bit more clinical.

Tasting notes: Sakè has a crisp pleasantly pungent veggie taste, vaguely like a dry, grassy Sauvignon Blanc. The dessert sakè is sweet yet crisp; think of a *very* light-bodied Muscat dessert wine. Prices are $5 for the sakè and $6.25 for the dessert wine.

Domaine Carneros • T$ GT ST

1240 Duhig Rd. (at Highway 121; P.O. Box 5420), Napa, CA 94558; (707) 257-0101. Daily 10:30 to 5:30 May through October, Friday-Tuesday 10:30 to 4:30 the rest of the year; MC/VISA. Sparkling wines sold by the glass for $3.50. Some wine-related gift items. Guided tours at 11, 1 and 3; self-guiding tours at other times.

An offspring of France's Champagne Tattinger, Domaine Carneros is among the valley's more elegant wineries. Styled after the Tattinger family's 18th century Chateau de la Marquetterie in the French Champagne district, it is an imposing presence, crowning a low hill in the heart of the Carneros. It was completed in 1987.

After admiring the portrait of Madame Pompadour, the beaded glass chandeliers, high coffered ceilings and the view, you can seat yourself in a cane-backed chair at a brass and glass table. Here, you are served a current sparkling offering (for a fee), with *hors d'oeuvres*, of course. On warm days, you can adjourn to a view deck.

Tours, conducted thrice daily, are thorough and informative, amounting to a cram course in sparkling wine production. If no tour is scheduled, you can step into a windowed gallery above the winery and watch the proceedings. Graphics, photos and historic exhibits help you along. Do try to arrive at tour time, however, or you'll miss a nicely done multi-media show, presented in a fashionable little drawing room with a window into the winery.

Tasting notes: The Sparkling Brut, Domaine Carneros' primary product, was pleasantly complex and mouth-filling, with a nice crisp Chardonnay finish. Prices are in the mid-teens.

Mont St. John Cellars • T GTA ⌆

5400 Old Sonoma Rd., Napa, CA 94558; (707) 255-8864. Daily 10 to 5; MC/VISA, AMEX. Most varieties tasted; no fee. Some wine logo gift items. A shaded public picnic area, plus a barbecue area available by reservation. Guided tours by prior arrangement.

The Louis Bartolucci family has been making Napa Valley wines since 1922. They moved to this small Spanish colonial facility in the 1970s, where they produce about 15,000 cases a year.

WINE TASTING

Your host in the wood-paneled tasting room likely will be lecturer James Walsh Meagher. Given half a chance, he'll happily talk your leg off about wines, the history of wine, the origin of many wine expressions and about life in general.

Tasting notes: Chardonnay, Sauvignon Blanc, Johannisberg Riesling, Gewürztraminer and Muscat di Canelli occupy the white list; Cabernet Sauvignon and Pinot Noir are the reds. The wines were uniformly good, with prices ranging from $6.50 to the early teens. A $12.75 Chardonnay was exceptional and the $6.50 Gewürztraminer was lush and rich without being sweet. Of the reds, we were impressed by the spicy-berry nose and complex flavor of the Pinot Noir.

Vintners choice: "Carneros is the ideal region for Chardonnay and Pinot Noir, and I would select those as our best wines," says Sue Bartolucci.

Carneros Creek Winery • T CT

1285 Dealy Lane, Napa, CA 94558; (707) 253-WINE. Daily 9 to 4:30; MC/VISA, AMEX. Most varieties tasted; no fee. A few wine logo items. Picnic area under an arbor.

"We like to enter into a dialog with visitors," says Carneros Creek's sales manager David A. Pramuk. This small winery is serious about Pinot Noir. Folks here like to talk with serious-minded wine enthusiasts, even offering tastes of rare library selections. Established in this region in 1972, specifically to pursue the Pinot, it is a leader in clonal research and has won numerous awards for its noble Burgundian-style wines.

The appearance of the place belies its serious intent. It resembles a suburban home with an oversized garage. To reach the tiny tasting room, one drives across a set of truck scales and parks near a picnic arbor.

Tasting notes: The list, not surprisingly, is mostly Pinot Noir, accompanied by Chardonnay, Merlot, Cabernet Sauvignon and Ruby Cabernet. We particularly liked the Fleur de Carneros Pinot, light yet complex with a powerful berry focus brought about by cloning. A Signature Reserve Pinot was spicy, peppery and awesome. (It's not normally offered for tasting; try begging a little.) The barrel-fermented Chardonnay was properly buttery and spicy, with a light finish. Prices start in the mid-teens and go beyond for library selections.

The Hess Collection • T$ ST

4411 Redwood Rd. (P.O. Box 4140), Napa, CA 94558; (707) 255-1144. Daily 10 to 4; MC/VISA. Cabernet Sauvignon and Chardonnay tasted for a $2.50 fee. Good selection of gift and art items. Self-guiding tour of the art museum, with views into the winery. Periodic slide shows about the winery and its founder.

Is it elegantly understated, or almost overdone? Are the smiling ladies in blue blazers a bit too much? The word "pretentious" came to mind when we stepped into this unusual blend of winery and art gallery. But the smiling ladies and the elegance of brass and beveled glass housed in an ancient stone winery soon won us over. It's one of the most impressive inner spaces in California's wine country, with its island-counter tasting salon, windows peeking into the winery and an art gallery with dazzling white walls set against old stone.

The art? It's on the leading edge of the modern movement which, like a dry martini, is an acquired taste.

The ninth generation of a Swiss brewing family, Donald Hess inherited a small fortune and soon turned it into a large one. He diversified into mineral water, restaurants and vineyards. His American wife encouraged him to establish a winery in California and it was she who suggested combining it with an art gallery.

"If one has the good fortune to be born rich, one should at least do something useful with it," Hess said.

The original winery was built at the turn of the century by Oakland businessman Theodore Gier. Then the Christian Brothers, a Catholic teaching order, purchased it in 1932 and established an adjacent novitiate. It functioned as the Mont La Salle Vineyards until Hess acquired the property in 1986 and began an extensive renovation. The winery was re-opened to the public in 1989.

Tasting notes: The winery bottles only Cabernet Sauvignon and Chardonnay, offering them in two styles: the upscale Hess Collection, suitable for aging, and the moderately priced Hess Select. Prices range from $9.50 to the high teens. A Hess Collection Chardonnay was lush, nutty and silky; while a Monterey County Hess Select was fruitier and less complex yet quite tasty. The Hess Collection Cabernet, peppery and spicy with a nippy tannic finish, was exceptional.

Chateau Potelle • T GTA ⌅

3875 Mount Veeder Rd., Napa, CA 94558; (707) 252-0615. Weekends only from noon to 5, other times by appointment, closed from November through March. Select varieties tasted; no fee. Picnic tables on wooden deck with a view; tours by appointment.

Potelle is a chateau in name only. Scattered over wooded slopes, this small facility more resembles an American hill country farmyard than a French manor. It's an appealing place in a woodsy sort of way, with a barn of a winery and small tasting room in a clapboard cottage. A deck offers impressive views of tilted vineyards and the surrounding hills.

The Fourmeaux family, late of France, started their winery in Menlo Park south of San Francisco in 1983, then moved to this remote site toward the end of that decade.

Vintners choice: "Sauvignon Blanc, Chardonnay and Cabernet—all elegant and well balanced," insists the winery's Susan Dicks. Actually, she named the entire list. Prices range from $9 to the mid-teens.

DOWN VALLEY WINERY TOUR • Finding wineries in this end of the valley requires no great navigational feat. They stand in ranks along Highway 29 and the paralleling Silverado Trail, or on crossroads that connect the two.

Since Highway 29 wineries may get crowded later in the day, we'll start you there first, then swing over to Silverado for the return trip. Of course, we don't expect you to cover them all in a single day. We certainly didn't.

We left you at the intersection of Redwood Road and Highway 29. Turn left (north) onto the highway, which is mostly a limited access expressway between here and **Yountville**. As you approach Yountville, take the Washington Street exit. You may want to explore the assortment of shops, boutiques and galleries in this tourist-oriented town. Many are in **Vintage 1870,** a former winery turned themed shopping center. Two visitors bureaus in Yountville provide assorted maps, brochures and publications: **Napa Valley Tourist Bureau** at 6488 Washington St. (Monday-Saturday 9 to 5 and Sunday 10 to 4), a commercial establishment that sells maps and books lodgings and tours; and the **Yountville Chamber of Commerce** in Washington Square at the north end of town (weekdays only, 10 to 3), with the usual collection of brochures and such.

Having done with Yountville, go west under the freeway on California Drive, then follow signs to the right to **Domaine Chandon.** Next, take the west side Highway 29 frontage road (Solano Avenue) about half a mile south to Hoffman Lane, turn right and follow it to **Lakespring Winery,** on your left.

Return to Yountville and continue north on Highway 29 (no longer an expressway). The wineries present themselves in quick order, so keep a wary eye: **Cosentino Winery** on the left, just beyond the popular Mustard's Cafe, then **DeMoor Winery,** also on the left, a few yards beyond; and **Robert Pepi Winery,** about a quarter of a mile farther, up a vineyard lane to the right.

Now, turn left onto Oakville Grade in the tiny hamlet of **Oakville** and drive about a mile up to **Vichon Winery** in the Mayacamas foothills. Along the way, you might stop at the **Carmelite Monastery** and browse through its gift shop, in a clapboard building below the monastery (open Tuesday-Sunday 11 to 3:30); the chapel above is generally open to th public only during mass, at 8 a.m. weekdays and 9 a.m. Sunday; phone 944-9408.

Return to Highway 29 and stop for a browse through the near-legendary **Oakville Grocery** on the corner of Oakville Cross Road. It's an old fashioned general store turned upscale deli, with cheeses, meats, breads, patès, prepared salads, a small produce section and a huge local wine selection. It's a one-stop picnic-builder.

From the grocery, follow Oakville Cross Road a mile east to **Silver Oak Wine Cellars**, up a lane to your right. (The sign is small; watch for an iron gate supported by decorative stone posts.) Retreat to Route 29, continue north and you'll soon encounter the Spanish mission-shaped **Robert Mondavi Winery** on the right. Half a mile beyond is **Sequoia Grove Vineyards** on the right; just beyond is the new **St. Supèry Winery.** As you enter **Rutherford**, look for Neibaum Lane on your left, leading up to **Inglenook-Napa Valley**. On the right in downtown Rutherford (what little there is of it), is **Beaulieu Vineyard**; **Grgich Hills Cellar** is just beyond, on the left.

A bit farther along, small **Rutherford Vintners** and large **Franciscan Vineyards** are across from one another—Rutherford on the left; Franciscan on the right. Just beyond is **Whitehall Lane,** on the left. A few hundred feet from Whitehall, turn right onto Zinfandel Lane, stop at **Raymond Cellars** up a gravel lane on your right, then continue on to the Silverado Trail. Swing south on Silverado and watch for Rutherford Hill Road, leading to the left through the posh **Auberge du Soliel** resort to **Rutherford Hill Winery.** A bit farther south on Silverado is **Conn Creek Winery** on the right, at the junction of Conn Creek Road (Highway 128). Go right on Conn Creek and follow it about half a mile to **Caymus Vineyards** on the left. Then backtrack to the Silverado Trail.

If you'd like to venture into the mountains and discover a couple of tucked-away wineries, follow Highway 128 (Sage Canyon Road) east from the Silverado Trail. You'll pass **Lake Hennessey,** Napa's water supply, then wind steeply into the flanks of the Vaca Range to **Nichelini Winery,** perched precariously on the right edge of the highway. Drive a short distance beyond, turn left onto Lower Chiles Valley Road and follow it into the bucolic Chiles Valley. After about 2.5 miles, you'll see **Rustridge Winery,** part of a scattered ranch yard on your right.

Return to Silverado and continue south; you'll soon encounter **Mumm Napa Valley** on the right, with **ZD Wines** practically next door. You have about a two-mile breather, then turn right onto Yountville Cross and drive a short distance to **S. Anderson Vineyard** on the left. Back on Silverado, **Robert Sinskey Vineyards** occupies a ridge just across the highway.

Pressing south, you enter the Stags Leap district in the Vaca foothills, whose sloping, rocky soils produce some of Napa's finest wines. The name comes from a rocky promontory above. On the valley side of the highway, crowning a hill rising from the valley floor is **Silverado Vineyards**, then **Pine Ridge Winery.** Coming up on the left are **Stag's Leap Wine Cellars, Chimney Rock Winery** and finally, **Clos Du Val.**

Probably having grown weary of all this, you can stay on Silverado, which will take you back to Napa. It bumps into Trancas Street and a right turn will take you to Highway 29.

Domaine Chandon • T$ GT 🎁 R

#1 California Dr., Yountville, CA 94599; (707) 944-2280. Daily 11 to 5 (closed Monday-Tuesday November through April); MC/VISA, AMEX. Sparkling wine sold by the glass, $3 to $3.50. Extensive gift selection. Tours every half hour from 11 to 5; champagne museum exhibits. Domaine Chandon Restaurant (see listing under "Wine country dining").

Occupying a garden-like setting just below the Yountville Veterans Home, Domaine Chandon is the first of the Napa Valley's three French sparkling wine houses. It's owned by the Louis Vuitton Moët-Hennessey conglomerate and, like its younger sister Domaine Carneros, produces only sparkling wine by *méthode champenoise.*

It more resembles a country club than a winery, bunkered into the landscaped terrain, with barrel arched roofs over stone, rimmed by moats, fountains, and patios. All it lacks is a golf course.

Tours assemble in the entry corridor, where graphics and exhibits trace the process of sparkling wine from Dom Pérignon's accidental discovery three centuries ago. ("I am tasting stars!" he exclaimed, after his wine underwent a second fermentation in the bottle.) Tour groups stroll past giant bullet-nosed horizontal fermenting tanks, watch a gyro-riddler in action and follow the 17 steps required to conduct sparkling wine's disgorging and bottling process. You can get a glass of bubbly—for a fee—in the tasting salon or on a sunny patio. Of course, thirsty souls can bypass the tour and go directly to the gift shop and salon.

Tasting notes: Our glass of Chandon Brut came with a plate of sourdough bread and cream cheese spread. All were excellent; we like the exploding effervescence of the brut and its lingering acidic finish. Domaine Chandon also produces Blanc de Noirs, Chandon Reserve and Chandon Club Cuvee, with prices from $13.50 to $20. Two non-sparklers are Panache apèritif wine and Fred's Friends Chardonnay for $7.50 and $6.50.

Lakespring Winery • T GTA ⛌

2055 Hoffman Lane, Napa, CA 94558; (707) 944-2475. Weekdays only, 10 to 3:30; MC/VISA, AMEX. Selected wines tasted; no fee. Small picnic area; tours by appointment.

Unlike many Napa Valley wineries, Lakespring doesn't go out of its way to pamper tourists. You enter a small conference room by way of the winery office for a sit-down tasting limited to one white and one red. However, if you exhibit proper enthusiasm, office/tasting room manager Kathy Kewell may offer a bit more.

You *should* be enthusiastic, since Lakespring is one of the valley's winningest small wineries. It often earns best of show and sweepstakes awards for its premium varietals. The Battat family of San Francisco established the facility and hired winemaker Randy Mason, who keeps those ribbons and medals coming.

Tasting notes: The list is short: Sauvignon Blanc, Chardonnay, Merlot, Cabernet Sauvignon and Elixa, a late-harvest sweet Chenin Blanc. The Sauvignon Blanc was elegant—spicy, fruity and mouth-filling with a wonderful aroma. A Merlot was excellent as well, soft and full of berries with a gentle tannic finish. Prices range from $8.50 to $14, modest for wines of this quality.

Cosentino Winery • T$ CT

7415 St. Helena Hwy. (P.O. Box 2818), Yountville, CA 94599. Daily 10 to 5:30; MC/VISA. Most varieties tasted for a $2 fee (which buys the glass or is applied toward wine purchase). A few wine-related gift items. Group tours by appointment.

Built in 1990, Cosentino Winery suggests a cross between a chateau and a French military barracks, with its flat, rather austere facade with dormer windows. There's nothing austere about the wines, however. Founder Mitch Cosentino has won 400 awards, including many best of show and sweepstake medals, in just ten vintages. He was America's first vintner to produce a red Meritage, the Bordeaux-inspired blend of Cabernet Sauvignon, Cabernet Franc and Merlot. It earned the sweepstakes award over 1,900 National Wine Competition entries in 1990.

Cosentino started out in Modesto in 1981, then moved to the Napa Valley to get closer to the grapes which had been gathering all those medals.

Tasting notes: "The Sculptor" Chardonnay was exceptional—spicy, nutty and silky with a hint of wood and gentle acid finish. Cosentino's Pinot Noir was light and fruity—suggestive of a young Zinfandel, while the Cabernet Franc was peppery yet soft, with a delicate tannin. Cabernet Sauvignon displayed classic chili pepper and berry attribute with hints of wood at the end. "The Poet," Cosentino's Meritage, was lushly soft and spicy, deserving of its sweepstakes award. Prices range from $13 to $30.

Vintners choice: "Meritage, Cabernet Sauvignon, Cabernet Franc and Merlot," says Mitch.

DeMoor Winery and Vineyards • T$

7481 St. Helena Hwy., Oakville, CA 94562; (707) 944-2565. Daily 10:30 to 5:30; MC/VISA, AMEX. Most varieties tasted for a $1.50 fee (includes glass). Good gift and wine logo selection. Shaded picnic area; winery innards visible from the tasting room.

A tasting room in a yurt? Genial tasting host Jack Bailey (probably not the TV emcee) insists it's a geodesic dome. Whatever its architectural pedigree, it's an upbeat place with Jack cracking jokes and deliberately mispronouncing wine names, while surfer music plays in the background.

The winery itself is more business-like, a large square structure just beyond the geodesic yurt. It was opened in 1973 and the first wines were produced five years later under the Napa Cellars label. It became DeMoor Winery in 1983.

Tasting notes: The wines exhibited an excellent overall quality. Sauvignon Blanc had a pleasant dusky nose and rich hint of raisins; Chenin Blanc was lush and fruity with a touch of acid at the end. Zinfandel was light and full of raspberries, unusually fruity for a Zin. The Cabernet was exemplary, big and complex with enough tannin to suggest letting it sleep for a few years.

Robert Pepi Winery • T$ GTA

7585 St. Helena Hwy. (P.O. Box 328), Oakville, CA 94562; (707) 944-2807. Daily 10:30 to 4:30; no credit cards. A choice of four wines tasted for a $2 fee (which buys the glass). Small gift selection. Guided tours by appointment.

The Pepi Winery is a handsome chateau-style stone and wood affair crowning a low hill above the vineyards. Carved doors beneath a stone arch lead into the tasting room. Windows offer peeks into the winery. It's a pleasant spot, offering nice valley views and a welcome retreat from the din of Highway 29.

Pepi established this facility in 1981. The small facility produces about 20,000 cases a year.

Tasting notes: The winemaker likes to focus on the fruit, with just a hint of wood. Thus, most wines are aged in 90-gallon French puncheons instead of smaller barrels. This style was particularly evident in a crisp Sauvignon Blanc (with a touch of Semillon) and a light yet spicy barrel-fermented Chardonnay. The Cabernet Sauvignon was peppery and full-flavored and, typically, with just a hint of wood. Completing Pepi's brief list is Dolcezza D'Oro, a botrytised Sauvignon Blanc with a sweet raisiny nose and rich, almost chewy flavor; it was akin to munching raisins. Prices range from $9 to the high teens.

Vintners choice: "Two-Heart Canopy Sauvignon Blanc, puncheon-fermented Chardonnay and Vine Hill Ranch Cabernet," says the winery's Donni Burke.

Vichon Winery • T GTA

1595 Oakville Grade, Oakville, CA 94562; (707) 944-2611. Daily 10 to 4:30; MC/VISA, AMEX. Four wines tasted free; fee for older vintages. A few wine logo items. Picnic area with impressive valley view. Guided tours daily at 10:30 and 2; appointment required.

Robert Mondavi's offspring—Mike, Tim and Marica—purchased this small ten-year-old winery in the mid-1980s. Despite its youth, its pink stucco Spanish colonial architecture and ivy-covered facade give it a venerable look. Barrel-potted flowers add a touch of color. The site is impressive; the winery is notched into a steep slope off Oakville Grade in the Mayacamas foothills. Views from the winery and from a laurel and oak-shaded picnic area are elegant.

The tasting room occupies a corner of the winery. It's a simple affair, decorated mostly with stacked boxes and a tier of barrels that look ready to topple. From here, you can take a quick visual tour of the facility.

Tasting notes: Vichon has won a generous share of awards for its select list, which includes Chevrignon (a Semillon and Sauvignon Blanc blend), Chardonnay, Cabernet Blanc, Cabernet Sauvignon and Merlot. The cabs were particularly noteworthy—classic studies in the red wine art. An unfiltered Cab was big and spicy while a filtered version was more gentle yet complex and light on the wood. A Stags Leap Cabernet offered tremendous body, spice and berries with a notable tannin finish. Prices range from $7.50 to the mid-teens, and go beyond for an extended library of older vintages.

Silver Oak Cellars • T$ GTA

915 Oakville Cross Rd. (P.O. Box 414), Oakville, CA 94562; (707) 944-8808. Monday-Friday 9 to 4:30, Saturday 10 to 4:30, closed Sunday; MC/VISA. Tasting for $5 fee (which buys the glass or is applied toward wine purchase). Guided tours by appointment at 1:30 weekdays.

A tree-lined lane leads through the vineyards to this comely Mediterranean style cut-stone winery, with a tile roof and dormer windows. The pleasant tasting room inside is paneled with redwood from old wine tanks.

Surprisingly, this fashionable facility is part of a made-over dairy barn. The winery was established in 1972 by Justin Meyer and Ray Duncan; the present facility was completed in 1982.

Tasting notes: Silver Oak produces only 100 percent varietal Cabernet Sauvignon, drawing grapes from Napa Valley and Sonoma's Alexander Valley. Interestingly, they're aged in American oak instead of the classic French, giving them a distinct spicy-soft wood finish. The Alexander Valley Cabernet, the only wine being tasted when we visited, was exceptional—gently complex and spicy with a light tannic finish. Prepare for sticker shock: Silver Oak's wines are in the $35 range and up. At least the glass—which you get to keep—is an impressively large thing, ideal for sloshing, sniffing and sipping.

Robert Mondavi Winery • T & T$ GT

7801 St. Helena Hwy. (P.O. Box 106), Oakville, CA 94562; (707) 963-9611. Daily 9 to 6 (10 to 6 from November through April); major credit cards. Periodic guided tours followed by free tasting; fee tasting without tour, from $1 to $3 per sample. Separate gift shop with good selection.

The Mondavi winery has a mission-like quality, perhaps appropriate to the owner's crusade to elevate wine's status and defend it from his "neo-prohibitionists." When he broke away from the family fold in the 1960s, he had three goals: to produce exceptional wines, to build the first winery designed

WARNING: WINE MAY BE GOOD FOR YOU

"Prohibitionists say that drinking is bad for you, but the Bible says that Noah made wine and drank it, and he only lived to be 950 years old. Show me an abstainer who ever lived that long."— Will Rogers

Recent medical studies appear to confirm what Noah and Will knew all along, that moderate wine consumption is good for you. Not just harmless, but *beneficial.* This comes as bad news to neo-prohibitionists who have succeeded in having every winery tasting room, wine price list and bottle tattooed with federal warning labels.

A couple of decades ago, a major statistical survey revealed that moderate users of alcohol live longer than teetotalers. Subsequent studies have shown that wine consumption, particularly red wine, may help prevent heart disease.

Research reported recently in the *Journal of Applied Cardiology* showed that wine consumption increases high density lipoprotein (HDL) in the blood. That's the so-called "good cholesterol" which helps clear low density cholesterol from arterial walls. Since red wine is more effective than white, researchers think fruit-rich polyphenols—tannins—may play a major role.

An earlier Canadian study suggests that red wine may help counteract cancer. In laboratory tests, doses of gallic acid (a tannin component) prevented carcinogenic agents from mutating chromosomes. Such mutations are precursors to cancer. Although wine's enemies want it labeled as a carcinogen, right up there with tobacco and burnt barbecued ribs, no study has found a positive link between moderate wine use and increased cancer rates. Laboratory rats kept constantly crocked have refused to become malignant.

Red wine plays another role, as an effective—although short-lived—disinfectant. In numerous tests, it has destroyed a variety of bacteria and viruses, including cholera and typhoid germs. It's not the alcohol, but the polyphenols, that kill the little critters. Ancient Greeks used wine as a disinfectant on combat wounds. Modern travelers add it to water in sanitation-poor countries to kill bacteria. Tests have shown that red wine concentrate can be effective against cold sores.

Louis Pasteur, noting that wine destroyed infection, called it "the most healthful and hygienic of beverages."

Statistics appear to confirm wine's role as a health aid. French and Italians, who drink nearly ten times as much wine as Americans, outlive us. Even poverty-level Italians live longer than the average American, despite poor medical care, sanitation and diet.

Other surveys show that people who get most of their spirits from wine have fewer heart attacks than those who drink mostly beer or hard liquor. Further, recent studies have found a positive link between exercise, moderate drinking and lowered cholesterol rates.

Writer Michael Brody speculated in an article in *Barons Weekly*: "This suggests that the best medicine for one's heart may be jogging from bar to bar—finally answering the question of how journalists manage to live so long."

for cultural offerings, and to enhance wine's public image. Along the way, he has propelled his facility into the third largest producer in the Napa Valley.

Your Mondavi experience begins with a tour, first to the adjacent vineyards, then inside the winery, housed in a wing of this Spanish style facility. It's designed as a shallow "V" that encloses a lawn area used for Mondavi's popular summer concerts and other functions. The arched central entrance, not accidentally, forms a natural podium for performers.

Tours end with a guide-conducted tasting of one white, one red and one dessert wine. If you wish to bypass the tour, you can buy an assortment of wines, by the glass, the bottle or the one-ounce sip.

Tasting notes: Mondavi was one of the first producers of Fumè Blanc, a Sauvignon Blanc with a distinctive but subtle smoky flavor. Indeed, the name translates as "white smoke." It's still one of our favorite Mondavi wines, crisp and clean with that dusky finish. The Cabernet was excellent, peppery with soft spices, good berries and a medium tannic finish. A Muscato D'Oro dessert wine had a rich honey nose and a focused yet curiously light taste. Other Mondavi wines include Chardonnay, Pinot Noir, a sweet Johannisberg Riesling botrytis and Sauvignon Blanc botrytis. Prices range from $8 to the twenties and well beyond for some reserve wines. Mondavi also markets a selection of varietal jug wines.

Sequoia Grove Vineyards • T ST

8338 St. Helena Hwy., Rutherford, CA 94573; (707) 944-2945. Daily 11 to 5; MC/VISA, AMEX. Most varieties tasted; $3 fee for some older wines. A few wine-related gift items. Small picnic area; self-guiding tour.

This small facility indeed sits in its own personal sequoia grove, a rustic island in time and space among its larger, sleeker winery neighbors. But it's big in reputation, having been picked recently as the winery of the year by the *International Wine Review*. Obviously, it wins a sizable share of medals.

A small tasting room is located in a corner of this weathered barn board and stone structure. From there you can peek or stroll into the surrounding winery. Although the venerable structure dates back several decades, the present winery is of recent vintage, founded in 1979 by James Allen.

Tasting notes: We were impressed by the low prices of the Allen Family label Chardonnay ($7.50), Gewürztraminer ($7) and Cabernet ($9). All three were exceptional wines. A Carneros Chardonnay ($14) had a nice mix of fruit, soft acid and spice, and an Estate Cabernet ($25) was exceptional with a great herbal nose, berry-like taste with a soft touch of wood and enough tannin to suggest laying it away.

St. Supèry Vineyards and Winery • T$ ST

8440 St. Helena Hwy., Rutherford, CA 94573; (707) 963-4507. Daily 9:30 to 4:30; MC/VISA. Selected wines tasted for a $2.50 fee. Good assortment of wine logo items. Self-guiding tour.

Don't be put off by the exterior look of this low-slung winery, which has all the charm of a government office building. Inside you'll find bright, carpeted corridors lined with art, photos and wine displays. St. Supèry offers the most informative self-guiding tour in the Napa Valley. Large windows offer peeks into the working winery and graphics explain in detail what you're seeing. Charts and maps discuss wine production in the Napa Valley, America and the rest of the world. A unique "essence" station gives you exaggerated whiffs of the aromas you should seek in a good Cabernet Sauvignon and Sauvignon Blanc.

Of you want to sip as well as sniff, purchase a ticket at the downstairs gift shop then adjourn to a tasting station upstairs. Wines also are available by the glass, to be sipped in a pleasant outdoor patio.

And who's Supèry? No saint, he was Edward St. Supèry, who owned a winery on this site in the last century. The present facility was launched by longtime valley winemaker Robert Skalli in 1988. Despite its youth, it's the valley's seventh largest producer. A comely gingerbread Victorian home adjacent to the winery is now a period museum, which can be toured by appointment.

Tasting notes: The overall character of the wines is light, fruity and gently acidic. A Chardonnay was soft and fruity, with a hint of wood and a Cabernet Sauvignon was gently spicy and light, with a subtle tannic finish. A Muscato dessert wine had a good crushed flower petal nose and a rich yet light taste. Prices range from $8.50 to the low teens.

Inglenook Napa Valley • T GT

1991 St. Helena Hwy. (P.O. Box 402), Rutherford, CA 94573; (707) 967-3358. Daily 10 to 5; MC/VISA, AMEX. Most varieties tasted; no fee. Separate gift shop with extensive selection. Guided tours on the hour and half hour.

Finnish sea captain and fur trader Gustave Nybom (later spelled Neibaum) put down roots here in the 1880s and built an impressive stone winery and elaborate Victorian mansion. Both survive as keystones of Inglenook's elaborate, manicured grounds, with a courtyard "large enough to accommodate several locomotives," according to one early-day writer. The facility, one of America's largest, is now owned by Heublein, Inc.

The great stone structure has a wonderful old library aroma, typical of well-aged wineries. Inside, you can browse through an extensive gift shop collection or adjourn to an adjoining room to taste Inglenook's offerings. Frequent tours take visitors through the ancient cellars.

Tasting notes: Unlike most valley wineries that tend to specialize, Inglenook produces a broad assortment of wines and most are available for tasting. Prices range from a modest five dollars to the high teens. We sipped a gentle, spicy Chardonnay; a crisply fruity Gravion (Sauvignon Blanc-Semillon blend); an excellent Merlot with soft, complex and berry-like flavors and sufficient tannin to encourage aging; and a complex, full-mouthed and nippy Cabernet Sauvignon.

Vintners choice: "Our most famous wine is Cask Cabernet Sauvignon," says Inglenook's Renae Cherry.

Beaulieu Vineyard • T GT

1960 St. Helena Hwy., Rutherford, CA 94573; (707) 963-2411. Weekdays 10 to 4, weekends 10 to 5; MC/VISA, AMEX. Select wines tasted free; older wines tasted in the Private Reserve Room for a fee. Separate gift shop with good selection; periodic guided tours; audio-visual show.

Beaulieu's corporate ownership by Heublein has not dimmed its historic reputation for wines. Its Cabernets are among the most honored in the country, and are consistent medal winners. Perhaps this consistency can be traced to winemaker Andre Tchelistcheff, who's been on the job for 40 years! The winery dates back to the turn of the century, founded by Georges de Latour. The original structure survives, a great stone fortress-like affair covered with decades of ivy.

The adjacent octagonal wood-paneled tasting room is one of the valley's more stylish. And it's wonderfully civilized. A smiling attendant hands you a sample of Chardonnay the moment you enter. You can seek more sips at a small tasting bar. An extensive gift and wine shop occupies a lower floor reached by a spiral stairway. An excellent audio-visual show tells the story of Beaulieu and its position in Napa Valley history. Thirty-minute tours are given periodically.

Tasting notes: Beaulieu's list is large, accommodating most of the premium varietals. We particularly savored the Beaufort Chardonnay with a nutty, rich and buttery flavor. The Beautour Cabernet had a classic chili pepper nose, fine berry-cinnamon taste and softly acidic finish. Equally appealing was a Pinot Noir with a fruity nose and pleasing raspberry flavor. The Muscat de Frontignan dessert wine was cherry like, spicy and nutty—so intense it could pose as a liqueur. Prices range from $7.25 to the mid teens.

Vintners choice: "Georges de Latour private reserve," states tasting room manager Craig Root.

Grgich Hills Cellar • T GT

1829 St. Helena Hwy. (P.O. Box 450), Rutherford, CA; (707) 963-2784. Daily 9:30 to 4:30; no credit cards. Most varieties tasted; no fee. Small selection of gift items. Tours at 11 and 2 weekdays and 11 and 1:30 weekends.

Yugoslav-born Miljenk Grgich's name may be unpronounceable, but it's on the tongue of every serious wine aficionado in the country. His medium-sized winery is a consistent award winner; a Grgich Chardonnay once beat out serious French competition to be declared the world's best. Winemaker Grgich, who looks more like poet with a soft, round face topped by a beret, says simply: "I baby my wines."

Grgich Hills Cellar wasn't named for mountains. Mike Grgich and Austin Hills are its founders, establishing the facility on the Fourth of July, 1977. The vaguely Spanish-style structure, trimmed with ivy, houses a small, wood-paneled tasting room decorated mostly with press notices. It's easy to tour the winery visually, standing at the tasting counter, glass in hand. Or you can join a walking one, twice a day.

Tasting notes: We discovered one of our favorite Zinfandels here, from a Sonoma vineyard, naturally, with a luxuriously peppery aroma and wonderful berry flavor. The Napa Valley Cabernet had a wonderful nose. a mixed banquet of spice, pepper, berries and soft wood, with a flavor to match. A Napa Valley Fumè Blanc was more flowery than smoky, with a buttery, almost Chardonnay-like taste. And the Chardonnay itself? Crisp, spicy, soft and silky. The wines range from $11 to $20; higher for library selections.

Vintners choice: The winery's Bob Hattaway's statement says nothing and therefore everything about the Grgich philosophy: "Each wine is treated as a special child—none better or less than the other."

Rutherford Vintners • T

1673 St. Helena Hwy., (P.O. Box 238), Rutherford, CA 94573; (707) 963-4117. Daily 10 to 4:30; MC/VISA. Selected tasted; no fee. A few wine-related gift items.

The Skoda family's small facility is a folksy island of intimacy afloat in a sea of larger-than-life wines and wineries. Evelyn Skoda herself, with a smiling face suggestive of Julia Childs, may stroll out of her cluttered office to pour the wines. The tasting room is a simple cottage-like affair; the Skodas decorate it mostly with medals they've won. The winery itself is back among the vineyards, basic and vine-covered.

Bernard Skoda grew up in Alsace-Lorraine, France, and brought his wine expertise to California in the 1950s. After working for others, he planted his own vineyards in 1968 and started Rutherford Vintners in 1976. He's been winning gold medals ever since.

Tasting notes: Rutherford's wines are good buys, ranging from $8 to the mid-teens. A Johannisberg Riesling aged in German oak was soft on the palate, with a nice fruity nose and light finish. The Cabernet Sauvignon was subtly spicy, berry-like and full-flavored. A nice crushed flower petal aroma emerged from the Muscat of Alexandria dessert wine; the flavor was predictably intense. Incidentally, serious collectors can find select wines ranging as far back as 15 years.

Franciscan Vineyards • T & T$

1178 Galleron Rd. (P.O. Box 407), Rutherford, CA 94573; (707) 963-7111. Daily 10 to 5; MC/VISA, AMEX. Select varieties tasted; free on weekdays, small fee on weekends. Extensive gift shop selection.

Franciscan's fee schedule contains a message: come on a weekday when the large, vaulted-ceiling tasting room is less crowded and the samples are free. On weekends, you might get caught up in a tour bus crowd, surging to the counter to cash in on a 20 percent wine discount they earned by taking a hot air balloon ride.

The middle-sized winery, producing 120,000 cases a year, sits on landscaped grounds alongside Highway 29 (despite the Galleron Road address). It was started as a simple shed by Peter Eckes and Agustin Huneeus in 1973 and has since grown into a more picturesque redwood-sided structure.

Tasting notes: Franciscan's prices are modest for the Napa Valley, ranging from $7 to the mid-teens; a bit higher for library selections. The wines were light and palate-pleasing, focusing more on fruit than wood. Our agreeable samples included a gentle but intensely flavored Gewürztraminer, a good buy at $7; a light, subtly spiced Chardonnay, also modestly priced at $9; a soft and herbal Cabernet Sauvignon and a peppery, raspberry-like Zinfandel with a good crisp finish.

Vintners choice: The winery's Andrea Sanjek ticked them off without adjectives: "Meritage, Merlot, Cabernet Sauvignon, Chardonnay."

Whitehall Lane Winery • T$ GTA & CT

1563 St. Helena Hwy., St. Helena, CA 94574; (707) 963-9454. Daily 11 to 5; MC/VISA, DISC. All varieties tasted for $2 fee (includes logo glass). A few wine oriented gift items. Tours by appointment or a peek into the winery, just off the tasting room.

Architect-winemaker Art Finkelstein designed the simple convergence of lines, angles and geometric shapes that comprise this gray and beige winery alongside St. Helena Highway. The tasting room is a cozy space, decorated mostly with bottles, medals and a few wine logo items.

Finkelstein and his brother Alan Steen planted vineyards here in 1979, built the winery the next year and opened the tasting room in 1982. The facility was purchased by Hideaki Ando of Japan in 1988; Finkelstein remains as general manager.

Tasting notes: Whitehall has won several awards with its balance of light, fruity wines. We liked crisp and fruity Le Petit Chardonnay and a spicy, soft Le Petit Merlot; plus a bolder, nutty-spicy Chardonnay and herbal-tannic Cabernet Sauvignon. Pinot Noir, Cabernet Franc and three sweeter wines—an off-dry Blanc de Pinot Noir, a rich Chenin Blanc and late harvest auslese-style Riesling complete the list. Prices range from $6 to $14.

Raymond Vineyard and Cellars • T GTA

849 Zinfandel Lane, St. Helena, CA 94574; (707) 963-3141. Daily 10 to 4; MC/VISA. Selected wines tasted free; fee for some library wines. Small giftware selection. Tours by appointment, generally at 11 a.m.

The Raymond family goes far back in Napa's winemaking history, although their modern winery dates from 1974. Right after Repeal, Roy Raymond started working at Beringer, where he met and married daughter Martha Jane. Their sons operate things now, with Walter making wine and Roy Junior marketing it. Although the winery is still family-run, a share was sold recently to Japan's Kirin Brewery, Inc.

Raymond produces mostly estate-bottled wines, drawn from vineyards surrounding their winery, which sits near the valley's geographic. The winery is a handsome low-rise structure, sort of a modern oversized bungalow, painted green to blend in with the surrounding vineyards. A bright, airy tasting room with grape theme grasscloth on its walls occupies one corner.

Tasting notes: Chardonnay, Sauvignon Blanc and Cabernet Sauvignon complete the Raymonds' premium list, plus red and white table wines. The Sauvignon Blanc was herbal and crisp with a nice tart finish and a three-year-old Chard was properly buttery and spicy, with a touch of oak. A Cabernet, two years in oak and two in the bottle, was smooth, complex with good berries and a touch of oak and tannin. Prices range from $9.75 to $17; higher for reserves.

Vintners choice: "Our Private Reserve Chardonnay and Cabernet; limited production; the best of each vintage," quoth the winery's Kas McGregor.

Rutherford Hill Winery • T$ GT

200 Rutherford Hill Rd., Rutherford, CA 94573; (707) 963-7194. Weekdays 10 to 4:30, weekends 10 to 5; MC/VISA, AMEX. Most varieties tasted for a $3 fee (includes the glass). Good choice of giftwares and wine logo items. Wooded picnic area with a valley view. Tours of caves and winery.

Rutherford Hill is a particularly striking facility, a monumental weathered wooden structure with flying buttresses, set in a wooded notch high above the valley. Tours take visitors through aging caves tunneled into the hillside, then into the state-of-the-art winery. Picnic areas are terraced and tree-shaded, with valley views.

The weathered wooden winery and aging caves suggest antiquity, yet the facility dates from the early 1970s. Tunneled by modern machinery and coated with gunnite, the cave network covers three-fourths of a mile; it may be the longest set of wine burrows in America. The tasting room is reached through tall cathedral-like doors at one end of the main winery. Heavy beams support the lofty ceiling. The atmosphere is that of a grand mountain ski chalet.

Tasting notes: The lists consists of Chardonnay, Cabernet Sauvignon, Merlot, Gewürztraminer, Sauvignon Blanc and a Zinfandel port. Several versions of Chardonnay and Cabernet are available. We particularly liked the fruity, toasty Cellar Reserve Chardonnay and nicely balanced, berry-flavored Library Reserve Cabernet. The Merlot had a spicy, herbal nose and good berries in the taste, with an acid nip at the end. The Zinfandel port was nutty and berry-focused—an exceptionally rich sipping wine.

Vintners choice: A voice from within said: "We call ourselves the Merlot winery."

Conn Creek Winery • T GTA

8711 Silverado Trail, St. Helena, CA 94574; (707) 963-9100. Daily 10 to 4; MC/VISA, AMEX. Most varieties tasted; no fee. Good gift and wine logo selection. Guided tours by appointment.

This prim little winery would look at home in Madrid, with its white stucco and Spanish arches. The Mediterranean theme carries into the tasting room, accented with iron chandeliers, carved wooden furniture and a rough tile floor.

A nicely filmed video tape espousing the winery's purpose plays on a TV set tucked among giftwares. Slices of the modern, efficient winery are visible through large windows.

Tasting notes: Sauvignon Blanc, Chardonnay, Zinfandel, Merlot, Cabernet Sauvignon and a late harvest Sauvignon Blanc comprise the list. Prices wander from $8 to $20. Our favorites were a subtly fruity and crisp Sauvignon Blanc, a complex and nicely finished Chardonnay and a fine Cabernet that was peppery, berry-like and velvety.

Vintners choice: "We're known as a Cabernet house," revealed the winery's Anne Salazar.

Caymus Vineyards • T$ GTA

8700 Conn Creek Rd. (P.O. Box 268), Rutherford, CA 94573; (707) 963-4204. Daily 10 to 4; MC/VISA. Most varieties tasted for a $2 fee (which buys the glass). A few wine logo items. Tours Saturday only at 1:30; limited to 20 people, so call ahead.

Although this unpretentious little winery was started in 1970, the founding Wagner family has been farming in this valley since 1906. They started making wine in 1915 and Charley Wagner, Sr., boasts that they carried on right through Prohibition. "We had a large basement," he recalls.

The complex, at the intersection of Conn Creek Road and Highway 128, hasn't changed much through the years. It's a busy cluster of buildings overwhelmed by grandfather trees and shrubs. The tasting room is a small, austere space off the office.

Wagner, somewhere near 80, is a crusty anomaly in this land of high-rollers, yuppies and corporate giants—an outspoken, down-to-earth dirt farmer who's probably forgotten more about wine production than wet-behind-the-ears Davis graduates have ever learned. He and his wife of more than half a century still run the place, assisted by their son Chuck.

Tasting notes: The ***Wine Spectator*** says Caymus produces the "best damned Cabernet in California." After tasting this deep purple, intense, berry-rich and tannic wine, we agree. The family also produces a good, honest raspberry-tasting Zinfandel, a rich and fruity Sauvignon Blanc and a lush and slightly sweet white called Conundrum, a blend of Sauvignon Blanc, Muscat Canelli, Chardonnay and Semillon. (Work on the pronunciation before you drink it.) Prices wander from $7 to $20; a line of modest-priced wines are released under the Liberty School label.

Vintner's choice: The winery's Mark Vaughn states: "Our Cabernets have garnered numerous accolades." That's not a word Charley would ever use.

Nichelini Winery • T CT ⚔

2950 Sage Canyon Rd., St. Helena, CA 94574; (707) 963-0717. Weekends only, 9 to 6 April-October and 9 to 5 November-March. MC/VISA. Most varieties tasted. Some wine logo gift items. Informal peeks into the winery; wooded picnic areas.

This delightfully rustic winery seems to cling to the edge of the highway, threatening to topple into a wooded canyon. However, it has managed to hold on since 1890, when it was founded by Italian-Swiss immigrant Anton Nichelini. His descendants still run the place, using a mix of ancient and modern equipment to produce notable wines—mostly reds. There's nary a vine in sight, however; the winery is surrounded by trees. The grapes flourish in nearby Chiles Valley.

On nice days, tasting is conducted outdoors; you can settle onto a nearby bench to sip your wine and listen to the soft sounds of the forest. Picnic tables are terraced about this charmingly weathered, sharply tilted winery complex.

Tasting notes: We particularly liked Nichelini's full-bodied, unfined Zinfandel, with a proper tannic nip at the end. The winery also does a white Zin with more oomph and berry flavor than most, plus full-flavored

Chenin Blanc, Sauvignon Blanc, Chardonnay and Johannisberg Riesling. Prices are modest, starting well below $10, and not going much beyond.

Vintners choice: "We pride ourselves in Zinfandel and white

Zinfandel because our mountain-located vineyards produce excellent grapes," says Carol Nichelini.

Rustridge Winery • T ⚔

2910 Lower Chiles Valley Rd., St. Helena, CA 94574; (707) 965-2871. Daily 9 to 4; MC/VISA. Most varieties tasted. Some wine gift items; shaded picnic area.

You'll have to drive through a pleasantly scattered ranch yard, past farm equipment and tired trucks, to find the winery and tasting room. Both occupy a cinderblock shed, sitting beside a couple of outdoor stainless steel fermentation tanks. The tasting room is just a wide spot in the middle of the small winery, which produces only a few thousand cases a year.

This remote winery, part of a working ranch and stud farm, was established in 1984 by Susan Meyer and her brother Stan. They also run a bed and breakfast, down at the ranch house. You won't always find someone in the tasting room, but yell or honk your horn and someone will come. A friendly farm hand climbed off a tractor to serve us.

Tasting notes: Chiles Valley's warm, wind-free climate produces *big* reds. We liked a full-flavored Cabernet, nearly black in color and with enough tannin suitable for aging; and an equally hefty Zinfandel with nice berries and a tannic nip. Others on the list included a soft and silky Chardonnay which was light, more of a Riesling style; and a Johannisberg Riesling, rich with a great crushed flower-petal nose and a tint of sweetness. Rustridge wines are produced from organically-grown, pesticide free grapes. Prices range from $5.50 to $18.50.

Mumm Napa Valley • T$ GT

1111 Dunaweal Lane (P.O. Drawer 500), Rutherford, CA 94573; (707) 942-4219. Daily 10:30 to 4:30; MC/VISA, AMEX. Sparkling wine by the glass, $3.50 to $4.50. Separate gift shop with good wine logo and book selection. Tours hourly on the half hour from 10:30 to 4:30.

France's legendary Mumm set up shop in the Napa Valley in the mid-1980s. Like the other French-owned producers, it doesn't call its stuff Champagne. It is sparkling wine, if you please. Advance scouting for a Napa Valley site, cleverly called "Operation Lafayette," began in 1979, and the the champagnery has grown in stages. The hospitality facility, a fashionable gift shop and airy tasting salon. was completed in 1990.

The structure is architecturally curious—a wood-sided creation suggestive of a king-sized California barn. It hovers low to the ground, and the guided tour reveals that much of it is underground, in true French champagnery fashion. The tour begins with an examination of a demonstration vineyard of Pinot Noir, Chardonnay and Muniere grapevines that are the basis for most premium sparkling wines. It then adjourns to the huge semi-submerged facility, where 30,000 cases are produced each year.

Tasting notes: We sampled three sparkling wines and agreed with a recent edition of ***The Wine Spectator,*** which rated Mumm as America's best bubbly. The Vintage Reserve was crisply perfect with a splendid finish; the Winery Lake was explosively fruity and the Blanc de Noir was soft with a strong hint of the parent Pinot Noir grape. Prices range from $14 to $23.

Vintners choice: Public relations manager Claudia Conlon leans toward the $23 Winery Lake.

ZD Wines • T$

8383 Silverado Trail, Napa, CA 94558; (707) 963-5188. Weekdays 10 to 12 and 1 to 4:30. Most varieties tasted for a $3 fee (includes glass).

ZD offers no picnic area, gift shop or tours. It makes up for this shortfall by offering tastings of fine, medal-winning wines. This small family facility is housed in a simple tile-roofed, vine-covered structure with a grape arbor entry to the tasting room. A tier of French oak towers threateningly over the tasting counter, but be at ease and enjoy your wine; there have been no reports of its toppling.

The winery started out as a hobby for engineers Gino Zepponi and Norman de Luze in 1969. After wine enthusiasts began taking them seriously, they moved to a serious winery in Sonoma and became full-time vintners. They shifted to the Napa Valley in 1979 and were scheduled to open a new facility in 1992. De Luze's son Robert is now the winemaker.

Tasting notes: It's a quick list: Chardonnay, Cabernet Sauvignon and Pinot Noir with not-so-modest prices ranging from $17 to $20. After tasting the wonderfully nutty-spicy Chard, the pepper berries of the Cab and the lushly herbal Pinot, we decided that they're worth it. The winery also produces, on occasion, a late-harvest Riesling, rich and raisiny, for $12.

S. Anderson Vineyard • T$ GTA$

1473 Yountville Cross Rd., Yountville, CA 94599; (707) 944-8642. Daily 10 to 5. Five wines tasted for a $3 fee. A few wine-theme gift items. Tours of wine caves by appointment for $3 per person.

Stanley and Carol Anderson started their vineyards in 1973, but didn't open their tasting room until 1990. It occupies a sort of glorified stone shed that once served as a pump house. More impressive are aging caves tunneled into a hill on the family estate. These stone rooms with lofty ceilings and cobbled floors are haven to nearly half a million bottles of sparkling wine and Chardonnay.

The caves and adjacent winery can be visited on twice-daily tours by advance reservation. Visitors to the tiny tasting room can adjourn tables on a landscaped terrace for more elbow room.

Tasting notes: Sparkling wine (which the Andersons dare to call Champagne) and Chardonnay make up the list. Prices range from $16 to $25. Our selection of five wines went thusly: A Stags Leap Chardonnay was spicy and balanced with enough acid for aging; Proprietor's Reserve Chardonnay was softer, more subtle and fruity with hints of oak; the Blanc de Noirs was surprisingly fruity and complex for a sparkling wine (Gorby got it at the White House); the Brut Champagne had a nice grapey nose with a fruit-rich flavor and gentle acid finish; the Rose Champagne was strong on the Pinot Noir berries, a sparkling mouthful.

Robert Sinskey Vineyards • T$ GT

6320 Silverado Trail, Napa, CA 94558; 944-9090. Daily 10 to 4:30; MC/VISA. Most varieties tasted for a $3 fee (includes glass or credit toward purchase). Some wine-related gift items. Guided tours at 11, 1 and 3.

Like many Silverado wineries, Sinskey occupies an impressive vantage point in the flanks of the Vaca Range. The winery is architecturally intriguing, with a high, ridge-like wooden center flanked by low stone-trimmed wings. The parking area is rimmed by a lattice colonnade with fieldstone walls, and a deck off the winery invites one to lounge (but not picnic) and enjoy a stellar view of the Napa Valley.

The winery interior is a nice mix of wood and stone. The tasting room's high ceiling is held aloft by a web-work of finished rafters; French doors offer a view of vats, barrels and stainless steel. Tours take visitors to a grapevine "petting zoo," through the winery and into caves tunneled into a nearby slope.

Opthamologist Robert Sinskey established the winery in the 1980s and completed the present facility in 1988. His son Rob is manager and marketing director. Tiny as Napa wineries go, with an output of 8,000 cases, it's nonetheless an attention-getter, having won numerous awards.

Tasting notes: Chardonnay, Pinot Noir, Merlot and a Bordeaux-style Claret complete the Sinskey list. The Aries Chardonnay was light but complex and silky, with a soft finish. The Aries Pinot Noir was soft as well, almost like a tasty Beaujolais. The best of the lot was RSV Carneros Claret with big berries, a nippy finish and enough tannin for aging. It should be good; the price tag read $28. Other wines range from $8 to the high teens.

Silverado Vineyards • T

6121 Silverado Trail, Napa, CA 94558; (707) 257-1770. Sunday-Friday 11 to 4, Saturday 11 to 4:30; MC/VISA, AMEX. Most varieties tasted; no fee. Some wine-related gift items.

Crowning a vineyard hill, Silverado is among the valley's more attractive wineries. Its fieldstone walls, Spanish arch colonnade and lofty ceilings give it the feel of an ancient abbey. The tasting room, occupying a portion of the main winery, is a study in old world refinement with a Spanish tile floor and wood panels. But why that stained glass portrait of Mickey Mouse in a transom?

Lillian Disney, widow of Mickey's creator, purchased several acres of Stags Leap vineyards in 1970, with her son-in-law and daughter, Ron and Diane Disney Miller. Construction of their winery followed in 1981. It was dedicated to the memory of Robert Louis Stevenson, who's *Silverado Squatters* inspired the name.

Winery tours take visitors into the heart of aging cellars where tomorrow's wines sleep to soften their tannins and absorb a touch of oak.

Tasting notes: John Stuart won a "winemaker of the year" title in 1987 for his small lots of "hand-crafted" wines. His list consists of Sauvignon Blanc, Chardonnay, Cabernet Sauvignon and Merlot. Several vintages of most wines may be purchased. We were impressed with the barrel-fermented Chardonnay, full and complex with a crisp acid finish, and a classic Cabernet Sauvignon with a wonderful spicy bouquet and lush, complex flavor, tannic and suitable for aging. Prices range from $9 to the early twenties, more for some reserves.

Pine Ridge Winery • T GTA

5901 Silverado Trail, Napa, CA 94558; (707) 253-7500. Daily 11 to 4; MC/VISA. Most varieties tasted; no fee. A few wine-related giftwares. Small picnic area with a swing set; tours of winery and caves 10:15 daily, by appointment.

Tucked into the pine-shaded hollow of a hill on the valley side of the highway, Pine Ridge is as folksy and casual as Silverado is elegant. It, too, has won many awards, most of which decorate the walls of the simple wood-paneled tasting room. You can peek into the winery and around a corner into several cooling caves, or arrange for a more formal tour.

Proprietor R. Gary Andrus, one of the valley's most respected winemakers, bought a Stags Leap vineyard in 1978, added more vines, then released his first wines in 1981. In a decade, he won 114 medals, particularly for his Cabernet Sauvignon.

Tasting notes: The list is brief: Chenin Blanc, Chardonnay, Merlot and Cabernet. Every wine we tasted was excellent: a lush, silky and spicy Knollside Cuvee Chard; an herbal, softly acidic Stags Leap Vineyard Chard; a Selected Cuvee Merlot with a giant of a berry nose, full and complex and ready to age; and a Stags Leap Vineyard Cab with enough complexity and tannic power to carry into the next century.

Vintners choice: "We're well known for our vineyard designated Cabernet," said the winery's Debi Haines.

Stag's Leap Wine Cellars • T$ GTA

5766 Silverado Trail, Napa, CA 94558; (707) 944-2020. Daily 10 to 4; MC/VISA. Most varieties tasted for $2 fee (includes glass). Good gift selection. Oak-shaded picnic area; guided tours by appointment.

When Warren and Barbara Winiaraski established their wine cellar in 1972, they added an apostrophe to Stag's Leap to separate it from the district name. Starting with one small structure, they've added to their complex as their wines gained favor. A new white wine facility was under construction when we visited.

Stag's Leap is tucked into a pleasantly wooded niche on the mountain side of Silverado. Gnarled oaks glamorize the modest-looking Spanish style complex. The tasting room is a simple counter in one end of the main winery building. From here, one can watch the business of winemaking. Tours are available by advance request.

Tasting notes: Stag's Leap is one of the larger Stags Leap producers, offering two wine lines: a cellar label and a less expensive Hawk Crest series. From the Stag's Leap cellar list, we tasted an outstanding Cabernet, big and complex with a brisk tannic finish; and a nutty, silky Chardonnay with a gentle ending and a hint of wood. Prices range from $10 to $28. The Hawk

Crest wines are good buys: a nice peppery Cabernet for $9, a spicy Chardonnay, also at $9, and a bright, light and fruity Sauvignon Blanc for $6.50.

Chimney Rock Winery • T$ GTA

5350 Silverado Trail, Napa, CA 94558; (707) 257-2461. Daily 10 to 4; MC/VISA, DISC. All current releases tasted for $2.50 fee (includes glass, or can be applied to wine purchase). Small selection of gift items; guided tours by appointment.

With its ornate Dutch Colonial architecture, Chimney Rock is one of the valley's most striking small wineries. The two-building complex was fashioned after a winery in the Cape Colony of South Africa. Note the elaborate frieze on the main building, portraying Ganymede, cup bearer to Zeus and other Mount Olympus celestials. Chimney Rock's tasting room and hospitality center is a study in old world elegance, with gleaming white walls, polished wood trim and 19th century furnishings. It's surrounded by manicured lawns and slender poplars.

All this is the creation of Sheldon and Stella Wilson, who purchased half of the Chimney Rock Golf Course in 1980 and converted it into a vineyard. The winery complex was completed in 1990. (The golf course, still in business, is now a nine-holer.)

Tasting notes: The intent here is to match wines with foods, making them soft and gentle, says winemaker Doug Fletcher. The Chardonnay is evidence of this philosophy—silky and almost honey-like, with only a slight hint of oak. We also tasted an herbal, complex and nicely balanced Cabernet Sauvignon and a bright, crisp Fumè Blanc with just a hint of duskiness. Prices range from $10 to $25.

Clos du Val • T GTA ⩙

5330 Silverado Trail (P.O. Box 4350), Napa, CA 94558; (707) 252-6711. Daily 10 to 4; MC/VISA. Three wines tasted from the list of current releases; no fee. Selected wine-oriented gift items including whimsical Ronald Searle posters and postcards. Oak-shaded picnic tables; tours by appointment.

Sitting upslope in a wooded grove, cathedral-like Clos du Val is one of the first of the valley's grand "new-generation" wineries. It was established in 1972 by John Goelet and French winemaker Bernard Portet; they had in mind a noble yet rather simple chateau. Both men are still principles in the operation.

The tasting room is a grand space—a stunning abbey-like affair with 50-foot ceilings, accented by ornate woods, conglomerate walls and tile floors. Lofty windows offer views into the working winery.

Tasting notes: Several Cabernet vintages top the award-winning list. We tasted an outstanding, complex and spicy eight-year-old Cab and one of Napa's better Zinfandels—herbal, complex and drinkable, with enough tannin to encourage aging. A Chardonnay was crisp, clean and pleasantly light. Merlot, Semillon and an inexpensive Le Clos White complete the list. Prices range from $10 to the mid-twenties. Buyers can select from a range of six or seven vintage years of most of the wines.

THE BEST OF THE BUNCH

The best wine buys • Mont St. John Cellars in the Carneros; Nichelini Winery in the Chiles Valley; Lakespring Winery, Sequoia Grove

Vineyards, Inglenook-Napa Valley, Rutherford Vintners and Franciscan Vineyards along Highway 29.

The most attractive wineries • Domaine Carneros in the Carneros; The Hess Collection on Mount Veeder; Domaine Chandon, Robert Mondavi Winery and Inglenook-Napa Valley on Highway 29; Rutherford Hill Winery, Silverado Vineyards, Chimney Rock Winery and Clos du Val on the Silverado Trail.

The most interesting tasting rooms • Domaine Carneros in the Carneros; Domaine Chandon and Beaulieu Vineyard on Highway 29; Conn Creek Winery, Rutherford Hill Winery, Silver Oak Cellars, Silverado Vineyards, Chimney Rock Winery and Clos du Val on the Silverado Trail.

The funkiest tasting rooms • Nichelini Winery and Rustridge Winery in the Chiles Valley.

The best gift shops • The Hess Collection on Mount Veeder; Domaine Chandon, Robert Mondavi Winery, Inglenook-Napa Valley, Beaulieu Vineyard and Franciscan Vineyards on Highway 29 and Mumm Napa Valley on the Silverado Trail.

The nicest picnic areas • Chateau Potelle on Mount Veeder; Vichon Winery on Oakville Grade; Rutherford Hill Winery, Pine Ridge Winery, Stag's Leap Cellars and Clos du Val on the Silverado Trail; Nichelini Winery in the Chiles Valley.

The best tours • Domaine Carneros (guided or self-guiding) in the Carneros; The Hess Collection (self-guiding) on Mount Veeder; Domaine Chandon (guided), St. Supèry Winery (self-guiding) and Beaulieu Vineyard (guided) on Highway 29; Rutherford Hill Winery (guided) and Mumm Napa Valley (guided) on the Silverado Trail.

BEYOND THE VINEYARDS

Wine's the thing in the southern end of the valley, but the area has a few other lures as well. **Napa**, which we bypassed in our eagerness to reach the vineyards, offers several attractions. It's the valley's commercial center and home to 56,000 souls—half the county's population.

Although its suburbs are typical shopping center-service station Americana, the oldstyle downtown area shouldn't be overlooked. The business district is well-kept and attractive, with tree-lined streets, brick-enhanced sidewalks and shops tucked into revitalized false-front stores.

First and Main streets are the heart of old Napa; to reach it take the First Street exit east from Freeway 29. Carefully restored **Victorian homes** rim the downtown area. Many are concentrated along Jefferson, Clay and Polk streets, northeast of downtown. Also, visit the **Napa County Historical Society Museum** at 1219 First Street. For **walking tour maps** of historic Napa, contact Napa City Hall, Second and School streets (252-7711).

Mountains cradling the Napa Valley lure lovers of winding roads and solitude. Pick any east-west route and you'll soon be surrounded by silence, whispered through pine and redwood forests and oak groves clustered on tawny hillsides.

Oakville Grade offers a good excuse to wind among the heights on your way to neighboring Sonoma Valley. Highway 121 twisting northeast of Napa takes you to **Lake Berryessa,** a large reservoir offering the usual boating, water-skiing, camping, swimming, fishing lures. You can check into one of seven resorts, get provisions at lakeside marinas and rent houseboats, fishing boats and other water toys. Call 966-2111 for details.

If you follow Highway 128 west from Berryessa, then turn right onto Lower Chiles Valley Road, you'll pass high meadows, forests and vineyards of the secluded **Chiles Valley.** Beyond that, you encounter **Pope Valley,** another prime vineyard area.

The tiny, prim Seventh-Day Adventist village of **Angwin** is home to **Pacific Union College** and a lot of good Christians. Interestingly, in this little hamlet in the hills above California's most famous wine country, one can't get a drink, since Adventists forswear alcohol, tobacco and caffeine. Most are vegetarians and you'll find no meat or fish in the **College Market**. Its bulk food section, brimming with legumes, spices, whole-grain flour, dried fruits and candies is one of the largest in California.

Down Valley activities & attractions

Antique car tours • Antique Auto Adventures, 520 California Blvd., #17, Napa CA 94559; 226-3988.

Boat tours • Jackson's Charters, Napa, 257-0257; Napa Riverboat Company (sternwheeler), 1200 Milton Rd., Napa CA 94558; 226-2648.

Boating at Lake Berryessa • Spanish Flat Resort with ski boat, patio boat, sailboard and jet ski rentals, 966-7700; Lake Berryessa Marina Resort with ski boat, fishing boat and patio boat rentals, 966-2161; Markley Cove, offering houseboat rentals, P.O. Box 987, Winters, CA 95694, (800) 242-6287 or 966-2134.

Bicycling • Bryan's Napa Valley Cyclery (bike tours), 4080 Byway East, Napa, CA 94558; Napa Valley Bike Tours, 255-3377.

Helicopter tours • Helicopter Network International, P.O. Box 10007, Napa, CA 94581, (800) 662-6886 or (707) 255-5135; Napa Valley Helicopter Tours, 1475 Fourth St., Napa, CA 94559; (800) 876-5559 or (707) 252-7874.

Horseback riding • Wild Horse Valley Ranch (five miles east of Napa), trail rides and barbecues, 224-0727.

Hot air ballooning • This is a great way to see the Napa Valley, which has the greatest concentration of hot air balloonists in California, maybe in the country. To take advantage of the still air, most balloonists launch early in the morning.

Among Down Valley's operators are: Above the West, P.O. Box 2290, Yountville, CA 94599, (800) 627-2759; Adventures Aloft, Box 2500, Yountville, CA 94599, (707) 255-8688; American Balloon Adventures, Box 6891, Napa, CA 94581, (800) 333-4359 or (707) 944-8117; Balloon About the Napa Valley, Box 10001, Napa, CA 94558, (707) 257-1001; Balloon Aviation of Napa Valley, Box 3298, Napa, CA 94559, (800) 367-6272.

Balloons Above the Valley, Box 3838, Napa, CA 94558, (800) 233-7681; Bonaventura Balloon Co., Box 5176, Napa, CA 94581, (707) 944-2822; Napa Valley Balloons, Box 2860, Yountville, CA 94599, (800) 253-2224; Napa's Great Balloon Escape, Box 4197, Napa, CA 94558, (707) 253-0860; and Napa Valley Balloon Safaris, (800) 255-0125.

Museum • Napa County Historical Society Museum, 1219 First St., Napa; 224-1739. Tuesday and Thursday, noon to 4; local history exhibits.

Napa Valley Wine Train • 1275 McKinstry St., Napa, CA 94559; (800) 522-4142 or 253-2111.

Wineland events • Wine appreciation courses sponsored by the Napa Valley Wine Library Association (see box in Chapter 6); 963-3535. Napa Valley Wine Auction, first weekend of June; 963-5246. Mondavi Pops Festival and Summer Music Festival, June-August; 963-9611. Napa County Fair in Calistoga, featuring local winery exhibits, early July; 942-5111. Home Winemakers Classic, tasting of amateur vintners' wines, late July; 253-0224.

Napa Town & Country Fair in Napa, featuring local winery exhibits, early August; 253-4900. Napa Wine Festival and Crafts Faire, mid-September; 257-0322. Harvest Festival at Charles Krug Winery, mid-September; 253-2353. Napa Valley Wine Festival, early November; 253-3563. Individual wineries also sponsor various events throughout the year.

Wine country tours • Napa Valley Tourist Bureau, 258-1957; Napa Valley Bike Tours, 255-3377; Antique Auto Adventures, 226-3988.

Wine country maps • ***Napa Valley Tour Map***, available at many wineries and gift shops for $2.50 or contact Napa Valley Art Studio, 1028 Summit Ave., Napa, CA 94559; 253-0204. Mattioli's ***In Your Pocket Guide*** to Yountville, Oakville and Rutherford, listing wineries, lodging, shops, restaurants and recreation, one dollar; available in many gift shops and tasting rooms, or call 965-2006.

MUSIC IN THE VINEYARDS

WINE COUNTRY DINING

Since it draws hundreds of thousands of visitors including many San Francisco Bay Area regulars, the Napa Valley supports some of northern California's better restaurants. This list covers dining from Yountville south to Napa; those from St. Helena north are in the next chapter.

California Cafe • ΔΔ $$$ ØØ

6795 Washington St. (Washington Square), Yountville; 944-2330. California-Southwest; dinners $12 to $20; full bar service. Monday-Thursday 11:30 to 9, Friday-Saturday 11:30 to 10, Sunday 10 to 9:30. Informal to casual; reservations accepted. Major credit cards. Contemporary cafe with an Art Deco look; eclectic menu touches on on grilled fresh fish, chicken and chops and pastas, enlivened with Mexican and Mediterranean touches. The cafe is smoke-free.

Compadres Mexican Bar & Grill • ΔΔ $$ Ø

6539 Washington St. (in Vintage Estate), Yountville; (707) 944-2406. Mexican; dinners $8 to $19; full bar service. Weekdays from 10 a.m., weekends from 9 a.m., various closing times. Casual; reservations accepted. Major credit cards. The usual smashed beans and rice dishes, plus specialties such as *Huajolote* (charbroiled turkey breast marinaded in chilies, spices and tequila) and grilled fresh fish topped with tomato salsa. The look is bright, cheery upscale California-Mexican; patio dining.

Domaine Chandon Restaurant • ΔΔΔΔ $$$$ ØØ

California Drive, Yountville; (707) 944-2892. California-French; dinners $25 to $40; wine and beer. Open daily; lunch 11:30 to 2:30, dinner 6 to 9:30. Dressy to informal; reservations essential (two weeks in advance for weekends). Major credit cards. At Domaine Chandon winery; one of the valley's more striking restaurants, with glass walls offering vineyard views. *Nouveau menu* ranges from from roasted pork tenderloin with fava bean purèe and sweet garlic to venison *tournedos* wrapped in pancetta with potatoes and Merlot-juniper essence. Extensive California wine-list; smoke-free dining room.

The French Laundry • ΔΔΔΔ $$$$ ØØ

Washington and Creek Streets (P.O. Box 0), Yountville; (707) 944-2380. California-French country; prix fixe dinners $46; wine and beer. Wednesday-Sunday, dinners only. Dressy to informal; reservations essential (well in advance). No credit cards. Fashionable French Country cafe in a century-old brick laundry building, with fireplace, European antiques, artworks and gardens. One seating nightly for five-course dinners, such as artichokes with garlic mayonnaise, soup *du jour*, duckling with a current glaze and apricot chutney, accompanied by a stir-fry of baby bok choy and shiitake mushrooms, salad and dessert. Smoke-free dining room.

The Garden Grill Restaurant • ΔΔ $$ Ø

1140 Rutherford Rd. (at Rancho Caymus Inn), Rutherford; (707) 963-1777. Light American fare; meals $8 to $12; wine and beer. Daily 8 a.m. to 2 p.m. Informal to casual; MC/VISA. Grilled entrèes, pastas, sandwiches and salad served indoors and out in this early California-style restaurant. Local wines are a specialty.

Mustards • ΔΔΔ $$$Ø

7399 St. Helena Hwy. (just north of Yountville), Napa; (707) 944-2424. California-American upscale grill; dinners $15 to $20; full bar service. Daily 11:30 to 10. Informal to casual; reservations essential. MC/VISA, DC. Near-legendary California *nouveau* cafe with Yuppie American grill look. Changing menu features smoked and grilled fish, fowl and beef served with fresh vegetables and innovative seasonings. Offerings include calves liver with caramelized onions, Mongolian pork chops with sweet and sour cabbage and chicken breast with chili chocolate, black beans and papaya chutney.

Ristorante Piatti • ΔΔΔ $$$ Ø

6480 Washington St. (downtown), Yountville; (707) 944-2070. Regional Italian; dinners $8 to $17; full bar service. Monday-Thursday 11:30 a.m. to 10 p.m. (closed 2:30 to 5), Friday 11:30 to 11 (closed 2:30 to 5), Saturday noon to 11, Sunday noon to 10. Informal to casual; reservations advised. MC/VISA. A branch of the Sonoma *trattoria* with bright, airy California decor and a versatile Italian menu. Specialties include angel hair pasta, spaghetti with duck ragout, black and white pasta with fresh mussels and grilled seafoods. Outdoor tables; smoke-free dining room.

VINELAND LODGINGS

Resorts, hotels and motels

Although Napa has numerous motels and hotels, we're focusing primarily on those near the vineyards.

Auberge du Soleil • ΔΔΔΔΔ $$$$$ Ø

180 Rutherford Hill Rd, Rutherford, CA 94573; (707) 963-1211). Doubles $275 to $325, singles $275, suites $425 to $7255, including continental breakfast. MC/VISA, AMEX. Opulent 48-unit Mediterranean style resort in a 33-acre olive grove; valley view suites in cottages on extensive grounds; TV movies, room phones, kitchens, wet bars, fireplaces and other amenities. Pools, health spa with masseuse and steam rooms, whirlpools and tennis. **Auberge du Soleil Restaurant** serves "California wine country cuisine"; breakfast 7 to 10:30, lunch 11:30 to 2:30, dinner 5:30 to 10:30; "wine country cuisine" featuring Continental-California fare; prix fixe dinner $52 or entrèes from $23 to $30; full bar service. The restaurant is smoke-free.

Best Western Inn • ΔΔΔ $$$$ Ø

100 Soscal Ave. (Imola Street), Napa, CA 94558; (800) 528-1234 or (707) 257-1930. Doubles $69 to $99, singles $65 to $79, suites $119 to $149. Major credit cards. Attractive 68-unit motel with TV movies, phones, in-room coffee and balconies; some room refrigerators. Pool, spa. **The Grape Steak** restaurant serves 6 a.m. to 10 p.m.; American; dinners $8 to $15; wine and beer; non-smoking areas.

The Chablis Lodge • ΔΔΔ $$$$ Ø

3360 Solano Ave. (Highway 29 at Redwood Road), Napa, CA 94558; (800) 443-3490 or (707) 257-1944. Doubles and singles $74 to $99, kitchenettes $74 to $84, rooms with spa $84 to $104. Major credit cards. A 34-unit motel at the edge of the wine country; rooms with TV movies, phones, wet bars, refrigerators, coffee makers. Swimming pool and spa.

The Chateau • ΔΔΔ $$$$ Ø

4195 Solano Ave. (Highway 29 at Trower), Napa, CA 94558; (800) 253-6272 in California only or (707) 253-9300. Doubles $80 to $95, singles $70 to $85. Major credit cards. A well-situated 115-unit motel on the edge of the wine country. Rooms with TV movies and phones, some with refrigerators. Pool and spa.

Clarion Inn Napa Valley ΔΔΔΔ $$$ Ø

3425 Solano Ave. (Highway 29 at Redwood Road), Napa, CA 94558; (800) 333-7533 or (707) 253-7433. Doubles $55 to $115, singles $45 to $105, suites $175 to $425. Major credit cards. Courtyard-style, 191-unit inn on the edge of the wine country; rooms with TV movies and phones. Lighted tennis courts, spa and swimming pool. Wine cellar style **Signature Restaurant** serves 7 a.m. to 10 p.m.; Continental-American; dinners $7 to $23; full bar service; non-smoking areas.

Inn at Napa Valley • ΔΔΔΔ $$$$$ Ø

1075 California Blvd. (at Highway 29), Napa, CA 94559; (800) 433-4600 or (707) 253-9540. All suites, $109 to $164, including full breakfast and afternoon cocktails. Major credit cards. The former Embassy Suites, this 205-room courtyard inn sits near the vineyards. Nicely-furnished rooms with TV movies, phones, wet bars, refrigerators and microwaves. Indoor-outdoor pool, spa, sauna, private sun decks, courtyard pond. **Caffe 1991**serves 11 a.m. to 10 p.m.; California *nouveau*; dinners $14 to $25; full bar service; non-smoking areas.

John Muir Inn • ΔΔ $$$$ Ø

1998 Trower Ave. (Highway 29, near vineyards), Napa, CA 94558; (800) 522-8999 or (707) 257-7220. Doubles and singles $75 to $90, kitchenettes $80 to $95, suites $105 to $130 (rates higher on weekends). Major credit cards. A 60-unit inn with TV movies, room phones, in-room coffee; some with kitchenettes, refrigerators and wet bars. Free continental breakfast; pool, spa.

Napa Valley Lodge Best Western • ΔΔΔ $$$$$ Ø

Madison Street at Highway 29 (P.O. Box L), Yountville, CA 94599; (800) 368-2468 or (707) 944-2468. Doubles $122 to $152, singles $115 to $142, suites and fireplace rooms $145 to $165; rates include breakfast. Major credit cards. New 55-room lodge with TV, room phones, in-room coffee, refrigerators and patios. Pool, spa, sauna, exercise room.

Napa Valley Travelodge • ΔΔ $$$ Ø

853 Coombs St. (Second Street, downtown), Napa, CA 94559; (800) 255-3050 or (707) 226-1871. Doubles $55 to $80, singles $50 to $75, suites $150 to $175. Major credit cards. A 44-room motel; TV, room phones; heated pool; morning coffee. Near Napa Valley Wine Train depot.

Silverado Country Club • ΔΔΔΔΔ $$$$$ Ø

1600 Atlas Peak Rd. (Monticello, above the vineyards), Napa, CA 94558; (800) 532-0500 or (707) 257-0200. Suites $160 to $225. Major credit cards. Long-established luxury resort with 18-hole PGA golf course, tennis courts, volleyball, cycling, jogging paths, spa. Suites and cottages have kitchens, TV movies, phones and other resort amenities. Three restaurants—**Vintners**

Court, Royal Oak and **Bar and Grill**, with continental, American regional cuisine and steak house; breakfast, lunch and dinner; $20 to $30 for dinner; full bar service; non-smoking areas.

Vintage Inn Napa Valley • ΔΔΔΔ $$$$$ Ø

6541 Washington St. (downtown), Yountville, CA 94599; (800) 351-1133 in California, (800) 982-5539 elsewhere; (707) 944-1112. Doubles $134 to $179, singles $124 to $179, suites $174 to $189. Major credit cards. American country style resort with 80 rooms; TV movies, phones, in-room coffee, wine, spa tubs; rates include buffet breakfast; tennis; pool; spa. Two restaurants, **Drums** (California) and **Compadres** (Mexican); breakfast, lunch and dinner; $12 to $18 for dinner; full bar service; non-smoking areas.

Bed & Breakfast Inns

Arbor Guest House • ΔΔΔ $$$$ Ø

1436 G St., Napa, CA 94559; (707) 252-8144. Doubles $85 to $135. Five rooms, all with private baths; full breakfast. MC/VISA, AMEX. Remodeled turn-of-the century Colonial home with period antiques; Amish quilts on oldstyle beds; three rooms with fireplaces. Breakfast served in patio garden.

Beazley House • ΔΔΔ $$$$ ØØ

1910 First St. (Warren), Napa, CA 94559; (707) 257-1649. Doubles $95 to $165, singles $82.50 to $152.50. Ten rooms, all with private baths; full breakfast. MC/VISA, DISC. Napa's first B&B in an historic landmark Edwardian mansion; rooms furnished with American and Victorian antiques; room phones available. Some rooms have fireplaces and spas. Extensive lawns and gardens.

Blue Violet Mansion • ΔΔΔ $$$$ Ø

443 Brown St. (Oak and Laurel), Napa, CA 94559; (707) 253-BLUE. Doubles $90 to $160. Six rooms, all with private baths; full breakfast. MC/VISA. Newly-remodeled 1886 mansion listed on the National Register of Historic Places. Nicely furnished rooms with early American and Victorian antiques. Afternoon tea, dessert buffet and wine tasting.

Coombs Residence Inn • ΔΔΔ $$$$ Ø

720 Seminary St. (Third Street), Napa, CA 94559; (707) 257-0789. Doubles $90 to $125, singles $60 to $95. Four rooms, two with shared baths; full breakfast. MC/VISA. An 1852 Victorian on the National Register of Historic Places; American and European antiques. Afternoon wine and cheese served in parlor; swimming pool, spa; bicycles available.

Churchill Manor • ΔΔΔ $$$$ Ø

485 Brown St. (off Oak Street) Napa, CA 94559; (707) 253-7733. Doubles $70 to $145. Eight rooms, all with private baths and room phones; buffet breakfast. MC/VISA, AMEX. An 1889 Victorian columned mansion, on the National Register of Historic Places. Italianate and American antiques, chandeliers, oriental rugs; nicely furnished rooms. Extensive gardens; afternoon snacks, tea, wine and cheese.

The Goodman House • ΔΔΔ $$$$$ ØØ

1225 Division St. (between Third and Coombs), Napa, CA 94559; (707) 257-1166. Doubles from $95 to $130. Four rooms, all with private baths; full

WINE TRAIN OR WHINE TRAIN?

When wealthy Bay Area entrepreneur Vince DeDomenico proposed running an excursion train through the Napa Valley in mid-1980, residents and many vintners threw a collective fit. "Too disruptive!" they cried. "Too tacky! We're too crowded already!"

Original plans for the Napa Valley Wine Train were scaled back to meet the many objections. Instead of disgorging loads of tourists at various wineries, it merely chugs from Napa to St. Helena and back, serving lunch or dinner en route. It is essentially a mobile restaurant.

Having taken a luncheon excursion, we are prepared to answer your questions. The train trip is $29; meals are extra—$22 for lunch or brunch and $45 for dinner, plus 12 percent service. You can opt for the less expensive "deli car" that offers light snacks, although we weren't told that when we made reservations. Meals are served in two sittings. While waiting, you can relax in a lounge car and watch the vineyards crawl past, or sample wines at a tasting bar ($5 for four samples). The trip lasts about three hours and covers 36 miles. You can call (800) 427-4124 to make reservations.

Question: Is it "relaxed elegance on one of the world's most magnificent trains," as the brochure claims, or is it tacky?

Answer: "Magnificent" is an overstatement, although the refurbished oldstyle coaches are nicely appointed, with "polished mahogany, brass and etched glass," as the brochure says. Dining cars are set with silver, china and crystal over white nappery. But having your picture taken before boarding, to be purchased later? *That's* tacky.

Q: Is the meal "a deliciously crafted culinary and wine experience," as the brochure claims?

A: No. Our salmon poached in court bullion was good but slightly overdone. Our designer salad was artfully presented but small, without enough veggies to keep a rabbit regular. The wine list was locally focused and good, although by-the-glass offerings were limited.

Q: Did you "glide gently past world famous vineyards?"

A: The train follows the same route as cars on Highway 29, so you will see nothing new. We certainly did glide gently, poking along at about 30 miles an hour—presumably to allow enough time for the two meal sittings.

Q: Was it "an unforgettable...relaxing journey through California's historic and scenic wine country?"

A: The train follows the route established by flamboyant Sam Brannan in 1864, although it goes only halfway. We may have been getting some local history over the speaker system, but the relaxed dining room chatter drowned it out.

Q: Could you sum up your Napa Valley Wine Train experience in ten words or less?

A: A pleasant little diversion, particularly if you like old trains, but rather expensive.

Q: That's thirteen.

A: Sorry.

breakfast. MC/VISA, AMEX. An 1880s Victorian; nicely-done rooms furnished with European and American antiques; three with fireplaces and one with spa. Parlor with grand piano and fireplace. Afternoon snacks and wine.

Hennessey House Bed & Breakfast • ∆∆∆ $$$$ ØØ

1727 Main St. (downtown), Napa, CA 94559; (707) 226-3774. Doubles $85 to $150. Ten rooms, all with private baths; full breakfast. No credit cards. A Queen Anne Victorian with extensive grounds; on the National Register of Historic Places. Rooms in main house and carriage house; each with different decorator theme. Two with fireplaces, four with whirlpool tubs. Belgian and English antiques. Sun porch and sauna.

La Belle Epoque • ∆∆∆ $$$$ Ø

1386 Calistoga Ave. (Seminary Street), Napa, CA 94559; (707) 257-2161. Doubles $95 to $135. Six rooms, all with private baths; full breakfast. MC/VISA, AMEX. An 1893 Victorian with stained glass windows, antique furnishings; near "Old Town" Napa. Breakfast served in a formal dining room with fireplace or on a sun porch; wine cellar with afternoon tasting.

La Residence Country Inn • ∆∆∆∆ $$$$ Ø

4066 St. Helena Highway (north of town, beyond Salvador Avenue), Napa, CA 94558; (707) 253-0337. Doubles $75 to $160. Twenty rooms, 18 with private baths; full breakfast. MC/VISA. An 1870 French-style mansion with adjacent "barn". Guest rooms in both buildings; American antiques in mansion and European country antiques in barn; 15 rooms with fireplaces. Two-acre landscaped grounds with pool, spa, gazebo and brick patios.

Magnolia Hotel • ∆∆∆ $$$$ Ø

6529 Yount St., Yountville, CA 94599; (707) 944-2050. Doubles $89 to $169. Twelve rooms, all with private baths; full breakfast. No credit cards. Restored 1873 stone and brick hotel with Victorian antiques; five rooms with fireplaces. Gardens and decks with pool and spa.

Napa Inn • ∆∆∆ $$$$$ Ø

1137 Warren St. (between First and Jefferson), Napa, CA 94559; (707) 257-1444. Doubles $100 to $150. Five rooms, all with private baths; full breakfast. MC/VISA. Spacious bedrooms in an 1899 Queen Anne; furnished with turn-of-the-century antiques and collectibles. Formal dining room, parlor with fireplace; landscaped grounds.

Oleander House • ∆∆∆ $$$$$ ØØ

7433 St. Helena Hwy. (near Mustards Grill), Yountville, CA 94599; (707) 944-8315. Doubles $115 to $145. Four rooms, all with private baths; full breakfast. MC/VISA. Contemporary country French style home with designer furnishings; high-ceiling rooms with fireplaces and private patios or balconies. Spa in landscaped patio garden.

Sybron House Bed & Breakfast • ∆∆∆ $$$$$ ØØ

7400 St. Helena Way (1.5 miles from Yountville), Napa, CA 94558; (707) 944944-2785. Doubles $100 to $150, singles $50 to $100. Four rooms, three with private baths; expanded continental breakfast. MC/VISA, AMEX. A new made-to-look Victorian home, decorated with a mix of modern and antique furniture; one bedroom with fireplace. Spa, tennis courts, nicely landscaped grounds. On a hill with a valley view.

Tall Timbers Chalets • ∆∆ $$$$$ ØØ

1012 Darms Lane (off Highway 29), Napa, CA 94559; (707) 252-7810. Individual cottages, $105; all with TV and private baths; continental breakfast. A refurbished 1940s resort with cozy cottages tucked among the trees. All are mini-suites with a bedroom, sitting room, bathroom and kitchen, suitable for romantic a get-away. Walking trails, bike rentals; golf nearby.

Down Valley information sources

Napa Chamber of Commerce, 1556 First St., Napa, CA 94559; (707) 226-7455.

Yountville Chamber of Commerce, 6795 Washington St., Yountville, CA 94599; (707) 944-0904.

Napa Valley Tourist Bureau, 6488 Washington St., Yountville, CA 94599; (707) 258-1957 (A commercial firm offering maps for sale, plus reservations for lodging and wine country tours).

Napa Valley Wine Library Association, P.O. Box 207, St. Helena, CA 94574; (707) 963-3535. (See box in Chapter 6.)

"A broad wine, with enough maturity to drink now. Cedar, blackberry and herb flavors are supported by medium tannins and a decent acid balance, but a dusty, tired aroma holds it back."

—Description of an Iron Horse Sonoma County Brut

Chapter Six

NAPA: UP VALLEY

Northern area, from St. Helena to Calistoga

St. Helena is the maternity ward of the Napa wine industry. The valley's oldest wineries were born hereabouts and many still function. Among its 19th century dowagers are Charles Krug, Schramsberg, Inglenook and Beaulieu.

However, not one is in the hands of a founding family, and some endured long periods of Prohibition-inspired dormancy. St. Helena's story, then, is one of history with hiccups. The oldest family-owned facility is Louis M. Martini Winery, dating back—appropriately—to 1933, the year of Repeal. Second and third-generation family members now operate it. The senior Martini was a giant among vintners, one of the movers and shapers of the valley's modern wine industry and a founder of the Wine Institute, the wine trade's leading watchdog organization.

Many of St. Helena's wineries are monumental structures, built when labor was cheap and owners had a sense of Victorian grandeur. Today, they are the state's most-visited wineries. As many as 300,000 tourists a year are processed by efficient and friendly guides, given quick doses of history and quick sips of wine at the end of the tour. Indeed, some of these are called "history tours," for they take visitors through outmoded stone castles and grandiloquent mansions used now only for aging cellars and for show.

St. Helena is a picturesque and prim community that doesn't appear to be completely at ease in the tourist spotlight. The Napa Valley Wine Library is based here (see box) and shops and cafes are plentiful, yet the town tends to pull in its sidewalks early, to the frustration of many visitors. When the last nearby tasting room has closed, most of the town's boutiques, antique shops and its only decent deli have closed as well. Restaurants remain open, of course, along with the ubiquitous Safeway and a good-ole-boy saloon called The Pastime, smelling of stale cigarette smoke and yesterday's spilled beer.

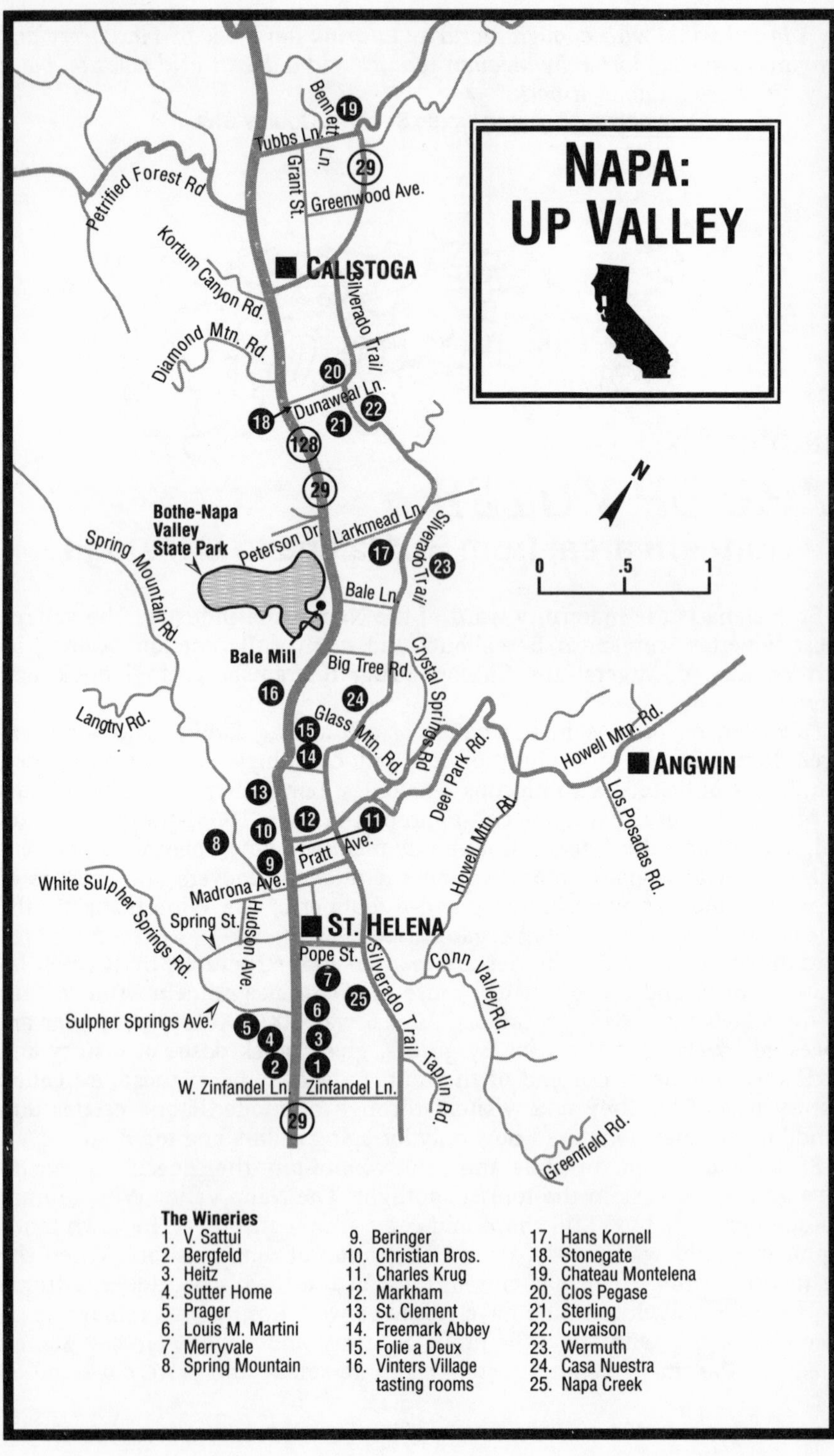

NAPA:
UP VALLEY
N
0 .5 1
Calistoga
St. Helena
Angwin
Bothe-Napa Valley State Park
Bale Mill
Tubbs Ln.
Bennett Ln.
Grant St.
Greenwood Ave.
Petrified Forest Rd
Kortum Canyon Rd.
Silverado Trail
Diamond Mtn. Rd.
Dunaweal Ln.
Peterson Dr.
Larkmead Ln.
Spring Mountain Rd.
Bale Ln.
Big Tree Rd.
Crystal Springs Rd.
Langtry Rd.
Glass Mtn. Rd.
Deer Park Rd.
Howell Mtn. Rd.
Los Posadas Rd.
Pratt Ave.
Madrona Ave.
White Sulpher Springs Rd.
Spring St.
Hudson Ave.
Pope St.
Conn Valley Rd.
Sulpher Springs Ave.
Taplin Rd.
W. Zinfandel Ln.
Zinfandel Ln.
Greenfield Rd.
29
128
The Wineries
1. V. Sattui
2. Bergfeld
3. Heitz
4. Sutter Home
5. Prager
6. Louis M. Martini
7. Merryvale
8. Spring Mountain
9. Beringer
10. Christian Bros.
11. Charles Krug
12. Markham
13. St. Clement
14. Freemark Abbey
15. Folie a Deux
16. Vinters Village tasting rooms
17. Hans Kornell
18. Stonegate
19. Chateau Montelena
20. Clos Pegase
21. Sterling
22. Cuvaison
23. Wermuth
24. Casa Nuestra
25. Napa Creek

The town's shops are worth a browse. We'd recommend breaking off from your winery touring with sufficient time to stroll its spotless sidewalks and nod pleasantly at the locals, who don't seem to mind all the hubbub. And certainly take time to visit the **Silverado Museum** which honors Robert Louis Stevenson's 1880 honeymoon stay and contains one of the world' largest collections of Stevenson lore.

After the shops have closed, use the last of the daylight to drive St. Helena's tree-lined residential streets. Admire handsome Victorian homes that speak of the days when adventuring Finnish sea captains, hard-working Italians and no-nonsense German immigrants built some of America's grandest mansions and wineries.

Calistoga, the other Up Valley community, is known more for mineral water and mud baths than for Merlot. The wineries are not far away, however, as new vineyards march ever northward. Founded as a resort by that capitalistic Mormon Sam Brannan, it wears its touristic mantle comfortably, quite pleased to be the Napa Valley's final visitor stop.

The town basks contentedly in the shadow of Mount St. Helena which, unlike its recently-rambunctious Washington state name-twin, is not volcanic. Its conical shape with a dip in the top has fooled many a brochure writer and author, including Stevenson. It is composed of faulted igneous rock, including silver-bearing cinnabar, but it was never a volcanic cone.

Like St. Helena, Calistoga is a comely little community, kept prim and prosperous by its place in tourism's limelight. It has the predictable assortment of boutiques, antique shops, restaurants and bed and breakfast inns. One can sink into a sensuously gooey mud bath or soar on wings of eagles by signing on at the Calistoga Glider Port (see box). Several attractions draw visitors to the area—an exhibit of a Sam Brannan resort cottage at Sharpsteen Museum, "Old Faithful" geyser on Tubbs Lane, the nearby Petrified Forest and Robert Louis Stevenson State Historic Park, a few miles up the mountain.

The Up Valley winery tour is simple, since most of the tasting rooms stand alongside either Highway 29 or the Silverado Trail. We'll first send you up Highway 29 from St. Helena, then down the Silverado from Calistoga.

HIGHWAY 29 WINERY TOUR • We stopped at Zinfandel Lane just south of **St. Helena** in the last chapter. Your first tasting room encounter north of Zinfandel is **V. Sattui Winery** on the right, then **Bergfeld Winery** on the left, followed by **Heitz Cellars** on the right.

Sutter Home Winery comes up quickly on the left, and **Prager Winery and Port Works** is just up Lewelling Lane, behind Sutter Home. Back on Highway 29, **Louis M. Martini Winery** is across the street. Then, after about a quarter of a mile, you reach **Merryvale Vineyards** on the right, on the outer rim of St. Helena. At the edge of town, turn right onto Charter Oak (at the old stone, vine-covered Tra Vigna restaurant building) and follow it two blocks to **Napa Valley Olive Oil Manufacturing Co.**

Why? Because it's a wonderfully cluttered Italian deli, awash with the sights and smells of cheeses, spiced meats, fresh pasta and olive oil. The walls are papered with thousands of calling cards and the "cash register" is a rolltop desk, into which your money is casually tossed after you've made your purchases.

Highway 29 becomes Main Street in St. Helena. On the left is the **Napa Valley Museum** at 473 Main, with changing exhibits on the valley's history, art and sociology. The **St. Helena Chamber of Commerce** is on the right, at Main and Pope streets. To reach the **Silverado Museum,** turn right at Adams, drive two blocks to the end, then go left on Library Lane.

Return to Main Street (Highway 29) and follow it to Madrona Avenue (the town's last stoplight), go left for three blocks, then right onto Spring Mountain Road. Signs posted by neighbors (to save people the trouble of inquiring) will tell you where you're headed: **Falcon Crest.** The fictional TV winery is **Spring Mountain Vineyards**; you encounter it in the wooded foothills of Spring Mountain, shortly after leaving St. Helena's suburbs.

Beyond the winery, the road winds ever higher, past a few vineyards and other wineries (which require appointments), and eventually down the other side to Santa Rosa. Assuming you prefer to stay in the Napa Valley, return to St. Helena and continue north on Highway 29.

You'll drive through a sheltering canopy of Dutch elms as three of the valley's largest and most historic wineries appear in quick succession: **Beringer Vineyards** with its fabled Rhine House and castle-like **Christian Brothers Greystone Cellars,** both on the left, and then **Charles Krug Winery** on the right. Just beyond Krug is **Markham Winery** on the right, then **St. Clement Vineyards,** in an attractive Victorian just uphill on the left. **Freemark Abbey** comes next, on the right; it's in a busy complex, with a winery, two restaurants and several shops. Beyond, up a narrow lane to the right, is **Folie á Deux Winery**.

Next comes **Vintners Village,** a shopping center on the left, with a raft of tasting rooms, then **Bale Grist Mill State Historic Park** and just beyond, **Bothe-Napa Valley State Park,** both on the left. Opposite the park, follow Larkmead Lane a short distance to **Hans Kornell Champagne Cellars** on the right, then return to Highway 29. Dip briefly to the right onto Dunaweal Lane for **Stonegate Winery**. From Stonegate, you can see Sterling Vineyards, a Moorish-looking winery cresting a hill. We're saving that one for the back nine, since it's nearer the Silverado Trail.

V. Sattui Winery • T ST

1111 White Lane (Highway 29), St. Helena, CA 94574; (707) 963-7774. Daily 9 to 6 (closes at 5 in winter); MC/VISA, AMEX. Most varieties tasted, no fee. Extensive gift, wine logo, deli and specialty foods selection; picnic grounds surrounding winery. Self-guiding tours of the stone wine cellars.

It looks like everyone here's having a picnic—the picnickers at dozens of outdoor tables, visitors thronging the tasting room-gift shop and the employees happily punching cash registers. Sattui is the supermarket of tasting rooms, busy with people tasting this and buying that. On a summer weekend, they're lining the long tasting counter and elbow-to-elbow in the exten-

---

WINERY CODES • T = tasting with no fee; **T$** = fee for tasting; **GT** = guided tours; **GTA** = appointment required for tour; **ST** = self-guiding tours; **CT** = casual tours or a peek into the winery; = picnic area; = separate gift shop or good giftware selection. Price ranges listed in tasting notes are for varietals; jug wines often are available for less. **DINING & LODGINGS • ØØ** = smoke-free establishment; Ø = non-smoking tables or rooms.

sive gift shop and deli.

One gets two quick impressions here, and they're both wrong. 1: The rugged stone castle-like tasting room and winery don't date back to King Arthur's day; they were built in 1976. It took $3 million and a lot of stone to make them look ancient. 2: This isn't a big corporate operation, but a family winery founded by Vittorio Sattui in to 1885. It was closed for several decades after Prohibition, then Vittorio's great-grandson Daryl got things rolling in the 1970s. Despite its apparent size, the winery produces only 30,000 cases a year, and it's all sold in that busy tasting room. Which isn't difficult, since the winery records about a quarter million visitors a year.

Tasting notes: A winery designed with tourists in mind doesn't necessarily make ordinary wine. Sattui has its share of medal winners. The list includes most of the white and red standard-bearers. We particularly like a soft, lush and rich Johannisberg Riesling, so silky it was suggestive of a Chardonnay; and a Suzanne's Vineyard Zinfandel, with great berries, soft and complex with a nice touch of wood. Good chili pepper aromas leaped from a five-year-old Napa Valley Cabernet; it was gentle enough to drink and tannic enough to age. Prices range from $7.25 to the mid-teens. An extensive selection of older wines, mostly Cabernets, is available at appropriately higher prices.

Vintners choice: "Preston Vineyard Cabernet," says the winery's Tom C. Davies. "Since the 1980 vintage, no Preston Vineyards Cab has failed to win one or more gold medals in major competitions."

Bergfeld Winery • T$ GTA ⌅ 🎁

401 South St. Helena Hwy., St. Helena, CA 94574; (707) 963-2335. Daily 10 to 4 (longer hours in summer); MC/VISA. Most varieties tasted for a $3 fee (includes the glass). Nice giftware selection. Picnic tables with mountain and vineyard views; guided tours on Fridays by appointment.

The old Napa Valley Wine Co-op is all dressed up in new clothes, with an airy, modern Swiss chalet-style tasting room, and with two new wine labels. Still functioning as a co-op, it now markets wines under the Bergfeld line and the lesser-priced J. Wile & Sons label. The winery's roots go back to 1885; the Bergfeld name dates from 1891, when the facility was purchased by San Franciscan Robert Bergfeld. It became a co-op in 1935, and now draws its grapes from more than 100 growers.

The facility is bright and cheerful, with a pitched shingled roof, cathedral ceiling, high arched windows and tiled floors. Picnic tables are placed about a lawn and on a back patio. Of interest to tasting room glass collectors: Bergfeld's goblets are quite pleasing, with floral patterns and a subtle tint.

Tasting notes: The prices are modest, even in the upscale Bergfeld line. These include Sauvignon Blanc, Chardonnay, Chenin Blanc, Pinot Noir, Merlot and Cabernet Sauvignon, ranging from $6 to $14. The J. Wile list consists of Sauvignon Blanc, Chardonnay, white Zinfandel and Cabernet Sauvignon, from $6 to $9. Of the Bergfeld line, we liked a spicy Sauvignon Blanc; a nutty, full-flavored Chardonnay and a peppery, full-bodied Merlot. In the Wile wines, we were moved by a fruity and silky Chardonnay and an aromatic, spicy and full-flavored Cab; both go for only $9. Incidentally, the Bergfeld Red Table Wine is one of the best *vin ordinaire* buys in the valley, at $5 a bottle.

Vintners choice: "Merlot and Sauvignon Blanc," says the winery's Denise Boyd. "The Sauvignon is 50 percent barrel fermented and the Merlot grapes come from the best Merlot area in the valley."

Heitz Wine Cellars • T$ GTA

436 South St. Helena Hwy., St. Helena, CA 94574; (707) 963-3542. Daily 11 to 4; no credit cards. Selected wines tasted; $5 tasting fee. Small wine logo selection; tours by appointment on weekdays.

Joe Heitz is a relative newcomer among the valley's "veteran" vintners, arriving in 1961. The no-nonsense winemaker has since made a name for himself as one of the area's premier Cabernet Sauvignon producers, as well as award-grabbing Chardonnay and Zinfandel. The mid-sized facility, producing about 40,000 cases a year, is run by Joe and four family members.

Visitor facilities are rudimentary, consisting of a simple cottage near the winery, where visitors gather around a carved walnut table to sip Joe's latest offerings.

Tasting notes: Only two wines were open when we stopped by, and both were excellent. A three-year-old Chardonnay was lush, spicy and buttery with a soft finish; a four-year-old Zin was soft, lightly spiced with good berry flavor and subtle tannin. We know from previous tastings that the Cabernets are excellent, particularly from Heitz' Martha's Vineyard and Bella Oaks Vineyard. Prices range from $8.75 to the mid-teens; higher for a selection of older Cabs.

Sutter Home Winery • T

277 South St. Helena Hwy. (P.O. Box 248), St. Helena, CA 94574; (707) 963-3104. Daily 10 to 4:30; major credit cards. Most varieties tasted, no fee. Extensive gift selection in new "Victorian Gallery."

You read the Bob Trinchero story in the rosé box in Chapter 3. He developed a blush version of Zin, called it white Zinfandel and catapulted Sutter Home from one of the valley's smallest to one of its largest wineries. Still dominating the white Zin market, it ships about four million cases a year. The winery gets its name from Lina Sutter Leuenberger, daughter of an early Napa Valley vintner. Her husband Emil established Sutter Home at the turn of the century. The Trinchero family purchased it in 1947, and it's still a family-run operation.

Wine tasting occurs in a new Victorian-style hospitality center and mini-museum opened in mid-1990. Graphics, photos and old winery artifacts tell the Sutter Home story. Visitors can browse through assorted gift items and gather at an island tasting bar. The elaborate Victorian home of the original owners, purchased by the Trincheros in 1986, stands nearby on the immaculately landscaped grounds. It isn't open to visitors, but some of its original furnishings are on display in the Victorian Gallery.

Tasting notes: The fabled white Zinfandel *is* nearly white, unlike its pinker counterparts; it's crisp and light and we'd regard it as a good picnic wine. Hearty, full-bodied and serious Zinfandels emerged from here as well, produced mostly from Amador County grapes. We tasted a particularly berry-like and softly tannic four-year-old Amador County Reserve, priced at $9.75. A lighter Zin, which we often use as an everyday dinner wine, goes for around $4.50—a very good buy. Chardonnay, Chenin Blanc, Cabernet

Sauvignon, Triple Cream Sherry and a sweet but light Muscat Alexandria complete the list. Prices stay below $10.

Vintners choice: "Reserve Zinfandel and white Zinfandel," said the winery's Diana Brown—not surprisingly.

Prager Winery and Port Works • T CT ⌶

1281 Lewelling Lane, St. Helena, CA 94574; (707) 963-PORT. Daily 10:30 to 4:30; MC/VISA. Most varieties tasted; no fee. A few wine logo gift items. Informal tours, consisting of a "3.5 minute glance around the winery."

Bewhiskered Jim Prager, who needs only a bourbon complexion to resemble Ernest Hemingway, may greet you halfway up the walk when you approach his battered little winery. If the tasting room isn't crowded—meaning there aren't more than three other people—he'll sit you down in a squeaky old captain's chair and ply you with his Zinfandels, Cabernets and ports. Between sips, you can admire a dusty corkscrew collection and old currency tacked on the walls. Between samples, you can walk two paces to the sink to rinse your glass.

A former insurance broker, Prager began the winery in 1980 as his "midlife crisis." He specializes in ports, 75 percent of his production, and he's grafted some traditional Portuguese vines onto a tiny vineyard in the front yard. His production is small, about 3,600 cases a year.

Tasting notes: A two-year-old Zinfandel was big and full-flavored, yet soft for such a young red. A five-year-old Cabernet Sauvignon, with four years in French oak, had a pleasant chocolatey aroma and complex flavor with high tannin, suitable for laying away. His Petit Syrah Port was rich but not sticky sweet, with a soft tannic nip. A late-harvest Chardonnay was honey-like and nutty, almost like liquefied dried fruit. Prager's not bashful about marketing: "How about two? One to kill and one to look forward to." Prices range from $16 to $30 and he signs each bottle he sells. For those prices, maybe he should include dinner. Are they worth it? Only your palate knows, and you can try before you buy. His stuff is sold only at the winery.

Vintners choice: "Our specialty is port," Prager said simply.

Louis M. Martini Winery • T & T$ GT ⌶

254 South St. Helena Hwy., St. Helena, CA 4574; (707) 963-2736. Daily 10 to 4:30; MC/VISA, AMEX. Most varieties tasted free; a $5 fee for a selection of reserve wines (includes glass). A few wine-logo gift items; picnic area; daily guided tours.

As a teenager, immigrant Louis Martini peddled wines along with clams and mussels on the streets of San Francisco shortly after the 1906 earthquake. He and his parents rented a winery in Pleasanton in 1911, then Louis established a grape products company in the San Joaquin Valley in the middle of Prohibition. After Repeal in 1933, he opened his Napa Valley winery. A founder of the Wine Institute, the "grand old man" was a leading figure in California's wine history until his death in 1974 at the age of 87.

Still family-owned, the winery does about a quarter million cases a year. Louis' original ivy-covered red brick winery still stands alongside Highway 29. It shelters aging cellars and a simple wood-paneled tasting room, trimmed with family history exhibits. Picnic tables rest beneath ancient oaks outside.

Tasting Notes: Several wines can be tasted free, but we recommend buying that $5 logo glass and doing a side-by-side sampling to compare regular releases with reserve wines. It's interesting to check the fruity, soft flavor of a Louis M. Martini Chardonnay ($8.99) with the spicier, more complex and buttery Napa Valley Reserve Chardonnay ($13.20). A smooth, berry-flavored seven-year-old Louis M. Martini Cabernet Sauvignon ($8.99) held up well beside a peppery, powerful eight-year-old Monte Rosso Vineyard Cabernet ($17.20). Although the winery has long been known for its reds, third-generation winemaker Michael Martini also earns recognition and medals for his whites. The list covers most popular varietals including a rarely-produced California Barbera, plus several sherries. Prices are modest for the quality, ranging from $6 to the mid-teens. Older vintages are available at higher prices.

Vintners choice: "Our vineyard-designated selections: Monte Rosso Cabernet, La Loma Pinot Noir, Las Amigas Chardonnay and Los Vinedos del Rio Merlot," says the winery's Bonnie Vanderschoot.

Merryvale Vineyards • T$ GTA

1000 Main St., St. Helena, CA 94574; (707) 963-2225. Daily 10 to 5:30; major credit cards. Most varieties tasted for $3 fee (refunded with purchase). A few gift items. Free Saturday wine seminars by appointment.

Old timers will remember this vine-entwined masonry building as Sunny St. Helena, the winery where Cesare Mondavi got his start shortly after Repeal. In 1986, William Harlan, John Montgomery and the late Peter Stocker, owners of the Napa Valley's posh Meadowood Country Club, bought the old place. They combined it with their already-active Merryvale Vineyards.

The large, uncrowded tasting room, in the heart of the old winery, is one of the most esthetically pleasing in the wine country. It's softly lit by dozens of votive candles, perched on every available barrel head, niche, shelf and unoccupied wine bottle. Although it's above ground, it has the look, aroma and feel of an ancient wine cellar.

Tasting notes: Two labels are offered—moderately-priced Sunny St. Helena wines and the more upscale Merryvale Vineyards line. Tastings are intelligently conducted and—as at Louis Martini—one has the opportunity to compare two styles of the same varietal. Prices range from $7 to the low teens for Sunny St. Helena and $12 and up for Merryvale. In the "Sunny" line, we particularly liked a fruity and soft Gewürztraminer and a young Zinfandel with a proper berry nose and flavor and a crisp tannic finish. Others are Chardonnay, Chenin Blanc, Sauvignon Blanc, Cabernet Sauvignon, a *Nouveau* and Muscat Canelli dessert wine. The Merryvale line is limited to Chardonnay, Cabernet Sauvignon, Meritage White and some remarkably good red blends. A five-year-old Bordeaux style red was soft and full flavored, sort of a Meritage without portfolio. The Starmont Chardonnay was buttery and gently spicy and the Meritage White was medium-bodied, rich and nicely herbal.

Spring Mountain Vineyards • T$ GT$ & GTA

2805 Spring Mountain Rd., St. Helena, CA 94574; (707) 963-5233. Daily 10 to 4:45. Three or more varieties tasted for a $3 fee. Good giftware selection. Free winery tours at 10:30 and 4:30, by appointment only; "Falcon Crest" tour $4, hourly from 11 to 4, no appointment needed.

*Angela's lair in television's **Falcon Crest** was Michael Robbins' stately Victorian home at Spring Mountain Winery.*

Michael Robbins says he just wants to make good wines—which he does—and forget all about that *Falcon Crest* foolishness. But tourists want to see the porch where icy-witted Angela sipped tea and plotted her day's deviltment, and the swimming pool where poor Maggie drowned. So visitors happily pay $4 to tour the exterior of the Robbins' Victorian mansion and landscaped grounds that served as the home of the fictional TV winemaking family.

During the show's run from 1981 to 1987, the production crew, Jane Wyman and other cast members were there only briefly, to film exteriors and establishing shots. The rest was done on a set in Hollywood. Still, fanatical fans would sneak onto the property, hoping for a glimpse or a souvenir. One lady tried to wrestle a piece of furniture off the porch, fell and broke her leg. Another was discovered sitting in the library, waiting for Angela to get home. Robbins once found a party of TV fans skinny-dipping in "Angela's" swimming pool. (Looking for the ring?)

This grand estate was established in 1889 by Tibercio Parrott, who dabbled in everything from olives to winemaking until his death in 1899. The place remained vacant for decades, then San Francisco businessman Robbins bought the property in 1973, refurbished the mansion and built a winery. Lorimar TV producers showed up in 1981, wanting to use the site for a series. The show's name comes from the outline of a parrot in a stained glass window on the mansion (symbolizing the Parrott family), which a Lorimar official mistook for a falcon.

Spring Mountain's tasting room is in a attractive winery above the mansion. That, too, may look familiar. Robbins styled it after the ornate architecture of Disneyland's Main Street. A gift and sales shop are in a nearby cottage.

Tasting notes: The list is short and excellent: Cabernet Sauvignon, Chardonnay, Pinot Nor and Sauvignon Blanc, with prices ranging from $10.50 into the twenties. An eight-year-old Cab was smooth with properly married flavors, like an aged Bordeaux. A seven-year-old Chardonnay that spent six months on oak was nice and silky, with hints of spice and wood. The Sauvignon Blanc was unusually buttery and complex, with a nice crisp finish. Yes, Robbins did yield to temptation and produce a Falcon Crest line. These wines weren't being tasted when we visited.

Vintners choice: "Our award-winning Cabernet Sauvignon and Chardonnay never fail to win great applause," boasted the winery's Kathleen Hamberis.

Beringer Vineyards • T & T$

2000 Main St., St. Helena, CA 94574; (707) 963-7115. Daily 10 to 6; 9 to 5 in winter; major credit cards. Free tasting following tour; tasting of reserve wines in Founders Room for a fee. Extensive giftware selection. Tours every half hour.

One of the valley's vintage landmarks, the winery was founded in the 1870s by immigrant brothers Frederick and Jacob Beringer. It remained in the family until Nestlè Chocolate (aka Wine World Estates) bought it in 1969. Its centerpiece is the stunning half-timbered Rhine House, an elaborate mansion styled after the brothers' German home. It now accommodates the gift shop and tasting room and it's easily one of the most gorgeous hospitality centers in all of California's wine country.

Tours begin near the original winery, an elaborate stone facade over caves dug by Chinese laborers into the steep slopes of Spring Mountain. They fill up quickly in the summer so get your wine label "ticket" as soon as you get there; it's free. The place lures about 200,000 visitors a year.

Although most wine production occurs across the highway, an intelligent commentary provides a good understanding of the process as you tour the ancient cellars. Most of the caves have been shored up and gunnited; however, one has been left undisturbed since 1937. With lichen-stained ceilings and tiers of bottles covered with decades of dust and cobwebs, it suggests a wonderfully spooky Edgar Allan Poe scene.

Tasting notes: Three gratis samples are offered at the tour's end. We sipped a nice, fruit-busy Sauvignon Blanc; a five-year-old Cabernet Sauvignon that was a typical Bordeaux blend, with a good peppery nose, softly complex flavors and a hint of wood; and a fruity and slightly sweet but not sticky Gewürztraminer. The Beringer list covers most varietals, with prices ranging from $7.50 to the high teens. Serious sippers can sample special reserves, mostly Cabernets, in the Founders Room for $2 to $3 per two-ounce sample.

Vintners choice: "Chardonnay and Cabernet, reserve and estate," says the winery's Bill Knox. "There's wonderful fruit in both."

Christian Brothers Greystone Cellars • T & T$ GT

2555 Main St., St. Helena, CA 94574; (707) 963-0763. Daily 10 to 4; MC/VISA, AMEX. Free wine tasting after tour; barrel tasting for $5 fee. Extensive gift shop collection. Frequent tours daily from 10 to 4.

This imposing structure has passed through several hands since it was built in 1888, and it may pass to another by the time you read this. Castle-like Greystone, measuring 60 by 400 feet, was the world's largest stone wine cellar when it was constructed by multi-millionaire gold baron William Bowers Bourn. The Christian Brothers, a Catholic teaching order, bought the winery in 1950 and turned it into one of the valley's largest producers. It was sold in the late 1980s to Heublein, Inc., and rumor has it that the baronial winery is on the market again.

The tour, like that of Beringer's next door, offers a mix of history and wine-making lore. It also fills up quickly in summer, so get your spot early. Good graphics and historical exhibits enliven the 40-minute stroll through this medieval-style wine castle. It ends with a tasting in a large hospitality facility. Make it a point to view the large corkscrew and wine paraphernalia collection, gathered by the Christian Brothers' much-venerated winemaker, Brother Timothy.

Tasting notes: Four wines are poured at the end of the tour and we view them thusly: Sauvignon Blanc—pleasant herbal-fruit nose and nice citrusy flavor; white Zinfandel—typical of the type with light raspberry flavor and thin finish; Cabernet Sauvignon—nice peppery nose, full-flavored yet soft with gentle tannin; Muscat de Frontignon—caramel color, brandy nose, rich nutty flavor approaching a cream sherry. Prices are moderate, ranging from $4.25 to the mid-teens. The extensive list covers most varietals and includes sherries and brandies. One can taste wines still aging in their barrels at a facility off the gift shop, for a $5 fee.

Vintners choice: "Cabernet, Chardonnay, white Zinfandel and Sauvignon Blanc—all from premium Napa Valley grapes," says the winery's Mary Keogh.

Charles Krug Winery • T & T$ GT

2800 North St. Helena Hwy., St. Helena, CA 94574; (707) 963-5057. Daily 9:30 to 4:45; MC/VISA, AMEX. Free tasting following tour; also a fee tasting for $3 (includes glass). Good giftware selection in separate gift shop. "Historical Tours" hourly on the three-quarter hour from 10:45 to 3:45.

The venerable Charles Krug winery offers choices: You can take a tour, followed by a gratis tasting. Or you can march right through the large gift shop to a tasting room in the rear of the hospitality center and sip wines for a fee. The glass you get to keep is a nice-sized one, incidentally. The tour through the massive old stone winery focuses mostly on history, since most wine production is conducted in newer facilities.

Despite the Krug name, the winery is the bastion of the Peter Mondavi family. It was established by Charles Krug in 1861 as the valley's first major winery, and it was operated by his heirs until Prohibition. Cesare Mondavi bought the empty facility in 1946 and ran it with his sons Peter and Robert until his death in 1959. After a family spat in the 1960s, Robert went his own way to start his down-valley winery; Peter is now Krug's president.

Tasting notes: The Mondavis pioneered cold fermentation and used the valley's first bladder press to produce crisp, fruity whites. It's evident in the citrusy, light and subtly acidic Sauvignon Blanc and fragrant, soft Chenin Blanc. A two-year-old Zinfandel was gentle with medium body, an herbal nose and light finish; a five-year-old Cabernet Sauvignon aged in American oak had a proper chili pepper nose and spicy, berry-like flavor with light tannin. Prices range from $6.75 to the mid-teens; higher for vintage Cabernets.

Markham Winery • T ST

2812 North St. Helena Hwy. (P.O. Box 636), St. Helena, CA 94574; (707) 963-5292. Daily 11 to 5; major credit cards. Selected wines tasted, no fee. Good selection of gift items; self guiding tours in balconies above the winery.

The old stone Markham winery should have a new look by the time this book reaches your hands. You may be greeted by fresh landscaping and a new gift shop and tasting room, instead of bulldozed earth and the sounds of construction.

Dating from 1876, the original winery was built of locally-quarried stone by a Bordeaux Frenchman named Laurent. It later became a small co-op. Advertising executive Bruce Markham bought the crumbling old structure in 1978, overhauled it and started making wine. Present Markham owners Bryan Del Bondio and Bob Foley are going a big step further, adding extensive wings onto the venerable structure. Mid-1992 is the target for completion.

Tasting notes: "Overall excellent quality" reads the note at the bottom of our wine-splotched tasting sheet. To be more specific: Sauvignon Blanc—fruity nose and taste, full-mouthed and crisp; Chardonnay—excellent, spicy, nutty with big grape flavor; Muscat Blanc—fruity nose, rich yet light; Cabernet Sauvignon—soft, spicy and pleasant, chili pepper nose and flavor, nippy tannic finish with a soft touch of wood. Prices range from $8 to the twenties.

St. Clement Vineyards • T GTA

2867 North St. Helena Hwy. (P.O. Box 261), St. Helena, CA 94574; (707) 963-7221. Daily 10 to 4; MC/VISA, AMEX. All varieties tasted, no fee. A few wine-logo items; guided tours by appointment.

An immaculately restored Victorian home with a witch's hat tower houses the tasting room of this old-new winery. Old because it was the eighth in the valley, bonded in 1879; new because it was re-opened by Dr. William Casey in the mid-1970s after a long period of dormancy. In the interim, the house served as a physicians' home and office. The winery, once owned by Spring Mountain's Michael Robbins, is now held by principles of Japan's Sapporo Beer Company.

The main winery, a rugged stone-faced affair, is tucked against the hill behind the house, reached by appointment-only tours. Some of the aging cellars are in the basement of the Victorian home. The tasting room, flawlessly restored, went public at the start of this decade.

Tasting notes: Prices range from $10 to $18 for St. Clement's short list. We tasted the lot and they were fine: Sauvignon Blanc—nice fruity-veggie nose, fruit-spice flavor, light acid; Chardonnay—very buttery, spicy-nutty, crisp finish; Merlot—lush, spicy nose, big berry flavor and tannic finish, to drink now or age; Cabernet Sauvignon (five years old)—wonderful nose, spicy and berry-like, soft tannins, drink it or age it.

Freemark Abbey Winery • T$ GTA

3022 North St. Helena Hwy., St. Helena, CA 94574; (707) 963-9694. Daily 10 to 4:30; Major credit cards. All current releases tasted for $5 fee (includes glass). Gift selection in tasting room; also gift shops nearby. Picnic area for winery patrons. Tours at 2 p.m. by appointment.

One of the first tourist-oriented facilities in the valley, Freemark Abbey dates from the mid-1960s. The complex includes a gift shop, candle shop and two restaurants. This doesn't detract from the wine quality, or from its history. The original winery was built in 1886 by Josephine Tychson, California's first woman vintner.

A seven-man partnership that re-established the winery in the 1960s still runs things today. The restaurants and gift shops in this attractive, wooded complex are leased out to others.

Tasting notes: Current releases are Chardonnay, Johannisberg Riesling, Cabernet Sauvignon and Cabernet Bochè (from the John Bochè vineyard near Rutherford). The Chardonnay had a fruity aroma, with a very spicy nutty-wood flavor; nice stuff! A four-year-old Cab was medium-bodied, with a great peppery nose and light, spicy flavor. The five-year-old Bochè offered a nice balance of berries and wood, with gentrified tannin at the end. Prices run from $8.50 into the twenties; older Chardonnays and Cabs are available at higher prices.

Vintners choice: "Bottle aged Chardonnay and Edelwein Gold, a late-harvest, botrytis Johannisberg Riesling," says Freemark's Marybeth Egner.

Folie á Deux Winery • T GTA

3070 North St. Helena Hwy., St Helena, CA 94574; (707) 963-1160. Daily 11 to 5; most major credit cards. Selected wines tasted; no fee. A few giftware and logo items. Picnic tables near tasting room; guided tours by appointment.

Is it shared fantasy or pleasant reality? You're sitting in a comfortable chair, sipping good wine in a tasting room that more resembles an early American living room, being watched by a window-sitting cat with a Cheshire grin. You pick up the bottle and rotate it slowly in your hand. The label is an ink-blot test, suggesting dancing maidens in a scene from the fourth act of Shakespeare's *The Winter's Tale.* "I'll have another flagon of wine, please. Why is that cat staring at me? Am I in his chair?"

Folie á Deux was founded in 1981 by mental health professionals Evie and Larry Dizmang. They bought an old sheep ranch with the intention of making wine, and two thoughts struck them at the time: 1. A person has to be crazy to go into the wine business. 2. Wine brings out the celebrative spirit in people. Folie á Deux, then, is not a name borrowed from a Bordeaux chateau; it translates as "a shared fantasy or delusion by two closely-linked people."

The tasting room in an old yellow cottage provides quiet escape from the busy Napa Valley, if not from reality. The grounds, shaded by oaks and poplars, still has that bucolic ranch feel. Fortunately, the sheep are gone.

Tasting notes: The Dizmang's winemaker Rich Tracy (not Dick Tracy; this is reality) crafts small lots of Chardonnay, Chenin Blanc and Cabernet Sauvignon. Specialties include Muscat á Deux dessert wine and a *methodè champenoise* sparkling wine called—what else?—Fantasie. A double award-winning Chenin was fittingly fruity, full-flavored and crisp; a four-year-old Cab had nice cherry-berry flavors and a light tannic finish. The Muscat á Deux was one of the better dessert wines we've tasted, surprisingly crisp and light, despite its rich flavor.

Vintners Village • T$ ⌅

3111 N. North St. Helena Hwy., St. Helena, CA 95474; (707) 963-4082. Daily 10 to 5; MC/VISA, AMEX. Several tasting rooms with wines offered from local wineries; tasting fee $5.

Not a winery, Vintners Village is a collection of tasting rooms, plus a deli, restaurant and several boutiques and galleries.

Hanns Kornell Winery • T GT

1091 Larkmead Lane (P.O. Box 249), St. Helena, CA 95474; (707) 963-1237. Daily 10 to 4:30; most major credit cards. Selected sparkling wines tasted after tour, no fee. A few wine logo items. Guided tours about every 20 minutes, from 10 to 3:45.

What's the farthest one can get from a Nazi concentration camp? How about to a successful champagnery in California? Hanns Kornell made that remarkable transition, fleeing Nazi Germany in 1939 and arriving flat broke in New York. He managed to work his way to California and, after years of saving and winemaking, opened his own sparkling wine facility in 1952. Now eighty or so, he still keeps his hand in things but leaves most of the work to daughter Paula and other family members.

Kornell's frequently-departing tours teach you everything you ever wanted to know about making sparkling wine. You then return to a simple, cottage style hospitality center to put to the taste what you've learned.

Tasting notes: We've long felt that Kornell's sparklers were among the best made for their price—under $12. We liked daughter Paula's crisp, fruitier versions even better. The Hanns Kornell Brut, with Pinot Noir and Pinot Blanc, revealed good grape character and a near-dry crispiness. Extra Dry (that wonderful winetalk antithesis) has a touch of sweet, while keeping that fruit flavor. A Muscat Alexandria dessert wine was rich and big-bodied, full of the grape with an almost liqueur character.

Stonegate Winery • T & T$ GTA ⌅

1183 Dunaweal Lane, Calistoga, CA 94515; (707) 942-6500. Daily 10:30 to 4:30; MC/VISA, AMEX. Most varieties tasted free on weekdays, $1.25 fee on weekends and holidays (includes glass). A few wine-related giftwares. Small picnic area; guided tours by appointment.

Jim and Barbara Spaulding started this small family winery in 1973 and have gradually built up to a 4,500-case production. Son David is now involved in the operation. Stainless steel tanks sit outdoors beside a vineyard; casks and other wine-creating gear are tucked inside a modest winery structure.

The tasting room is reached via a small stone arch, which also appears on the label. It's friendly and cozy inside. A sign advises: "Limit 12 persons; if the door is locked, it should be a short wait." The picnic area consists of a single table. As we said, it's a cozy, friendly place.

Tasting notes: Cabernet Sauvignon, Merlot, Chardonnay, Sauvignon Blanc and a late harvest blend comprise the list. Prices range from $12.50 to $14. A five-year-old estate Cabernet had a spicy nose and subtly peppery taste, rich in berries with soft tannins. The Merlot, four years old, was full-flavored, dusky and mellow—the pleasant taste of an old wine cellar. The Late Harvest, a partly botrytised Sauvignon-Semillon blend, had a nice aroma of new mown hay and a honey-toasty flavor, sweet yet crisp.

LEARNING THE WINE GAME

You say you can't tell a Chardonnay from a Charbono? Are you taunted by vintage verbosity? Do you yearn to get comfortable with a wine list?

Special high-intensity courses sponsored by the Napa Valley Wine Library Association take the mystery out of the grape. They teach enthusiasts how wine is made, and how to evaluate and appreciate it.

Classes are conducted by Napa Valley winemakers and other industry professionals, beginning on Friday afternoon and continuing through the weekend. Held in and about St. Helena, these sessions feature wine sampling, vineyard and winery tours and wine-tasting meals.

Introductory Wine Weekend courses focus on sensory evaluation, grape varieties, wine production and wine with food. They include field trips to vineyards and wineries, wine-tasting luncheons and panel discussions about wine consumerism.

Advanced Wine Weekend courses are for serious aficionados. They feature tastings from undiscovered wineries, panel discussions on current wine issues, consumer trends and surveys of Napa Valley appellations and their grape varieties. Wine luncheons and dinners are included.

The association also sponsors one-day seminars with tastings of specific grape varieties, and field trips during the crush.

Association membership is $20 per year; it includes a periodic wine information newsletter and access to the 5,000-volume Napa Valley Wine Library collection, housed in the St. Helena Public Library. Class prices are $275 for advanced and $175 for introductory courses, and $95 for one-day seminars. For information, contact the Napa Valley Wine Library Association, P.O. Box 207, St. Helena, CA 94574; (707) 963-3535.

CALISTOGA-SILVERADO TRAIL WINERY TOUR • Assuming you returned to Highway 29 and continued north, you're now in **Calistoga**, trying to choose between a mud bath and another tasting room. Plan plenty of time in this neat old community at the foot of St. Helena; it offers many diversions. We'll cover most of them in the "Beyond the vineyards" department below, after we've finished with our final Napa Valley winery selections.

From the western edge of Calistoga, drive north on Highway 128 as if you're Geyserville-bound. After about 1.8 miles, turn right onto Tubbs Lane and follow it past **Old Faithful Geyser** (the signs won't let you miss it) and thence to **Chateau Montelena.** It's reached by a short, twisting drive that takes you quickly into a wooded thicket.

Continue a short distance on Tubbs Lane to Highway 29 and follow it south a mile, branching to your left onto the Silverado Trail. After a bit more than a mile, turn right onto Dunaweal Lane, then right again into the temple-like **Clos Pegase.** Just below, on the left, is **Sterling Vineyards,** crowning a hill and reached by a sky tram.

Return with us now to Silverado and you'll see Spanish-style **Cuvaison Winery** on the left. Two miles more, and you reach tiny **Wermuth Winery**; look for the small sign on the left. Another mile or so takes you to **Casa Nuestra,** a bit off the highway on your right then, after a mile and a half, you encounter **Napa Creek Winery,** also on the right.

Chateau Montelena Winery • T$ GTA

1429 Tubbs Lane, Calistoga, CA 94515; (707) 942-5105. Daily 10 to 4; MC/VISA. Selected wines tasted for $5 (credited toward wine purchase). Some wine-oriented gift items. Guided tours by appointment at 11 and 2.

Sheltering trees, a mini-medieval castle and an Oriental lake provide one of the valley's most serene winery retreats. It's a place of discoveries, where visitors are invited to stroll the perimeter of Jade Lake, cross bright red arched bridges to tiny islands (when they're not occupied), converse with ducks, encounter stone knights guarding adjacent vineyard and pause under the quietude of Japanese maples.

Its mixed heritage comes from two sources. In the 1880s, Alfred L. Tubbs, entrepreneur and state senator, hired a French architect to build a classic winery chateau, really more of a castle, with turrets and gun ports. Like many, it fell to ruin after Prohibition. The property was bought by a wealthy Chinese, Yort Franks, in the 1950s. He didn't revive the winery but he created an Asian showplace with a lake reminiscent of the old country. An investment group bought the place in 1972 and resumed making wine.

Tasting notes: The wines were uniformly excellent. We tasted a fine two-year-old Chardonnay focused more on the fruit than spice and oak. A ten-year-old Cabernet Sauvignon was aged to near perfection, smooth yet still peppery and complex, with a soft oak-tannin finish. A young Johannisberg Riesling, available only at the winery, was light and fruity with a hint of sugar. The Cabs and Chards have won scores of awards, including a 1976 Chardonnay victory over tough French competitors; it was so significant that it was reported in *Time Magazine.*

Vintners choice: Brazenly boasted Montelena's Eric Swan: "Our Chardonnay and Cabernet Sauvignon have been generally reckoned among the very best for nearly two decades."

Clos Pegase • T$ GTA

1060 Dunaweal Lane, Calistoga, CA 94515; (707) 942-4901. Daily 10:30 to 5. Selected wines tasted for $3 fee (includes glass). A few wine logo items. Guided tours by appointment; wine and art lectures the third Saturday of each month, by appointment.

When multi-millionaire publisher Jan Shrem decided to build a shrine to wine and art in the 1980s, he sought logical sources. From Beaulieu's honored Andre Tchelistcheff he requested winemaking advice, and he asked the San Francisco Museum of Modern Art to sponsor an architectural competition. Tchelistcheff recommended Bill Pease as a winemaker and the museum selected Princeton architect Michael Graves to design a "temple of wine."

The result: Clos Pegase wines consistently win awards and Graves' impressive salmon-colored post-modern Greek-Roman-Aztec wine temple is the darling of new-wave architects. It's at once imposing and stark—a towering, columned presence enclosing a simple courtyard. A giant mural of Bacchus rises behind the counter in the large tasting room, taunting you to another sip. Although the huge winery appears to stand alone above the vineyards, it's actually built against a small, steep hillside with caves cut into the cliff. They can be seen on reservation-only tours.

Tasting notes: A Sauvignon Blanc was so lush and spicy it could have passed for a Chardonnay, while a Los Carneros Chardonnay was fruity and honey-like, with little spice, as if the two had switched roles. Perhaps the best wine was a three-year-old Cabernet Franc with a touch of Merlot, berry-like and spicy with soft tannins. Prices range from $9.50 to the high teens.

Sterling Vineyards • T$ ST

1111 Dunaweal Lane (P.O. Box 365), Calistoga, CA 94515; (707) 942-4219. Daily 10:30 to 4:30; MC/VISA, AMEX. Tram ride $5 (includes tasting of three wines; $2 credited toward wine purchase). Extensive gift and book selection. Self-guiding tours.

Sterling gleams from a hillock among the vines hill like a misplaced Moorish monastery. It's reached in rather novel fashion: one buys a $5 sky tram ticket and rides above tawny, tilted meadows and oak clusters to this "winery in the sky." Once there, the Moorish impression continues. Sterling is a gleaming collection of white stucco walls, sunny patios, stainless steel tanks and dimly-lit wine cellars that seem older than they are. The self-guiding tour is among the best of the California wine country, adorned with explanatory graphics, historic wine art reproductions and wonderful quotes about the grape. Never mind the sky bucket access; once on top, the place exudes an aura of artistic class.

After touring, one adjourns to a spacious tasting room or outside terrace, where three wines are served. An adjacent gift shop offers a good selection of wineware, books and such.

The winery was created in 1969 by four owners of a San Francisco-based paper company, then it became part of the Coca-Cola Company's wine venture in 1977. It was sold in 1983 to Seagram Classics Wine Company, the present owners.

Tasting notes: Sauvignon Blanc, Chardonnay, Cabernet Blanc, Merlot, Cabernet Sauvignon and Pinot Noir comprise the list. Prices range from $8 to the mid-teens; more for reserve and vineyard-designated wines. Our notes on the three tasted wines: Sauvignon Blanc—lush with soft fruit, almost a Chardonnay character; Chardonnay—spicy, complex and mouth-filling, an excellent wine; Cabernet—huge peppery nose, lush and spicy flavor with soft wood at the end.

Cuvaison Winery • T$ GTA

4550 Silverado Trail (P.O. Box 384), Calistoga, CA 94515; (707) 942-6266. Daily 10 to 5; MC/VISA, AMEX. Most varieties tasted for $2.50 fee (includes glass). Good giftware selection. Shaded picnic area near tasting room; guided tours by appointment.

We've always regarded Cuvaison as the little jewel of the Napa Valley. It's a pleasing, Spanish mission-style winery with a matching tasting room, sheltered by ancient oaks. The tasting room is a comfortable space, trimmed in oak, roomy yet busy with bottles, cases and giftwares. A woodsy picnic area on a downslope offers views of vineyards and the distant Mayacamas Mountains.

Cuvaison, which is the French term for fermenting red wines on their skins, was started in 1969 by two engineers, who sold it to New York publisher Oakleigh Thorne in 1974. It's presently owned by the wealthy Schmidheiny family, major stockholders of Swissair; they purchased it in 1979.

Tasting notes: Four wines make up the list, and they've received considerable recognition in the wine world: Chardonnay, Cabernet Sauvignon, Merlot and Zinfandel. Prices range from $13.50 to the mid-twenties. Cuvaison's style is light and fresh, evident in a soft, buttery Chard and a fresh, berry-filled Zin. A three-year old Cab was a bit more assertive, an outstanding wine with chili peppers and berries, hints of wood and tannin; good for drinking or laying away.

Wermuth Winery • T CT

3942 Silverado Trail, Calistoga, CA 94515; (707) 942-5924. Daily 10 to 5; MC/VISA. Most varieties tasted, no fee. Casual tours (a peek into the winery); small picnic area.

This tiny winery is housed in a couple of pink corrugated sheds beside Ralph and Smitty Wermuth's home on the upside of the Silverado Trail. One of the valley's smallest wineries open to drop-in visitors, it produces about 4,000 cases a year. Tastings are conducted in a properly dusty barrel aging room. Pipe-smoking, soft-spoken Ralph, who started the winery about ten years ago, will sign your purchase.

Tasting notes: Prices are $8, $8.50 and $9.50 for Wermuth's three wines. Sauvignon Blanc—light and fruity, crisp acidic finish; dry Colombard—spicy nose, hint of licorice and peppermint in the flavor, interesting but not awesome; Napa Valley Gamay—nice berry nose, soft and light flavor like a *nouveau.* "It goes well with chocolates," Ralph says, offering a tin of Hershey's kisses. He was right.

Casa Nuestra • T GTA

3473 Silverado Trail, St. Helena, CA 94574; (707) 963-5783. Friday-Sunday 11 to 5; MC/VISA. Most varieties tasted. A few wine-related gift items. Shaded picnic area; group tours by appointment.

"Step into the house and I'll pour you a glass of wine." This is the message you perceive, and not subliminally, when you drop into this little yellow cottage. Once a farmhouse, it's now Casa Nuestra's tasting room, complete with fireplace and easy chairs, where you sit to sip your wine. The name, appropriately, is Spanish for "our house."A tree-shaded picnic area, complete with hammock, reinforces the laid-back, down-home impression.

The winery was bonded in 1980 by former civil rights attorney Gene Kirkham and his wife Cody. The San Francisco-born Kirkham became fed up with the pin-stripped city life, so he bought this small farm, grew a Mormon beard and started making wine. Learning the trade by trial and error, consulting county farm advisors and friendly neighbor vintners, he and his wife have become what the local paper once described as "happy farmers."

Tasting notes: No, Tinto isn't the Lone Ranger's effeminate Indian companion. It's Casa Nuestra's red blend, made from a polyglot of grapes: Zinfandel, Cabernet, Gamay, Pinot Noir, Mondeuse, Carignan, Alicante and possibly Pfeffer, coexisting in a tiny vineyard. Our sample suggested a big Chianti, with lots of berries and spice yet curiously gentle; it has won a couple of gold medals. Others on the list are a Dry Chenin Blanc, crisp and fruity and nicely tart; Johannisberg Riesling, off dry yet with nice acid; a sweet Chenin Blanc, obviously fruity and rich; and Cabernet Franc, a lively, spicy wine with big berry flavor and a light finish. Prices range from $7 to $12.72.

Napa Creek Winery • T CT

1001 Silverado Trail, St. Helena, CA 94574; (707) 963-9456. Daily 10:30 to 4:30; MC/VISA, AMEX. Most varieties tasted, no fee. A few wine-related gift items. Casual tours.

The breezeway through Napa Creek's small masonry winery once held sides of beef suspended from hooks; this facility began life as a meat packing plant. When Jack and Judy Schulze turned it into a winery in 1980, it suited their needs just fine. Packing plants are designed to be kept cool, so they're ideal places for producing and aging wines. Fortunately, this one smells like a winery, not like a meat factory.

A simple tasting table is set up amidst barrels and boxes. The winery "tour" consists of walking down that breezeway from the parking lot to the tasting area.

Tasting notes: We started with a barrel fermented Chardonnay that was more fruity than herbal, with a nice buttery texture and light finish. A Johannisberg Riesling was semi-dry with a hint of spice. Merlot was peppery and full of berries, soft with a gentle tannic finish; an excellent wine. Flavors of a decade-old Cabernet were nicely merged, with lots of berries, touches of spice and soft tannin. Prices range from $8.50 to $20.

Vintners choice: "A recent Chardonnay that won a gold in a major New York competition, and our Merlot," reports Jack.

THE BEST OF THE BUNCH

The best wine buys • Sutter Home Winery, Louis M. Martini, Christian Brothers Greystone Cellars, Charles Krug Winery, Freemark Abbey Winery and Casa Nuestra.

The most attractive wineries • V. Sattui Winery, Spring Mountain Vineyards, Beringer Vineyards, Christian Brothers Greystone Cellars, Chateau Montelena, Clos Pegase, Sterling Vineyards and Cuvaison Winery.

The most interesting tasting rooms • Bergfeld Winery, Sutter Home Winery, Merryvale Vineyards, Beringer Vineyards, Folie á Deux Winery and Clos Pegase.

The funkiest tasting rooms • Prager Winery and Port Works, and Casa Nuestra.

The best gift shops • V. Sattui Winery, Sutter Home Winery, Beringer Vineyards, Christian Brothers Greystone Cellars, Charles Krug Winery, Freemark Abbey Winery and Sterling Vineyards.

The nicest picnic areas • V. Sattui Winery, Cuvaison Winery, Freemark Abbey Winery and Casa Nuestra.

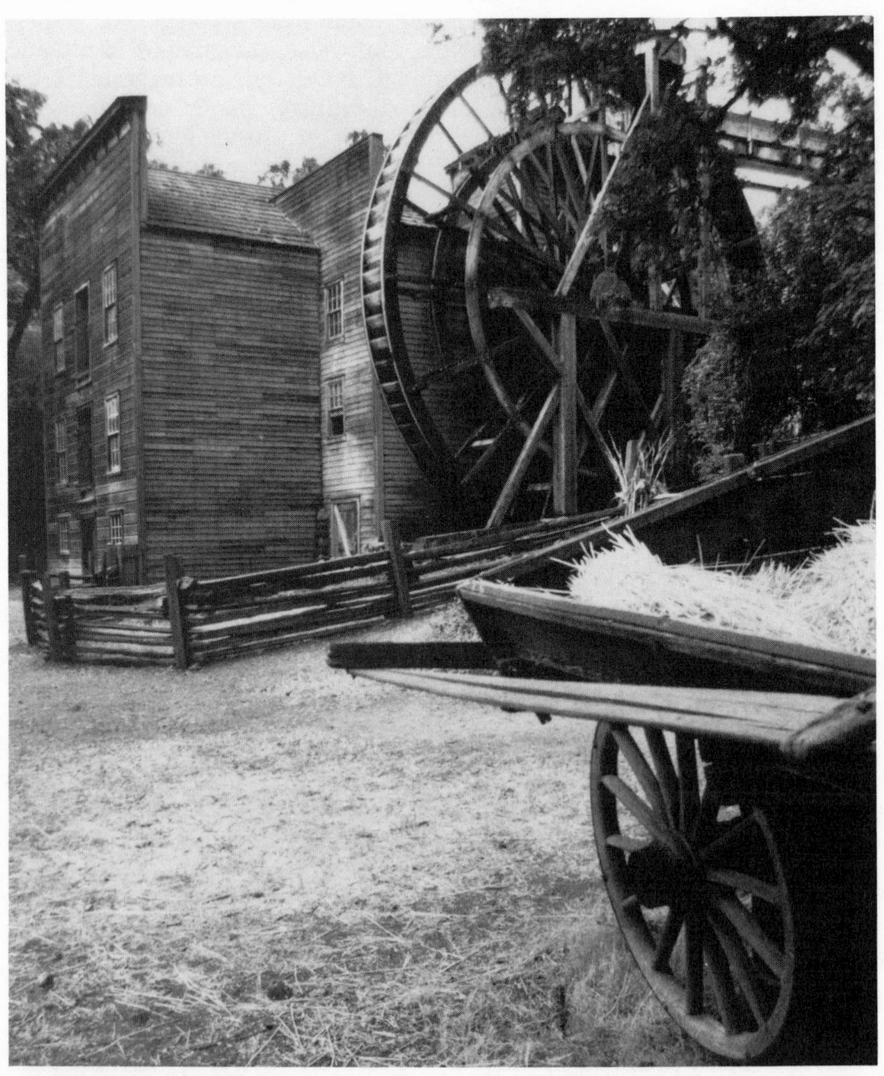

Dr. Edward Bale's grist mill ground flour for the Napa Valley's earliest settlers. The 1846 mill is now a state historic park.

The best tours • Spring Mountain Vineyards (guided winery and "Falcon Crest" tours), Beringer Vineyards (guided), Christian Brothers Greystone Cellars (guided), Hanns Kornell Champagne Cellars (guided, sparkling wine) and Sterling Vineyards (self-guiding).

BEYOND THE VINEYARDS

Up Valley offers more non-winery attractions than the lower end. They're focused mostly around Calistoga, which was a spa before the valley became America's best known wine-producing region.

St. Helena has its share of lures as well, including the **Napa Valley Museum** and **Silverado Museum** (listed below). If you like scenery with a twist (in the roads), follow Spring Mountain Road northwest from St. Helena until it dizzily tops the Mayacamas ridge. After it bumps into Calistoga Road, turn right and follow that north. It blends into Petrified Forest Road and gets you to Calistoga.

In case you didn't visit **Angwin** in the previous chapter, take Deer Park Road east from St. Helena. It's a quaint little Seventh-Day Adventist town and home to **Pacific Union College.** You can get great health foods at the **College Market** but no wine; Angwin is a dry town. From here, continue north on Howell Mountain Road into bucolic **Pope Valley**, an hidden enclave of vineyards and high meadows rimmed by wooded mountains. Chiles-Pope Valley Road loops south and then west, back toward the Napa Valley.

As you drive North Highway 29 from St. Helena to Calistoga, visit the restored water wheel-driven grist mill at **Bale Grist Mill State Historic Park.** Just above is **Bothe-Napa Valley State Park,** offering swimming, picnicking, camping and a good assortment of hiking trails. A particularly nice—if occasionally steep—hike is from the Bothe-Napa Valley picnic area to the Grist Mill; it's just under two miles.

High-living Mormon entrepreneur Sam Brannan made Calistoga famous when he opened a spa, then he built a railroad to Napa to bring in the tourists. Those rails still exist (traveled part-way by the Napa Valley Wine Train), and the town continues to be a mecca for fans of mud baths and mineral water hot tubs. Resort operators tout the supposed therapeutic value of Calistoga's mineral water, neck-deep mud baths and "European body wraps" to "purge your skin of toxins and restore its elasticin." (These aren't endorsements; we're merely quoting from brochures.) Calistoga's spas are listed below, under "Up Valley attractions & activities."

If you'd rather drink mineral water than sit in it, you can get samples of **Crystal Geyser's** product—straight or flavored—at 501 Washington Street. Calistoga Mineral Water Company also is located here, on the Silverado Trail at the edge of town, but it has no public facilities. If you prefer more kick to you fizz, **Napa Valley Brewing Company** operates a microbrewery at in the old water tower of the Calistoga Inn at 1250 Lincoln Avenue (see listing under lodgings).

Calistoga is busy with shops and boutiques. Several are clustered in the refurbished **Depot Restaurant and Shops.** Others are strung along Lincoln Avenue, the main drag. Specifics of these Calistoga tourist lures are listed under "Up Valley attractions" below: **Petrified Forest, Old Faithful Geyser** and the **Sharpsteen Museum and Sam Brannan cottage.**

A seven-mile drive into the flanks of Mount St. Helena on Highway 29 takes you past the **Calistoga Glider Port** to **Robert Louis Stevenson State Park.** It's undeveloped, but fun to explore (see box). If you press north on Route 29, you'll witness a lot of mountain scenery and eventually wind up in Lake County. It's home to huge Clear Lake and several wineries described in Chapter 2. Another pretty route out of Calistoga is Highway 128 northwest, which delivers you to Mendocino County and its wineries, also covered in Chapter 2.

Up Valley activities & attractions

(Also check Down Valley listings in Chapter 5)

Bicycle rentals • Jules Culver Bicycles, 1227 Lincoln Ave., Calistoga, CA 94515, 942-0421; and St. Helena Cyclery, 1156 Main St., St. Helena, CA 94574; 963-7736.

Glider rides • Calistoga Gliders, 1546 Lincoln Ave., Calistoga, CA 94515; 942-5000.

Hiking, swimming • Bothe-Napa Valley State Park, 3801 North St. Helena Hwy., Calistoga, CA 94515; 942-4575.

Hot air balloon rides • Once In a Lifetime Balloon Co., 1458 Lincoln Ave. (The Depot), Calistoga, CA 94515; 942-6541.

Hot springs, mud baths & spas • **With lodging:** Calistoga Spa Hot Springs at 1006 Washington St., 942-6269; Dr. Wilkinson's Hot Springs at 1507 Lincoln Ave., 942-4102; Golden Haven Spa at 1713 Lake St., 942-6793; Indian Springs Resort at 1712 Lincoln Ave., 942-4913; Calistoga Village Inn and Spa at 1880 Lincoln Ave., (800) 543-1923 or (707) 942-4636; and Nance's Hot Springs at 1614 Lincoln Ave., 942-6211. **Without lodging:** International Spa at 1300 Washington St., 942-6122; and Lincoln Avenue Spa at 1339 Lincoln Ave., 942-5296.

Museums, historic exhibits & attractions •

Bale Grist Mill State Historic Park, Highway 29, three miles north of St. Helena; 963-2236. Daily 9 to 5; admission fee. Restored grist mill built by Dr. Edward T. Bale in 1846.

Calistoga Depot, 1458 Lincoln Ave., Calistoga, CA 94515; one of California's oldest train depots, built in 1868 for Sam Brannan's Napa Valley Railroad; a state historic landmark, now restored as a themed shopping complex.

Napa Valley Museum, 473 Main St., St. Helena, CA 94574; 963-7411. Monday-Friday 9 to 12 and 1 to 4. Changing exhibits of the valley's history, art and sociology.

Old Faithful Geyser, 1299 Tubbs Lane, Calistoga, CA 94515; 942-6463. Daily 9 to 6 in summer, 9 to 5 the rest of the year; admission fee. Smaller than Yellowstone's but reasonably faithful, erupting about every 40 minutes; picnic area, gift and snack shop.

Petrified Forest, Petrified Forest Rd. (five miles west), Calistoga, CA 94515; 942-6667. Daily 9 to 6 in summer, 9 to 5 the rest of the year; admission fee. A scattering of petrified trees, museum, gift shop and picnic area.

Robert Louis Stevenson State Historic Park, seven miles above Calistoga on Highway 29. Site of the author's 1880 honeymoon; undevel-

ON WINGS OF EAGLES

The cool rush of wind through the vent reminds me that I'm simply a mortal, borne aloft not on wings of eagles or fantasies of Icarus, but on soft summer air, rising from the floor of the Napa Valley.

I am tucked under the Plexiglas dome of a Schweizer 232, sitting beside my son Dan who, at age 16, consists mostly of arms and legs. He is too absorbed in flight to notice that his right elbow seems intent on sinking my floating rib.

The two-passenger glider is a cozy fit, but neither my rib nor I notice. We are engaged in the purest form of flight, riding afternoon thermals that crawl invisibly up the flanks of Mount St. Helena like lazy, friendly ghosts. I have flown in most things with wings, several with rotors, one dirigible and three hot air balloons. Nothing matches the sensual, silent aerial ballet of a glider.

Our pilot Artie Sveum—who looks like the retired math teacher that he is, but seeks out thermals with the instincts of an eagle—puts his craft into a lazy spiral. The world rotates below; we are in perfect suspension, held in place by the gentle yaw of the glider. Then the left wing drops and the rocky crags of the Palisades rise up to greet us.

"Do you want to get closer?" Artie asks over his shoulder, noticing that I've unholstered my Nikon.

"Sure!" Dan answers before I can respond.

We sweep the face of the Palisades, then drift toward a ridge and lift effortlessly over it with all the grace and none of the noise of a helicopter. Later, after exploring the ramparts of St. Helena, Artie slips the glider off the afternoon thermals; the vineyards and glossy roofs of the Napa Valley sweep into view. Calistoga is an orderly grid, the glider port a streak of gray between the green fields and vines.

"Gliders use a steeper approach than airplanes," says Artie, who's been doing this for 25 years, in addition to teaching math.

The craft swoops downward like a fishhawk after a salmon, then levels off and scuttles across the asphalt. We jolt gently to a stop and Artie pops the canopy. Twenty minutes have passed in the blink of an eagle's eye.

Calistoga Gliders offers one and two-passenger flights from 9 a.m. to 6 p.m. daily. On summer weekends, they continue until sunset. Twenty-minute rides are $75 for one and $95 for two; a bit more for longer flights. Morning trips are more smooth, while afternoon thermals provide a livelier ride. Generally, you can catch a flight on short notice during the week; it's best to make reservations on weekends. Contact Calistoga Gliders, 1546 Lincoln Ave., Calistoga, CA 94515; (707) 942-5000.

oped, but with several hiking trails and a monument at the honeymoon cabin site.

Sharpsteen Museum and Sam Brannan Cottage, 1311 Washington St., Calistoga, CA 94515; 942-5911. Daily 10 to 4 from April to October, noon to 4 the rest of the year. Historic museum with scale model of Sam

Brannan's resort and a restoration of one of his cottages.

Silverado Museum, 1490 Library Lane (P.O. Box 409), St. Helena, CA 94574; 963-3757 or 963-3002. Noon to 4 daily except Mondays and holidays. Excellent collection of objects concerning Robert Louis Stevenson and his 1880 honeymoon visit to the Napa Valley.

Wine country maps • ***Napa Valley Tour Map***, available at many wineries and gift shops for $2.50, or contact Napa Valley Art Studio, 1028 Summit Ave., Napa, CA 94559; (707) 253-0204. Mattioli's ***In Your Pocket*** guides to St. Helena and Calistoga, listing wineries, lodging, shops, restaurants and recreation, one dollar; available in gift shops and tasting rooms, or call (707) 965-2006.

Wineland events • Napa Valley Wine Library Association courses (see box), 963-3535; Napa Valley Wine Auction, first weekend of June, 963-5246; Napa County Fair in Calistoga, featuring local winery exhibits, early July, 942-5111; Home Winemakers Classic, tasting of amateur vintners' wines, late July, 253-0224; Napa Valley Wine Festival, early November, 252-7122. Individual wineries also sponsor various events throughout the year. Also see listings in Chapter 5.

WINE COUNTRY DINING

Brava Terrace • ΔΔ $$ Ø

3010 St. Helena Hwy., St. Helena; (707) 963-9300. French-American bistro; dinners $8 to $15; wine and beer. Daily 11:30 to 9. Informal to casual; reservations advised. MC/VISA, DISC. Charming bistro featuring local meats and produce and fresh pasta on its eclectic menu, which varies from roast chicken thighs with pistachio nuts to pork tenderloin with bell peppers and cilantro. Outdoor dining terrace.

Depot Restaurant • ΔΔ $$

1458 Lincoln Ave. (in the Calistoga Depot); (707) 942-6411. American; dinners $6 to $15; wine and beer. Monday-Thursday 7 a.m. to 9 p.m., Friday-Sunday 7 to 10. Informal to casual; reservations accepted. MC/VISA, DISC. Dining inside the historic Calistoga depot or in a wine garden. Family-style atmosphere, basic American menu featuring steaks, prime rib, chops and seafood; salad bar.

Showley's at Miramonte • ΔΔΔ $$$ Ø

1327 Railroad Ave. (between Hunt and Adams), St. Helena; (707) 963-1200. California cuisine; dinners $16 to $24; full bar service. Open daily, lunch 11:30 to 3, dinner 6 to 9:30. Informal to casual; reservations advised. Major credit cards. Housed the 1858 Miramonte Building, one of St. Helena's oldest structures. Blend of oldstyle and upscale decor. Creative California menu hops from grilled duck breast with green peppercorn sauce to salmon fillets in parchment with julienne vegetables. Outdoor dining.

Trilogy • ΔΔΔ $$$ Ø

1234 Main St. (Hunt Street), St. Helena; (707) 963-5507. California nouveau; dinners $18 to $30; wine and beer. Lunch Tuesday-Friday noon to 2, dinner Tuesday-Saturday from 6 p.m. Informal to casual; reservations advised. MC/VISA. Cozy little place offering interesting fare from an often-changing *nouveau* menu. Outdoor dining; large wine list featuring valley labels.

Triple S Ranch Restaurant • ∆∆ $$

4600 Mt. Home Ranch Rd. (off Petrified Forest Road), Calistoga, CA 94515; (707) 942-6730. American; dinners $12 to $20; full bar service. Casual; reservations advised. MC/VISA. Down-home atmosphere in a Western style family restaurant in the hills west of Calistoga. Menu with rural Americana tilt, leaning toward steak, chicken and ham, with a couple of seafood items. At a family resort with wooded grounds, a pool and hiking trails.

WINELAND LODGINGS

Hotels, motels & resorts

Calistoga Inn • ∆ $$$

1250 Lincoln Ave. (Cedar), Calistoga, CA 94515; (707) 942-4101. Doubles $50 to $55, singles $48 to $55, including continental breakfast. MC/VISA. An oldstyle 17-room inn with shared baths and no-frills "American comfortable" furnishings; it dates from the turn of the century. **Napa Valley Brewing Company** microbrewery and restaurant are part of the rustic complex. Restaurant opens at 8 a.m. (various closing times), serving American fare; dinners $8 to $19; wine and beer, including—of course—its own brews.

Calistoga Village Inn & Spa • ∆∆ $$$ Ø

1880 Lincoln Ave. (Silverado Trail), Calistoga, CA 94515; (707) 942-0991. Doubles $65 to $175, singles $55 to $150. Most major credit cards. A 42-room inn with spa, featuring mud baths, mineral baths, massages and facials; swimming pool. Room have TV movies and phones. **Jamee's Restaurant** serves dinners only, Tuesday-Sunday 5:30 to 9; California cuisine; dinners $20 to $30; wine and beer; intimate candlelight decor; all non-smoking.

Comfort Inn • ∆∆ $$$ Ø

1865 Lincoln Ave. (near downtown, off Grant Avenue), Calistoga, CA 94515; (800) 228-5150 or (707) 942-9400. Doubles $90 to $120, singles $80 to $110. Major credit cards. A 54-unit motel with landscaped grounds, mineral water pool and spa, plus a sauna and steam room. Rooms have TV movies and phones.

Dr. Wilkinson's Hot Springs • ∆∆ $$$ Ø

1507 Lincoln Ave. (Fairway), Calistoga, CA 94515; (707) 942-4102. Doubles $49 to $94, singles $44 to $84, kitchenettes $56 to $84. MC/VISA, AMEX. A 42-room motel and spa; TV and room phones. Full spa facilities with three mineral pools, massages, facials and mud baths.

El Bonita Motel ∆∆∆ $$$ Ø

195 Main St., St. Helena, CA 94574; (707) 963-3216. Doubles $53 to $95, singles $48 to $91, kitchenettes and suites $71 to $98. Major credit cards. A 41-room art deco motel, recently remodeled, with landscaped grounds; on edge of St. Helena, near wineries. TV, room phones and some room refrigerators. Pool, spa, volleyball court.

Golden Haven Spa & Resort • ∆∆ $$$

1713 Lake St., Calistoga, CA 94515; (707) 942-6793. Doubles and singles $49 to $99, kitchenettes $65 to $75, suites $75. MC/VISA, AMEX. A 30-room motel and mineral spa. TV, no room phones; some rooms have Jacuzzi tubs

"...AND THE WINE IS BOTTLED POETRY"

A sign at the Napa Valley's entrance quotes a troubled, tubercular young Scottish writer who spent the summer of 1880 in the valley's upper end, seeking refuge from the damp fogs of San Francisco.

Robert Louis Stevenson had pursued Fanny Osbourne, a married American woman, from France to California, trying to convince her to leave her husband and marry him. She finally relented and they chose the Napa Valley for their honeymoon, accompanied by her son Samuel and their dog Chuchu. Not yet published, Stevenson was almost peniless, so they moved into an empty bunkhouse on the tailing dump of the old Calistoga Silver Mine on Mount St. Helena.

"The place was open like the proscenium of a theatre," he wrote, "and we looked forth into a great realm of air, and far and near on wild and varied country."

Stevenson, ever the poet, called their honeymoon haven Silverado. Traveling about the valley, they visited still-surviving landmarks such as Bale's Grist Mill, Schramsberg Winery and the Petrified Forest, where he found its owner, Charley Evans, to be a "far more delightful curiosity" than the stone trees.

Despite his illness, he hiked up Monitor Ledge to the top of the mine shaft to witness the stunning vista of the Napa Valley, often covered with a cottony fog blanket. "That vast fog-ocean lay in a trance of silence, nor did the sweet air of morning tremble with a sound."

Stevenson kept a diary called "Silverado Journal," and from this he compiled ***The Silverado Squatters***, his first published work.

The honeymoon site is now part of **Robert Luis Stevenson State Historic Park**, reached by a seven-mile drive north from Calistoga on Highway 29. It's undeveloped, with no camping, water or other facilities. However, a few picnic tables sit near the concrete foundation of a former toll house below the mine. A one-mile hiking trail switchbacks up the mountain to the cabin site. The bunkhouse is gone; a monument erected by Napa Valley women's clubs marks the spot.

A difficult scramble over broken rock will deliver you to the mine, which is more of a slot cut into the silver-bearing ridge. A trail from the monument joins a forestry road that takes you to the top of the ridge. From there, you can enjoy Stevenson's dramatic Napa Valley view.

Memorabilia of Stevenson and his Napa Valley visit are preserved in the **Silverado Museum** at 1490 Library Lane, St. Helena, in the city library building. Hours are Tuesday through Sunday from noon to 4. Admission is free; phone (707) 963-3757.

Stevenson left his Silverado after two months. In renewed health and spirits, he became one of history's great authors. Sadly, he died just 14 years later. An inscription on the women's club monument, taken from one of his poems, marks his passage:

Doomed to know not Winter, only Spring,
A being trod the flowery April blithely for a while,
Took his fill of music, joy of thought and seeing,
Came and stayed and went, nor ever ceased to smile.

or saunas. Spa includes mud baths, massages, hot water mineral pool and Jacuzzi; swimming pool.

Hideaway Cottages • Δ $$$

1412 Fairway (Lincoln), Calistoga, CA 94515; (707) 942-4108. Doubles $47 to $91, singles $40 to $81, kitchenettes $72 to $74, suites $76 to $91. MC/VISA, AMEX. Fifteen room cottage-style motel with TV; mineral water swimming pool.

Indian Springs • ΔΔΔ $$$$$

1712 Lincoln Ave., Calistoga, CA 94515; (707) 942-4913. Rooms $105 to 140, large house $300. Early California style resort with 18 units in hotel rooms and cottages; TV, refrigerators, coffeemakers in rooms. Pool with poolside cafe. Compete health spa with mud baths, mineral baths, facials and massages. Hot spring pool open to public for a fee.

Meadowood Napa Valley• ΔΔΔΔΔ $$$$$

900 Meadowood Lane, St. Helena; (800) 458-8080 or (707) 963-3646. Rooms and suites $215 to $500; major credit cards. Luxurious, secluded French country style resort with opulently-furnished rooms. Extensive landscaped grounds; golf, tennis, pool, spa and hiking trails. **Starmont Restaurant** features California cuisine; **Fairway Grill** is a bistro-style cafe; meal service daily from 11:30 to 10; dressy at Starmont, informal at Fairway Grill; dinners $23.50 to $35.50; full bar service; reservations essential.

Pine Street Inn and Spa • ΔΔ $$$$

1202 Pine St., Calistoga, CA 94515; (707) 942-6829. Doubles and singles $75 to $85, including continental breakfast. MC/VISA. California ranch-style inn with 16 rooms; mix of antique and modern furnishings. Spa facilities including whirlpool, mud baths and facials.

Wine Country Inn • ΔΔΔ $$$$

1152 Lodi Lane (Highway 29), St. Helena, CA 94574; (707) 963-7077. Doubles $92 to $188, singles $72 to $168, including continental breakfast. MC/VISA, AMEX. New 25-room inn fashioned like an elegant oldstyle American country home. Stylish rooms and common areas with wood paneling and print wallpaper; antique furnishings.

Bed & breakfast inns

Calistoga's Wine Way Inn • ΔΔΔ $$$$ ØØ

1019 Foothill Blvd. (off Highway 29), Calistoga, CA 94515; (707) 942-0680. Doubles $70 to $110, singles $65 to $106. Six rooms with private baths; full breakfast. MC/VISA, AMEX. A handsomely renovated early American home with multi-level decks, rimmed by a wooded yard. American antiques, leaded glass trim, fireplace in parlor. Gazebo with view of Calistoga.

Calistoga Country Lodge • ΔΔ $$$$ Ø

2883 Foothill Blvd. (Highway 128, 1.5 miles north), Calistoga, CA 94515; (707) 942-5555. Doubles and singles $85 to $105. Six rooms, three with private baths; continental buffet breakfast. MC/VISA, AMEX. A 1917 ranch house with Southwestern decor; Navajo rugs, Indian artifacts and American furnishings. Pool and patio; vineyard view. Evening wine and snacks.

Cinnamon Bear Bed & Breakfast • ΔΔ $$$$ Ø

1407 Kearney St. (Adams), St. Helena, CA 94574; (707) 963-4653. Doubles $65 to $145, singles $55 to $145. Four rooms with private baths; full breakfast. MC/VISA. Early 20th century redwood home with shady front porch. Former mayor's residence; furnished with antiques and early American arts and crafts; teddy bear theme. Comfortable living room with fireplace.

Culver's, a Country Inn • ΔΔ $$$$ ØØ

1805 Foothill Blvd. (Highway 128), Calistoga, CA 94515; (707) 942-4535. Doubles and singles $95 to $115. Six rooms, some private and some shared baths; full breakfast. No credit cards. An 1875 Victorian with a mix of Victorian, art deco and art *nouveau*; fireplace and player piano in living room. Pool, spa and sauna.

The Elms Bed & Breakfast • ΔΔΔ $$$$ Ø

1300 Cedar St., Calistoga, CA 94515; (707) 942-9476. Doubles and singles $95 to $200. Five rooms with private baths and TV; full breakfast. No credit cards. Elegant 1871 mansard-roofed Victorian, former judge's home, on the National Register of Historic Places. Nicely done room with European and Asian antiques; separate honeymoon cottage with kitchenette. Extensive landscaped grounds. Afternoon wine and cheese.

Forest Manor • ΔΔΔΔ $$$$$ ØØ

415 Cold Spring Rd. (Deer Park Road), Angwin, CA 94508; (707) 965-3538. Doubles and singles $105 to $175. Three rooms with private baths; continental breakfast. MC/VISA. Striking English Tudor home on 20-acre estate, in the mountains above the Napa Valley. English antiques, Oriental art and Persian rugs; vaulted ceilings; verandas; billiard room; pool and spa. Large suites, some with fireplaces, one with spa.

Erika's Hillside • ΔΔΔ $$$$ ØØ

285 Fawn Park (off Silverado Trail), St. Helena, CA 94574; (707) 963-2887. Doubles $75 to $165, singles $55. AMEX. Three rooms with private baths; continental breakfast. Remodeled century-old Swiss chalet on wooded, landscaped three-acre estate; European furnishings; hand-painted rosemaling decor. Large rooms with private entrances; hot tub.

The Ink House • ΔΔΔ $$$$$ ØØ

1575 St. Helena Hwy. (Whitehall Lane), St. Helena, CA 94574; (707) 963-3890. Doubles and singles $125 to $165. Four rooms with private baths, TV and phones; continental breakfast. No credit cards. Elegant 1884 Italianate mansion listed on the National Register of Historic Places. American and English antiques; 12-foot ceilings; large guest rooms and common rooms. Spa and sauna; roof observatory with 360-degree valley view.

Larkmead Country Inn • ΔΔΔ $$$$$ ØØ

1103 Larkmead Lane (between Highway 29 and Silverado), Calistoga, CA 94515; (707) 942-5360. Doubles $100 to $115, singles $75. Four rooms with private baths; continental breakfast. No credit cards. Imposing 1918 early California winery estate furnished with English antiques, Persian carpets and artworks. Extensive landscaped grounds with mature hardwoods. Vineyard and mountain views.

Meadow Lark Country House • ΔΔΔ $$$$$ ØØ

601 Petrified Forest Rd. (Foothill Road), Calistoga, CA 94515; (707) 942-5651. Doubles and singles $100 to $125. Four rooms with private baths; full breakfast. Restored 1886 American country home set on 29-acre wooded, landscaped grounds. English country antiques and contemporary furnishings. Pool; forest paths; nearby horse training ring.

Shady Oaks Country Inn • ΔΔ $$$$ Ø

399 Zinfandel Lane (Highway 29), St. Helena, CA 94574; (707) 963-1190. Doubles $85 to $145, singles $75 to $145. Four rooms with private baths; champagne breakfast. No credit cards. An 1887 winery building with cut stone walls, fashioned into a farm style bed and breakfast inn; American antique furnishings. On secluded two-acre grounds.

Silver Rose Inn • ΔΔΔ $$$$$ ØØ

351 Rosedale Rd. (Silverado Trail), Calistoga, CA 94515; (707) 942-9581. Doubles $110 to $175. Five rooms with private baths and TV; full breakfast. MC/VISA, DISC. Stylish modern-rustic country home on oak knoll with valley views from all guest rooms. Done in early American, Oriental and modern decor. Landscaped grounds with pool, flagstone paths and rock garden.

Up Valley information sources

Calistoga Chamber of Commerce, 1458 Lincoln Ave. (in the Calistoga Depot), Calistoga, CA 94515; 942-6333.

Calistoga Resort Owners' Association, P.O. Box 3, Calistoga, CA 94515.

Napa Valley Wine Library Association, P.O. Box 207, St. Helena, CA 94574; 963-3535.

St. Helena Chamber of Commerce, P.O. Box 124 (Main and Pope streets), St. Helena, CA 94574; 963-4456.

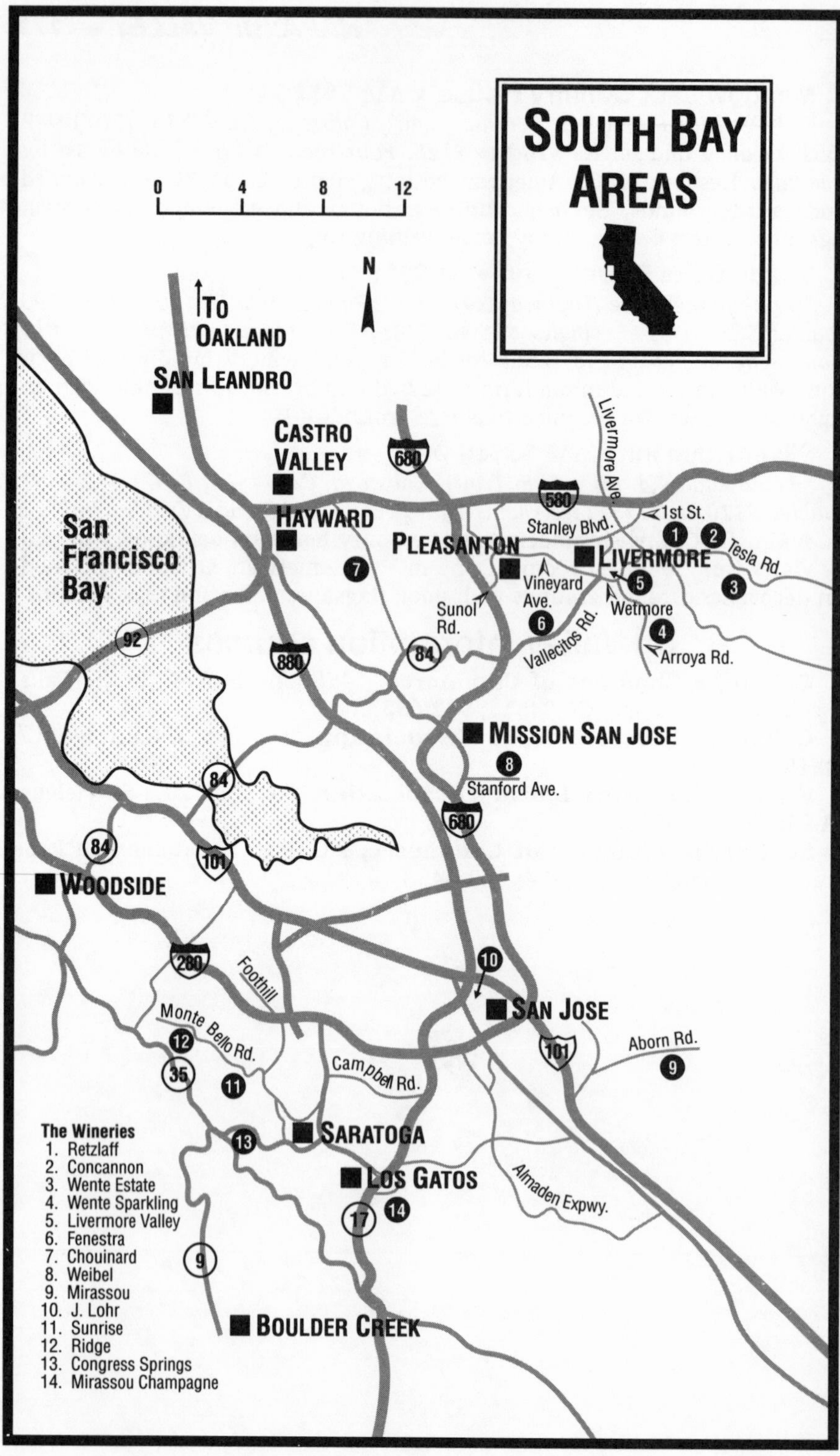

SOUTH BAY AREAS
0
4
8
12
N
To OAKLAND
SAN LEANDRO
CASTRO VALLEY
HAYWARD
San Francisco Bay
PLEASANTON
LIVERMORE
Livermore Ave.
1st St.
Stanley Blvd.
Tesla Rd.
Vineyard Ave.
Sunol Rd.
Wetmore
Vallecitos Rd.
Arroya Rd.
680
580
880
92
84
MISSION SAN JOSE
Stanford Ave.
101
WOODSIDE
280
Foothill
SAN JOSE
Monte Bello Rd.
Campbell Rd.
Aborn Rd.
35
SARATOGA
LOS GATOS
Almaden Expwy.
17
9
BOULDER CREEK
The Wineries
1. Retzlaff
2. Concannon
3. Wente Estate
4. Wente Sparkling
5. Livermore Valley
6. Fenestra
7. Chouinard
8. Weibel
9. Mirassou
10. J. Lohr
11. Sunrise
12. Ridge
13. Congress Springs
14. Mirassou Champagne

"Weedy black currant and olive flavors are complemented by hints of plum in this balanced wine; the vegetal notes don't dominate, but rather blend in."

—Description of a 1987 Concannon Livermore Valley Reserve Cabernet Sauvignon

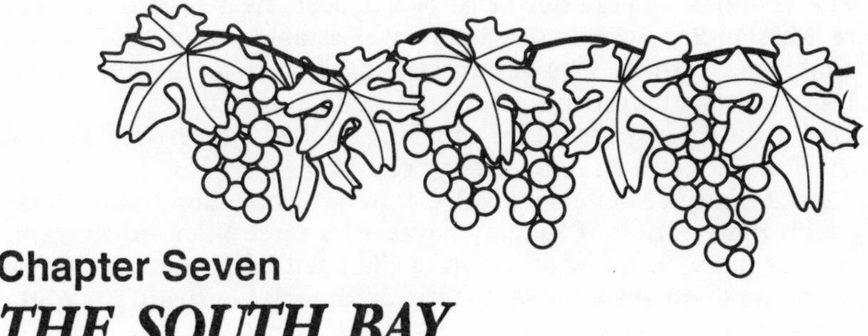

Chapter Seven
THE SOUTH BAY
Southern Alameda & northern Santa Clara counties

Silicon chips and suburbs have prevailed over Sauvignon Blanc and Semillon in southern Alameda and northern Santa Clara counties. However, many noteworthy wineries survive. Some—such as Concannon, Wente and Mirassou—date back more than a century. Mirassou, in fact, is the oldest family-owned winery in California.

These venerable establishments and several newcomers have survived the suburban spread in various ways. Some have set up shop in the foothills, or retreated even higher, particularly to Montebello Ridge of the Santa Cruz Mountains, southwest of San Jose. Others have remained firmly in place, with their wineries and tasting rooms surrounded by tract homes. They surrendered their vineyards to subdivisions and planted new vines in Monterey County to the south or Mendocino County to the north.

A few, such as the long-popular Paul Masson facility in the heart of Silicon Valley, simply closed up shop and moved elsewhere.

These two wine-producing areas on the lower rim of San Francisco Bay appear on some of the earliest pages of California's history.

Livermore Valley on the southeastern edge of the bay was settled by English sailor Robert Livermore, who picked up two Mexican land grants in 1830. He had grapes growing by the 1840s. Charles A. Wetmore, who served as California's chief viticultural officer, established Cresta Blanca Winery in 1882, followed by the arrival of Carl H. Wente and James Concannon the next year.

To the southwest, The Santa Clara Valley's history goes back even further. San Jose was born in 1777 as the state's first civil settlement; it served as the first capital from 1849 to 1851. By the mid-1850s, San Jose was a major wine producer and its surrounding Santa Clara Valley was called the "Garden Spot of the World." French vineyardist Pierre Pellier started a winery here in 1854. His daughter married Pierre Mirassou in 1881, beginning the Mirassou wine dynasty that persists to this day. At the turn of the century, the Santa Clara Valley had more than 100 wineries and nearly 9,000 acres of vines. The usual triple whammy of the 1870s depression, phylloxera and Prohibition closed all but the most obstinate of these early wineries.

The Santa Clara and Livermore valleys—and the borders of Santa Clara and Alameda counties—merge northeast of San Jose, near present-day Fremont. Here, Mission San Josè de Guadalupe was established in 1797 (to the constant confusion of those who assume the mission is in the city of San Jose). In 1869, railroad baron and politician Leland Stanford and his brother Josiah started a winery just east of the mission. The Swiss-born Weibels took it over in 1940 and it's still a family enterprise.

Santa Clara County's Montebello Ridge wineries came along much later, beginning with the creation of Ridge Vineyards by three Stanford Research Institute couples in 1959. A few others have since settled in these steep, forested hills. Among them are Sunrise Winery, occupying the rustic site of the 1880s Picchetti Ranch winery.

Livermore and Santa Clara valleys, cooled by bay breezes, are known mostly for their whites; Cabernet Sauvignon and Petit Sirah are grown here as well. Montebello Ridge, higher but warmer, produces some excellent Zinfandels.

LIVERMORE VALLEY WINERY TOUR • It's best to plan this outing on a weekend since two of the more interesting wineries, Fenestra and Chouinard, are open Saturdays and Sundays only.

Most folks find get their bearings in **Livermore** at the flag pole, which occupies a small swatch of green in the old downtown area, at the merger of Livermore Avenue and First Street. Coming from the Bay Area, take the Livermore Avenue turnoff and go south into town. Approaching from the east on I-580, First Street will get you there. From the south, take State Highway 84 east from I-680.

Follow Livermore Avenue south until it kinks to the left after about a mile and becomes Tesla Road. Right at that kink, you'll see a sign on the left identifying small **Retzlaff Vineyards.** At this point, you've shed most of Livermore's suburbia and are traveling through a mix of vineyards and farm fields. Tawny rolling hills stand on the horizon. Continuing southeast on Tesla, you soon encounter **Concannon Vineyard** on the left and, less than a mile beyond, **Wente Brothers Estate Winery** on the right.

Retrace your path along Tesla Road then, just beyond Concannon, take a hard right onto Wente Street. It curves into Marina Avenue, which bumps into Arroyo Road. Go left and you'll soon pass, on the right, **Ravenswood Historical Site,** an elaborate country estate and former winery. It's now administered by the Livermore Area Recreation and Park District.

Continuing along Arroyo Road, you encounter **Wente Brothers Sparkling Wine Cellars and Restaurant** on the left. Reverse your route for about a mile, then take a hard left onto Wetmore Road and you see **Livermore Valley Cellars** on the right. Wetmore does a 90-degree right turn and becomes Holmes Street. Within a few hundred yards, take a sharp left onto Vallecitos Road (State Highway 84). You're now well into the country, taking a gentle roller-coaster ride through undulating hills.

After less than a mile, you see **Fenestra Winery,** housed in a wonderful old tattered barn on your right. Pressing on, you wind steeply over a set of low hills, then cross Interstate 680. Stay with Highway 84, which becomes Niles Canyon Road. (Avoid getting on I-680, although the Livermore Valley Winegrowers map implies that you jog south on the freeway.)

Pass the dinky community of **Sunol** and follow Highway 84 through scenic, winding **Niles Canyon.** Its Alameda Creek waters offer a popular weekend retreat for locals. After about four miles, turn right up Palomares Road and take its steep, winding course about three miles to **Chouinard Vineyards.** Look for the bright red barn on your left.

From here, retrace your route to I-680, then go south about four and a half miles to the Mission Boulevard exit. Follow it east past **Mission San Josè** to Stanford Road; a left turn takes you up to **Weibel Champagne Vineyards.**

Retzlaff Vineyards • T ⌆

1356 S. Livermore Ave., Livermore, CA 94550; (510) 447-8941. Monday-Friday noon to 2 and weekends noon to 5; AMEX. Most varieties tasted. A few wine logo items; picnic area shaded by pepper trees.

A graveled lane flanked by vineyards and pepper trees takes you to this small winery in a weathered farm complex. Park beside a lawn picnic area and stroll to the tasting room in a small cottage. It's likely that lively little Pi Matthews, sort of a mini-grandmother type, will serve you on a red-checker tablecloth tasting bar. Dried statice hanging from ceiling rafters gives the place a nice herbal aroma.

The winery was started in 1978 by home winemaker and chemist Bob Taylor and his wife Gloria Retzlaff Taylor. They began with the intention of selling grapes, then decided to produce their own wines, at the rate of about 3,000 cases a year.

Tasting notes: The three wines we tasted, comprising the entire list, were quite pleasant. A Gray Riesling had a nice herbal nose; it was soft and buttery on the palate. A Chardonnay was very fruity and silky, with only a hint of wood. A two-year-old Cabernet offered a peppery nose, herbal flavor and soft finish. Prices range from $7 to $11.

Concannon Vineyard • T$ GT ⌆ 🎁

4590 Tesla Rd., Livermore, CA 94550; (510) 447-3760. Weekdays 10 to 4:30, weekends 11 to 4:30; MC/VISA. Most wines tasted for $3 fee (refunded with purchase). Good wine-oriented gift selection. Nice picnic area; tours weekends at 1, 2 and 3 and weekdays on request. Horse carriage tours of vineyards by appointment.

The story goes that Irish immigrant Joseph Concannon, printer by trade, was asked by San Francisco Archbishop Joseph S. Alemany to make some good altar wine. Being a proper Catholic, Joe complied and thus started the

---

WINERY CODES • T = tasting with no fee; **T$** = fee for tasting; **GT** = guided tours; **GTA** = appointment required for tour; **ST** = self-guiding tours; **CT** = casual tours or a peek into the winery; ⌆= picnic area; 🎁 = separate gift shop or good giftware selection. Price ranges listed in tasting notes are for varietals; jug wines often are available for less. **DINING & LODGINGS • ØØ** = smoke-free establishment; Ø = non-smoking tables or rooms.

first Gaelic winery in California. For generations, Concannons and Wentes were friendly rivals, making honest wines and sending their kids to the same schools. It remained thus until 1981, when Concannon was bought out by Deinhard and Partners, obviously non-Irish.

Like the Concannons before them, the new owners maintain a lively schedule of special events and wine-tasting dinners. The extensive gift and deli shop offers something unique to the wine country—hot lunches to be consumed with Concannon wine on the landscaped lawn picnic area. The tasting room is housed in one of the century-old winery buildings. It's all done up in brick and wormwood paneling, decorated by quilts hanging like rural tapestries.

Tasting notes: The list tilts toward reds; those we tasted had strong varietal character, without excessive fining and filtering. A Sauvignon Blanc was subtly nutty with a nice acid finish; Petite Sirah had a good berry nose and flavor; a five-year-old Cabernet Sauvignon was inky in color with a strong chili pepper nose and a lush taste. A Concannon specialty, Assemblage—a blend of Sauvignon Blanc and Semillon—had a spicy fruitiness similar to a Chardonnay. Prices range from $7.50 to the high teens.

Wente Brothers Estate Winery • T GT

5565 Tesla Rd., Livermore, CA 94550; (510) 447-3603. Monday-Saturday 10 to 4:30, Sunday 11 to 4:30; MC/VISA, AMEX. Most varieties tasted. Good selection of wine logo and specialty food items. Picnic area beside tasting room. Tours Monday-Saturday at 10, 11, 1, 2 and 3 and Sundays at 1, 2 and 3.

The Wentes and Concannons started their wineries in 1883. After more than a century, fourth-generation Wentes are still at the helm. Only the Mirassou clan claims a longer California winery lineage. C.H. Wente, his son Ernest and grandson Karl were major forces in shaping the valley's wine industry. Karl's wife Jean and their children carry on today.

Although most of the vineyards have moved south to Monterey County and to the Livermore foothills, a few vines still embrace the neat, businesslike winery complex. The tasting room and adjoining gift shop are housed in an adobe block and wood double octagon. It's one of the more appealing winery structures in the area. Like their longtime Concannon neighbors, the Wentes sponsor frequent special events.

Tasting notes: Wente offers a very intelligent tasting form, useful in directing you and keeping track of your sips. The list covers most major varietals; the wines are quite tasty and reasonably priced, ranging from $5 to $9 for current releases and to $20 for reserves. The signature wine is Gray Riesling, named by the founder a century ago; it was fruity, light and dry—a good picnic wine. Sauvignon Blanc was oaky and spicy; Semillon had a herbal nose and flavor and a crisp, almost tart finish; Chardonnay was spicy and nutty with a soft touch of wood; Zinfandel revealed a big raspberry nose, medium body and nippy tannic finish. A three-year-old Estate Cabernet Sauvignon offered a big bell pepper aroma, nice peppery-berry flavor and medium tannin.

Vintners choice: "We were the first producers of Chardonnay here, with 57 consecutive vintages," said Wente's Michael Perry. "We offer a lot of different styles and prices."

Wente Sparkling Wine Cellars • T GT ⌆ R

5050 Arroyo Rd., Livermore, CA 94550; (510) 447-3603. Monday-Saturday 10 to 4:30, Sunday 11 to 4:30; MC/VISA, AMEX. Wente Brut and some still wines tasted at no fee; $2 for tastes of Grand Brut. Good selection of wine logo and specialty food items. Tours Monday-Saturday at 10, 11, 1, 2 and 3 and Sundays at 1, 2 and 3. Restaurant adjacent.

The Wentes have blended history, architectural beauty and state-of-the-art sparkling wine making at this Spanish-style facility. Started in 1882 as Charles Wetmore's Cresta Blanca Winery, it was purchased by the Wente family in 1981. After extensive rehabilitation, it was reborn as a modern champagnery housed in glossy white stucco and tile-roofed buildings. The complex is accented by mature trees, lawns, landscaped gardens, cork trees and an herb garden. Here, chefs from the adjacent Restaurant pluck their seasonings.

The tasting room is housed in an enclosed former courtyard, with lofty ceilings held up by imposing square columns. Tours take visitors through the modern champagnery and into 650 feet of aging caves tunneled into a hillside. Re-excavated and gunnited by the Wentes, they still have that wonderfully musty mushroom farm smell of ancient caverns.

Tasting notes: Wente Brut has won impressive awards, considering its modest $10 price. A typical blend of Pinot Noir, Pinot Blanc and Chardonnay, it was perfectly crisp, practically floating over the palate, with subtle flavors of the fruit. A few of Wente's other wines are tasted here as well.

The Restaurant • ΔΔΔΔ $$$ ØØ

At Wente Sparkling Wine Cellars; (510) 447-3696. Regional American; dinners $14 to $22; wine and beer. Daily 11:30 to 2:30 and 5:30 to 9. Informal to casual; reservations advised. Major credit cards. Stylish dining room with warm woods, cane-back chairs and linen nappery. Fixed-priced dinners with wine pairings are offered Monday and Tuesday evenings and periodic winemakers dinners are scheduled. Emphasis on "estate beef," since the Wentes own a cattle ranch. Other entrees include chicken *paillard* with white beans, escarole and salsa verde; calzone with pepperoni, artichoke, goat cheese and herbs; and charcoal grilled swordfish with red lentils, fire roasted peppers and olive pesto. Smoke-free dining room; patio dining.

Livermore Valley Cellars • T ⌆

1508 Wetmore Rd., Livermore, CA 94550; (510) 447-1751. Daily 11:30 to 5; MC/VISA. All varieties tasted. A few wine logo items; small picnic area.

The smallest and scruffiest of the area wineries, Livermore Valley Cellars occupies a weathered old farmyard up a graveled lane. When we visited, a vineyard up front was unattended, a victim of California's prolonged drought. Owner Chris Lagiss decided not to prune it, since he's a dry farmer and he felt there wasn't sufficient water to bring in a decent crop. Wines haven't been produced here for three years. However, the little 2,000-case winery isn't out of business; the family intends to buy grapes and resume production in the early 1990s.

Tasting notes: Livermore Valley Cellars produces only whites. Because of the production lag, most of those we tasted were several years old and a bit tired. They're still quite drinkable and moderately priced, from $6 to $12.

We found a six-year-old Chardonnay to be quite very tasty, with nice spices and subtle oak, and a six-year-old Gray Riesling was lush and full-bodied, a good buy at $5.95.

Fenestra Winery • T ⌅

83 E. Vallecitos Rd., Livermore; mailing address—P.O. Box 582, Sunol, CA 94589; (510) 862-2292. Weekends only, noon to 5; MC/VISA. Most varieties tasted. A few wine logo items; shaded picnic area.

All it lacks is a Mail Pouch tobacco sign painted on the roof. Fenestra Winery occupies one of the most wonderfully weathered old barns in California. Bunkered into a hollow, surrounded by gnarled oaks and wild oats, this concrete and wooded barn is a classic of American country Gothic. It was built in 1889 by a pioneer farmer named George True.

Inside, soft-spoken chemist Lanny Replogle makes wines while his wife Fran handles marketing. It's a weekend job, since Lanny teaches at San Jose State University; he started winemaking in 1976. On pleasant days, tastings are convened outside, beside the rustic oak-shaded picnic areas.

All this may be spruced up in coming years, since the area will be part of a large golf course, vineyard and housing complex called Signature Hills, headed by golfer Jack Nicholas. Developers promise to leave the historic barn intact. Hopefully, they it will leave it properly scruffy as well. Paint would ruin the effect.

Unless they decide to paint a Mail Pouch tobacco sign on the roof.

Tasting notes: When it comes to winemaking, Lanny the chemist is no mad scientist. His wines are straightforward, full bodied and excellent, certainly not test tube products. They've won a good share of medals. He produces most of the popular whites, plus Merlot and Cabernet Sauvignon. Our wines of choice were a nutty and spicy Semillon, an herbal and complex Pinot blanc, a Chardonnay with deep and intense buttery flavor, a young Merlot with rich berry flavor and a four-year-old cab with a spicy nose and mellow berry-rich taste. Lanny's "user-friendly" everyday drinking wine has a great double entendre label to honor the barn-builder: True Red. Overall prices are modest, ranging from $6 to the low teens.

Chouinard Vineyard and Winery • T GT ⌅

33853 Palomares Rd., Castro Valley, CA 94552; (510) 582-9900. Weekends and some holidays from noon to 5; MC/VISA. Most varieties tasted. Some wine logo items. Shaded picnic area. Tours on request during tasting room hours.

Tucked into a wooded slope and housed in a bright red barn, Chouinard Winery could pose for a Grandma Moses painting. Its pleasant grounds and vineyards are terraced up a shallow ravine, high above the Livermore Valley—so high that it's in the Castro Valley postal zone. The tasting room is in a cozy loft in the eaves of the red barn winery. Picnic tables rest beneath oaks, maples and redwoods nearby. We'd suggest arriving with a picnic lunch, buying a bottle of wine and spending a couple of hours in this pleasantly wooded mountain retreat.

Architect George Chouinard, his wife Caroline and their sons Rick and Daimian started their vineyards in 1978. They became intrigued with wine after living in France for several years. They opened their tasting room in 1985 and often host special events at this mountain retreat.

Pioneer George True's rough stone and wood barn near Livermore provides properly rustic shelter for Fenestra Winery.

Tasting notes: Chardonnay, Semillon, Johannisberg Riesling, Gewürztraminer, Zinfandel, Cabernet Sauvignon and Granny Smith apple wine comprise the list. Prices range from $7 to $12.50. Wines are full-bodied, complex and quite tasty. Our choices included an 80 percent malolactic Chardonnay with a nutty aroma and nice spicy, buttery taste; a Johannisberg with a flower petal nose and fruity, crisp flavor; a young Zinfandel with a great raspberry nose and taste; and a powerful four-old Arroyo Seco Cab with a nice chili pepper nose and rich tannins; definitely one to age.

Vintners choice: "Chardonnay and our Granny Smith Apple wine; both are award-winners," says George.

Weibel Vineyards • T GT

1250 Stanford Ave. (P.O. Box 3398), Mission San Jose, CA 94539; (510) 656-2340. Daily 10 to 5; MC/VISA. Most varieties tasted. Gift shop with wine logo items; arbor-shaded picnic area. Tours on request from 10 to 3 weekdays.

The Swiss family Weibel took over the old Leland Stanford Winery in 1940. They planted vineyards in these sunny, gently sloping hills between the Livermore and Santa Clara valleys, just east of Mission San Jose. The slopes are still sunny, but they're now covered with houses instead of vines. One new subdivision, appropriately, is called Vineyard Hills.

Most of Weibel's vines have been shifted north to Mendocino County, although some winemaking operations continue here. They can be witnessed during periodic tours. We've always liked the ruggedly handsome Spanish-style Weibel tasting room, called "The Hacienda." Its chapel-like architecture compliments old Mission San Josè, just down the road a bit.

Tasting notes: The Weibel family bottles half a million cases a year and their list includes most major varietals. Overall style is light and ready-to-drink. They also produce tasty and inexpensive sherries and ports. Overall wine prices are modest, ranging from $5 to $10. From the lengthy list, we particularly liked a light and fruity Chardonnay; a rich yet crisp and dry Gewürztraminer suitable as a good picnic wine; a three-year old Cabernet with a spicy nose, complex and soft flavor and low tannin; and a gentle ten-year Pinot Noir Reserve. The cream sherry and Rare Port were rich, lush and nutty, good buys at $8.

Vintners choice: "Sherry and ports are consistent gold medal winners," says Diana Weibel. "And we have very inexpensive sparkling wines."

SANTA CLARA VALLEY-MONTEBELLO WINERY TOUR • The valley wineries are open daily, but some of the Montebello Ridge places have limited hours, so plan accordingly.

One of California's largest cities now stands where hundreds of acres of vines once flourished. San Jose is pushing a million population and its suburbs push far and wide into the Santa Clara Valley. Two wineries thrive here, however. Venerable Mirassou remains firmly rooted to the spot where it began more than a century ago. And latecomer Jerry Lohr decided to join them instead of fight them; he started a winery right in the middle of a San Jose industrial district.

The area's other wineries seek refuge in nearby hills, beyond reach of the commotion below. Our tour thus takes you from thick civilization to near-wilderness.

Mirassou is the first stop in this urban-mountain winery trek. From the Bayshore Freeway (U.S. 101), take the Capitol Expressway northeast for a couple of blocks, then go right on Aborn Road and follow it past shopping centers and subdivisions to the winery.

Return to the Bayshore, go about six miles north to Interstate 880, then head south, following Santa Cruz signs. Drive about two miles, exit onto The Alameda (State Highway 82) and go left under the freeway. After a mile of pleasant older suburbs, you'll enter a commercial area. At the old Towne Theatre (you can't miss that violet facade), turn left onto Lenzen Avenue and the **J. Lohr Winery** appears. It's in a brick building on your right.

Get back to I-880, continue south for just over a mile to the I-280 interchange and follow it right (west) toward Cupertino. After about seven miles, exit at the Foothill interchange and go left under the freeway on Foothill Boulevard. You'll quickly escape civilization and begin climbing into the Santa Cruz Mountain foothills.

This area offers more winding roads than wines, but it's a pretty drive and the wineries are interesting. Foothill Boulevard becomes Stevens Canyon Road, toiling through brushy slopes toward Stevens Creek Reservoir. Shortly after passing the dam, take a sharp right up Montebello Road, which twists and turns up to **Sunrise Winery.** It's on the historic Picchetti Ranch in the Monte Bello Open Space Reserve. A graveled trailhead parking lot also provides parking for the tasting room.

Continue climbing and spiralling up Montebello Road, enjoying panoramic valley vistas if you dare look. You'll see more trees than vines here, although an occasional vineyard is spotted, clinging to these steep slopes. When it seems that you've climbed halfway to heaven, you see **Ridge Vineyards** crowning the ridge that provided its name. It's one of the most dramatically situated wineries in the country.

Retreat down Montebello to Stevens Canyon Road and turn right. After a couple of miles, fork to the left and upward onto Mount Eden Road. (Don't miss the fork; Stevens Canyon dead-ends into a wilderness.) You soon pass the mountain winery of **Paul Masson**. It's home to special vineyard events but is otherwise closed to the public. Its tasting room is in Chapter 10, at Monterey's Cannery Row.

Mount Eden blends into Pierce Road, which continues downhill and bumps into Congress Springs Road (Highway 9). Turn right and drive about a mile to **Congress Springs Vineyards**, up a lane to your left. Then, reverse your route on Congress Springs Road (which becomes Big Basin Way) and follow it to the wooded foothill community of **Saratoga.** En route, you'll pass the **Santa Clara County Arboretum** and **Hakkone Gardens**, both worth a browse. Also, you may want to explore a few Saratoga boutiques and shops before continuing.

Follow Saratoga-Los Gatos Road (still Highway 9) southeast to Los Gatos. Once there, turn right onto University Avenue (at a stoplight, just short of the Highway 17 freeway) and follow it about six blocks to Main Street. Go left on Main, cross the freeway and quickly turn right onto College Avenue (near a gray apartment building). College winds steeply into wooded hills, taking you to the **Novitiate of Los Gatos,** on whose grounds resides **Mirassou Champagne Cellars.**

Like Saratoga, Los Gatos is a lushly-wooded foothill town busy with boutiques, yuppie shops and restaurants. You may want to explore its **Old Town** Spanish flavored shopping mall.

Mirassou Vineyards • T GT 🎁

3000 Aborn Rd., San Jose, CA 95135; (408) 274-4000. Monday-Saturday 10 to 5, Sunday noon to 4; MC/VISA, AMEX. Most varieties tasted free; library reserves tasted at $1. Wine-related gift selection. Tours Monday-Saturday at 10:30, noon, 2 and 3:30; Sunday at 12:30 and 2:30.

If you count in-laws, the Mirassou family traces its geneological vines back to 1854, when Pierre Pellier planted grapes in the Santa Clara Valley, then married his daughter to a Mirassou. Their descendants still make wine on that plot of ground planted by Great, great-grandfather Pellier.

Most of the vines have shifted southward to Monterey County. Only 20 acres survive here, a small Cabernet vineyard forming a thin green line between the winery and encroaching subdivisions. The venerable winery grounds are stately, with weathered, properly ivy-covered buildings shaded by mature trees. The large and attractive wood-paneled tasting room is housed in one of the winery structures. Inside, you can peek through windows at giant redwood casks.

Tasting notes: We *like* the way Mirassou conducts tastings. You fetch a large tulip-shaped glass from a wall rack and walk past several tables, where samples of nearly everything on the lengthy list are poured. Nearly all popular California varietals are produced by Mirassou. Prices are modest, ranging from $6.50 to the mid-teens; some library wines go higher. The Mirassou style is light, crisp and clean. Among our choices were a lightly spicy Chardonnay; a fruity and crisp Monterey Riesling; a spicy and medium bodied Cabernet Sauvignon, excellent for its $9.75 price; and young Pinot Noirs and Zinfandels, both refreshingly fruity with fine berry aromas.

Vintners choice: "Chardonnay, Pinot Noir, Pinot Blanc and Monterey Riesling," says publicity director Steve Wilson. "The cool climate of our Monterey County vineyards brings out the best in these grapes."

J. Lohr Vineyards & Winery • T GT

1000 Lenzen Ave., San Jose, CA 95126; (408) 288-5057. Daily 10 to 5; MC/VISA. Most varieties tasted. Good selection of wine logo gift items. Tours Saturday and Sunday at 11 and 2.

Despite its industrial-strength location, Jerry Lohr's urban winery presents an attractive picture. Hedges and bushes grace the narrow space between the sidewalk and the square-shouldered brick winery. The redwood paneled tasting room is spacious and inviting; barrels, vats and other winery trappings are just beyond. In one corner, a video cassette recites the J. Lohr story.

That story began in 1974 when Jerry started making wine in this facility, which once housed the Falstaff and Fredericksburg breweries. Much of the winemaking occurs in the field, however. Lohr's crew has done much of the pioneering in night harvesting and field pressing to start the process when the juice is cool and fresh. Output has grown rapidly, now topping 300,000 cases a year.

Tasting notes: Lohr wines have won an array of medals, particularly the lush and fruity whites. They come in two labels—the modestly priced Cypress line, from $5.75 to $7.75 and the J. Lohr Estates wines, $7.25 to $12.25. We favored the nutty, spicy and silky Estates Riverstone Chardonnay, the Wildflower Monterey Gamay, with great raspberry nose and flavor (a major medal winner) and a lush, peppery Seven Oaks Cabernet. Of the Cypress line, we liked a fruity, crisp and light Fume Blanc; spicy and subtly oaky Merlot and the Blush White, with a brisk berry flavor. It's not a rosè, but a white-red blend, made with Chenin Blanc, Riesling, Petit Sirah and Merlot.

Vintners choice: "Our Chardonnays, Rieslings and Gamay from Monterey County and Paso Robles Cabernet Sauvignon," said a winery voice.

Sunrise Winery • T CT

13100 Montebello Rd., Cupertino, CA 95014; (408) 741-1310. Friday-Sunday 11 to 3; MC/VISA. Most varieties tasted. A few wine logo items. Picnic area near tasting room; informal tours.

From urban J. Lohr, the pendulum swings bucolic. Sunrise occupies old stone and wooden buildings at the Picchetti Ranch, where a pioneering family made wine more than a century earlier. Ronald and Rolayne Stortz started the present-day operation, moving from their Felton location in 1983. The setting is so oak-shaded rural Americana that it's often used as a movie location. It will remain unchanged, for the Picchetti Ranch is part of the Montebello Ridge Open Space Preserve.

The winery is reached by a farmyard lane from a large graveled parking lot that also serves as a trailhead for open space hikers. The tasting room, a small table and a few wine logo items, is a tiny presence in a huge wooden-floored barn. Quiet conversation echoes to far, empty corners. Standing there sipping wine, we felt the place needed something more. A barn dance, perhaps.

Tasting notes: Chardonnay, Pinot Blanc, Sauvignon Blanc and white Riesling comprise the white list; reds are Pinot Noir, Zinfandel and Cabernet. We liked the nutty, lush flavor of the malolactic barrel-fermented Chardonnay and the herbal, grapey flavor of the Riesling. A five-year old Pinot Noir was medium bodied with a nice berry flavor and tannin nip. A 12-year old Cabernet was lush, fully integrated and excellent, with chili pepper undertones. Prices range from $7.50 to $20.

Vintners choice: "Pinot Blanc, Pinot Noir and Estate Zinfandel" was Rolayne's roll call.

Ridge Vineyards • T GT ⌅

17100 Montebello Rd. (P.O. Box AI), Cupertino, CA 95015; (408) 867-3233. Weekends only, 11 to 3; MC/VISA, AMEX. Selected wines tasted. A few wine logo items. Hilltop picnic area with dramatic views; tours by appointment the third Saturday of the month.

Ridge, indeed. Several Stanford Research Institute scientists retreated to this lofty perch in 1959. They built an earthy yet technologically advanced winery and began producing some of the finest Zinfandels in California. Paul Draper, called by some the state's most intellectual winemaker, joined the crew in the late 1970s. He's still there, intellectually and poetically creating Zin—perhaps with a bit of Zen.

The Ridge structures are rudimentary, appropriate to this final base camp of the vintners' art. If the winemaking approach here is inward, the view is outward—spectacular and more than panoramic. On a rare clear day, when vehicle exhaust and silicon dust have settled in the valley below, one can see San Francisco's highrises, 40 miles away. There's a feeling of Oz about this place. It's like sitting on a vineyard cloud, peering down at a reality that can't touch you.

Bring lunch and buy a bottle. Picnic tables are at the highest point of Oz, sitting among 40-year old Cabernet vines, like gnarled old guardian angels. You won't want to leave.

Tasting notes: The Zinfandel list has been expanded considerably to include Cabernet Sauvignon, Chardonnay, Merlot and Petite Sirah. In fact, Cabs now dominate. Several vineyard-designated and vintage-year selections appear on the list, and a few are picked each weekend for tastings. We happened upon an incredibly lush and spicy eight-year-old Jimsomare Cabernet, a lush and nutty Santa Cruz Mountains Chardonnay and a raspberry-rich, mellow and subtly spicy eight-year-old Lime Kiln Zinfandel. A pepper-spice 10-year-old Petite Sirah completed our day on the mountain.

Congress Springs Vineyards • T GT ⌅

23600 Congress Springs Rd., Saratoga, CA 95070; (408) 867-1409. Daily 11 to 5; MC/VISA. Most varieties tasted. A few wine logo items; picnic area. Guided tours by appointment.

Down off the ridge but still in a nice wooded setting, Congress Springs occupies a shallow, sheltered hollow. Redwoods and other conifers guard this little vineyard valley, reached by a short, tree-canopied drive from Congress Springs Road. Vineyards tumble down a gentle slope and wine is made in a century-old concrete building farther up the hill. Tasting happens in an appealing old wood frame building with rough log rafters.

A French-owned winery dating back to 1910, the facility was reactivated by the Dan Gehrs and Vic Erickson families in 1976. It's now operated by Anglo American Agriculture, Inc., with founder Gehrs as winemaker.

Tasting notes: On the list are Pinot Blanc, Chardonnay, Pinot Noir, Merlot, sparkling Blanc de Noir and Blanc de Blancs. A medal-winning Pinot Blanc offered a nice fruit-acid balance and a spicy flavor; Pinot Noir and Merlot were both soft and full flavored. A San Ysidero Chardonnay was lush and fruity with a crisp ending. Prices range from $9.50 to the mid-teens.

Vintners choice: The winery's Joe Andrè said simply: "We make premium Chardonnays."

Mirassou Champagne Cellars • T GT

300 College Ave. (at the Novitiate of Los Gatos), Los Gatos, CA 95032; (408) 395-3790. Daily noon to 5; MC/VISA, AMEX. Good selection of wine logo items. Guided tours at 12:30, 2 and 3:30.

Like Wente, Mirassou found an historic site for its sparkling wine operation. It leased the 1888 Novitiate cellars, where Brother Corte produced memorable wines until a decade ago. The Novitiate of Los Gatos still owns the property; it has chosen to leave the winemaking to others.

This is indeed a handsome spot, tucked into a mountain shelf, half a mile above Los Gatos. Visitors enter through a formal gate and follow a tree-lined passage to the white-washed, tile-roofed Colonial Spanish complex. The tasting room, housed in a bold cut-stone building, is reached via a glowering stone archway right out of an Indiana Jones movie set. But the airy hospitality room is quite cheerful. Tours take visitors through the ancient winery buildings and pleasantly musty aging caves burrowed into surrounding hills.

Tasting notes: Mirassou produces four sparkling wines, all by *mèthode champenoise*. We enjoyed a crisp and dry Au Naturel made from Pinot Noir and Chardonnay; a light, lean and clean Blanc de Noirs of 100 percent Pinot Noir; and a Brut with just a hint of sweetness and a nice touch of the grape.

THE BEST OF THE BUNCH

The best wine buys • Wente Brothers Estate Winery and Fenestra Winery in Livermore Valley; Weibel Vineyards at Mission San Jose; and J. Lohr Winery in San Jose.

The most attractive wineries • Wente Brothers Sparkling Wine Cellars and Chouinard Winery in Livermore Valley; Ridge Vineyards (site) on Montebello Ridge; and Mirassou Champagne Cellars in Los Gatos.

The most interesting tasting rooms • Concannon Vineyard and Wente Brothers Estate Winery in Livermore Valley; Weibel Vineyards at Mission San Jose; J. Lohr Winery in San Jose; and Congress Springs Vineyards near Saratoga.

The funkiest tasting rooms • Retzlaff Vineyards and Fenestra Winery in Livermore Valley.

The best gift shop • Wente Brothers Estate in Livermore Valley.

The nicest picnic areas • Retzlaff Vineyards, Concannon Vineyard and Chouinard Winery in Livermore Valley; Ridge Vineyards on Montebello Ridge.

The best tours • Wente Brothers Sparkling Wine Cellars in Livermore Valley and Mirassou Champagne Cellars in Los Gatos.

BEYOND THE VINEYARDS

As you have noted, the southern Bay Area is a mix of spreading suburbia laced with hide-away canyons, beige hills and wooded ridges of the Santa Cruz Mountains.

While in the Livermore Valley, you might take a break at **Del Valle Regional Park** at the end of Arroyo Road. It offers swimming, boating and picnicking. **Pleasanton,** Livermore's next-door neighbor, has a pleasing early American look to its downtown area, with some interesting boutiques. As you work southwestward in your winery quest, check out the **San Francisco Water Temple** just off Sunol Road at the head of **Niles Canyon**. The canyon itself, as we noted earlier, has nice spots for picnicking, swimming and bank-sitting. **Mission San Josè de Guadalupe** in the Warm Springs district of Fremont is certainly worth a visit.

The **San Jose-Santa Clara** area has several major attractions, ranging from **Great America** amusement park to musueums and missions. Write to the sources at the end of this chapter for details.

If you've come here from the Bay Area and you aren't weary of winding roads, consider returning via the Coast Range's skyline ridge. **Skyline Boulevard** follows the ridgeline all the way to Belmont. There, you can pick up Highway 92 and go east to the Bayshore or west to U.S. Highway 1 and continue into San Francisco. To reach Skyline (Highway 35) take State Route 9 north from Saratoga; it intersects with Route 35 at Saratoga Gap. Views to the east and west are impressive from this remote path high above the densely populated Bay Area.

South Bay vineyard area attractions

Hot air ballooning • Professor Muldoon's Hot Air Balloon Co., P.O. Box 867, Pleasanton, CA 94566; (800) 822-3333 or (510) 449-4490.

Farm products • Maps listing farms and wineries selling directly to the public. ***Alameda County Farm Trails,*** available at many wineries and farm trail participants, or send a stamped, self-addressed business-sized envelope to: Alameda County Farm Trails, 658 Enos Way, Livermore, CA 94550. ***Country Crossroads,*** listing outlets in Santa Clara and Santa Cruz counties; available at farm and winery members or send a stamped, self-addressed business-sized envelope to: Country Crossroads, Santa Clara County Farm Bureau, 1368 N. Fourth St., San Jose, CA 95112.

Attractions near the vineyards•

Hakkone Gardens, 21000 Big Basin Way, Saratoga; (408) 867-3438, ext. 43. Weekdays 10 to 5, weekends 11 to 5; donation requested. Formal Japanese gardens in 15-acre park.

Lawrence Livermore Laboratory Visitors Center, Greenville Rd., Livermore; (510) 422-9797. Weekdays 9 to 4:30, weekends noon to 5; free. Exhibits and slide show concerning the search for new energy sources.

Mission San Josè de Guadalupe, 43300 Mission Blvd., Fremont; (510) 657-1797. Daily 10 to 5; free. Mission chapel and museum with pioneer artifacts.

Villa Montalvo, Montalvo Road, off State Highway 9 southeast of Saratoga; (408) 741-3421. Weekdays 8 to 5, weekends 9 to 5, shorter hours for gallery; free. Lush gardens around a Mediterranean villa with an arboretum, art gallery and theater.

Wineland events • Summer vineyard concerts at Paul Masson's Mountain winery, (408) 741-5182; Wente Winery summer concert series featuring major stars, (510) 443-1500; Harvest Celebration sponsored by Livermore Valley Winegrowers, Labor Day weekend, (510) 443-1500;

Winery touring maps • ***Livermore Valley Winegrowers Map***, free at valley wineries or call (510) 443-1500. ***Wines of Santa Clara Valley***, free at wineries or contact Santa Clara Valley Wine Growers Association, P.O. Box 1192, Morgan Hill, CA 95037; (408) 779-2145 or (408) 778-1555. ***Winetrails of the Santa Cruz Mountains,*** listing mountain wineries between Woodside and Santa Cruz, free at participating wineries.

South Bay information sources

Since South Bay wineries are rather spread out, few lodgings or restaurants are within the vineyard areas, with the notable exception of The Restaurant at Wente Sparkling Wine Cellars, listed above. There are, of course, hundreds of restaurants and lodgings in the communities of this thickly populated area. Sources below will happily provide long lists of them.

Livermore Chamber of Commerce, 2157 First St., Livermore, CA 94550; (510) 447-1606.

Pleasanton Chamber of Commerce, 450 Main St., Suite 202, Pleasanton, CA 94566; (510) 846-5858

Los Gatos Chamber of Commerce, 50 University Ave., Los Gatos, CA 95030; (408) 354-9300.

San Jose Chamber of Commerce, 180 S. Market St., San Jose, CA 95113; (408) 998-7000.

San Jose Convention & Visitors Bureau Tour and Travel Information Center, 333 W. San Carlos St., San Jose, CA 95110; (408) 295-9600.

Saratoga Chamber of Commerce, 20460 Saratoga-Los Gatos Rd., Saratoga, CA 95070; (408) 867-0753.

"A tough wine, but the focused cherry and raspberry flavors manage to make themselves heard above the tannic din."

—Description of a 1985 Parusso Barolo from Barbaresco, Italy

Chapter Eight

SOUTHERN SANTA CLARA

Friendly family wineries in garlic country

Southern Santa Clara Valley ranks with northern Sonoma County as one of our favorite winery touring areas. The wines are excellent and affordably priced, the wineries are easy to find and the folks are friendly.

The region's focal point is Gilroy, a town of about 25,000 that's better known for garlic than for wine. Indeed, it produces a lot of both.

Community leaders don't mind being kidded about Gilroy's garlicky reputation. In fact, they encourage it; highway signs proclaim the town to be the Garlic Capital of the World. It's a rightful claim, since 90 percent of America's garlic is produced thereabouts. If that statistic doesn't take your breath away, the aroma during the annual Gilroy Garlic Festival will.

"It's the only town in America where you can marinate a steak by hanging it on a clothesline," Will Rogers once quipped.

During the festival, held in late July, citizens present their "scented pearls" in every conceivable format, from garnishes to garlands. Events include a *Tour de Garlique* bicycle run, Garlic Gallop, Garlic Squeeze Barn Dance and—hold your breath for the grand finale—the Great Garlic Cookoff. The *Los Angeles Herald Examiner* called it the "ultimate summer food fair."

You needn't wait for the festival to immerse yourself in the scented pearl—or the stinking rose, depending on your attitude regarding garlic breath. Two stores on U.S. 101 just south of town, Garlic World and The Garlic Shoppè, will sell you garlic-laced relish, mustard, marinade, jam, butter, ice cream and—clear your palate—garlic wine.

With all that garlic and all that wine, can Italians be far behind? The list of wineries reads like a Milano phone book: Fortino, Conrotto, Rapazzini, Pedrizzetti and Guglielmo. Names like Kirigin, Kruse, Blocher of Live Oaks Winery, Vanni and Wilson of Solis and Yamaki of Sycamore Creek have been stirred in to create an international brew of winemakers.

Mostly they make red. The sloping hills and sheltering mountains provide the proper soils and warm climate for Zinfandel, Grignolino, Carignan, Petit Sirah, Cabernet and Merlot. You'll find fine whites as well, particularly more full-flavored types such as Chardonnay, Johannisberg Riesling and Sauvignon Blanc.

Wineries of the South Santa Clara region are conveniently packaged. Most stand alongside Hecker Pass Highway west of Gilroy and in the Uvas Valley to the north. Others are within minutes of U.S. 101 freeway between Gilroy and Morgan Hill.

Despite their easy access, they're rarely crowded. On a typical day, you'll find few other visitors in the tasting rooms, and the person pouring your wine might be the one who made it. These are mostly family operations, ranging from third-generation vintners of Guglielmo Winery to the newly-arrived Dave Vanni of Solis.

Neither garlic nor Italians figure in the early history of this area. In the mid-19th century, a dour Scotsman named John Cameron went AWOL from a British ship in Monterey Bay and scampered northward. Using his mother's maiden name of Gilroy (presumably to avoid being shanghaied back to his ship), he befriended the Ortega ranching family, married one of its daughters and settled down. The Ortega-Gilroys planted orchards and raised cattle, gradually forming the hub of a community.

Just up the trail, an Irishman named Martin Murphy acquired a chunk of Rancho Ojo de Agua de la Coche in 1845. In 1882, his granddaughter Diana married wealthy San Franciscan Morgan Hill, and they built a lavish ranch estate. Thus, the town bordering the northern edge of this wine country was named for a gentleman, not a mountain.

Hills do occur in abundance, however. The lower Santa Clara Valley is cradled between the Diablo Range to the east and the Madonna ridge of the Santa Cruz Mountains westward. Highway 152, slicing west to east through this area, spirals over two noted passes—Hecker and Pacheco.

SOUTHERN SANTA CLARA VALLEY WINERY TOUR • This is another area you might prefer to tour on weekends, since some of the wineries have limited weekday hours. A good number are open daily, however.

After going through urban San Jose and Montebello Ridge contortions, this route is simple, and relatively flat. It's also relatively rural, since most of the area is still beyond the circle of suburbia that spreads like rings of disturbed water from greater San Jose.

Driving along U.S. 101, you pass by checkerboard agricultural lands and an occasional vineyard. In **Morgan Hill**, go east from the freeway on Dunne Road, immediately turn left onto Condit Road and follow it less than a mile to Main Avenue. Turn right and you'll soon arrive at **Emilio Guglielmo Winery** (pronounced *Goo-YELL-mo),* just across the road from a high school. Obviously, Morgan Hill have encroached, but vineyards and farm fields still stretch to the east.

Re-trace your route down Main and go south on Condit beyond Dunne Road to San Pedro Avenue, the next cross street. A left turn brings you shortly to **Pedrizzetti Winery.** Return yet again to Condit and continue south to Tennant Avenue and turn right, which gets you back on the freeway.

You might want to continue into Morgan Hill; its downtown area along Monterey Road is spruced up with landscaped sidewalks, brick crosswalks

and street plantings. A few boutiques and antique shops may tempt you to explore. Most of Morgan Hill is contained between Tennant Road and Main Avenue. Until the freeway was completed a few years ago, U.S. 101 carried its heavy burden of traffic along Monterey Road through Morgan Hill, San Martin (pronounce it *Mar-TEEN*) and Gilroy. Freed from freight trucks and weekend traffic jams, the towns have redeveloped much of this stretch. Progress produces casualties, however. The long-popular **San Martin Winery** tasting room in the town of that name closed its doors recently for lack of *patròns.*

From Morgan Hill, either stay on Monterey Road (if you don't mind a few stoplights), or continue south on U.S. 101 to **Gilroy** and take the Highway 152 exit to the right. It does one zig and one zag through town: left onto Monterey Road and right onto First Street. As you clear Gilroy's suburbs,

First Street becomes Hecker Pass Highway, which delivers you to most of the area's wineries. It's one of south Santa Clara's nicest drives, passing vineyards, flower and tree nurseries and winding toward forested Madonna ridge, often capped with a soft halo of clouds.

Your first encounter is **A. Conrotto Winery,** on the left, just beyond Santa Teresa Boulevard. A bit farther is **Goldsmith Seeds, Inc.,** which presents a spectacular quilt of blooming flowers in summer. Visitors are welcome to stroll among its brilliant fields and admire its striking geometric floral displays. Take your camera. **Hecker Pass family amusement park** is just beyond, followed by **Western Tree Nursery,** with great forests of potted trees.

The wineries now come thick and fast. You encounter **Live Oaks Winery** on your right, **Solis Winery** (*SOLE-lees*) on your left and **Sarah's Vineyard** (open by appointment only) on the right. **Thomas Kruse Winery** is on the left, opposite the Watsonville Road turnoff, and **Fortino** winery is just beyond, on the right. The final Hecker Pass Highway winery, appropriately called **Hecker Pass Winery,** is next to Fortino, also on the right.

Backtrack briefly to Watsonville Road, turn left and you'll encounter **Kirigin Cellars** after about 2.5 miles; it's on the right, just beyond Day Road. A bit past Kirigin, fork left onto Uvas Road and you'll quickly see **Sycamore Creek Vineyards.**

Return now to downtown Gilroy and follow either Monterey Road or U.S. 101 south. Just beyond the point where the two merge, you'll see **Garlic World,** then **Rapazzini Winery** and **The Garlic Shoppè,** all on the left. We'd recommend taking Monterey Road through old downtown, some of which is being redeveloped. The **Gilroy Visitors Bureau** is on the left, two blocks south of First Street at Monterey and IOOF Street. Nearby, also on the left, is the wonderful old **Gilroy City Hall** with its fantasyland clock tower.

Emilio Guglielmo Winery • T

1480 E. Main Ave., Morgan Hill, CA 95037; (408) 779-2145. Weekdays 9 to 5, weekends 10 to 5; major credit cards. Most varieties tasted. Good wine logo and specialty foods selection. Picnic patio near vineyards.

Immigrant Emilio Guglielmo started making wines in 1925, and this handsome facility is the one of the oldest of the Southern Santa Clara Valley wineries. However, that's rather recent in the family time-line; Guglielmo winemakers have been traced back to Roman times. The family enterprise is presently run by Emilio's son George and his two sons, Gene and Gary, with yet another generation coming along.

The Guglielmo tasting room/gift shop is an inviting space, Spanish style with thick tile floors, warm woods and brick trim. Picnic tables sit beside the vineyards on an attractive patio. As roomy as it seems, all this soon will be expanded into a Mediterranean-style hospitality center, says Gene.

Tasting notes: Guglielmo wines, straightforward and full bodied, have won a good share of awards. Issued under three labels, Guglielmo Reserve, Mt. Madonna and Emile's, they cover most of the red, white and blush spectrum. Our favorites were a light, crisp picnic-style Mt. Madonna Pinot Blanc and several Guglielmo Reserve wines—a fruity, nutty-flavored Chardonnay with a soft finish; a spicy and full-bodied Zinfandel and a big, peppery and herbal Cabernet Sauvignon. A Grignolino, rarely found as a varietal, had a lively berry nose and good spicy-fruity flavor. Prices are modest, ranging from $7 to $12.

Pedrizzetti Winery • T CT ⌶

1645 San Pedro Ave., Morgan Hill, CA 95037; (408) 779-7389. Daily 9 to 5, major credit cards. Most varieties tasted. A few wine logo items. Small picnic area; casual tours.

We'd pulled winemaker Allen Kreutzer off the bottling line to sample some wines, and he seemed rather intense. Which was fine, because so were his wines—intensely straightforward and excellent.

"Wine should be clean but not pristine," he said. "Every time you fine a red, you take something out of it."

After tasting, it was evident that Kreutzer had put a lot of skill into his wines, and taken very little out of them.

Ed and Phyllis Pedrizzetti started this winery in 1945 and it's still family-owned, with Kreutzer doing the creative work. It's a simple affair. The winery is housed in a basic masonry building and the tasting room is in a tiny space that more resembles a wine shop than a hospitality center.

Tasting notes: Although it's a small operation, Pedrizzetti generates an impressive array of wines, including most of the premium varietals, several fruit wines, a sherry, port, brandy and sparkling wine. We particularly liked a full-bodied, spicy Chardonnay with a nice crisp finish; a peppery and light but complex Zinfandel; and a Cabernet Sauvignon with a great chili pepper nose and lush flavor with a nice tannic nip. A raspberry wine was delicious; it was like drinking crushed berries. Wines are very modestly priced, from $5 to $9.75.

A. Conrotto Winery • T ⌶

1690 Hecker Pass Highway, Gilroy, CA 95020; (408) 842-3053. Weekends only 11 to 5 (11:30 to 5 in winter), MC/VISA, DISC. Most varieties tasted. A few wine logo items. Small picnic area.

Housed in a cute little red shed, Conrotto's rustic tasting room looks out over an orchard, not a vineyard. A deck invites visitors to linger. A small vineyard of Symphony grapes up front reminds visitors that this is indeed a winery.

This pocket-size, bucolic winery is one of the area's oldest, founded by Anselmo Conrotto in 1926. It's presently run by his two daughters and their husbands, Jim and Jean Burr and Gerald and Jermaine Case; they produce about 6,000 cases a year.

Tasting notes: The Conrotto list is small: Zinfandel, Burgundy, Chablis and Rosè, all made in a hearty full-flavored Italian style. The Burgundy is an excellent spaghetti wine, a blend of Grenache, Carignan and Barbara. Petit

---

WINERY CODES • T = tasting with no fee; **T$** = fee for tasting; **GT** = guided tours; **GTA** = appointment required for tour; **ST** = self-guiding tours; **CT** = casual tours or a peek into the winery; ⌶= picnic area; 🎁= separate gift shop or good giftware selection. Price ranges listed in tasting notes are for varietals; jug wines often are available for less. **DINING & LODGINGS • ØØ** = smoke-free establishment; **Ø** = non-smoking tables or rooms.

The Fortino Winery peeks through a veil of its vineyards along Hecker Pass Highway near Gilroy.

Sirah, Sauvignon Blanc and an award-winning cream sherry sometimes appear on the list. Prices are modest, staying well under $10.

Live Oaks Winery • T ⚔

3875 Hecker Pass Highway, Gilroy, CA 95020; (408) 842-2401. Daily 8 to 5, MC/VISA, AMEX. Most varieties tasted. Picnic area near tasting room.

Oak-shaded Live Oaks Winery began life in 1912 as the project of one Eduardo Scagliotti. His original winery, bunkered into the side of a hill, now houses the tasting room and aging cellars. Present-day owners are Richard and Barbara Blocher.

You must wander through an old farm yard and follow a graveled road down into a hollow to find the rustic little place. Once there, you step into a long, rudimentary tasting room whose walls are lined—not with wine—but with glossies of TV and movie stars. Tasting room manager Al Whitaker collects celebrity photos, claiming an accumulation of about 20,000. He sells them, along with wines, in the tasting room. If you need the latest pic of Tom Selleck or a vintage photo of ex-President Reagan as a drugstore cowboy, this is the place.

Tasting notes: Live Oaks offers several whites that lean toward the sweet side and some rather light reds. Of the whites, only Chenin Blanc and Chardonnay were dry; both were crisp with light finishes. A Zinfandel was subtly peppery and a Cabernet Sauvignon was gently herbal; both were light in tannin. Prices are modest, ranging from $4.50 to $8.

Solis Winery • T ⌆

3920 Hecker Pass Hwy., Gilroy, CA 95020; (408) 847-6306. Open daily January to April and Wednesday through Sunday May to December, 11 to 5; major credit cards. Most varieties tasted. A few wine gift items. Picnic area with vineyard view.

This winery with an up and down history is up again. After a period of silence, it was dusted off and reopened in 1990 by Watsonville nurseryman Dave Vanni. Young U.C. Davis graduate Cory Wilson makes the wine and his wife Laura runs the business end. The facility dates back to 1917, when it was started by the Alfonso Bertrero family. It managed to survive Prohibition and Berteros ran it until 1980, then it was operated by a corporation as Summerhill Winery until recently.

Solis, which produces about 5,000 cases a year, has one of the most appealing tasting rooms in the area. A curved tasting bar is matched by a curving bay window that offers a CinemaScopic view of vineyards and distant forested ridges.

Tasting notes: Winemaker Cory likes to produce big fruit flavors with light woods. The list includes Sauvignon Blanc, Chardonnay, Pinot Noir, Merlot and Zinfandel, plus a Muscat Canelli and proprietary red. We especially liked the Sauvignon Blanc, crispy and subtly spicy; a Santa Clara Pinot Noir with a nice dusky nose and big berry-like flavor; and a San Luis Obispo County Zinfandel with a great raspberry nose and lush taste. Prices range from $6.50 to $12.50.

Vintners choice: "Our Sauvignon Blanc and Johannisberg Riesling," says Cory. "Of the reds, I favor the Pinot Noir and Merlot."

Thomas Kruse Winery • T$ GTA ⌆

4390 Hecker Pass Hwy., Gilroy, CA 95020; (408) 842-7016. Weekends 12 to 5; no credit cards. Most varieties tasted for $1 fee (refunded with purchase). Small picnic area. Guided tours by appointment or informal tours on the spot.

Tom Kruse is regarded as a renaissance man of the wine business. A laconic, philosophical muse, he started the winery in 1971, some years after fleeing the tumult of Chicago. He reactivated a winery originally built in 1910 by the Caesar Roffinella family; it had lain idle since 1946.

His wines and his operation are simple and forthright. Some of his labels are hand-written; one featured a detailed cost breakdown, from grape to foil cap, to suggest that some in the business are charging too much. His laid-back wineyard is a casual scatter of rudimentary equipment—an old red tractor, plastic jugs and barrels for fermenting, a canoe paddle for stirring. Tastings occur on a plank inside a battered winery structure, or on a barrel head outside. "No loose pets, ill behaved children, bicyclists or large groups of Republicans," advises a sign.

Tasting notes: Kruse produces about 3,000 cases a year, focusing on dry and crisp whites and reds that retain the fruity flavor of the grape. The list is mostly red—a rarely-found varietal Grignolino, Zinfandel, Cabernet

Sauvignon, Pinot Noir, Carignan and good old Gilroy Red. Its companion, Gilroy White, and Chardonnay cover the white side of the ledger, plus a bottle-fermented sparkling wine aptly called Insouciance.

Vintners choice: "Dorky question," he responded laconically.

Fortino Winery • T GTA

4525 Hecker Pass Hwy., Gilroy, CA 95020; (408) 842-3305. Daily 9 to 6; MC/VISA. Most varieties tasted. Gift shop with good selection of wine related items and specialty foods, plus a smaller boutique. Deli with cheeses, sliced meats and other fare. Guided tours by appointment. Shaded picnic area.

Fortino is the largest, busiest and most versatile of the Hecker Pass wineries. One can buy picnic fare from the Italian deli or have a hefty sandwich constructed, pick out a bottle of wine or a soft drink, and adjourn to a tree-shaded picnic area beside a vineyard.

Ernie and Marie Fortino have created all this in 20 years, after buying the old Cassa Brothers Winery in 1970. Like many of his Italian neighbors, Ernie is an immigrant from the old country, but one of recent vintage. Arriving in 1959, the amiable workaholic began building his version of the American dream. Typical of vintner families, the Fortinos are starting a dynasty. Son Gino, daughter Terri and her husband Brian Dauenhauer are now helping run things. New daughter-in-law Jenny, on the staff of the local newspaper, hasn't yet been lured into the business.

Tasting notes: Ernie's list ranges from red and white varietals to sparkling wine and cream sherry. He's noted for fine full-bodied reds; not fancy yuppie creations, but honest, forthright wines. They've won a good share of awards. This list includes Carignan, Ruby Cabernet, Pinot Noir and Charbono. Our favorites were a rich, spicy and berry-like Petit Syrah; a Cabernet Sauvignon, soft and lush yet with enough tannin to encourage aging; and a fine Zinfandel with a great raspberry nose and taste. His Burgundy Reserve is one of our regular daily wines. Of the whites, we liked a lush Chardonnay with a gentle nip at the end and a Johannisberg Riesling with a nice floral nose and complex flavors. Prices are modest, ranging from $5.50 to $12.50.

Vintners choice: Ernie flashed one of his impish grins and thought for a moment. We could see that he didn't want to commit himself to a favorite. "They're all good. What can I say?"

Hecker Pass Winery • T GTA

4605 Hecker Pass Hwy., Gilroy, CA 95020; (408) 842-8755. Daily 9 to 6; MC/VISA. Most varieties tasted. Some wine logo gift items. Picnic area; guided tours by appointment.

Pardon the pun, but the Fortinos seems to have bottled up the western end of the Gilroy wine country. Ernie's brother Mario Fortino and his wife Frances opened their Hecker Pass Winery in 1972. The two brothers, both "back to basics" winemakers, engage in friendly competition. Like his brother, Mario is noted for his robust, full-bodied reds.

"Let the wine be wine," Mario said. "Chemists have no place in the wine business."

The tasting room is a simple affair, with wood paneling decorated mostly with award ribbons. A pleasant picnic area sits beside the vineyards, near the wooded slopes of Mount Madonna.

Tasting notes: Mario's reds dominate the list, and they're excellent—uniformly spicy and full-bodied; all are 100 percent varietal. The Zinfandel was nicely herbal with a good berry flavor and nippy tannic finish; Carignan had a spicy taste with big but not harsh tannins; and Petit Sirah had a nice herbal-berry flavor. Of the more mellow wines, we liked Mario's Red Velvet, a "secret blend" that was soft, yet full-flavored with a gentle finish. Chablis, Blanc de Blanc, Grenache Rosè, Carignan Ruby and a generic burgundy complete the list. Prices are very modest, from $5 to $7.

Kirigin Cellars • T GTA ⌆

11550 Watsonville Rd., Gilroy, CA 95020; (408) 847-8827. Daily 10 to 6; MC/VISA. All varieties tasted. Attractive picnic area. Tours by appointment.

The Gilroy countryside is populated by philosophical winemakers.

"Dinner without wine is like a date without kissing," said 73-year-old Nikola Kirigin Chargin, in his soft middle European accent.

He claims to be semi-retired, although he makes 2,000 cases of wine a year and he still greets visitors in his pleasantly spartan tasting room. A good talker, he'll tell you that the wine industry, wine writers and wine judges make too much fuss about things. He refuses to enter competitions because he thinks judging is silly.

"How can someone else judge your taste?"

Mostly, he gets upset about government intervention, mandated warning signs, and a general American indifference to their country. He has good reason. He left his native Croatia in disgust after it became Communist Yugoslavia and the government took over his family winery. After working for several vintners, he bought the old Uvas Winery in 1976, at an age when most men are contemplating retirement.

He still talks about retiring, while continuing to host his tasting room visitors. Incidentally, the Kirigin facility is quite nice, built around a stylish old country home, with picnic tables under sheltering trees.

Tasting notes: Out of respect to Nikola, who dislikes winetasting verbosity even more than we do, we'll keep it simple: The list includes Sauvignon Blanc, Chardonnay, Sauvignon Vert, Gewürztraminer, Malvasia Bianca, Pinot Noir, Cabernet Sauvignon and Zinfandel. Whites are nice and full-bodied, not processed to blandness; reds are lush, tasting like the grapes they came from. Our favorites were Sauvingon Blanc, Chardonnay, Cabernet, Zinfandel and a delicious dessert wine called Vino de Mocca. It's made of wine, cocoa, chocolate and orange. Prices are modest, ranging from $5.50 to $8.50 and they haven't changed in six years.

Is that simple enough, Nick?

Vintners choice: Nick looked at me as if I were crazy, then he smiled. "Why do you care what I like? You tell me what *you* like!"

Sycamore Creek Vineyards • T ⌆

12775 Uvas Rd., Morgan Hill, CA 95037; (408) 779-4738. Weekends only, 11:30 to 5; MC/VISA, AMEX. Most varieties tasted. A few wine-related items.

This small winery sits in a bucolic little hollow, surrounded by vineyards and shaded by an assortment of mature trees. Neat white-painted wooden outbuildings and trim landscaping give it the look of a prosperous, well-maintained old farm. The winery dates back beyond Prohibition, when it was started by the Marchetti family. Later abandoned, it was rehabilitated by Terry and Mary Kay Parks, who operated it until the late 1980s.

A Japanese winemaking firm called Koshu Budoshu Honpo bought the facility in 1989 and sent winemaker-manager Hideki "Mike" Yamaki to run things. Winemaking was no problem; he'd been doing that in Japan for more than a decade. The real challenge was to learn English. He's done so with remarkable speed and you'll be interested in his comments about Japanese wines compared with those made in America. Japanese prefer sweet wines, and Mike is building a strong following for this style at Sycamore Creek.

Tastings—sweet and dry—occur in a pleasing, country-style tasting room with plank floors, wormwood walls and views of vines and trees.

Tasting notes: Yamaki recently won a gold medal for a semi-sweet Gamay Blanc. We liked its rich, honey-like flavor. He earned a silver for a perfumey and tasty semi-sweet Johannisberg Riesling. His "Romeo and Juliet" dessert wine was so rich it was like drinking liquid fruit. Mike can make 'em dry, as well. We especially liked a spicy and fruity Sauvignon Blanc and a crisp, light Chardonnay. A selection of soft, flavorful reds—Carignan, Zinfandel, Cabernet Sauvignon and Pinot Noir—compete the list. Prices range from $6 to $15.

Vintners choice: Not surprisingly, winemaker Yamaki favors his medal-winning Gamay Blanc and Johannisberg Riesling.

Rapazzini Winery • T

4350 Highway 101, Gilroy, CA 95020; (408) 842-5649. Daily 9 to 6 in summer and 9 to 5 the rest of the year; MC/VISA. Most varieties tasted. Extensive giftware and specialty food selection, with emphasis on garlic products. Tasting and specialty foods also at the Rapazzini-owned Garlic Shoppè, a few hundred feet south.

It requires a good sense of humor to get serious about garlic, and Jon P. Rapazzini's family has done so. They opened their winery in 1962, and expanded to include a long list of garlic-laced specialty foods. "Mama Rap" Rapazzini has added the spicy pearl to just about everything imaginable: relish, sauces, mustards, mayonnaise, chips, dressings and yes—even chocolate, jelly and ice cream. Several of these items can be sampled at the two tasting rooms.

Finally, are you ready for garlic wine? After sampling the above, can you tell the difference? It's a French Colombard, which the family has had the courage to name *Château de Garlic.* It's crisp and subtly fruity with a lingering—*definitely* lingering—finish.

"It goes well with garlic-spiced foods," our hostess said with a straight face.

The tasting room is quite handsome, made of cut stone, with a long copper tasting bar and a fireplace dominating one corner.

Tasting notes: Really, folks, these are serious wines, with medals to prove it. The list contains Sauvingon Blanc, Chardonnay, a couple of blushes, Merlot, Cabernet Sauvignon, Petit Sirah, Zinfandel and some specialty dessert wines including a rich cream sherry. We liked a dry, subtly nutty Chardonnay; a Merlot with medium body, raspberry flavor and a hint of oak; a soft peppery Cabernet Sauvingon with light tannins; and a big Zinfandel, aged to perfection with a lots of berries and spice. Most of the reds are held six to ten years before release. Prices range from $6.50 to the mid-teens. Take home *Château de Garlic* for a mere $6.

THE BEST OF THE BUNCH

The best wine buys • Southern Santa Clara wines are among the best buys in California; prices are very uniform among the various wineries. It was difficult to select overall "price leaders." So we didn't.

The most attractive wineries • Kirigin Cellars and Sycamore Creek Vineyards.

The most interesting tasting rooms • Guglielmo Winery, Solis Winery, Fortino Winery, Sycamore Creek Vineyards and Rapazzini Winery.

The funkiest tasting room • Thomas Kruse Winery.

The best gift shops • Emilio Guglielmo Winery, Fortino Winery and Rapazzini Winery.

The nicest picnic areas • Emilio Guglielmo Winery and Kirigin .

BEYOND THE VINEYARDS

Wine is the main draw to this area, along with the seductive aroma of the scented pearl. Since the region is cradled between two mountain ranges, forests and their attendant hiking trails, campgrounds and picnic areas are but a short drive away.

Pressing beyond the wineries on Highway 152, you'll climb Hecker Pass Highway into pine and redwood country. Near the pass is **Mount Madonna County Park** with beautiful redwood groves, camping, picnicking and hiking trails. It is, incidentally, one of the prettier mountain parks in northern California, and it's rarely crowded. Just beyond is **Mount Madonna Inn** (see dining listing below), a longtime landmark offering impressive views to the west. From here, you tumble down to Watsonville and—take your pick—the coastal resort communities of Santa Cruz to the north or Monterey to the south.

Heading inland on Route 152, you climb wooded **Pacheco Pass**, which takes you into the broad San Joaquin Valley. Enroute, you might like to pause at **Casa De Fruta** (listed below under attractions). Continue down to **San Luis Reservoir,** with boating, swimming, picnicking and bird-watching; it's a state recreation area and wildlife refuge.

If you like wilderness areas, head east from Gilroy on Leavesley Road, following signs toward **Henry W. Coe State Park**. It's mostly undeveloped, with hiking trails and primitive camping. Once-famous **Gilroy Hot Springs**, near the park entrance, is to be restored to its former glory in the mid-1990s.

South Santa Clara activities & attractions

Family parks •

Casa de Fruta, 10031 Pacheco Pass Hwy., Hollister, CA 95023; 842-9316. Gift shop, wine and cheese tasting, small zoo, ball fields, train ride, RV park and motel (listed below).

Hecker Pass Family Adventure, 3050 Hecker Pass Hwy., Gilroy, CA 95020; 842-2121. Call for hours; admission fee. Train ride, zoo, water park, restaurant and such. Under construction and open only to groups at press time.

Farm products • ***Country Crossroads*** map lists farms and wineries selling directly to the public. Available at farm and winery members or send a stamped, self-addressed business-sized envelope to: Country Crossroads, Santa Clara County Farm Bureau, 600 Main St., Suite 2, Watsonville, CA 95076.

Garlic shops • **Garlic World**, 4800 Monterey Hwy. (U.S. 101), Gilroy; (800) 537-6122 or (408) 847-2251. Garlic-laced specialty foods, garlic souvenirs and a fruit and produce section. **The Garlic Shoppè**, 4350 Highway 101, Gilroy; 848-3646. Described above under Rapazzini Winery listing.

Hot air ballooning • The Gentle Adventure, P.O. Box 1617, Morgan Hill, CA 95038; 778-1945.

Museums •

Gilroy Historical Museum, in the old Carnegie Library building at Fifth and Church Streets, Gilroy; check Chamber of Commerce (842-6436) for hours. Early-day history exhibits.

Wagons to Wings Museum, 15060 Foothill Ave., Morgan Hill; 227-4607 or 779-4136. Wednesday-Sunday 10 to 8; free. Interesting collection of vehicles, from stagecoaches to rare old airplanes. To reach it, go east on San Martin Avenue from San Martin, then north on Foothill Avenue. **Flying Lady** aviation-theme restaurant is adjacent.

Wineland events • Gilroy Garlic Festival, mostly garlic but with winery participation, last full weekend of July, 842-1625; Fall Harvest Festival of the Southern Santa Clara Valley Vintners Assn., at Hecker Pass Family Adventure Park in mid-October, 842-6436.

Winery touring maps • ***South Santa Clara Wine Region*** map available at wineries or from Gilroy Convention & Visitors Bureau, 7780 Monterey St., Gilroy, CA 95020; 842-6346. ***Wines of Santa Clara Valley***, free at wineries or contact Santa Clara Valley Wine Growers Association, P.O. Box 1192, Morgan Hill, CA 95037; 779-2145 or 778-1555.

WINE COUNTRY DINING

Cielito Lindo Restaurant • ΔΔ $

7460 Monterey St., Gilroy (between Fifth and Sixth); (408) 842-7724. Mexican; dinners $5 to $8; wine and beer. Weekdays 10 a.m. to 9 p.m., weekends 8 to 10. Casual; reservations for groups only. Most major credit cards. Brightly decorated local favorite. Serves the usual smashed beans and rice dishes, plus specials such as sizzle-platter *fajitas, chimichangas* and *menudo.*

Harvest Time • ΔΔΔ $$$ Ø

7397 Monterey St. (Sixth Street), Gilroy: (408) 842-7575. California-continental; dinners $14 to $21; full bar service. Lunch weekdays 11:30 to 2, dinner nightly. Informal to casual; reservations accepted. MC/VISA. Stylish Victorian restaurant featuring local veggies—and garlic specialties, of course—from co-owner Don Christopher's ranch. Typical entrèes are stuffed chicken breast with feta, mahi mahi and garlic-stuffed blackened filet mignon. Crystal chandeliers, hunter green columns and Queen Anne furnishings. Patio service on weekends.

Mount Madonna Inn • ΔΔΔ $$ Y Ø

1285 Hecker Pass Hwy., Watsonville; (408) 724-2275. American; dinners $10 to $21; full bar service. Thursday-Saturday 4 to 10 p.m., Sunday 10 to 10. Informal to casual; reservations advised. Major credit cards. Long popular inn perched atop Hecker Pass, offering far-away views. Nights sparkle with the twinkle of a dozen cities. The menu ranges from pastas to assorted steaks, veal, chicken and seafood.

VINELAND LODGINGS

Best Western Inn • ΔΔ $$$ Ø

360 Leavesley Rd. (just off freeway), Gilroy, CA 95020; (800) 528-1234 or (408) 848-1467. Doubles $46.50 to $70.50, singles $42.50 to $52.50, family units $72.50 to $98.50. Major credit cards. A 42-unit hotel with TV movies, room phones, refrigerators. Spa, pool, coin laundry.

Casa de Fruta Motel • ΔΔ $$

10031 Pacheco Pass Hwy., Hollister, CA 95023; (408) 548-3813. Doubles $44 to $46, singles $42. MC/VISA. Country-style motel with TV, room phones and refrigerators; swimming pool. (See listing under "Family parks" above.)

Country Rose Inn Bed & Breakfast • ΔΔΔ $$$$ ØØ

455 Fitzgerald Ave. (Monterey Road), San Martin (mailing address: P.O. Box 1804, Gilroy, CA 95021-1804); (408) 842-0441. Doubles $85 to $149. Five rooms, all with private baths; full breakfast. MC/VISA, AMEX. Restored Dutch Colonial home on landscaped grounds shaded by ancient oaks. Rooms are a nice blend of antique and modern decor. In a rural setting on the edge of San Martin.

Forest Park Inn • ΔΔΔ $$$ Ø

375 Leavesley Rd., Gilroy, CA 95020; (800) 237-7846 or (408) 848-5144. Doubles $49 to $60, singles $37 to $41, suites $76 to $92. Major credit cards. Nicely-maintained 77-unit motel with TV movies, room phones, some refrigerators. Sauna, spa, pool. Lyons Restaurant serves American fare; dinners $7 to $11; open 24 hours; full bar service; non-smoking areas.

Super 8 Motel • ΔΔ $$ Ø

8435 San Ysidro (just off freeway), Gilroy, CA 95020; (800) 800-8000 or (408) 848-4108. Doubles $40 to $46, singles $34 to $38, suites $41 to $53. Major credit cards. A 53-unit motel with TV movies, room phones, some refrigerators. Continental breakfast, pool.

Southern Santa Clara Valley information sources

Gilroy Visitors Bureau, 7780 Monterey Rd., Gilroy, CA 95020; (408) 842-6436.

Morgan Hill Chamber of Commerce, 17875 Monterey Rd., Morgan Hill, CA 95037; (408) 779-9444.

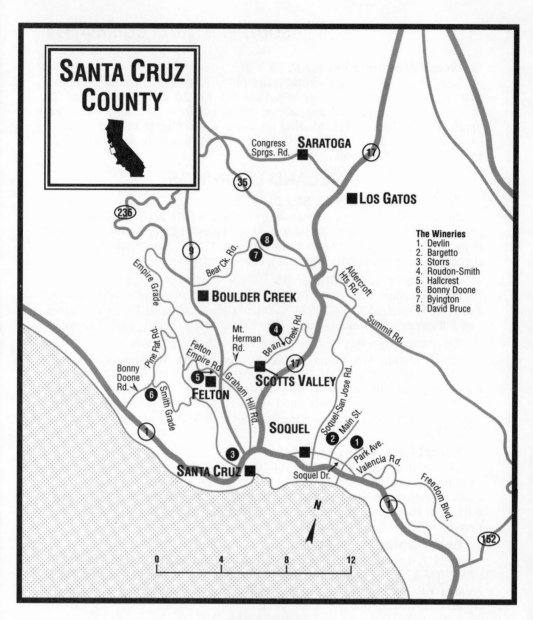

SANTA CRUZ COUNTY

Congress Sprgs. Rd.
SARATOGA
17
35
LOS GATOS
236
9
Bear Ck. Rd.
Empire Grade
Aldercroft Hts Rd.
BOULDER CREEK
Summit Rd.
Pine Flat Rd.
Mt. Herman Rd.
Bean Creek Rd.
Felton Empire Rd.
Graham Hill Rd.
SCOTTS VALLEY
Bonny Doone Rd.
Smith Grade
FELTON
Soquel-San Jose Rd.
Main St.
SOQUEL
1
Park Ave.
Valencia Rd.
SANTA CRUZ
Soquel Dr.
Freedom Blvd.
N
152
0 4 8 12

The Wineries

1. Devlin
2. Bargetto
3. Storrs
4. Roudon-Smith
5. Hallcrest
6. Bonny Doone
7. Byington
8. David Bruce

"It lumbers rather than dances. Of marginal quality for a wine of this pedigree, but some may find its funkiness appealing."

—Description of a 1988 Corton-Charlemagne white from Burgundy

Chapter Nine
SANTA CRUZ COUNTY
Pinot in the pines

Santa Cruz County is one of the neatest little packages in California. In one small space, it offers miles of lonely beaches, miles of busy beaches, some remarkably charming little communities, an excellent university, silent redwood forests—and some little jewels of wineries.

Although the county is on the rim of the San Francisco Bay Area, the thick wedge of the Santa Cruz Mountains keeps it relatively isolated. Only 225,000 people live here and its largest city, Santa Cruz, numbers about 45,000. It's a popular tourist destination, although many visitors stay on Highway 101 and go shooting past, landing in easier-to-reach Monterey.

The two are aquatic neighbors. Santa Cruz occupies the northern curve of huge Monterey Bay and Monterey has settled in the southern arch. This can cause confusion if you left your Boy Scout compass home and assume the ocean is west. Much of coastal Santa Cruz faces south.

Because of its sheltered southward position, the popular Santa Cruz seaside resort is often fog-free while Monterey is veiled in the mists. Expect the beaches to be cheek-to-cheek bikinis on a summer weekend. You'd best stay to the high ground if you want to avoid Coney Island West.

Which is just fine, because that's where you'll discover most of the wineries and all of the vineyards. If you've come looking for beaches and tawny young women and rustic piers and a great old art deco fun zone called the Santa Cruz Beach Boardwalk, you're in the wrong guidebook.

Actually, we encourage you to enjoy it all—the wineries, the woods *and* the beaches. I happen to like cheek-to-cheek bikinis.

The sheltering mountains spared this area from much of California's tumultuous history. The Spanish, waving their crosses and crossbows, did take the trouble to establish Mission Santa Cruz in 1791, naming it for the sacred cross. But they stuck it in the wrong place, on a narrow mountain-hugged coastal shelf instead of the fertile river delta to the south. It didn't fare well and when Mexico took California from Spain and secularized the missions, Santa Cruz was the first to go.

Americans came during the 1849 gold rush and did their best to rid the Santa Cruz Mountains of redwoods, since that was the lumber of choice for booming San Francisco and busy Monterey. Fortunately, they missed a few and several stands are now preserved in large parks.

When California joined the Union, gringo farmers began clearing the flood plain around present-day Watsonville and vintners sought suitable vineyard sites in the mountains. Commercial winemaking began in 1863 but it never was a major enterprise. All of the county's small wineries perished during Prohibition.

One of the first to crop up after Repeal was Bargetto Winery in Soquel. It's alive and well, still run by Bargetto descendants. It had few followers, however. Only three wineries were functioning by the 1960s. Then the wine boom of the '70s encouraged several solitude-seeking entrepreneurs to carve out vineyards in the steep slopes of the Santa Cruz Mountains. These heights offer cool micro-climates suited to Pinot Noir, Cabernet Sauvignon, Chardonnay, Gewürztraminer and Johannisberg Riesling.

Most wineries are still small and virtually all are family owned. Davis Bruce is the largest, with an output of 30,000 cases. They probably spill more wine than that at Gallo.

SANTA CRUZ COUNTY WINERY TOUR • You have to work to tour the county's wineries, since most are scattered among the trees. But it's nice work, taking you to the coastal resort of Santa Cruz, then high into its namesake mountains. Further, you'll discover some exceptional wines. Plan this outing for a weekend, since several of the wineries have limited hours.

Pay attention now, because the mountain portion involves a lot of twisting and turning.

Since we left you in Gilroy in the last chapter, you might as well come on down by following Hecker Pass over the Mount Madonna ridge to **Watsonville**. This is rich farming country, on the Pajaro River delta and one of the few flat places in the county.

Pick up Highway 1 and head north past artichoke stands, through Aptos to **Capitola** and **Soquel**. The two small towns flank Highway 1, which is a freeway at this point. Take the Park Avenue exit and head north (right) into the hills. The route quickly clears the suburban edge of Soquel and becomes a narrow lane, climbing steeply into wooded slopes. After less than a mile, you pass through a gate and wind up in someone's yard. Fortunately, it's the **Devlins'** yard, and they operate a small winery here.

Come back down Park Avenue (there's no alternative) and take a right onto Soquel Avenue at a stoplight, just short of the freeway. Drive north for less than a mile and turn right again onto Main Street (at a Unocal service station). This takes you to **Bargetto Winery** on your left.

Retrace your route on Main Street, crossing Soquel Avenue and staying aboard until Main curves into Porter Street. Go left, then quickly right and you're back on the freeway. Continue into **Santa Cruz,** staying to the left on Highway 1 at the Freeway 17 interchange. You'll sweep into a wide right-hand cloverleaf, then hit a stoplight at freeway's end.

This is River Street; turn left, then slant right onto Potrero Street after about three blocks. Within a block, you'll see a light industrial and shopping complex called **The Old Sash Mill.** Take the second right into the facility and you've found **Storrs Winery.**

Return to River Street, backtrack to Highway 17, follow it north about three miles and take the Mount Hermon Road exit into **Scotts Valley**. This hamlet sits on the edge of the wooded ramparts of the Santa Cruz Mountains. This is a pleasant region, interlaced with winding, redwood-canopied lanes. Don't expect a wilderness, however. Chalet-style homes, mountain lodges and RV parks poke through the trees every mile or so, but it's still a far cry from downtown Des Moines.

Fork right onto Scotts Valley Road; after one block, turn left onto Bean Creek Road. A twisting two miles up Bean Creek takes you to **Roudon-Smith Vineyards,** on the left. Watch for the sign, which is quite small.

Now, return to Scotts Valley and follow Mount Hermon Road to **Felton,** a town of about 5,000, scattered among the trees. It still shows some traces of its 1960s role as a hippie haven, although boutiques now outnumber health food stores. From Mount Hermon, cross Highway 9 onto Felton Empire Road (at the stop light) and you'll see **Hallcrest Vineyards** on your left, within a quarter of a mile.

Continue on Felton-Empire, winding steeply upward. This is mostly mountainous woodland, but an occasional small vineyard will remind you of your purpose. After about three miles, you hit a stop sign at Empire Grade. Continue forward onto Ice Cream Grade and follow it about 2.5 miles until it dead-ends into Pine Flat Road. You're now in the hamlet of **Bonny Doon,** although you wouldn't know it. It's not a town with a business district, but a collection of hideaway homes tucked among the trees. Go left onto Pine Flat and follow it to its junction with Bonny Doon Road. **Bonny Doon Winery** is on your left, opposite the junction.

Our next destination is Boulder Creek. If you have a detailed map, you'll note that several roads wander vaguely in that direction. Some are startlingly steep and winding. For simplicity's sake, we'll return to Felton and press northward on Highway 9.

Once you pass **Ben Lomond** and achieve tree-sheltered **Boulder Creek**, drive through its small business district, then turn right onto Bear Creek Road. After what seems an eternity of winding, you see the striking new chateau of **Byington Winery** on the right. It's about six miles from Boulder Creek. Half a mile beyond, on the left, is **David Bruce Winery,** terraced into a steep slope.

If you yen now for the flatlands, the quickest escape—albeit a twisting one—is to continue on Bear Creek Road, which winds down to Freeway 17 just south of Los Gatos.

Devlin Wine Cellars • T GTA ⌆

3801 Park Ave. (P.O. Box 728), Soquel, CA 95073; (408) 476-7288. Weekends noon to 5, MC/VISA. Most varieties tasted. Some wine logo gift items. Lawn picnic area; guided tours by appointment.

Many California wines win sweepstakes awards, and some have the honor of being served to the President. But few small, new wineries reach these heights. U.C. Davis graduate Chuck Devlin and his wife Cheryl started their winery on a Soquel hilltop in 1978. They've since gathered a remarkable collection of major awards and their wines were among those selected to accompany former President Reagan on his China tour.

The Devlins' facility occupies a lofty hilltop perch. Wines are tasted in a small cottage beside their attractive but modest country home; the winery is just up the hill a bit. The front lawn serves as a picnic area, with a fine view down the valley.

Tasting notes: The list is short and certainly impressive. Prices are remarkably reasonable for such quality: $4.50 to $13, often with specials at $3. A four-year-old Beauregard Ranch Zinfandel had a nice spicy-berry nose, a pronounced raspberry flavor and light tannin finish. An award-winning six-year-old Central Coast Merlot was subtly dusky, complex and delicious, with a touch of oak. A three-year-old Chardonnay had a light floral nose, spicy and crisp flavor with soft tannins. The Devlins also do a Sauvignon Blanc, Chenin Blanc, Cabernet Sauvignon and white Zinfandel.

Vintners choice: "Merlot and Cabernet; we've won sweepstakes for both," says Chuck.

Bargetto Winery • T GT

3535 Main St., Soquel, CA 95703; (408) 475-2258. Tasting room also located on Cannery Row in Monterey. Monday-Saturday 9:30 to 5, Sunday noon to 5; MC/VISA. Most varieties tasted. Good wine logo, gift and wine book selection. Tours daily at 11 a.m. and 2 p.m.

The Bargetto winery's neat and trim shingled structures appear to sit alongside a residential street, but that's a facade. Step inside and you'll see that the winery borders the wooded Soquel Creek bank. The buildings shelter a cozy creekside courtyard, often used for art exhibits and sometimes as a tasting area. Visitors enter through a nicely-done gift shop and sales room, then step down to the handsome creek-bank tasting room. It's trimmed in barnwood and decorated with vintage winemaking tools. A large window offers creek views.

Philip and John Bargetto established the winery in 1933; John's son Lawrence and his family run things today.

Tasting notes: The Bargettos earned an early reputation for tasty yet light fruit wines and they still produce them. However, fine, complex, medium-bodied varietals are at the forefront of the list today. Our wines of choice were a dry and fruity Monterey County Gewürztraminer, a spicy and light Central Coast Cypress Chardonnay and a three-year-old Central Coast Cypress Cabernet, with a nice spicy-oaky nose and medium rich berry taste. Several Cabs are on the list, along with Sauvignon Blanc and Pinot Noir. Fruit wines are raspberry (our favorite), olallieberry, apricot and Mead. A late harvest Riesling dessert wine was so rich it didn't need an accompaniment; it *was* dessert.

Vintners choice: "Our specialties are Santa Cruz Mountains Chardonnay, Cabernet and our fruit wines," says Beverly Bargetto.

WINERY CODES • T = tasting with no fee; **T$** = fee for tasting; **GT** = guided tours; **GTA** = appointment required for tour; **ST** = self-guiding tours; **CT** = casual tours or a peek into the winery; = picnic area; = separate gift shop or good giftware selection. Price ranges listed in tasting notes are for varietals; jug wines often are available for less. **DINING & LODGINGS •** ØØ = smoke-free establishment; Ø = non-smoking tables or rooms.

Storrs Winery • T CT

303 Potrero St. (in the Old Sash Mill, #35), Santa Cruz, CA 95060; (408) 458-5030. Open noon to 5, daily except Wednesday in summer, Friday-Monday the rest of the year; major credit cards. Most varieties tasted. Informal tours on request.

Your first impression is that you've found one of those shopping center tasting rooms divorced from the main facility. However, Stephen or Pamela Storrs will happily show you their busy little winery. It's tucked into warehouse space behind the snug tasting room and spilling into a rear drive. Creatively cluttered, it's a marvel of compactness.

This is a husband-and-wife operation from crush to bottling; both are U.C. Davis graduates in enology and viticulture. They started their winery in 1988 to create Santa Cruz Mountain varietals. And create they have; the small 2,000-case winery has won an impressive array of awards.

Tasting notes: The Storrs specialize in *les mèthodes anciennes,* classic European style winemaking, utilizing barrel fermenting and *sur lie* aging. The result: full-flavored wines with soft touches of oak. They focus on Chardonnays and the spicy, crisp Vanamanutagi Vineyards selection we tasted was exceptional. We also favored their lush and honey-like white Riesling and a Rhône-style, soft San Miguel

Petit Sirah with subtle tannins and wood. Prices range from $7.50 to $9.

Vintners choice: "Our Santa Cruz Mountains Chardonnays—filled with aromas of fruit and toasty oak," says Pamela. "We create four different vineyard-designated varieties."

Roudon-Smith Vineyards • T CT ⌶

2364 Bean Creek Rd., Santa Cruz, CA 95066; (408) 438-1244. Weekends only, 10 to 4; MC/VISA. Selected wines tasted. Small picnic area; informal tours.

This trim little wooden winery is tucked into a wooded slope, encircled by sheltering trees. It's a bit hard to spot because of those trees and because of its small sign, so be watchful. It's probably best to call and get directions. Also, since it's a family operation, the place may be closed on rare weekends. However, the winery does have as tasting room on Monterey's Cannery Row, open daily. (See the next chapter.)

The double-joined name comes from Bob and Annamaria Roudon and Jim and June Smith. They started their small winery elsewhere in 1972 and settled here six years later. Production is about 10,000 cases.

Tasting notes: We especially liked the big, spicy reds, which the Roudon-Smiths let rest a few years before release. A four-year-old Santa Cruz Mountains Pinot Noir exhibited a nice berry nose and complex flavor; and a six-year-old Sonoma Mountain Cabernet Sauvignon was aged to tasty smoothness, yet it had a crisp tannic finish. Of the whites, we tilted toward a nutty-silky five-year-old Santa Cruz Mountains Estate Chardonnay. Others on the list are Johannisberg Riesling, Petite Sirah and Zinfandel. Prices range from $8.85 to the mid-teens, less for some table wine blends.

Vintners choice: "Estate grown Chardonnay and Santa Cruz Mountains Pinot Noir," says Jim Smith. "And we add a touch of Chardonnay to our Petite Sirah to soften the tannins and add finesse to the wine."

Hallcrest Vineyards • T GTA ⚒

379 Felton Empire Rd., Felton, CA 95018; (408) 335-4441. Daily 10 to 5:30; MC/VISA, AMEX. Most varieties tasted. A few wine logo and picnic items. Nice picnic area with a view of Felton.

The casually arrayed but neat buildings of Hallcrest occupy a wooded slope just above the town. A Riesling vineyard adds authenticity to the setting. The tasting room is a deliberately cute cottage with a schoolhouse-style bell tower. A grassy picnic area is just below; it's shaded by a huge gnarled oak right out of the forest scene from *Snow White*.

Hallcrest's career started in 1941 when it was established by Charles Hall. It functioned as Felton-Empire Winery in the late 1970s. Then, John and Lorraine Schumacher and John's sister Shirin bought the facility in 1987 and restored the original name. A U.C. Davis grad, John has been making wines since he fiddled with fermenting fruit from the family orchard as a teenager.

Tasting notes: It's an interesting menu, starting with Chardonnay, white Riesling, Zinfandel and Cabernet Sauvignon. In addition, John makes a lightly sweet yet tart Napa Valley Fumè Blanc that's completely organic, with no sulfites. This was one of our favorites, along with an excellent soft, spicy-berry young Zinfandel and a rich, complex and gently tannic three-year-old Cabernet Sauvignon. Prices range from $7.50 to $18.50. Hallcrest also produces a line of lush, tasty non-alcoholic Muscat and white Zinfandel grape juices.

Vintners choice: "white Riesling, our *Clos de Jeannine* red table wine that has won many medals, and our Cabernet Sauvignon," says Lorraine.

Bonny Doon Vineyard • T GTA ⚒

10 Pine Flat Rd., Bonny Doon; Mailing address: P.O. Box 8376, Santa Cruz, CA 95061; (408) 425-3625. Open noon to 5 daily except Tuesday from May through September, and Friday through Monday the rest of the year; MC/VISA, AMEX. Most varieties tasted. Wine logo gift items. Picnic area. Informal guided tours by appointment.

As long as you're making serious wine, you might as well have fun with the labels. That appears to be the philosophy of Randall Grahm, MD, owner of Bonny Doon Vineyard. His labels range from Art Deco to New Wave to zany.

One, with Randall and his employees jammed into a storm-tossed boat, is labeled "Grahm Crew." Another offers details about the wine that can't be read until the bottle is empty; it's printed on the backside of the front label. His newsletters are both erudite and off the wall. A recent one bore the words to Dr. Grahm's "opera"—*Don Giovese in Bakersfield*, sort of an ode to Grignolino.

These serious wines shielded by campy labels are tasted in a funkily pleasant wooden cottage at roadside in the Bonny Doon forest. The winery and a scatter of tree-shaded picnic tables are just upslope. The tasting room's best feature, in addition to its wines, of course—is its T-shirt collection. Many memorable Grahm labels have been captured for torso display.

Tasting notes: You won't find many varietal labels, since most of Grahm's wines are creative blends. We found them to be excellent, for the most part. Prices are all over the court—$6.50 to $20. He also does fruit wines and a pot-still brandy. Grahm Crew Vin Blanc, should you wonder, is a honey-like botrytis Grenache Blanc. Vin Gris de Cigare is a Rhône blend of Grenache, Pinot Noir and Mourvèdre and Pinot, a pink with more character and fruit than most blushers. We took heavily, perhaps too heavily, to Clos De Gilroy, a fruity and spicy Grenache that, says Grahm, is "exceptionally well-suited to heavily garlicked preparations." His Chardonnay was spicy and delicious and we've found someone who shares our disdain for silly tasting descriptions. To quote from the tasting sheet:

"There is a beautiful floral and tropical component to the wine buttressed by a rich, buttery nuance that makes the wine popular with *todo el mundo* and permits us to charge big bucks."

Vintners choice: "We specialize in Rhône style wines made from northern and central coastal California grapes," says tasting room manager Rebecca Foulk. "We also produce unique dessert wines and distilled spirits."

Byington Winery and Vineyard • T GTA

21850 Bear Creek Rd., Los Gatos, CA 95030; (408) 354-1111. Daily 11 to 5; MC/VISA. Most varieties tasted. Giftware selection, mostly wine-logo items. View picnic area with barbecue; tours by appointment.

Prepare for a double-take. After visiting quaint, prim and funky family wineries of Santa Cruz, you'll be pleasantly startled by the Italianate chateau of Bill Byington. Tile-roofed and multi-gabled, it's the county's most imposing winery, occupying carefully-groomed grounds in a wooded knoll, amidst young vineyards. The tasting room is a high-ceiling elegant space with tiled floors and arched windows.

Tours, by appointment, take you into the cutting-edge winery and upstairs to opulent meeting and entertainment rooms, often the scene of weddings and other notable events. Views from the winery grounds are awesome, over redwood forests to Monterey Bay and the Pacific. They're yours if you opt for a picnic; the winery staff will even provide charcoal and a barbecue pit.

Byington, owner of the West Coast's largest steel treatment plant, bought the land here in 1962, began producing wine in 1974, and completed his impressive facility in 1990. His winemaker is Greg Bruni, a U.C. Davis grad whose family once owned the San Martin Winery.

Tasting notes: The Byington list is short and selective: Fumè Blanc, Chardonnay, Cabernet and Pinot Noir. Bruni also produces white and red table wines and a sparkling wine. We favored the herbal nose and spicy flavor of a Monterey County Fumè Blanc and a complex, nutty Chardonnay. A Napa Valley Cabernet Sauvignon was properly peppery, medium bodied and quite tasty. Prices range from $7.65 to the mid-teens.

David Bruce Winery • T

21439 Bear Creek Rd., Los Gatos, CA 95030; (408) 354-4212. Thursday-Sunday noon to 5; MC/VISA. All varieties tasted. Picnic area on a grassy shelf overlooking the mountains.

Dr. David Bruce, noted for his medal-winning wines and no-nonsense approach to winemaking, has constructed a facility that matches his attitude. The winery is a no-frills affair, where visitor amenities are secondary to wine production. Tasting room decor consists of stacked boxes of wine; plain walls exhibit the medals they've won. Classical music issues from a boom box stuck in a corner. One thing *is* visually impressive: the winery is terraced into steep slopes, surrounded by trees and its own vineyards, with views to the far-away bay.

Bruce, a physician, was among the first new-generation Santa Cruz winemakers. He started his hillside facility in 1964 and gradually built it up to its present output of 30,000 cases a year—the largest in the county.

Tasting notes: An impressive assortment of wines is available for tasting. Chardonnay accounts for 70 percent of the output and the Santa Cruz Mountains version was outstanding, buttery-crisp and nutty with a nice oak finish. We discovered some fine reds as well—an Estate Pinot Noir with a spicy nose and flavor and busy tannic finish, and a four-year-old Cabernet with big chili pepper flavor. Bruce also does a very drinkable "Mr. Boggins" Grenache and Petit Sirah blend; plus a Shandon Red, a "serious spaghetti wine" of Petit Sirah, Cabernet Pfeffer and Carignan. Prices range from $8.50 to the high teens.

THE BEST OF THE BUNCH

The best wine buys • Devlin Wine Cellars and Bargetto Winery.

The most attractive winery • Byington Winery.

The most interesting tasting rooms • Bargetto Winery and Byington Winery.

The funkiest tasting rooms • Storrs Winery and Bonnie Doon Vineyard.

The best gift shop • Bargetto Winery and Bonnie Doon Vineyard (wine label T-shirts).

The nicest picnic areas • Devlin Wine Cellars, Hallcrest Vineyards, Byington Winery and David Bruce Winery.

The best tour • Bargetto Winery (guided).

BEYOND THE VINEYARDS

It's tempting to suggest that wine is the tip of the tail that wags Santa Cruz County's tourism dog. As we have seen, the area shelters some neat little wineries, but most folks come for the beaches and redwood forests.

Your trek to the wineries has taken you through its forested mountains. We'll now suggest a route that exposes its coastal lures. Begin at a familiar place—River Street and Highway 1. Drive south on River Street through the heart of Santa Cruz. You'll pass **Pacific Garden Mall,** devastated by the 1989 Loma Prieta earthquake. Some of it has been rebuilt and shops are open. When we visited, however, parts of it still awaited reconstruction.

River Street changes to Front Street and takes you to the primary Santa Cruz attractions—the **Municipal Pier,** the **Beach Boardwalk** and of course, the beach. Head eastward from here (remembering that it's a south-facing beach), staying close to the shoreline. Follow Beach Street which turns into Riverside Avenue and swings inland, then turn right onto **East Cliff Drive**. This will keep you tucked close to the shore for the most part. You'll see fine old beachfront homes, lots of sand and seagulls and an occasional sea lion.

With luck, you'll reach **Capitola,** a cute little town of cliff-perched Victorian homes and beachside boutiques. A **pedestrian path** along Soquel

Creek is quite pleasant. Park Avenue will return you to U.S. 1 freeway. From here, with the aid of a local map, you can work southwestward, dipping down to the bayfront where streets permit. An assortment of state and local beaches invite sunning and surf-sloshing.

If you prefer more beach and less congestion, go west (eventually north) on Highway 1 from our River Street starting point. After a mile or so, turn right onto Bay Street and follow signs to the forested campus of the **University of California at Santa Cruz.**

Return to U.S. 1 and press on, taking time for a stop at **Natural Bridges State Beach.** Other beaches will crop up frequently as you follow this relatively unspoiled coastal stretch toward San Mateo County.

Santa Cruz vineyard area attractions

Family lures •

Mystery Spot, 1953 N. Branciforte Dr., Santa Cruz; 423-8897. Daily 9:30 to 4:30; admission fee. It's one of those magnetic field places where folks seem to tilt at odd angles.

Roaring Camp & Big Trees Railroad, Graham Hill Road, Felton; 335-4400. Various hours; admission fee. Steam train rides through the redwoods; also site of the **Felton Covered Bridge.**

Santa Cruz Beach Boardwalk, at the beach; 423-5590. Opens at 11 a.m. daily in summer, on weekends and holidays only the rest of the year. Free admission; fees for rides. Nicely restored oldstyle amusement park, one of the few beachfront fun zones left in America.

Santa Cruz Municipal Wharf, Beach Street, Santa Cruz; 429-3628. Busy, rustic wharf with restaurants, seafood shops and such.

Farm products • Farms and wineries selling directly to the public are listed in ***Country Crossroads***. Available at farm and winery members or send a stamped, self-addressed business-sized envelope to: Country Crossroads, Santa Cruz County Farm Bureau, 600 Main St., Watsonville, CA 95076; 724-1356.

Redwood parks •

Big Basin Redwoods State Park, north of Boulder Creek; 338-6132; entrance fee. Camping, hiking and picnicking.

Henry Cowell Redwoods State park, off Graham Hill road near Felton; 335-4598; entrance fee. Camping, hiking, picnicking, restaurant, snack bar and curio shop.

Forest of Nisene Marks, Aptos Creek Road, Aptos; 335-4598; no fee. Wilderness park with hiking and biking trails.

Wilder Ranch State Park, 1401 Coast Rd., Santa Cruz; 688-3241; entrance fee. Restoration of a turn-of-the-century ranch.

Wineland events • Santa Cruz County Vintners Festival, late June, 458-5030; Passport Saturday, with "passport" tickets to wine and foods at various wineries, late July, 458-5030; Capitola Art & Wine Festival, mid-September, 688-7377.

Winery touring maps • ***Fine Wines of Santa Cruz*** brochure, available at wineries and visitors bureaus or contact: Santa Cruz Winegrowers, P.O. Box 3222, Santa Cruz, CA 95063; 458-5030. ***Winetrails of the Santa***

Cruz Mountains, listing mountain wineries between Woodside and Santa Cruz, free at participating vintners.

Santa Cruz County information sources

The county offers scores of places to eat, sleep, swim, surf and play. The Conference and Visitors Council will happily provide you with pounds of information. Ask specifically for the ***Santa Cruz County Visitor Guide, Accommodations Guide*** and ***Dining Guide.***

Santa Cruz County Conference and Visitors Council, 701 Front St., Santa Cruz, CA 95060; (800) 833-3494 or (408) 425-1234.

For south county information, contact the **Watsonville Chamber of Commerce,** 318 Main St. (P.O. Box 470), Watsonville, CA 95076; (408) 724-3900.

AN INFORMAL TOUR

"Assertive, tannic and flavorful, with weedy dill and slight menthol aromas and flavors that compete with the modest currant note."

—Description of a 1987 Joullian Carmel Valley Cabernet Sauvignon

Chapter Ten

MONTEREY COUNTY

Sun-soaked vines in Steinbeck Country

Noted primarily for tourism, Steinbeck novels and golf tournaments, Monterey County has a vineyard surprise. It contains nearly 30,000 acres of premium wine grapes—more than any California county except Napa and Sonoma.

They aren't all that evident. The visitor will find no great gathering of wineries, and the only concentration of tasting rooms is in that mother of all tourist traps, Cannery Row.

So, where's the grapes? Most are in the cool, flat and wind-brushed Salinas Valley below Salinas. A drive south on Highway 101 won't reveal many vines, although this is one of California's major agricultural areas. Grapes prefer the good drainage offered by slopes, so many of the vineyards are coved into the benchlands of the Gavilan Mountains to the east and the Santa Lucia section of the Coast Range to the west. A few vines also grow in the Carmel Valley, inland from Carmel.

Monterey County is rich with the lore of early California. However, it had nothing to do with wine, other than the usual mission grapes stomped by the padres for sacramental sipping. Father Junipero Serra started California's second mission near Carmel in 1770, and it served for decades as headquarters for the 21-mission chain. The only record of early grape planting was at Mission Soledad, established in the Salinas Valley in 1791. No trace of those vineyard remain.

It wasn't until 1960 that the Salinas Valley was seriously regarded as a premium wine-producing area. Until then, it was thought to be too dry and windy. Aided by researchers from the University of California at Davis, growers solved the wind problem by planting grapes parallel to the prevailing breezes. Drilling proved that the Salinas River—mostly underground—had plenty of water.

This is a relatively cool area, kept that way by those winds, so it's ideal for whites, which account for three-fourths of the plantings. Among those that thrive are Chardonnay (the most commonly planted variety), Sauvignon

Blanc and Gewürztraminer. Cabernet Sauvignon is the most popular red; Zinfandel, Pinot Noir, Petite Sirah and Merlot are among its companions.

Despite its youth, this newcomer to the California wine world has won an impressive number of medals. Monterey County Chardonnays are particularly strong in competitions.

The first vintners were South Bay refugees such as the Wente Brothers, Mirassou, Alamden and Paul Masson, whose vines were being crowded out by subdivisions. Since they already had elaborate production facilities to the north, they built no wineries here.

The Monterey Vineyard was the first major new facility built here. Owners opened the doors to its classy winery and tasting room in the Salinas Valley in 1974.

MONTEREY COUNTY WINERY TOUR • As we wrote this, only nine county vintners had tasting rooms that kept regular hours, and most of these are disconnecting from the wineries. The rest are in Monterey and Carmel, which makes good business sense, since those areas attract hundreds of

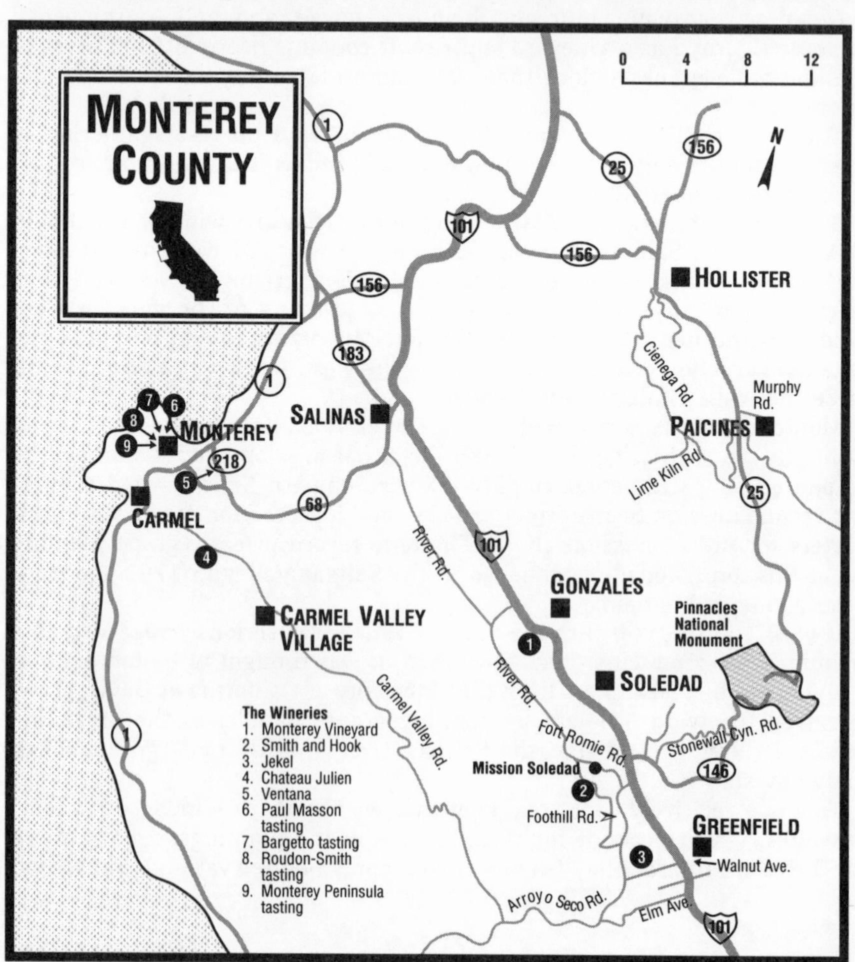

thousands of tourists a year—particularly Cannery Row.

Of the tasting rooms still married to their wineries, three are near U.S. Highway 101, south of Salinas. While this small number may not be worth a special trip from some great distance, they offer a nice diversion if you happen to be headed that way.

Your tour thus begins somewhere on Highway 101, with your compass set for **Gonzales.**

Gonzales?

Exit the freeway at Gloria Road just south of town, follow the frontage road north and you shortly arrive at the impressive structure of **The Monterey Vineyard.** From here, continue into Gonzales and turn left (west) onto Gonzales River Road. After 2.5 miles, you'll bump into River Road. Head south about six miles and fork to the right onto Foothill Road. Go another three miles, turn right and follow a road to **Smith and Hook,** cradled among vineyards in the Santa Lucia foothills.

Backtrack briefly on Foothill to Mission Road, turn right, follow it about a mile to Fort Romie Road and turn right again. You soon see the ruins of **Mission Soledad,** worth a brief perusal. Are you superstitious? It's interesting to note that this was the thirteenth California mission established, one of the least successful and one of the few that fell to complete ruin. Only fragments of adobe walls and a modern-day chapel mark this spot, now surrounded by farm fields.

From here, continue south on Fort Romie, following signs back to U.S. 101. Eight miles will fetch you into **Greenfield.** Ignore the first exit and take the second one right (west) onto Walnut Avenue and follow it a mile through vines and veggies to **Jekel Vineyard.**

You've now done the Salinas Valley vineyards. Two other tasting rooms are just outside Carmel and Monterey; they're easy to find once you're in the neighborhood. **Chateau Julien** is about five miles out Carmel Valley Road from Carmel. Look for the castle-like structure on your right. **Ventana Vineyards'** tasting room is at the junction of the Monterey-Salinas Highway (Route 68) and State Highway 218, about 2.5 miles from Highway 1 above Monterey. It's in the northwest corner of that junction, in a tree-sheltered fieldstone complex called the "Old Stone House," which contains a couple of other businesses.

The other four tasting rooms are on Monterey's **Cannery Row**. We won't bother with driving instructions; just park and walk. If it's a weekend, get there early. Otherwise, you'll have trouble parking and you'll be lined up five deep at the tasting counters.

Paul Masson and **Bargetto** tasting rooms are in an old pier-piling cannery structure; it's opposite Steinbeck Plaza parking lot at Cannery Row and Prescott streets. To reach **Roudon-Smith** from here, walk two blocks

---

WINERY CODES • T = tasting with no fee; **T$** = fee for tasting; **GT** = guided tours; **GTA** = appointment required for tour; **ST** = self-guiding tours; **CT** = casual tours or a peek into the winery; ⨯ = picnic area; 🎁 = separate gift shop or good giftware selection. Price ranges listed in tasting notes are for varietals; jug wines often are available for less. **DINING & LODGINGS • ØØ** = smoke-free establishment; Ø = non-smoking tables or rooms.

along Cannery Row toward the **Monterey Bay Aquarium.** You'll find the tasting room upstairs in a structure at the corner of David Street.

Now, go one block up David to Wave Street, turn left and walk a block to Irvin. **Monterey Peninsula Winery's** tasting room is in an old Victorian cottage on your left. Incidentally, at any one of these tasting rooms, you can pick up a blue card-map with directions to the others.

The Monterey Vineyard • T GT

800 S. Alta St. (P.O. Box 780), Gonzales, CA 93926; (408) 675-2316. Daily 10 to 5; MC/VISA, AMEX. Selected wines tasted. Good assortment of gifts, crystal, books and wine logo items. Ansel Adams photographic gallery. Frequent tours; landscaped picnic areas.

The Monterey Vineyard's park-like facility is one of the most attractive in California's winelands. Geese glide along placid ponds, picnickers spread their fare on lawn tables and sippers sip in an opulent Spanish style tasting room. Tours depart frequently for close-ups of a state-of-the-art winery, in a Mediterranean-modern building.

A gallery features works of contemporary photographers and a permanent exhibit of Ansel Adams' black and white study, "Story of a Winery," commissioned by Seagrams in 1960. Most of the photos are of the Paul Masson winery. Why Paul? Because Seagrams Classics Wine Company owns both wineries, and the Masson facility is not open to the public.

Tasting notes: This is a fine place to sample Monterey County varietals because winemaker Cary Gott uses only local wines. His list includes Johannisberg Riesling, Chenin Blanc, Chardonnay, Cabernet Sauvignon, Gamay Beaujolais, Merlot and a brut sparkling wine. The Chardonnay and Chenin Blanc were full-bodied and complex with lots of fruit, and a five-year-old Cabernet was nicely mellowed, with hints of tannin still evident. The jug wines are quite good here. We especially liked the full flavor of Classic Red, a blend of Cab, Merlot and Pinot Noir. Prices are moderate, ranging from $5.75 to the early teens. Some limited release wines are available, also inexpensive, between $9 and $16.

Smith and Hook • T CT

37700 Foothill Rd., Soledad, CA 93960; (408) 678-2132. Daily 11 to 4. Additional tasting room on Steinbeck Court in the Crossroads Shopping Center, 217 Crossroads Blvd., Carmel, CA 93921; (408) 625-6480. Monday-Saturday 10 to 6 and Sunday noon to 5. MC/VISA. Wine logo items and picnic area in Soledad; more extensive gift selection in Carmel.

Of the two Smith and Hook tasting rooms, we prefer the original, fashioned from an old redwood wine vat. The Carmel tasting room, in a shopping center off Highway 1 just south of Carmel Valley Road, is useful if you're in the Monterey Bay area, and it has a nice gift selection.

The ranch-style winery sits in the Santa Lucia foothills, a refreshing escape from the flatlands of the Salinas Valley. You'll find no Smiths nor Hooks there today. The winery gets its name from owners of the former horse ranch that occupied this site. The Nicolaus Han family established the winery in 1979 and preserved much of the rustic look of the ranch.

Tasting notes: The Santa Lucia Highlands are warmer than the valley floor and thus ideal for reds. S&H has won scores of awards for its peppery, medium-bodied Cabernet Sauvignon and Cabernet Franc, among the best

Monterey County reds we tasted. We also liked a three-year-old Merlot, so big and spicy it could have passed for a Cab. Whites on the list are Gewürztraminer, Riesling and a light, yet lush and fruity Chardonnay. Prices are moderate, ranging from $6 to the mid-teens.

Jekel Vineyard • T GTA ⌶

40155 Walnut Ave. (P.O. Box 336), Greenfield, CA 93927; (408) 674-5522. Daily 10 to 5; MC/VISA. All varieties tasted. Picnic area beneath arbor. Fair selection of wine-related items. Tours by appointment.

Upscale American Gothic might describe the trim, prosperous looking Jekel winery. The main facility is housed in a neat red barn with white trim. The adjacent cheerful tasting room is sheltered by an arbor dripping with wisteria; an impressive array of medals add to the decor. All this is accented by carefully-tended landscaping. Surrounding vineyards complete this prim picture.

William and August Jekel built the winery in 1978, six years after planting their vineyards. It's now part of the Vintech Wine Group, with Steve Pessagno as winemaker.

Tasting notes: Cabernet Franc, a big award winner for Jekel, had a nice bell pepper nose and herbal, berry taste. A Private Reserve Cabernet was surprisingly big and powerful for a Salinas Valley red. Of the whites, we liked a rich, buttery and spicy five-year-old Chardonnay. Several Rieslings, dry, semi-dry and late harvest, complete the list. Prices range from $4.50 for the Rieslings to the mid-teens for most of the others.

Vintners choice: "Chardonnay and Johannisberg Riesling do exceedingly well in our cool, dry climate," said the winery's Leigh Togneth.

Chateau Julien Winery • T GTA

8940 Carmel Valley Rd. (P.O. Box 221775), Carmel, CA 93923; (408) 624-2600. Weekdays 8:30 to 5, weekends 11 to 5; MC/VISA, AMEX. Most varieties tasted. Wine-oriented giftwares; guided tours at 10:30 and 2:30 weekdays by reservation.

If King Arthur had yearned to make wine instead of fussing about Lancelot, he might have created Chateau Julien, a modern fairy castle set in affluent Carmel Valley. This Camelot is complete with a tower, but presumably no Repunzel resides therein. The tasting room is properly Arthurian, with a carved tasting table—not round but more or less oval—arched windows and a crackling fireplace.

A modern winery is sheltered within, which can be explored by reservation, followed by a tasting intelligently conducted by the tour host. All this opulence was conceived in 1983 by a corporation with a name no less modest than its creation—Great American Wineries, Inc.

Tasting notes: The list of medals is considerably longer than the roster of wines. Varietals are Chardonnay, Merlot, Cabernet Sauvignon, Sauvignon Blanc, Gewürztraminer and Johannisberg Riesling. They're full-bodied creations, often made *sur lie* to add to their complexity. We favored a young and spicy barrel fermented Chardonnay, a dry but fruit-filled *sur lie* Semillon and a soft, complex Merlot. A cream sherry was nutty and sensuously lush. Prices range from $6 for the whites to the high teens.

Vintners choice: "Chardonnay, Merlot and Cabernet Sauvignon, consistent gold and silver medal winners," says the corporation's Patricia Bower.

Ventana Vineyards • T

2999 Monterey-Salinas Highway, Monterey, CA 93940; (408) 372-7415. Daily noon to 5; no credit cards. Most varieties tasted. Sheltered picnic deck.

Some years ago, former Vietnam fighter pilot J. Douglas Meador decided he wanted to go into the wine business. He cleared and planted a 400-acre vineyard in gravelly soil along the Arroyo Seco River, between Soledad and Greenfield. In 1978, when he began making his wines, perhaps even he was amazed. According to a winery source, Ventana has won more awards than any other single-vineyard winery in America.

You won't see this remarkable vineyard, because the winery offers no tours. You can taste the wines in a handsome hospitality center in a rough-stone, vine-covered complex called "the Old Stone House" just east of Monterey.

Tasting notes: Most premium whites appear on Doug's list, along with Cabernet Sauvignon, Pinot Noir, a sparkling *Cuvee Natural* and a couple of dessert wines. His flagship Sauvignon Blanc was excellent, fruity and spicier than most Chardonnays; his barrel-fermented malolactic Chardonnay was—predictably—spicier still. Of the reds, we liked a rich, peppery young Cabernet Sauvignon with a typical Bordeaux blend of Cabernet Franc and Merlot; and a Pinot Noir Reserve rich with berries. Prices are modest for such award-winners—ranging from $5 to the high teens.

Vintners choice: "Sauvignon Blanc, Chardonnay and Riesling," ticked off the winery's Connie Winners.

Paul Masson Tasting Room • T

700 Cannery Row, Monterey, CA 93940; (408) 646-5446. Daily 10 to 7 in summer, 10 to 6 the rest of the year. Most varieties tasted free; also wines by the glass at $3. Extensive wine logo, giftware and tourist souvenir selection.

We said earlier in this book that we prefer our tasting rooms at the winery. Ambiance and all that sort of thing. We're ready to make an exception for the Paul Masson Wine Tasting Room, Gift Shop & Museum. That's the full name, and it's all here.

The Masson facility occupies one of Cannery Row's best perches. On the second floor of an old cannery, reaching over the water on pilings, it commands a striking Monterey Bay view. One can purchase a glass of wine and snacks and relax in chairs before a window-wall to the bay. The gift area rivals the other Cannery Row curio shops in its selection of specialty foods, giftwares and tourist doodads. Soft classical music gives this glittering place a properly subdued aura. The museum portion contains old wine paraphernalia and photos tracing the history of the winery, which was founded in 1900 by rotund and robust Frenchman Paul Masson in the hills above Saratoga. An excellent film relates Masson's story, interlaced with rare historical footage of America and its wine industry.

Incidentally, the founder bears a resemblance—in circumference at least—to Orson Wells, who advises us solemnly in his TV commercial that no Masson wine is sold before its time.

Tasting notes: From a list covering most premiums and a lot of specialty wines, we chose these for comment: A Sauvignon Blanc was light and crisp, yet with spicy overtones; a Pinot Noir had a pleasingly fruity nose and good berry flavor; a Cabernet Sauvignon was nicely tannic and peppery for

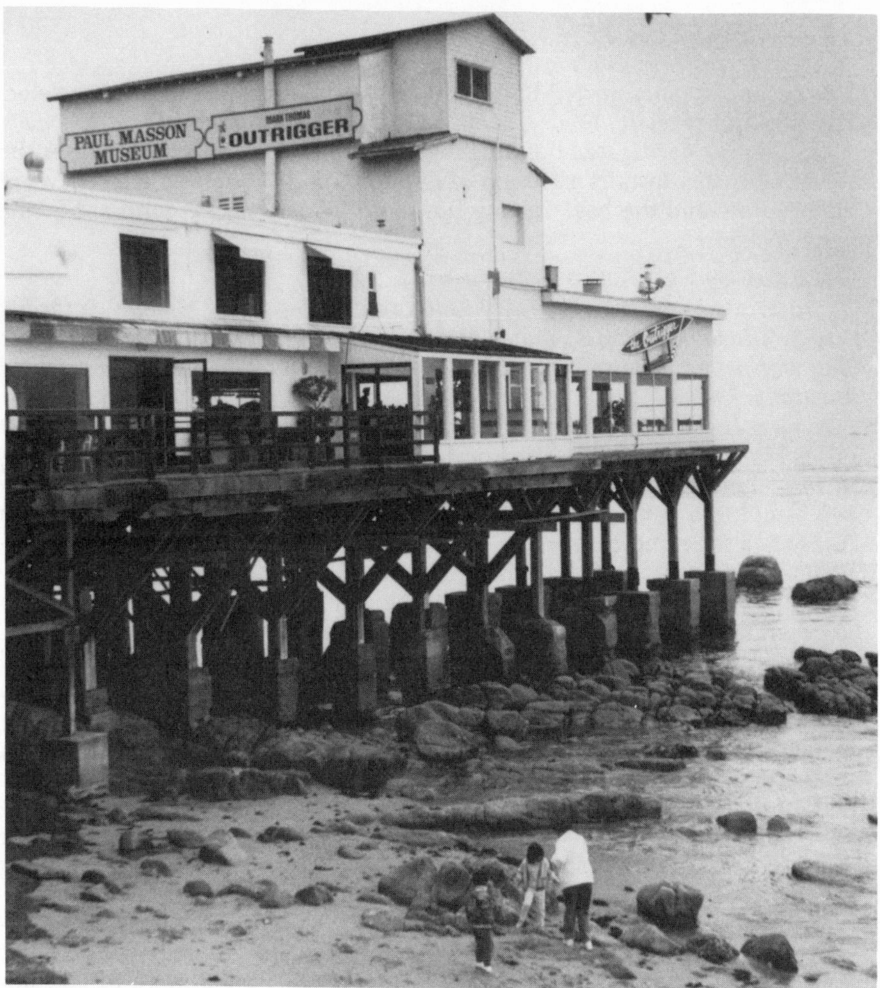

Many of Monterey County's tasting rooms are divorced from their wineries; four are along Cannery Row of John Steinbeck fame.

its $9 price tag. Perhaps an even better buy was a fruity, soft $5 Zinfandel. To end this round, while watching a pair of pigeon guillemot on the railing outside, I sipped a rich, nutty Rare Cream Sherry, excellent at $7 a bottle.

Bargetto Winery Tasting Room • T

700 Cannery Row, Monterey, CA 93940;(408) 373-4053. Daily 10 to 6; MC/VISA. Most varieties tasted. Extensive wine logo, giftware, specialty foods and souvenir selection.

Bargetto's tasting room is on the ground floor of the building containing the Masson facility. It, too, offers a large gift selection, and a particularly good choice of specialty food items and cookware. Tasting notes and winery background are in the previous chapter.

Roudon-Smith Vineyards Tasting Room • T

807 Cannery Row, Monterey, CA 93940; (408) 375-8755. Monday-Friday

11 to 6, Sunday noon to 6; MC/VISA. Most varieties tasted. Wine logo selection; gifts and specialty foods in adjacent shops.

An old pink corrugated building near Monterey Bay Aquarium houses the pleasantly rustic upstairs gift shop of Roudon-Smith. Windows offer views of Cannery Row and the bay. Tasting notes and winery background are in the previous chapter.

Monterey Peninsula Winery • T$

786 Wave St., Monterey, CA 93940; (408) 394-2999. Monday-Saturday 10 to 5, Sunday noon to 5; major credit cards. Most varieties tasted for a fee; along with wines from several other Monterey County wineries. Wine-oriented giftwares.

A pleasant old clapboard Victorian one block up from Cannery Row houses Monterey Peninsula Winery's offerings. Plans were afoot at this writing to include tastings from several other small area wineries, so you may have a multiple choice by the time you read this. The Monterey Peninsula Winery has never been far from its tasting room. Deryck Nuckton and Roy Thomas started the facility in the late 1970s in a structure at the Monterey County Airport. They moved in 1986 to a warehouse in Sand City, just up the beach from Monterey. Grapes, obviously, come from elsewhere.

Tasting notes: This outfit makes *big* wines. Whites were full-bodied and complex; many of the reds were husky and hearty, with enough tannin for aging. Both a Doctors Reserve Pinot Blanc and Sleepy Hollow Chardonnay were spicy, lush and subtly tart. Several Zinfandels occupy the red list, ranging in ages from four to ten years; all displayed strong varietal character and tannin accents. A Doctors Reserve Cabernet Sauvignon was herbal, complex and fruity and a non-vintage Black Burgundy had lots of pucker power; it was a Petite Sirah-Zinfandel blend. Prices range from $7 to the high teens for varietals; lower for blends.

Vintners choice: "Merlot, for which we've won numerous gold medals," said the winery's John C. Olds. "Also, our Barbera aged in oak and Pinot Blanc, fermented and treated like a Chardonnay." He had more to list, but we had to cut him off.

THE BEST OF THE BUNCH

The best wine buys • The Monterey Vineyard, Smith and Hook, Ventana Vineyards and Paul Masson.

The most attractive wineries • The Monterey Vineyard, Jekel Vineyard and Chateau Julien Winery.

The most interesting tasting rooms • Smith and Hook (Soledad), Ventana Vineyards and Paul Masson.

The best gift shops • The Monterey Vineyard, Paul Masson and Bargetto Winery.

The nicest picnic areas • The Monterey Vineyard and Jekel Vineyard.

The best tour • Chateau Julien Winery.

BEYOND THE VINEYARDS

From a visitor standpoint, Monterey and Santa Cruz have much in common. Both have namesake cities bordering on huge, crescent shaped Monterey Bay and both are major tourist draws. The **Monterey Peninsula** is a play land for the rich, who tee off at Pebble Beach (now with Japanese consent, only), gallop their horses on the back trails of **Carmel Valley** and play tennis at luxury resorts. The wanna-be-rich shop the boutiques of **Carmel**, prowl **Fishermans Wharf** and **Cannery Row** in Monterey and hang out, scantily clad, at an assortment of beaches.

The more esoteric seek soulful peace on stormy strands and in the wilds of **Los Padres National Forest** to the south, particularly in the area with that mystical name, **Big Sur**. (Utter the phrase and you can almost see Liz Taylor scuffing along the beach, eyes downcast, in *The Sandpiper*.)

Monterey County attractions

Museums, missions and such •

Mission Nuestra Senora de la Soledad, Fort Romni Road, Soledad; 678-2586. Wednesday-Monday 10 to 4; donations asked. Fragments of original mission walls and chapel with museum.

Mission San Carlos Borromeo del Rio Carmelo, 3080 Rio Rd., Carmel; 624-3600. Monday-Saturday 9:30 to 4:30, Sundays and holidays 10:30 to 4:30. Former headquarters of the California missions, with museum, chapel, courtyard and history exhibits.

Monterey Bay Aquarium, 886 Cannery Row, Monterey; 648-4888. Daily 10 to 6; admission charge. One of America's leading aquariums with 23 habitat exhibits and tide pools.

Monterey State Historic Park, 20 Custom House Plaza, Monterey; 649-2836. Daily 10 to 5 in summer, 10 to 4 in winter; admission charge, covers all exhibits and museums. A collection of historic structures tracing Monterey's history as the Spanish, then Mexican capital of California.

Point Lobos State Reserve, four miles south of Carmel off Highway 1; 624-4909. Daily 9 to 7 in spring and summer, 9 to 5 in fall and winter; modest admission charge. Wildlife preserve on beautiful seacoast peninsula with beaches, picnicking and hiking.

Scenic drive • Seventeen-Mile Drive takes visitors through the green seacoast ramparts from Pacific Grove to Carmel; 624-9585; toll charge.

Wineland events • Masters of Food and Wine, Carmel Highlands in late February, 624-3801; Monterey Wine Festival, mid-March, (800) 525-3378.

Winery touring maps • ***Monterey Wine Country*** passport, Monterey Wine Country Associates, 375-9400. A "passport," available from most wineries, will—when completed with stamps from participating tasting rooms—earn the bearer an invitation to a wine celebration.

Monterey County information source

Few lodgings and restaurants are near Monterey's wineries, which are located for the most part in rural areas, away from primary visitor areas. For a comprehensive compendium of what to do and see, where to play, eat and sleep, get a copy of the ***Monterey Peninsula Visitors Guide*** from: **Monterey Peninsula Visitors & Convention Bureau,** P.O. Box 1770, Monterey, CA 93942; 649-1770.

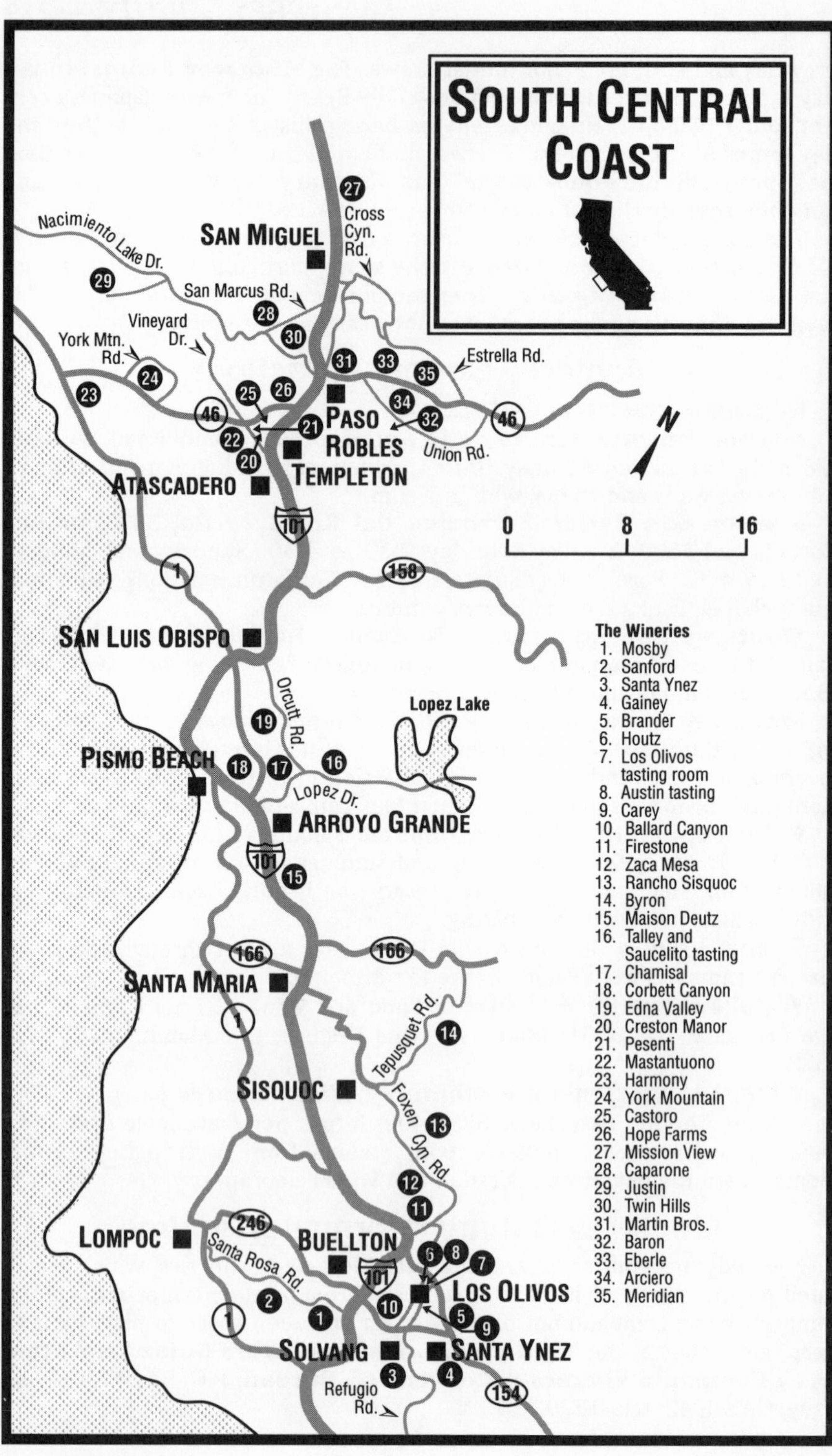

SOUTH CENTRAL COAST
N
0
8
16
SAN MIGUEL
Cross Cyn. Rd.
Nacimiento Lake Dr.
San Marcus Rd.
Vineyard Dr.
York Mtn. Rd.
Estrella Rd.
PASO ROBLES
Union Rd.
ATASCADERO
TEMPLETON
SAN LUIS OBISPO
Orcutt Rd.
Lopez Lake
PISMO BEACH
Lopez Dr.
ARROYO GRANDE
SANTA MARIA
Tepusquet Rd.
SISQUOC
Foxen Cyn. Rd.
LOMPOC
Santa Rosa Rd.
BUELLTON
LOS OLIVOS
SOLVANG
SANTA YNEZ
Refugio Rd.
The Wineries
1. Mosby
2. Sanford
3. Santa Ynez
4. Gainey
5. Brander
6. Houtz
7. Los Olivos tasting room
8. Austin tasting
9. Carey
10. Ballard Canyon
11. Firestone
12. Zaca Mesa
13. Rancho Sisquoc
14. Byron
15. Maison Deutz
16. Talley and Saucelito tasting
17. Chamisal
18. Corbett Canyon
19. Edna Valley
20. Creston Manor
21. Pesenti
22. Mastantuono
23. Harmony
24. York Mountain
25. Castoro
26. Hope Farms
27. Mission View
28. Caparone
29. Justin
30. Twin Hills
31. Martin Bros.
32. Baron
33. Eberle
34. Arciero
35. Meridian

"Rich and highly extracted, with plum and chocolate flavors, but lacks acidity and lift and cruises to a listless finish of alcohol and wood."
—Description of a Burgess 1988 Napa Valley Zinfandel

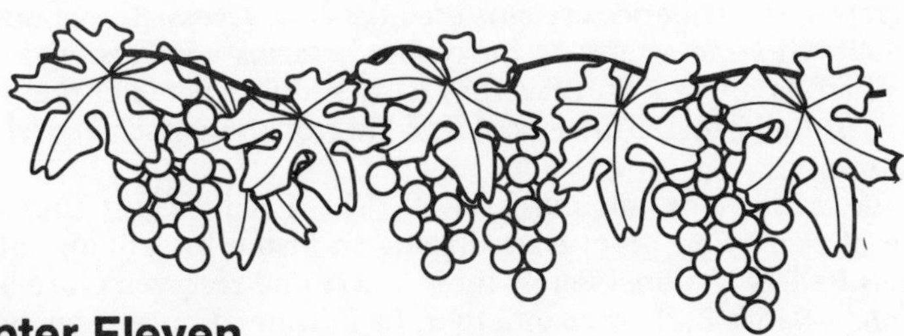

Chapter Eleven
THE SOUTH CENTRAL COAST
San Luis Obispo and Santa Barbara counties

"Whaddya mean, our wines are as good as the Napa Valley's?" growled lanky Al Nerelli. It was his gruff way of agreeing with me. "Hell, we *are* the Napa Valley!"

I looked at him curiously.

"They've bought up half the damned area," he continued. "Bob Mondavi and those people. You drink Napa Valley wine, and it's a good bet you're drinkin' south coast wine!"

Nerelli, one of the owners of Pesenti Winery near Paso Robles, was right on target. "Those people" from Napa, Sonoma and other north coast wineries have discovered a new vineland, equal to their own. Robert Mondavi, Kendall-Jackson, the huge Wine World, Inc., conglomerate and others have bought generously into Santa Barbara and San Luis Obispo counties.

Local folks have known for years what outsiders are just discovering: the south central coast provides ideal conditions for premium wine grapes. This is hill country, seamed by rough ridges that cradle river valleys leading to the sea. Cooling breezes and morning fogs temper the summer sun, creating a proper grape-growing climate. Chardonnay, Merlot, Cabernet Sauvignon and Zinfandel do exceptionally well here.

Vines and wineries are focused in four areas, two in each of the counties. Santa Barbara's vinelands are in the Santa Ynez Valley around Solvang and Buellton and in the Santa Maria Valley, east of the town by that name. Although most of the wineries are in the Santa Ynez Valley, 6,000 of the county's 10,000 vineyard acres are on the Santa Maria flood plain.

San Luis Obispo County's vinelands are concentrated in the Edna Valley inland from Arroyo Grande, and the around the Paso Robles area. Whites thrive in the cooler Santa Ynez, Santa Maria and Edna valleys while reds become big and bold in Paso Robles' summer warmth.

Compared with Sonoma and Napa, the south central coast became a major premium wine producer overnight. Among wineries open to visitors, only

Pesenti and York Mountain date back more than two decades. Most of the others have emerged since the late 1970s. New ones were blooming even as we prowled about the area.

All of this adds up to good tasting and touring for the visitor. Like tightly bunched grapes, the wineries are clustered for easy access. They range from elegant, moneyed wine estates to funky family farms with tasting counters laid across barrels on end. Further, they're tucked into some of the prettiest hill country in California. This is a classic slice of the oak-chaparral woodland climate zone.

Manmade attractions abound as well. The Pacific coast provides an abundance of recreation, from clam-digging in Pismo to sunning off Santa Barbara. Los Padres National Forest lures hikers and reservoirs lure boaters. Five missions—Santa Barbara, Santa Inez, La Purisima Concepcion, San Luis Obispo and San Miguel—are havens of California history.

SANTA BARBARA COUNTY

Despite the youth of the area's wine industry, vines go deeply into its historic roots. The first cuttings likely were planted shortly after the founding of Mission Santa Barbara in 1786. Other vines followed with the establishment of Mission Santa Inez in 1804 in the Santa Ynez Valley.

Rancher Don Jose de Ortega pre-dates the missions; he arrived in 1769 and built up the largest rancho in the county. During the late 1700s, he planted extensive vineyards and sold wine to his neighbors and to folks in the emerging pueblo of Santa Barbara.

The Santa Ynez Valley contained hundreds of acres of vines and several wineries when Prohibition shut them down. They weren't re-established after Repeal. Following an extended dry spell, the first major vineyards were planted by Richard Sanford in 1971, followed by Brooks Firestone in 1974. A member of the huge tire and rubber family, Firestone decided he'd rather make wine than whitewalls.

The Santa Barbara coastline is curiously shaped, taking a sharp right-angle turn at Point Conception to face south instead of west. This invites a west-to-east Pacific air flow that moderates the summer sun, providing proper temperatures for Chardonnay, Riesling, Merlot and other cool-weather grapes. The valley now has nearly 20 wineries; more than half host visitors.

However, more people come to see the deliberately cute Danish village of Solvang than to tour the wineries. A group of Danes arrived in 1910 to establish a colony and school beside Mission Santa Inez. The name of their hamlet is Danish for "Sunny Field." Since World War II, this collection of Scandinavian architecture has grown into one of the largest themed villages in America. Cross-timbered buildings abound and windmills creak in the wind, pumping nothing but atmosphere. Scores of shops sell import giftwares, restaurants serve *aebleskivers* and *smorrebrod*, and gas lamps flicker images of old Copenhagen.

The valley also shelters the lifestyles of some of the rich and famous. Luminaries such as Ronald and Nancy Reagan, Bo Derek and Mike Nichols own ranches and horse farms here. As you drive about the valley, you'll encounter Chateau-like country estates behind neat white-painted fences.

Enough of this. We came to visit the wineries.

SANTA YNEZ VALLEY WINERY TOUR • Begin not in Solvang but in **Buellton**, a neat and prim little town four miles west on Highway 101. Its primary presence is **Anderson's,** a large restaurant and gift shop dating back to 1924 when Juliette Anderson came up with a pretty tasty recipe for split pea soup. Anderson billboards, with Sweet-Pea and Ha-Pea splitting peas, are common throughout the state. A cellar tasting room offers three samples of sweet fruit wines for a dollar.

From Anderson's, follow the town's wide Avenue of the Flags south, then swing west onto Santa Rosa Road. You quickly encounter **Mosby Winery at Vega Vineyards** on the left, within sight of the freeway. A couple of miles beyond is **Sanford Winery**, also on the left.

Now backtrack to Buellton, follow State Highway 246 to and through **Solvang**, then turn right onto Refugio Road. **Santa Ynez Winery** soon appears on your right. Return to Highway 246 and continue east to **The Gainey Vineyard.** It's on your right, just short of the 246-154 junction.

Swing left onto State Highway 154 and drive about three and a half miles to Roblar Avenue. Turn right and follow signs to **The Brander Vineyard.** Now, put it in reverse, cross Highway 154 on Roblar Road, then fork left onto Exterior Road and follow signs to **Houtz Vineyards.** Return to Roblar and follow it into the Victorian-style town of **Los Olivos**; Roblar makes a right turn into Grand Avenue. Among the avenue's 18th century buildings and storefronts, you'll find two tasting rooms, detached from their vineyard moorings—**Los Olivos Tasting Room** and **Austin Cellars.** Los Olivos offers sips from small area wineries with no tasting rooms. For $3, you can try up to ten samples.

From Los Olivos, follow Alamo Pintado Road south, past oak woodlands, pasturelands, vineyards and ranch estates to **Carey Cellars,** on your right. Continue on Alamo Pintado and you're back in Solvang, probably ready to hit some gift shops and then graze through a *smorrebrod*. Incidentally, the Santa Ynez Winery has a tasting room in a cellar shop at 448 Alisal Road.

Departing Solvang, head north on Chalk Hill Road, which blends into Ballard Canyon Road, another exceptionally scenic drive. **Ballard Canyon Winery,** which may or may not be open, is on your left. (We heard that it was closing when we were in the area.)

Ballard Canyon Road crosses Highway 154 and cleverly becomes Foxen Canyon Road. Continue on Foxen for just over four miles and take a hard left onto Zaca Mesa Road. This leads you to **Firestone Vineyard,** up a hill on your right. Return to Foxen and follow it a mile or so to **Zaca Mesa Winery** on your left.

Beyond Zaca Mesa, you leave the Santa Ynez Valley and approach the broad **Santa Maria Valley**. Eight miles from Zaca, take a sharp right turn (just below an old twin-steepled hilltop church) and follow a narrow lane to **Rancho Sisquoc Winery.** Then continue along Foxen Canyon for a mile, turn right onto Tepusquet Road and follow it across the usually dry Sisquoc River to **Byron Vineyard and Winery.** You'll note that the Santa Maria Valley has become a major vineyard area. Vines often extend from foothill to foothill on the broad, level floor of this flood plain.

From Byron, retrace your route on Tepusquet Road, then swing right onto Santa Maria Mesa Road, which blends into Foxen Canyon. That, in turn, blends into Betteravia Road, which puts you on U.S. 101 Freeway in **Santa Maria**. Head north across the Santa Maria River and you're in San Luis Obispo County.

Mosby Winery at Vega Vineyards • T CT ⩙

9496 Santa Rosa Rd. (P.O. Box 1849), Buellton, CA 93427; (805) 688-2415. Daily 10 to 4. All varieties except grappa *tasted; MC/VISA, DISC. Some wine-related gift items; a few picnic tables near the tasting room.*

The Mosby Winery occupies an old red barn with an attractive little tasting room tucked into one end. The pleasantly scruffy farmyard and a peeling 1853 adobe transport you—metaphysically, at least—far from the freeway rumbling nearby.

Bill and Jeri Mosby started *la petite* Vega Vineyards in 1979 and moved to this rustic spot a year later. Jeri likely will be running the tasting room, and she may permit a peek into the winery if things aren't too hectic.

Tasting notes: The short list tilts toward whites and the Mosby's produce some fine ones. Particularly interesting was the Mosby Chardonnay, deep straw colored, velvety and delicious. Several Rieslings were properly fruity and gentle on the acid and a lone red, Mosby Pinot Noir, was mellow, low in tannin and very big on the berry. A powerful Italian cognac-style brew called *grappa* is sold at the winery but not tasted. Prices range from $9 to $14; a 375ml of *grappa* will set you back $25.

Sanford Winery • T ⩙

7250 Santa Rosa Rd., Buellton, CA 93427; (805) 688-3300. Daily 11 to 4; MC/VISA. Most varieties tasted. Picnic area beside a creek.

This mid-sized winery occupies a bucolic creek hollow, just uphill from Santa Rosa Road. Scattered winery buildings are deliberately rustic; some were fashioned of scrap lumber from dairy barns that once stood here. The tasting room is distinctively funky, with weathered wood siding and a twig-roofed *ramada* out front. Books about wine and other subjects share shelf space with some impressive wine awards. A pot-bellied stove and comfortable chairs occupy one area of the room and a sleeping pooch usually occupies the doorway.

Richard and Thelka Sanford planted some of the valley's first grapes in 1971. They began making their own wine ten years later in San Luis Obispo County before moving to this part of the Santa Ynez Valley in 1983.

Tasting notes: The Sanfords' wines frequently gain *grand prix*, sweepstakes awards and platinum medals. The list is short and excellent: a flowery, crisp Sauvignon Blanc; nutty-spicy and complex Chardonnay and a soft, lush and low tannin Pinot Noir. Prices are $5.50 for the Blanc, $16 for the Chardonnay and $14.50 for the Pinot.

Vintners choice: "Our Chardonnay and Pinot Noir have both received international awards," boasts the winery's Shelley Smith.

Santa Ynez Winery • T ST ⚹

343 N. Refugio Rd., Santa Ynez, CA 93460; (805) 688-8381. Daily 10 to 5; MC/VISA. Also a tasting room in Solvang at 448 Alisal Rd., and on Stearns Wharf in Santa Barbara. Most varieties tasted; major credit cards. Wine-related items and specialty foods. Sheltered picnic area; self-guiding tours.

One can go on walkabout at the Santa Ynez Winery. A printed self-guiding tour explains what happens at the small facility, and helps the visitor identify varietal vines that fan out below the neat gray tasting room. Picnic tables on the vineyard-view porch offer an inviting rest stop.

This small facility, founded in 1979 as the Santa Ynez Valley Winery, is owned by Doug and Candace Scott family. It occupies the site and one of the cow barns of a former dairy.

Tasting notes: The list is extensive, ranging from a sparkling wine through assorted varietals to a good jug red. The Sparkling Brut made of Chenin Blanc and Johannisberg Riesling had a nice touch of fruit. The Chardonnays were soft and pleasantly busy with light touches of oak. Among the reds, the Zinfandel was our favorite, with a peppery nose and taste and medium tannin. Cabernet-Merlot had a nice chili-pepper nose and a soft, low acid finish. Prices range from $8 to $15.

Vintners choice: "Johannisberg Riesling, Chardonnay and Merlot," said winemaker Mike Blom. "The east-west orientation of the valley provides a cooling effect from the ocean."

The Gainey Vineyard • T GT ⚹

3650 E. Highway 246 (P.O. Box 910), Santa Ynez, CA 93460. Daily 10 to 5; MC/VISA. All varieties tasted in "flights" of three; most tastings are free, small fee for reserves. Picnic tables in a vineyard garden. Guided tours hourly on the half hour from 10:30 to 3:30.

This is a class operation. The winding, pepper tree-lined drive, the carefully landscaped Spanish style winery and its gleaming high-tech equipment speak of moneyed elegance. Wine columnist Robert Lawrence Balzer called Gainey "one of the most beautiful wineries in the world."

It also offers an excellent, educational tour, starting with a small demonstration vineyard exhibiting different varieties of grapes and different styles of trellising. From there, visitors pass through the high-tech winery, then return to the refined tasting room—furnished with French antiques—for a personally conducted tasting. One can bypass the tour and go straight to the tasting counter, where flights are started every fifteen minutes. Visitors are conducted through three select wines.

The Daniel Gainey family, owners of a 2,000-acre Arabian horse ranch, snipped their purse strings to create this artistic facility in 1984. Presumably, their investment has been returned, for their wines are winning a goodly share of awards.

Tasting notes: Herewith, the report on our flight: The Sauvignon Blanc was clean, crisp and wonderfully fruity. Chardonnay was spicy-nutty and lush with hints of oak. A Cabernet was full-bodied with strong tannin and a pleasant oak touch; suitable for laying away. Overall, the Gainey wines are excellent. Prices range from $8.75 to the early teens.

Vintners choice: "They're all great but our limited selection Pinot Noir is exceptional," exudes Karen Owens.

The Brander Vineyard • T GT ⌅

2401 Refugio Rd., Los Olivos, CA 93441; (805) 688-2455. Daily 10 to 5; MC/VISA, AMEX. Most varieties tasted. Some wine-related gift items; small picnic area. Guided tours when time permits.

At Brander, you're likely to encounter one of the valley's most spirited characters. Lovette Twobirds is the winery's Girl Friday—tasting room hostess, labeler, caretaker, gardener, tour guide and promotion director.

You'll find the tasting room either in the weathered barn of a winery, or in a simple pink Italianate chateau, built by C. Frederic Brander. He established this small winery in 1981 to produce only estate-bottled wines from classic French grapes. While he makes wines, lively Lovette—half Cherokee and half Irish—makes friends for the winery.

"Take two sips," she urges. "You need the second one to set up your taste buds, to make them work on the wine. Isn't that a nice Sauvignon Blanc? It's fun, it's fruity, it's a drink-it-tonight wine."

Tasting notes: Brander's wines are as exuberant as Lovette. The Three Flags Sauvignon Blanc was complex and fruity, with a subtle touch of oak. Tete de Cuvee Sauvignon Blanc was full-flavored with a nice acid nip. Tete

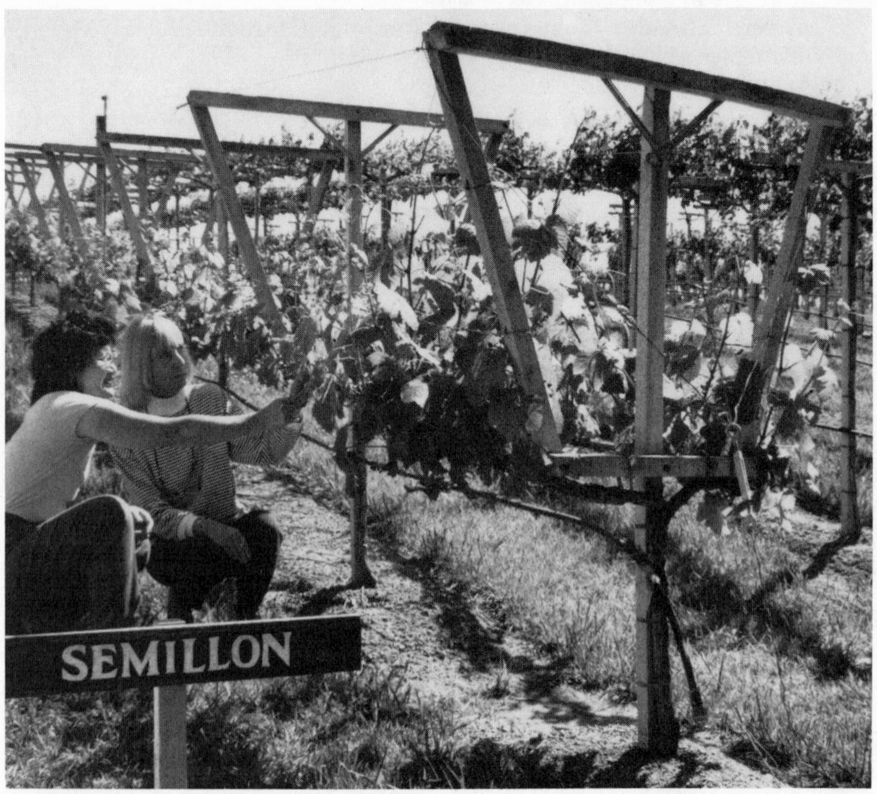

Demonstration plot at the Gainey Vineyard in Santa Ynez Valley exhibits grape varieties and trellis styles. Gainey's Margo Alexander and co-author Betty Woo Martin discuss Semillon's finer points.

de Cuvee Bouchet, a blend of Cabernet Franc and Merlot, was full of berries, with a spicy oak finish. Both whites and reds are barrel-fermented and aged, giving them a distinct complexity. Prices range from $6.50 to $20.

Vintners choice: "Our classic Bordeaux-style Sauvignon Blanc and blended red Bouchet," said Lovette.

Houtz Vineyards • T

2670 Ontiveros Rd., Los Olivos, CA 93441; (805) 688-8664. Weekends only, noon to 4; MC/VISA. Selected wines tasted. Pleasant picnic area by a pond.

This inviting hillside winery, built around a pool and rose gardens above the vineyards, was opened in 1985. However, owners David and Margy Houtz have raised other crops on this picturesque place since the late 1970s. The winery occupies a redwood barn, where they produce about 3,000 cases a year. The family pours selections from its small list in the cheery little tasting room. Guests are encouraged to wander out to the gazebo, glass in hand, to survey this spot the Houtz' call Peace and Comfort Farm.

Tasting notes: The Chenin Blanc was rich and fruity, with a light acid finish; the Chardonnay had a proper nutty-fruity taste. Cabernet was soft and ready to drink, full-flavored with a slight touch of oak. Prices are modest, ranging from $6 to $11.

Austin Cellars • T

2923 Grand Ave., Los Olivos, CA 93441; (805) 688-9665 or (800) 824-8584. Daily 11 to 5; MC/VISA, AMEX. Most varieties tasted. Good selection of wine-related items and specialty foods.

You miss the ambiance of the vineyards when you visit Austin Cellars tasting room in downtown Los Olivos. But you'll taste some excellent wines in the pleasant environment of a refurbished turn-of-the-century cottage. With luck, owner-winemaker Tony Austin may happen by and, in a burst of nervous energy, start discussing his wine-making philosophy.

"Passion is important in the wine business, in anything," he says. "It's what shades your world. And in this business, the winemaker *is* the winery."

His ancestors came to California for the Gold Rush then became northern Sonoma County winemakers. Fourth-generation Tony came south to make wines for Brooks Firestone. Needing more challenge, he started his own facility in 1983 and he's been winning awards ever since.

Tasting notes: Tony's Pinot Noir, powerful on the palette and berry-like with a pronounced tannin finish, is his best wine. He also produces some excellent Sauvignon Blanc and Johannisberg Riesling botrytis wines that are sweet, yet not sticky. His lighter whites were properly fruity with crisp acid finishes. A Cabernet Franc had a wonderfully spicy nose and a big berry flavor. Prices range from $6 to $12.

Vintners choice: "Pinot Noir, when I can get good grapes, and my botrytis wines. They're rich without being cloying," he said before sprinting out the door to fulfill some chore.

Carey Cellars • T GT

1711 Alamo Pintado Rd., Solvang, CA 93463; (805) 688-8554. Daily 10 to 4; MC/VISA. Most varieties tasted. Wine-related gift items; picnic tables with vineyard view. Tours on the half hour, by request.

Brooks and Kate Firestone, early arrivals on the Santa Ynez wine scene, recently purchased this handsome winery, tucked beneath giant oaks above hillside vineyards.

It isn't remarkable that the Firestones get a lot of press, since it's certainly a famous family name. Nor is it surprising that they had the means to purchase this facility, after developing their own Firestone Vineyard. What *is* remarkable is that Brooks and Kate are easy-to-meet, earthy people.

Kate, who manages Carey to keep its identity separate from Firestone Vineyard, is likely to pitch in at the tasting room when things get hectic. With her precise English accent and honest smile, the slender former ballerina talks enthusiastically of *her* winery. Then she may excuse herself and scamper away to complete preparations for an upcoming vineyard wedding.

Even if you don't meet Kate, you'll enjoy visiting this cute yellow and white trimmed cottage tasting room. Picnic tables occupy a deck shaded by a giant oak tree; the view down through the vineyards is a rural joy.

Tasting notes: Carey focuses on upper end varietals. We tasted two Cabernets, found one soft, berry-like and ready to drink and another much heartier, higher in tannin and suitable for laying away. Two whites, Chardonnay and Sauvignon Blanc, were fruit-filled and perfectly balanced, and a Pinot Noir Blanc was surprisingly rich and fruity for a blush wine. Prices range from $6 to the mid-teens.

Vintners choice: "We've been known for some of the best Cabernet Sauvignon in the area," says Kate. "We have two different vineyards which produce quite different styles. We're also known for our Sauvignon Blanc, Chardonnay and Merlot."

Firestone Vineyard • T GT ⌶

5017 Zaca Station Rd., Los Olivos, CA 93441; (805) 688-3940. Daily 10 to 4; MC/VISA. Selected wines tasted. Small gift item selection; courtyard picnic area. Tours from 10 to 4, every 30 to 45 minutes.

Brooks Firestone focused the wine world's attention on the Santa Ynez Valley when he produced the area's first post-Prohibition wines in 1975. He came here not as a winemaker, but as a businessman, to build a winery among vineyards purchased by his father, Leonard K. Firestone. The wines are created by Alison Green, among the growing ranks of women in the industry.

The winery, an intriguing complexity of rooflines, is a large brown presence on a benchland overlooking the vineyards. Tours through this facility provide dramatic views from a gallery of stainless steel tanks down into a cellar filled with French oak. Participants are then given a personal tasting in an intimate paneled room off the main tasting room. One can bypass the tour and step into the main tasting facility, which is properly stylish, located off a sheltered courtyard.

Tasting notes: The list is large for a Santa Ynez winery, with six whites, three reds, an excellent Rosè of Cabernet and a sparkling Blanc de Noirs. We discovered a consistency of crisp fruitiness in the Chardonnay, Johannisberg Riesling and Sauvignon Blanc. A Cabernet, Cabernet Reserve and Merlot were full flavored yet soft, with a gentle finish. Prices range from $7 to the early teens, going higher for some reserves.

Vintners Choice: "Johannisberg Riesling is our flagship wine," says promotions director Katie O'Hara. "Our Chardonnay, Merlot and Cabernet Sauvignon are consistently good."

Zaca Mesa Winery • T GT ⌆

6905 Foxen Canyon Rd. (P.O. Box 899), Los Olivos, CA 93441; (805) 688-3310. Daily 10 to 4; MC/VISA, AMEX. Most varieties tasted. Wine-related giftwares and specialty foods. Tours every hour on the half hour 10:30 to 2:30.

Zaca Mesa's appealing cedar-sided barn of a winery sits in a hollow off Foxen Canyon Road. Here, the view is primarily inward. The building's elongated U-shape forms three sides of a courtyard; sheltering oaks provide the fourth. One can picnic at tables tucked under a roof overhang. A large, appealing hospitality room occupies one end of the winery, where sippers gather at one of three tasting areas. We settled before an oversized walnut banquet table to work through the small list of six wines.

Owned by a realty corporation, Zaca Mesa is one of the area's earlier wineries, dating from 1978. Tours take visitors through the busy but well-organized facility, from crusher to ranks of American and French oak.

Tasting notes: Two Chardonnays showed markedly different styles, although both were excellent. The Zaca Mesa Chard was fruity, fresh and crisp while the reserve was more complex, nutty and buttery. A reserve Pinot Noir was soft and berry-like and a Syrah had a pronounced tannin nip, yet it was gentle and full-flavored. Prices range from $6 to $16.50.

Vintners choice: "Chardonnay, Reserve Chardonnay and Reserve Pinot Noir are our best wines," says Zaca's Jim Fiolek. "They're our focus Varietals."

Rancho Sisquoc • T CT ⌆

Foxen Canyon Road (Route 1, Box 147), Santa Maria, CA 93454; (805) 934-4332. Daily 10 to 4; MC/VISA. All varieties tasted. Tours if time allows; otherwise, one can peek into the small winery. Picnic tables on a lawn area.

Seeking out Sisquoc may require a brief search, since you might overshoot the turnoff. Look for the small, weathered Sisquoc Church on a low rise to your right, take a hard right onto a farm road and follow it two miles. You'll wind up in a large farmyard, the work center of a 38,000 acre cattle ranch. A sign identifies the weathered wooden cottage that houses the small tasting room. Once inside, you'll see the church again—a simple drawing on the winery's label.

After tasting fine barrel-aged wines and perhaps chatting with affable assistant winemaker and tasting room host Fausto Hernandez, you'll be glad you found the place. If things are slow, he'll take you on a brief tour of the adjacent winery, or at least encourage you to take a peek.

San Franciscan James Flood started this ruggedly handsome, hidden-away winery in 1977. The surrounding cattle ranch hearkens back to Spanish days.

Tasting notes: Most of the wines are aged in wood, giving even the whites a nice complexity. Barrel-fermented Sauvignon Blanc and Chardonnay were delicious, with nice spicy-fruity flavors. A Franken Riesling, uncommon in this area, was crisply fruity. Merlot and Cabernet Sauvignon had powerful peppery bouquets and flavors; both were big wines suitable for putting away. Prices range from $9 to $12.

Vintners choice: "We work on quality, not quantity," said Fausto of the 6,000-case winery. "I think they're all good; I guess I'd pick the Franken Riesling as my favorite."

Byron Winery • T GT ⯹

5230 Tepusquet Rd., Santa Maria, CA 93454; (805) 937-7288. Daily 10 to 4; most major credit cards. Wine-related gift items and picnic fare. Picnic tables overlooking Tepusquet Creek. Guided tours on request.

Byron represents Robert Mondavi's entry into the south central coast wine area. However, founder and managing partner Byron Ken Brown still runs the operation and makes the wine. It was established by Brown and several partners in 1984, and later purchased by the Mondavi family.

The winery is the most dramatically-situated in the county. Surrounded on three sides by vines, it perches on the wooded rim of a small ravine. Tepusquet Creek rustles beneath the trees 50 or so feet below. It's an appealing facility, a stylish wood-sided barn with vague Spanish-Oriental lines. The tasting room, tucked under a balcony at one end, is done in knotty pine. The landscaped picnic area on the edge of the ravine is a great spot for a lunch break; you can buy the wine and nibbles inside.

Tasting notes: Normally, a good bottle of wine shouldn't cost more than a good bottle of Scotch, but we'd willingly pay the $17 for Byron's silky, buttery Chardonnay Reserve. The 1988 version was voted best in the American Wine Competition. A Sauvignon Blanc was fruity and complex while the Pinot Noir had a pleasant peppery nose and gentle berry flavor. The Cabernet Sauvignon was a typical Bordeaux, well-rounded and full flavored with gentle hints of wood. Prices range from $9 to $18.

Vintners choice: The focus is on premium Burgundian varietals—Chardonnay and Pinot Noir, according to a winery source.

SAN LUIS OBISPO COUNTY

With a wider climatic range than Santa Barbara, San Luis Obispo County vineyards produce hearty, award-winning reds as well as whites. Edna Valley, open to Pacific breezes, is noted for its premium whites and full-flavored Pinot Noir. The Paso Robles-Templeton-San Miguel area is sheltered by the Coast Range, providing warmer climates for outstanding Zinfandel and Cabernet.

Edna Valley

Edna Valley wineries are the new kids on the block. This area northeast of Arroyo Grande shelters eight wineries and the oldest, Chamisal, dates only from 1981. Pacific breezes provide natural summer air conditioning; Chardonnay and Pinot Noir thrive in this benign climate.

EDNA VALLEY WINERY TOUR • Heading north on U.S. 101 freeway from **Santa Maria**, you'll see the modern **Maison Deutz** winery sprouting among hillside vineyards on your right. Continue north on the freeway, take the Grand Avenue exit and drive east into the oldstyle business district of **Arroyo Grande**. You might want to pause and browse through the shops tucked behind false front and brick facades in the prim, well-maintained downtown area.

Heading east on Grand Avenue, you'll go through several street name changes; stay your course by following signs to **Lopez Lake**. You'll blend from Grand to Branch Street to East Branch to Hausna and then turn left onto Lopez Drive. Still with us?

Clearing Arroyo Grande's suburbs, you enter bucolic **Edna Valley**, rimmed with softly contoured hills. They're green velvet in spring and French-bread beige in summer and fall. An occasional vineyard climbs toward the low horizon. After a couple of miles on Lopez Drive, you'll encounter **Talley Vineyards,** up a vine-covered rise to your left. It also houses the tasting facilities of **Saucelito Canyon Vineyard.** Retrace your route briefly on Lopez Drive and turn right (north) onto Orcutt Road. You soon discover **Chamisal Vineyard** on your left.

Now, backtrack on Orcutt, turn right onto Tiffany Ranch Road and right again onto Corbett Canyon Road (State Highway 227). **Corbett Canyon Vineyards** crests a hill to the left. Continue north on Corbett Canyon a bit more than a mile, turn right onto Biddle Ranch Road and you'll see **Edna Valley Winery** on the right. Continue northwest on Highway 227 and you'll emerge into the heart of **San Luis Obispo**, with its nicely restored mission. Signs will take you from there back to the freeway.

Maison Deutz • T$ ST & GTA ⚹

453 Deutz Dr., Arroyo Grande, CA 93420; (805) 481-1763. Daily except Tuesday 11 to 5; MC/VISA. Glass of sparkling wine and snack plate, $3.50. Some wine-related gift items; small picnic area. Peek into the winery, or guided tour by reservation.

Since this chateau-style hillside sparkling wine cellar doesn't open until 11, make it a lunch stop. The "tasting" consists of a glass of Brut Cuvee served with a plate of cheese spread, crackers, fruits, pistachios and other goodies. During the crush, you can nibble on freshly-picked wine grapes and perhaps sip a bit of free-run juice that—without your intercession—would have become fine sparkling wine.

A joint venture of the 150-year-old Champagne Deutz of France and America's Wine World, Inc., the facility was built in 1983. It's an impressive complex, emerging from its own vineyards above the highway. From the stylish cathedral-ceiling tasting room, one can see the Pacific, whose breezes create a perfect habitat for grapes that go into Deutz' sparkling wine. Barstools at the tasting counter and small tables in the spacious tile-floored room invite you to linger.

You can study the huge wooden *Coquard* French basket wine press in the adjacent crush room; it's the only one of its kind in America. Then, stroll down to a lower winery building cantilevered into the hillside for a peek at the aging barrels and *triages* of sleeping sparkling wine. Call ahead if you'd like a detailed tour.

Tasting note: The primary product is Cuvee Brut ($15), rated by wine judges among California's finer sparkling wines. After letting its tiny bubbles tickle our nose and enjoying its crisp, complex flavor, we agree. The tasting room also may have Brut Reserve ($22) and Brut Rosè ($21) available.

Talley Vineyards • T ⚹

3031 Lopez Dr., Arroyo Grande, CA 93420; (805) 489-0446. Noon to 5, daily in summer and Thursday through Sunday the rest of the year; MC/VISA.

Most varieties tasted. Wine logo gift items and specialty foods. Picnic tables in a gazebo and on a lawn near the tasting room.

A square-shouldered, two-story brown farmhouse first catches your eye. It stands, almost arrogantly, above the surrounding vineyards, without need of shielding vegetation. Closer scrutiny reveals an ancient adobe, now impeccably restored. El Rincon Adobe was built in 1863 as headquarters of a 4,000-acre rancho. It now houses the offices of Talley Vineyards, and tasting facilities for Talley and Saucelito Canyon Vineyard. The Saucelito winery is located farther up the valley, beyond Lopez Lake. El Rincon is a mini-museum as well as a tasting facility. An exhibit room has been furnished with Spanish and early American antiques.

The Talley family has owned this land for 40 years. The winery dates back to the late 1980s when Don and Rosemary and their son Brian began producing a select list of whites and a Pinot Noir.

Tasting notes—Talley: We sipped an excellent Chardonnay, full of buttery fruit, with a hint of oak, and a soft and fruity Sauvignon Blanc; both were barrel-aged. A Riesling was crisp and fresh, done in stainless steel. The lone red is a Pinot Noir, spicy and berry-like with a medium body and light tannin. Prices range from $8.50 to $16.

Vintners choice—Talley: "Our Chardonnay and Pinot Noir, both from the family vineyards," says the winery's Lori Hall.

Tasting notes—Saucelito Canyon: This winery focuses on Zinfandel. The 1988 version we tasted was excellent, berry-like and peppery with a subtle hint of wood.

Vintners choice—Saucelito Canyon: "We specialize in Zinfandel from our 110-year-old dry-farmed vineyard. Our wines are intense but drinkable upon release," quotes Nancy Greenough, who owns the small 2,000-case winery with her husband Bill.

PICKNICKING AMONG THE VINES

Chamisal Vineyard • T CT

7525 Orcutt Rd., San Luis Obispo, CA 93401; (805) 544-3576. Wednesday-Sunday 11 to 5; MC/VISA. Most varieties tasted. A few wine-related gift items, books and specialty foods; small picnic area.

The oldest and one of the smallest of the Edna Valley wineries, Chamisal occupies a simple stucco barn at the edge of a large vineyard. The Norman Goss family began crushing grapes here in 1981; the vineyards go back another ten years.

The tasting room is a simple square at a corner of the winery, dressed up a bit with wainscoting and rough wood paneling. The most impressive adornment is thatch of ribbons behind the tasting bar, proof of Chamisal's wine quality. Nice feature: this is one of the few tasting rooms with bar stools. The picnic area is as rudimentary as the rest of the place. A few tables stand beside the winery, sheltered from breezes by a board fence.

Tasting notes: The list is short. Two Chardonnays were complex, buttery and fruity with a proper acid nip at the end. A Cabernet Sauvignon Blanc displayed a lively peppery nose that carried into the taste. For a blush Cab, it had a surprisingly strong varietal flavor. We thought of Mexican food as we sipped. A sweet yet light aperitif made of Chardonnay, wine spirits and herbs completed the list. Prices range from $10 to $14.

Corbett Canyon Vineyards • T GT

2195 Corbett Canyon Rd. (P.O. Box 3159), San Luis Obispo, CA 93403: (805) 544-5800. Monday-Friday 10 to 4:30 and weekends 10 to 5; MC/VISA. Selected varieties tasted; usually six. Good assortment of gift items and wine-related books. Picnic area near the tasting room. Guided tours on weekends only, at 11, 1 and 3.

There's no denying that this is a winery; one of the more handsome in the south coast area, in fact. However, there's not a vineyard in sight; they're elsewhere in the county. Built in 1984 as the Lawrence Winery, it is now owned by the Wine Group, a corporation that has spent time and money upgrading the facility. It also has won more than its share of awards; *Wine and Spirits* and *Vanity Fair* have praised its wines.

The stucco Spanish style building is almost mission-like, with a tile roof and arched entry. The large tasting room is bright and cheery, done in salmon stucco, with a latticed skylight and colonnaded walls. Picnic tables sit beneath an arbor; the entire facility is nicely landscaped. It's no surprise that a local newspaper voted this as the county's most attractive winery.

Tasting notes: Corbett's list is larger than most, and they're all estate wines. We were struck by the fresh, fruity varietal flavor of the whites, a Coastal Classic Sauvignon Blanc, Chardonnay and Reserve Chardonnay. A Coastal Classic Pinot Noir was light and soft yet pleasantly spicy. The Merlot was equally spicy, more complex with a nice tannic finish. Prices are modest here, ranging from $4.25 to $11.

Vintners choice: Our tasting hostess informed us that they're particularly proud of their estate Chardonnay and Pinot Noir.

Edna Valley Vineyard • T CT

2585 Biddle Ranch Rd., San Luis Obispo, CA 93401; (805) 544-9594. Daily 10 to 4; MC/VISA. Most varieties tasted. Small picnic area; casual tours.

From showy, we come to austere. However, Edna Valley's wines don't play second fiddle to its more glitzy neighbor. The wines are excellent and the winery is—well—businesslike. You enter through a roll-down door and pass through a roomy emptiness that suggests this facility was built for expansion. The tasting area is a counter that appears to have been set up almost as an afterthought. Stacked boxes form a working background. The area is brightened, however, by a couple of vases of flowers on the counter.

Nearby is an oldstyle cellar where this mid-sized winery's 58,000-case production matures. Guided tours, available by prior arrangement, will get you there. Further, you'll learn that this "roomy emptiness" is strictly state of the art. The winery is owned by Chalone, Inc., which has a similarly straightforward facility in Monterey County.

Tasting notes: Chardonnay topped our list; it was buttery, spicy and crisp. A rarely-seen Pinot Noir Vin Gris was pleasantly tart and fruity. The Pinot Noir was lush, complex and rather light on the finish while the Cabernet Sauvignon had a proper chili-pepper nose, boldly complex flavor and a nice tannin finish. Edna's Sparkling Wine, Lot 2, was crisp and fruity with a hint of sweetness. Prices range from $6.50 to the mid-teens, going higher for some reserves.

Vintners choice: "Chardonnay and Pinot Noir," says the winery's Darlene Elderman. "We have ideal growing conditions for these wines, and make a Burgundian style Pinot."

Paso Robles and environs

In contrast to Edna Valley, the Paso Robles area has a long history in the wine business. We aren't just referring to the usual practice of Spanish padres sticking cuttings into the ground.

Indeed, founders of Mission San Miguel Archangel near Paso Robles *did* plant vines around 1797. Then in 1882, Andrew York established the York Mountain winery, followed by Adolph Siot's Rotta Winery in 1890. Both survived Prohibition and York still hosts visitors. Another old-timer is Pesenti Winery, started by Frank Pesenti in 1934 and still owned by the family.

About 25 wineries thrive today, and most host visitors. They're grouped along Vineyard Drive and State Highway 46 west of Templeton, above and below San Miguel and along Highway 46 east of Paso Robles. This is primarily red wine country, and vintners produce outstanding Zinfandel and Cabernet. Plan more than a day to visit this region's somewhat scattered wineries. They're in three separate areas, so we'll divide Paso Robles and neighbors into a trio of tours.

TEMPLETON AREA WINERY TOUR • This will be a loop, taking you west to the Pacific Ocean, then back along State Highway 46 to U.S. 101. Incidentally, there's a tasting room downtown at Sixth and Main streets called **Templeton Corner,** offering tastes from area wineries without their own facilities. It's open daily except Monday from 10 to 6.

What better street than Vineyard Drive to lead you to wineries? Take the Vineyard interchange from U.S. 101, just south of Templeton and head west, but not very far. Make a quick right to the **Creston Manor** tasting room, within sight of the freeway. As you continue west on Vineyard Drive, you'll pass upscale horse farms and fancy country homes similar to those in the Santa Ynez Valley. Some of California's finest breeding stables are hereabouts. You'll soon find **Pesenti Winery** on your left and then the chateau-like **Mastantuono Winery,** which shows up about the time Vineyard Drive blends into Highway 46.

Now, settle back for a 20-mile drive on Highway 46, through a parade of picturesque country. You'll pass a mix of meadows, pasturelands, clumps of oaks and madrones; stay alert and you can catch an occasional glimpse of the distant Pacific. Vineyards appear now and again to remind you that this is wine country. Forested hills of the Lucia Mountains of the Coast Range cradle you, marking the horizon on every side. Then you quickly break free and hurry downhill to the green headlands above the Pacific.

At Highway 1, turn left and drive about a mile to a tiny nest of rustic charm called Harmony. Once a busy dairy complex, this 130-year old hamlet tucked into a green hollow now boasts a population of 18. The weathered buildings—all five of them—are occupied by artists, boutiques, one good restaurant and the tasting room of **Harmony Cellars.**

Retrace your route on Highway 46; after about 12 miles, turn left at York Mountain Road to visit **York Mountain Winery.** Return to Highway 46, drive another eight miles or so and you'll see **Castoro Cellars** in a restored Victorian on the right at Bethel Road. A short distance beyond on Highway 46 is **Hope Farms Winery** on the left. That old familiar freeway is just ahead and you'll hit it between Templeton and Paso Robles.

Creston Manor Winery • T

Highway 101 at Vineyard Drive (P.O. Box 577), Templeton, CA 93465; (805) 434-1399. Daily except Wednesday 10 to 5; MC/VISA. Most varieties tasted. Good selection of gift and wine logo items. Picnic area near the tasting room.

Creston's tasting room occupies a prim little French-windowed cottage. It's been on this spot since the mid-80s, luring travelers off nearby Highway 101. Visitors can picnic under the shade of the cottage eaves.

The vines and winery are about ten miles inland, near Creston northeast of Atascadero. Creston Manor was established in 1981 by Larry and Stephanie Rosenbloom.

Tasting notes: Creston's list is small, with the requisite Chardonnay and Cabernet Sauvignon, plus a Pinot Noir and white Zinfandel. The Chard was properly fruity and silky with a nice acid nip to the finish; Cabernet was complex and mildly peppery, with enough tannin to encourage putting it down for a few years. The Pinot Noir was softer, ready to drink and the white Zin revealed a nice flowery palate. Prices range from $6 to $17.50.

Vintners choice: Chardonnay and Cabernet Sauvignon, said the tasting room host.

Pesenti Winery • T GTA

2900 Vineyard Dr., Templeton, CA 93465; (805) 434-1030. Monday-Saturday 8 to 5:30 and Sunday 9 to 5:30; no credit cards but out-of-town checks accepted. Most varieties tasted. Extensive giftware and wine logo selection. Guided tours by appointment.

Venerable Pesenti Winery's tasting list reads like a vintner's catalog. We counted 44 items! Everything from premium varietals to jug wines to hard cider to fruit and berry wines. The tasting room resembles a well-stocked wine shop, with shelves running from floor to ceiling.

In the early days, according to local legend, the Pesenti family would leave a few bottles and a sampler jug out front. If you liked the wine, you laid down a dollar and took a bottle home.

Pesenti is still a popular place to stop by for a bottle or two. In fact, that's the best way to get a real feel for the wine, since tastings are served in—good grief!—shot glasses. Ever try to swirl, slosh and sniff with a shot glass?

Frank Pesenti started the winery in 1934. Son Victor, his sister Sylvia and her husband Al Nerelli have been running things since the 40s. They're assisted now by younger Pesentis and Nerellis.

Tasting notes: Pesenti offers some of the best wine buys south of Sonoma. Maybe south of Seattle. Most of their reds are big and lusty, and the whites are classic examples of fresh fruitiness. A grand national champion Cabernet Sauvignon goes for $9.95, and a national champ Gray Riesling, their best seller, is yours for $5.95. An exceptional Zinfandel, winner of national and international medals, sells for $6.95. Other premium varietals are priced between $5 and $10; quite drinkable blends drop below $5.

And don't forget that hard cider; take it home for $4.

Vintners choice: Al thought for a moment, then said, flatly: "Our Zinfandels and Cabernets. They're some of the top wines in this area."

Mastantuono Winery • T

100 Oakview Rd. (Route 2), Templeton, CA 93465; (805) 238-0676. Daily 10 to 6; MC/VISA. Most varieties tasted. Extensive giftwares, stemware and deli foods. Picnic area.

Step inside Pat Mastantuono's wonderfully overdone tasting room and you expect to see jolly knights thumping their flagons on the bar, demanding refills. From afar, the place looks like a cross between a chateau and a castle. From within, it might be a Bavarian hunting lodge, with game trophies glaring from their wall mounts.

"*Italian* hunting lodge," corrected the gregarious founder of this place. Between sips of wine as robust as their creator, we get the Pasquale Mastantuono story. "I started a furniture business in L.A. With these hands; tool box and the whole thing. I wanted to make a million so I could retire at 39. So that's what I did."

With an exaggerated sweep of his left hand, he gestures around the tasting room. "*This* is my retirement. This is fun!"

Pat started having fun in 1976 when he began making wine commercially. His Italian forbearers had been doing it for three generations, so he figures it was in his genes. Actually, he says he doesn't make wine; he only guides it.

"The wine is made in the vineyard," he said, in refreshing contradiction to the modern school of test tube winemakers.

Tasting notes: Mastantuono's philosophy practically jumps from the glass. His reds are dry-farmed, unfined and unfiltered. The Zinfandels run a tasty gamut from light and berry-like to powerful and robust. A six-year-old Zin, aged three years in oak, was one of the best we've tasted. Chardonnays were crisp and spicy with a hint of wood and a Cabernet was rich and aged to proper smoothness. Also on the list were a fruity white Zin, a soft but nippy Carminello (from the Carmine grape, a U.C. Davis hybrid of Cabernet, Merlot and Carignan) and a silky, full-flavored port. Prices range from $6 to $20.

Vintners choice: The license plate on Pat's flashy boat-tailed Auburn displayed out front says it: "ZINMAN 1."

Harmony Cellars • T

10 Old Creamery Rd. (P.O. Box 2502), Harmony, CA 93435; (805) 927-1625. Daily 10 to 5; MC/VISA. Most varieties tasted. Wine logo gift items, plus several gift shops and boutiques nearby. Picnic tables in adjacent patio.

The tasting room shares the 19th century Harmony Valley Creamery Association building with a dinky post office, cafe and several boutiques. Wines are tasted over plank laid across barrel heads. A free-form stove occupies one wall, with a kinky Smoky Stover stovepipe writhing toward the ceiling. The wine tasting list is written on a chalkboard behind the bar.

This small winery's vineyards are out of sight, in the faraway hills. According to winemaker Chuck Mulligan, plans are afoot to build a new winery on a hillside niche above this rustic, harmonious little hamlet.

Tasting notes: The Chardonnay and Johannisberg Riesling displayed pronounced varietal character, strong on fruit, light on wood, with a crisp acid finish. The Pinot Noir was pleasantly oaky with a spicy nose and a good taste of berries while the Cabernet was lighter and somewhat herbaceous. A Zinjolais, a blend of Zinfandel and Beaujolais, was light yet rich with the flavor of the grapes, with a gentle acid finish. Prices range from $5.50 to $11.50.

Vintners choice: Mulligan likes to keep the fruit in his wine. Grapes for his favorite—Zinjolais—are hand picked right into a fermentation tank, where they're chilled with dry ice to retard fermentation and retain the fruity flavor.

York Mountain Winery • T CT

York Mountain Road (Route 2, Box 191), Templeton, CA 93465; (805) 238-3925. Daily 10 to 5; no credit cards. All varieties tasted; most free, $4 for samples of five reserves or 50 cents a sip. Good wineware selection, books and specialty foods. Tours by appointment, or one can peek into the winery.

York Mountain is aging gracefully. The venerable winery occupies an early American farmyard fringed by trees and vineyards high on the flanks of the Santa Lucias. The vine-entwined tasting room has the look of an old-style general store, with a wide selection of gifts, specialty foods and books. It's one of wineland's more intriguing tasting rooms, with a beamed ceiling, craggy stone fireplace and a 1910 New Era motorcycle parked along one wall.

As far as we could determine, York Mountain is the oldest surviving winery in all of southern California, dating from 1882, when it was established by Andrew York. Present owner Max Goldman bought it from the York family in 1970.

Tasting notes: York's busy list ranges from red and white jug wines and classic varietals to a sparkling wine and dry sherry. The Zinfandel, Pinot Noir and Cabernet Sauvignon were hearty and full-bodied with a strong taste of the grape. Chardonnay, the only varietal white, was crisp and light, while the jug white was nicely acidic—one of the better we've tasted.

Sherry, made from Chenin Blanc and French Colombard, was properly nutty. Prices range from $4.50 for the blends to the mid-teens for high end varietals.

Vintners choice: "We're in a red area," said Goldman simply.

Castoro Cellars and Comanche Creek Vineyard • T$

1480 N. Bethel Rd., Templeton, CA 93465; (805) 238-0725. Daily 11 to 5; MC/VISA, AMEX. All varieties tasted for $2 fee, including logo glass. Good selection of wine-related giftware and specialty food items. Picnic area near the tasting room.

This is a joint venture, with Niels and Bimmer Udsen's Castoro Cellars furnishing the wines and Dawn and John Hawley's Comanche Creek providing the tasting room. And what a room! It's housed in a former 1880 schoolhouse shaded by century-old oaks. The interior is as comfortable as an oldstyle living room with country French antiques and a fireplace that crackles warmly on chilly days.

The Udsen's family winery produces about 15,000 cases a year. Most varieties are available at the tasting room, which opened in mid-1990. The Hawleys intend to produce their own wines as well, under their Comanche Creek label.

Tasting notes: The Castoro Fumè Blanc, one of the few produced on the south central coast, was crisp and light with a nice acidic finish. A light touch of oak accented the Chardonnay. Of the reds, the Pinot Noir was full and complex yet soft. The Zinfandel also was on the light side, with typical raspberry flavor. A pretty cranberry-colored Gamay Nouveau had nice strawberry taste. Prices range from $6 to $12.

Vintners choice: "What we're really known for is our reds," commented winemaker Niels.

Hope Farms Winery • T$

2175 Arbor Rd., Paso Robles, CA 93446; (805) 238-6979. Daily 11 to 5; MC/VISA. All varieties tasted for a $2 fee, glass included. Extensive gift and specialty food selection; free food samples. Picnic area in a gazebo.

Built in 1990, the sparkling new Hope Farms tasting room is a study in 19th century rural elegance, with a stained glass entryway, coffered ceilings, Casablanca fans and lively fruit-print wallpaper. Dishes of cheeses, sauces, mustards and dips arrayed along the tasting counter are yours for sampling. You can buy what you like, both food and wine, and adjourn to a picnic area in a gazebo furnished with white wrought iron.

Two Hope couples, Chuck and Marilyn and Paul and Janet, planted vineyards in this area in 1978, then they opened their middle American country-style winery a decade later.

Tasting notes: The Hope Farm list consists of six varietals. The Chardonnay was light yet complex, Sauvignon Blanc was fruity and crisp with a nice acid finish and the white Zinfandel was soft with a hint of sweetness. Both the Zinfandel and Cabernet Sauvignon were berry-like, soft and ready to drink. The sixth entry, Muscat Canelli, is a sweet dessert wine, tasty enough to sip slowly or pour over fruit.

PASO ROBLES-SAN MIGUEL WINERY TOUR • Drive north on U.S. 101 and take the first turnoff into San Miguel. Follow the weathered old town's main street to **Mission San Miguel**, which is worth a pause. About half a mile beyond, turn right on River Road. It winds up into vineyard benchlands above the town, shortly reaching **Mission View Winery**. Return to U.S. 101 and head south. Watch for a small sign indicating San Marcos Road, on your right about a mile south of San Miguel. Follow this to **Caparone Winery** on the right, then continue on San Marcos to its junction with Nacimiento Lake Drive. After about two miles, fork right onto Chimney Rock Road and follow it seven miles to **Justin Winery.** Chimney Rock is a narrow country lane canopied with oaks and flanked by tawny and green mounds of the Santa Lucia foothills.

Retrace your route, this time staying on Nacimiento Lake Drive until you come to **Twin Hills Ranch** winery on the left. If you're continuing to the third wine area, follow Nacimiento back to Paso Robles. It crosses U.S. 101 and becomes State Highway 46, taking you into the Estrella River Valley.

Mission View Vineyards • T$ ⌅

13350 N. River Rd., San Miguel, CA 93451; (805) 467-3104. Daily 10 to 6. Most varieties tasted for a $2 fee. Picnic area on redwood deck overlooking the vineyards.

If you look carefully westward from the picnic deck of this winery perched atop a benchland, you do indeed have a Mission San Miguel view. The close-up view is nice, as well. The redwood-sided, blue tile-roofed winery is sort of Alpine-Spanish and its tasting room is definitely Spanish with beamed ceilings, tile floor and painted tile insets in the counter. The grounds are landscaped with terraced rose gardens and other bloomers.

This corporate-owned facility was completed in 1985 and currently bottles about 8,000 cases.

Tasting notes: Mission View produces big hearty Zinfandel and Cabernet with nice oak finishes; they're drinkable now and will improve with age. Chardonnay, fermented and aged in barrels, had a complex nutty flavor. The Sauvignon Blanc, also barrel-aged, displayed an ideal balance between fruit and acid with a hint of wood. The wines are consistent medal winners.

Vintners choice: "The hot summers here grow beautiful Cab and Zin grapes," said public relations director Betty Quigley.

Caparone Winery • T CT

2280 San Marcos Rd., Paso Robles, CA 93446; (805) 467-3827. Daily 11 to 5; no credit cards, checks accepted. All varieties tasted.

Don't be put off by the austere brown prefabricated metal shed that houses M. David and Mary Caparone's winery. The surprise is inside: an assortment of excellent red wines at affordable prices. Dave makes only reds and he makes them powerful, lush and high in tannin. Drink them now or lay them away. He racks his wines instead of filtering them to preserve their complexity to "let the big fruit come forward." Like Mastantuono, he feels the foundation for the wine is laid down in the vineyard.

A tour here consists of a glance around the cozy 4,500-case winery. Ebullient tasting room host Jack Strauch likes to guide visitors through a vertical tasting, including some barrel samples.

Tasting notes: Dave's big reds are easy on the wood, full flavored and lush with berries. The Zinfandel was predictably bold and fruity and the Cabernet was complex and tannic yet surprisingly soft. Merlot rounds out the short list; it exhibited a nice peppery nose and flavor, with a tongue-tickling tannic finish. Prices are a bargain, from $7.52 to $8.50. The Caparones also have yearly releases of ten-year-old wines, at higher prices, of course.

Justin Vineyards and Winery • T CT

11680 Chimney Rock Rd., Paso Robles, CA 93446; (805) 238-6932. Daily except Monday, 10 to 6; MC/VISA, AMEX. Most varieties tasted. Garden picnic area; tours if someone is available.

What's this? A French chateau in the Santa Lucia wilds? This grand symbol of affluence rises in striking contrast to its bucolic surroundings. Architecture of the multi-gabled wooden winery appears to be a mix between French manor house and a California seacoast hideaway. It's rimmed by formal English gardens, with picnic tables beneath an arbor. The tasting room features thick ceiling beams, rough terrazzo floors, an iron chandelier dangling above a glass-topped tasting table, a grand piano and walls of—uh—simulated marble. The whole vision swims somewhere between elegant and pretentious.

Former investment banker Justin Baldwin established the winery in 1987. He and winemaker Chris Johnson produce small lots of carefully crafted estate bottled wines.

Tasting notes: Justin's wines, which win an exceptional number of medals, often sell out. The Chardonnay was a classic—nutty, buttery and crisp. The Meritage, labeled simply as Estate Reserve, was lush and berry like, with a pleasant nip of tannin. Others on the select list are Merlot, Cabernet Franc, Cabernet Sauvignon and a sparkling Blanc de Noir. Prices range from $15 to $22.50.

Twin Hills Ranch Winery • T

2025 Nacimiento Lake Dr., Paso Robles, CA 93447; (805) 238-9148. Daily except Monday, 11 to 5; MC/VISA. Most varieties tasted. Shaded picnic area; good selection of wine logo items.

The copper roofed, cross-timbered tasting room is a curious—and pleasant—blend of Spanish and French, with touches of the plantation South. The winery owner, former aerospace executive Jim Lockshaw, used bricks and beams from an anti-bellum mansion in its construction. The interior is a comfortable living room setting of bentwood chairs, couches before a fireplace that sometimes crackles, and potted ivy perched on high shelves.

Another of the wine world's corporate drop-outs, Lockshaw started his winery in 1980, and produces about 10,000 cases a year.

Tasting notes: The wines are soft and ready to drink, with more accent on fruit than wood or tannin. The Chardonnay was light yet complex with a spicy flavor. The Zinfandel Rosè was excellent; not wimpy but brimming with berry flavor. The Zinfandel and Cabernet Sauvignon were soft and spicy. Prices range from $8 to $12.

Vintners choice: Twin Hills' Cathie Besheer went down her list of favorites: "Chardonnay, very light; Zinfandel Rosè, fruity and semi-dry; our California Beaujolais, light and fruity."

ESTRELLA RIVER VALLEY WINERY TOUR • This is shallow, softly contoured countryside, not as striking as the Nacimiento area with its steep oak-thatched hills and tilted meadows. You will be rewarded, however, with fine wines and some impressive looking wineries.

If you're just coming off the previous tour, continue across U.S. 101 on Nacimiento Lake Drive, which blends into State Highway 46. The first winery comes up quickly: **Martin Brothers** on your left. Drive about a bit over a mile and, at the Union Road sign, take a right and then an immediate left. Follow this two and a half miles to Penman Springs Road, turn right and you'll see the small **Baron Vineyard Cellars** on an upslope to the right.

Now, return to Highway 46 and continue east. The remainder of the wineries will present themselves without further search: **Eberle Winery** on the left, elegant **Arciero Winery** on the right, then, after a short drive, **Meridian Vineyards** on the left.

Martin Brothers • T GTA

Highway 46 at Buena Vista Drive (P.O. Box 2599), Paso Robles, CA 93447; (805) 238-2520. Daily 10 to 6 in summer, 10 to 5 the rest of the year; MC/VISA. All varieties tasted. Gift items, books, specialty foods and wine accessories. Picnic patio with white wrought iron tables and chairs. Guided tours by appointment at the winery, a mile away on Buena Vista Drive.

The Martin name is English-Scottish, as my own ancestors confirm, but Nick and Tom specialize in Italian-style wines. They've planted such old world varieties as Nebbiolo, Vin Santo and Aleatico. These can be sampled, along with others, at their neat gray and white-trimmed tasting room set in a formal garden. The airy, color-coordinated interior provides a pleasing sipping setting.

Nick and Tom Martin established their winery in 1986 and produce about 15,000 cases a year. They're so focused on their Italian wines that they open a booth each year at VinItaly, Verona's noted international wine trade show.

Tasting notes: The traditional whites and reds show strong varietal character; they're light and ready to drink. We were particularly interested in the Italian entrees. Nebbiolo is a crisp, tannin-rich red with a nice berry flavor. Vin Santo and Aleatico are dessert wines; the first with sweet apricot aroma and taste and the second a rich Muscat style. Prices range from $6.50 to the mid-teens. A Grappa de Nebbiolo goes for $40 and, understandably, isn't available for tasting.

Vintners choice: "Our Italian varietals—particularly the Nebbiolo, and our Chenin Blanc," says PR manager Cynthia Reed.

Baron Vineyard Cellars • T

1985 Penman Springs Rd., Paso Robles, CA 93446; (805) 239-1931. Daily 11 to 5; MC/VISA. Small picnic area; a few wine logo items.

This tiny winery, in an cottage-style structure on an upslope among the vineyards, produces only 2,000 cases a year. A new tasting room was rather spartan when we visited, but it may be more embellished when you arrive.

Former fireman Tom Baron and his wife Sharon began farming here in 1981 to escape Los Angeles traffic and smog. They came for the grapes, the rural life and the view of the Estrella River Valley and distant Santa Lucia range. From their hillside perch, it's rather impressive.

Tasting notes: Their two whites, Chardonnay and Sauvignon Blanc, are light and crisp, with low acid. Paso Panache, a rosè, is done in similar fashion. A Muscat Canelli is rich but not sticky, with a refreshing crushed flower petal taste. Prices are a modest $4 to $7.

Eberle Winery • T GTA

Daily 10 to 5, until 6 in summer; MC/VISA. All varieties tasted. Good selection of giftwares and books. Picnic tables on a view terrace; guided tours by appointment.

This attractive cedar, shake-roofed winery sits on a rise above its own vines, commanding a wide-angle view of the shallow river valley. The tasting room suggests a nicely furnished modern home with beamed ceilings, fabric walls and a fireplace. Formal landscaping completes a pleasant setting.

W. Gary Eberle established the winery in 1982. A "pioneer" in this young area, he studied winemaking at U.C. Davis and settled here in 1973, working initially with Estrella River Vineyards. He was named Central Coast Winemaker of the Year in 1990. The much traveled young wine pioneer also holds a master's in zoology and he was a defensive tackle for Penn State; he has the barrel chest to prove it.

Tasting notes: The Eberle wines we tasted were uniformly excellent. The Chardonnay was crisp, buttery and spicy, while the Cabernets were light yet lush with a peppery nose and nicely complex flavor. Zinfandel was powerful and fruity; with strong tannic accents, it will improve greatly with aging. For chuckles, Gary has created "Eye of the Swine," a pink blend of Cabernet, Zinfandel, Muscat Canelli and Chardonnay. This is no wimpy rosè; think of it as a blush wine with the heart of a defensive tackle.

Arciero Winery • T ST

Highway 46 at Jardine Road (P.O. Box 1287), Paso Robles, CA 93447; (805) 239-2562. Daily 11 to 5 (until 6 on summer weekends); MC/VISA, AMEX. Select varieties tasted. Extensive gift, wineware and deli selection. Self-guiding tour; racing car display.

This is how you build a family winery if you happen to be a family of millionaires. Visually, Arciero is one of America's great wine chateaux: a study in tile-roofed Spanish elegance set into a vineyard slope. A juniper-lined drive, extensive lawns, lavish landscaping and umbrella picnic tables create a setting of moneyed country refinement. The high ceiling tasting room is accented with glossy tile, chandeliers and a fireplace. An impressive horseshoe-shaped tasting counter is its focal point.

Excellent graphics take you on a self-guiding tour through the winery. Bunkered into the hillside, it rivals the luxury of the tasting room, with carved oaken doors, a brass chandelier in the entry and carpeted corridors. Large view windows allow peeks into assorted winery operations.

Brothers Frank and Phil Arciero made their fortunes in southern California construction, and ran a stable of racing cars as a pastime. Three of their cars, including an Indy Super Vee flown by Phil Hill, Dan Gurney and Al Unser, are displayed in the tasting room.

Tasting notes: Like the winery, the wines are uniformly upscale. Yet they're modestly priced, ranging from $3.69 for a good serviceable red table wine to $8.69 for excellent varietals. The Chardonnay was full bodied and nutty, with a nice hint of oak. Chenin Blanc was fruity and sweet; good if you like sweeter whites. Cabernet Sauvignon, Zinfandel and Petite Sirah were full-flavored and robust, suitable for immediate sipping or putting down.

Meridian Vineyards • T ⌅

Highway 46 (P.O. Box 3289), Paso Robles, CA 93447; (805) 237-6000. Wednesday-Sunday 10 to 5; daily in summer; MC/VISA. Most varieties tasted. Wine-related gift items. Picnic area near winery.

Starting from a small but well-financed base, Meridian is emerging as another major Paso Robles wine estate. Nestle's Wine World division is building this facility, which crests a hill with a fish-eye view of its own vineyards. Only the first phase, a rural-modern shingle-roofed winery and tasting room, were completed when we visited. The finished product will be impressive, a large U-shaped complex with stone facing, a landscaped courtyard and other amenities.

Most of its grapes are drawn from three vineyards owned by Meridian in Santa Barbara County; others are maturing right at the new winery's doorstep. The facility was started in 1988 and the tasting room opened in 1990.

Tasting notes: Both the Santa Barbara County and Edna Valley Chardonnays were excellent, fruity and toasty with crisp finishes and hints of oak. The Pinot Noir had a berry-like nose and taste; light in body and mouth-filling. Paso Robles Syrah was big, oaky and peppery; excellent if you like assertive wines. The Cabernet was softer, complex and spicy with a light tannin finish. Prices range from $6 to $14.75

Vintners Choice: "We're particularly happy with our Chardonnays and Syrah," said tasting room hostess Denise McLean.

THE BEST OF THE BUNCH

The best wine buys • Houtz Vineyards and Austin Cellars in Santa Ynez Valley; Corbett Canyon Vineyards in Edna Valley; Pesenti Winery in the Templeton area; Caparone Winery west of Paso Robles; and Baron Vineyard Cellars and Arciero Winery in the Estrella River Valley.

The most attractive wineries • The Gainey Vineyard in Santa Ynez Valley; Corbett Canyon Vineyards in Edna Valley; Justin Winery east of Paso Robles; and Arciero Winery in the Estrella River Valley.

The most interesting tasting rooms • Sanford Winery east of Buellton; the Gainey Vineyard in Santa Ynez Valley; Mastantuono Winery, Castoro/Comanche Creek and Hope Farms in the Templeton area; Twin Hills and Mission View near San Miguel; and Arciero Winery in the Estrella River Valley.

The funkiest tasting room • Harmony Cellars in Harmony.

The best gift shops • Mastantuono Winery, York Mountain Winery and Hope Farms in the Templeton area; Harmony Cellars (adjoining boutiques and shops); and Arciero Winery in the Estrella River Valley.

The nicest picnic areas • Houtz Vineyards, Carey Cellars and Firestone Vineyard in Santa Ynez Valley; Byron Winery in Santa Maria Valley; Harmony Cellars in Harmony; Hope Farm in the Templeton area; Justin Cellars east of Paso Robles; and Arciero Winery in the Estrella River Valley.

The best tour • The Gainey Vineyard (guided), in Santa Ynez Valley.

BEYOND THE VINEYARDS

The south central coast was a popular tourist area before the first Pesenti squeezed his first grape, and certainly before the new crop of high-tech wineries arrived. Without the tasting rooms, tens of thousands still would come to prowl about the missions, poke about Solvang's shops and toast themselves on Pacific beaches. Just over the ridge, architecturally gorgeous, tile-roofed Santa Barbara is one of California's major tourist lures.

Starting from **Solvang**, we'll suggest driving tours that will carry you to the two counties' touristic highlights. First, you'll likely want to go "shop-about" in Solvang, stuff your little faces with Danish pastries, ride the horse-drawn streetcar and perhaps catch a play at the **Festival Theater.** A repertory group performs summer-long in this outdoor playhouse. **Elverhoy Museum** in a Scandinavian-style building at 1624 Elverhoy Way (Second Street) recalls Solvang's Danish heritage. You'll also want to investigate the museum and ancient adobe halls of **Mission Santa Inez.**

From Solvang, head south on Alisal Road, which coils through some of Santa Ynez Valley's prettiest oak woodlands. Pause at lushly wooded **Nojoqui Falls County Park** for the short hike to the waterfalls, which may or may not be falling, depending on the season. Continue on Alisal Road to U.S. 101; you can follow it south to **Gaviota State Beach** and on to alluring **Santa Barbara**, or head north to **Buellton** of pea soup fame.

We'll focus on the northern route, which is closer to the vinelands. From Buellton, take State Highway 246 west to **La Purisima Mission State Historic Park** near Lompoc. It's the most authentically restored of California's 21 missions, having been reassembled as a WPA project during the Depression. Workers used the same tools as those employed by the Indians. The Lompoc area also is famous for its glittering Technicolor **flower fields** in spring and early summer. **Vandenberg Air Force Base,** noted for its missile launches, is out this way.

From Lompoc, head north on one of America's most scenic byways, State Highway 1. It will take you to the wide sandy beaches of **Oceano, Grover City** and clam-famous **Pismo Beach**. At the Grover City-Oceano section of **Pismo State Beach,** you can drive right along the surf, just like they do in the TV commercials—if your car has the proper tires. Be careful you don't get stuck; ask the ranger at the gate if the sand's firm enough for your car.

Highway 1 rejoins U.S. 101 freeway in Pismo, but avoid that and follow the ocean-front drive through **Shell Beach** to wonderfully funky old **Avila Beach.** It's a resort town right out of the Thirties with tiny stucco cottages and a beach walk. Just beyond, weathered **Port San Luis Pier** is host to a good seafood restaurant (listed below), a fish market, uncounted seagulls and an occasional visiting sea lion.

Return to U.S. 101/State Highway 1 and explore tidy and prim old **San Luis Obispo.** Its visitor offerings include **Mission San Luis Obispo;** several boutiques, restaurants and antique shops in SLO's clean-swept downtown area, just below the mission; and the comely campus of **California Polytechnic State University,** or simply Cal Poly. (Noted for its high-tech agricultural courses, it's sometimes unkindly called "Cow Piley.") It's rimmed by typical student cafes, bars and bookstores.

From SLO, take State Highway 1 northwest to **Morro Bay**, a seaside charmer with dome-shaped **Morro Rock** as its centerpiece. Two state parks, **Morro Bay** and **Montana de Oro**, preserve slices of rocky beaches, windy headlands and lush forests. Driving north on Highway 1, you'll skim the rough-hewn coastline and pass **Harmony,** the dairy town turned art colony. From here, you can continue north to aquatically rustic **Cambria**. Just beyond is **Hearst San Simeon State Historical Monument**, the lavish castle-home of newspaper baron William Randolph Hearst.

If you head south from Solvang, you'll want to visit Santa Barbara's many attractions. On the don't-miss-list are **Mission Santa Barbara,** the **County Courthouse** with its lavish Spanish-Moorish architecture, **El Presidio de Santa Barbara State Historic Park** for the flavor of early Mexico, old **Stearns Wharf** and the city's excellent expanse of beaches.

Incidentally, a nice approach to Santa Barbara from Solvang is on State Highway 154. It carries you past **Lake Cachuma County Park** with boating, fishing, hiking, camping, and picnicking; across the dizzying **Cold Spring Bridge,** one of the highest single-arch spans in America, thence over **San Marcos Pass** through the rugged Santa Ynez Mountains. As you spiral down from the hills into Santa Barbara, you'll enjoy impressive city and ocean views.

Santa Ynez Valley activities & attractions

Boating, swimming • Cachuma Lake Recreation Area; 688-4658.

Museums & historical exhibits •

Elverhoy Museum, 1624 Elverhoy Way, Solvang, CA 93463; 686-1211. Friday 11 to 4, weekends 1 to 4. Exhibits of Solvang's Danish heritage.

La Purisima Mission State Historic Park, Lompoc, CA 93436; 733-3713. Daily 9 to 5; modest admission charge. A faithful WPA reconstruction of an early California mission.

Mission Santa Inez, 1760 Mission Dr., Solvang, CA 93463; 688-4815. Weekdays 9 to 5, Saturdays 9 to 4:30 and Sundays noon to 4:30. Restored early California mission; self-guiding tour and museum.

Santa Ynez Valley Historical Society Museum and Carriage House, 3596 Sagunto St., Santa Ynez, CA 93460; 688-7889. Museum open Friday-Sunday 1 to 4 and carriage house Tuesday-Thursday 10 to 4 and Friday-Sunday 1-4. Chumash Indian, local history exhibits; carriage displays.

Theater • Solvang Theaterfest, June-September, outdoors in the Solvang Festival Theater; 922-8313. Pacific Conservatory of the Performing Arts Theaterfest, Allan Hancock College, Santa Maria; 922-8313.

Wineland events • Santa Barbara County Vintners' Festival, various wineries in the Santa Ynez Valley, April; 688-0881. Danish Days in Solvang includes some winery events, third weekend of September; 688-3317.

Winery touring map • ***Santa Barbara County Wineries***, available at area wineries or from the Santa Barbara County Vintners' Association, P.O. Box 1558, Santa Ynez, CA 93460-1558; 688-0881.

San Luis Obispo County activities & attractions

Museums & historical exhibits •

Mission San Luis Obispo, Chorro and Monterey streets, San Luis Obispo, CA 93405; 543-6850. Daily 9 to 5. Restored early California mission, self-guiding tours, museum.

San Luis Obispo County Historical Museum, 696 Monterey St., San Luis Obispo, CA 93405; 543-0638. Wednesday-Sunday 10 to 4. Historical exhibits in restored Carnegie Library.

Vineyard events • Paso Robles Wine Festival, third weekend of May; 238-0506. Central Coast Winetasting Classic, San Luis Bay Inn, Avila Beach, July; 544-5229 or 543-1323. Central Coast Wine Festival, Mission Plaza, San Luis Obispo, September; 543-1323. Individual wineries also sponsor events throughout the year.

Winery touring maps • ***Wineries of the Edna Valley and Arroyo Grande Valley***, available at area wineries or from: Edna Valley Arroyo Grande Vintners, P.O. Box 159, Arroyo Grande, CA 93420; 541-5868. ***Wine Tasting in Paso Robles***, available at area wineries or from: Paso Robles Wine Country, 548 Spring St., Paso Robles, CA 93446 or call the Paso Robles Chamber of Commerce at 238-0506.

WINE COUNTRY DINING

Santa Barbara County

A.J. Spurs • ΔΔΔ $$$ Ø

350 E. Hwy. 246 (just east of the freeway), Buellton; (805) 686-1655. Western barbecue; dinner $10 to $25; full bar service. Monday-Thursday 11:30 to 9:30, Friday-Saturday 11:30 to 10, Sunday 9 to 1 and 2 to 9:30. Casual; reservations accepted (except on Saturday). MC/VISA, AMEX. Housed in an oversized log cabin, abrim with Old Western atmosphere, contrived but nicely done. Cowboy curios, game trophies and geegaws to study while you chew. The menu is as Western as John Wayne's drawl—barbecued steaks, ribs and chicken, served with tortillas and beans. Live music nightly.

Anderson's Pea Soup Restaurant • ΔΔ $$ Ø

376 Avenue of the Flags, Buellton; (805) 688-5581. American; meals $9 to $15; full bar service. Daily 7 a.m. to 10 p.m. Casual. MC/VISA. Historic restaurant started in 1924, based on Juliette's recipe for split pea soup. It's still the most interesting thing on the menu, which features Americana steaks, chops and pot roast. Complex includes gift shops, fruit wine tasting and a quick study of Anderson family history.

Bit O' Denmark • ΔΔ $$ Ø

473 Alisal Rd. (Mission Drive), Solvang; (805) 688-5426. Danish-American; dinners $8 to $20; wine and beer. Daily 6 a.m. to 9 p.m. Casual; reservations accepted. Major credit cards. Popular Danish restaurant featuring breakfasts with a variety of pancakes; a full *smorgaasbord* spread for lunch and dinner. Local wines and international beers.

Cold Spring Tavern • ΔΔΔ $$$ ØØ

5995 Stagecoach Rd. (half an hour uphill from Solvang on Highway 154), Santa Barbara; (805) 967-0066. American; dinner $14 to $20; full bar service. Open daily; lunch 11 to 3, dinner 5:30 to 9 (to 10 weekends), breakfast weekends only from 8 to 11. Casual; reservations advised, essential on weekends. MC/VISA. Century-old stage stop tucked into the bottom of a ravine; a setting that's at once dramatic, romantic and rustic. Wagon wheel chandeliers, kerosene lamps and the like. Varied menu with large portions—steak, pasta, chop, venison, rabbit and chicken, with interesting seasonings and sauces. Smoke-free; live music on weekends.

Danish Inn Restaurant • ΔΔ $$ Ø

1547 Mission Dr., Solvang; (805) 688-4813. Danish-continental; dinner $10 to $32; full bar service. Daily 11:30 to 10. Informal to casual; reservations advised. Major credit cards. Scandinavian in architecture and menu, styled as an old world wayside inn. *Smorgaasbord* and assorted continental entrees. Live entertainment nightly in lounge.

The Hitching Post • ΔΔ $$$ Ø

406 E. Hwy 246 (half mile east of the freeway), Buellton; (805) 688-0676. Western barbecue; dinner $12 to $25; full bar service. Tuesday-Saturday from 5 p.m., Sunday from 4. Casual; reservations advised. MC/VISA. Long-established, locally popular place featuring barbecue specialties: steak, baby back pork ribs, grilled quail, chicken or duck and seafood. Decor is austere rural American.

The Little Mermaid • ΔΔ $$ Ø

1546 Mission Dr. (Fourth Place), Solvang; (805) 688-6141. Danish-American; dinner $8 to $14; wine and beer. Daily 7:30 a.m. to 8 p.m. Casual. MC/VISA. Cute Scandinavian-style cafe featuring serving *aebleskivers*, puffy round Danish pancakes. "Skiver-maker" works in full view, observable from within or without the restaurant. Breakfasts feature *aebleskivers* with a dollop of jam and a large, bland Danish sausage.

Massimi Ristorante • ΔΔ $$$ ØØ

1588 Mission Dr. (Petersen Village Square), Solvang; (805) 688-0027. Italian; dinner $14 to $25; wine and beer. Daily except Monday, 5:30 p.m. to 9 p.m. Casual; reservations accepted. MC/VISA, AMEX. Pleasingly decorated Italian chef-owned restaurant featuring fresh pastas, Osso Buco, seafood, veal and in-house desserts. Smoke-free; patio dining.

Mattei's Tavern • ΔΔΔ $$ Ø

Highway 154 (Grand Avenue), Los Olivos; (805) 688-4820. American; dinners $9 to $17; full bar service. Monday-Thursday from 5:30, Friday-Sunday from noon. Informal to casual; reservations advised on weekends. MC/VISA. An 1886 stage stop, refurbished and furnished with antiques and western America artifacts. Menu ranges from prime rib and steaks to fresh seafood and pastas.

Scandia Restaurant • ΔΔ $$$ Ø

420 Alisal Rd. (downtown), Solvang; (805) 688-8000. American-Continental; dinners $9 to $22; full bar service. 7 a.m. to 9 p.m. daily. Informal to casual; reservations accepted. Major credit cards. Danish-style restaurant with Scandinavian, other European and American fare. Buffet breakfast daily; brunch on Sunday. Live entertainment nightly.

The Viking Garden • Δ $ Ø

446-C Alisal Rd. (Copenhagen), Solvang; (805) 688-1250. Danish, German, American and Mexican; dinners $6 to $7, full-course early bird dinners $5.95 from 4 to 7; wine and beer. Monday-Friday 10 a.m. to 8 p.m., Saturday-Sunday 8:30 to 8. Casual; no reservations; no credit cards. Small restaurant with eclectic, inexpensive fare. Bargain "early bird" Danish dinners such as *Karbonander* (breaded pork patties and red cabbage). Indoor and outdoor dining.

San Luis Obispo County

All restaurants in the city of San Luis Obispo are smoke-free, by local statute.

A.J. Spurs • ΔΔΔ $$$ Ø

508 Main St., Templeton; (805) 434-2700. Western barbecue; dinner $10 to $25; full bar service. Monday-Thursday 11:30 to 9:30, Friday-Saturday 11:30 to 10, Sunday 9 to 1 and 2 to 9:30. Casual; reservations accepted (except on Saturday). MC/VISA, AMEX. See description under Santa Barbara County.

Berardi & Sons • ΔΔ $$ Ø

1202 Pine St., Paso Robles; (805) 238-1330. Italian; dinner $9 to $15; wine and beer. Lunch weekdays 11 to 2:30, dinner nightly 5 to 9:30. Casual; reservations advised, essential on weekends. No credit cards. Local hangout housed in a narrow, century-old brick store; busy and noisy most nights. Some interesting dishes include chicken *saltimbucca* stuffed with prosciutto and cheese and calamari *Diablo* with sweet peppers and onions. Local and extensive wine list.

Brubeck's • ΔΔ $$ ØØ

726 Higuera St. (Broad Street), San Luis Obispo; (805) 541-8688. California nouveau; dinners $10 to $13; full bar service. Open daily; lunch 11:30 to 3:30, dinner 5:30 to 10, Sunday brunch 9:30 to 3. Informal to casual; reservations advised. MC/VISA, AMEX. Lively local hangout in old brick, perched over a creek bank. Menu ranges from fresh fish, coconut fried prawns and grilled lamb chops to assorted pastas. Extensive list of local and other California wines.

Carmel Beach Restaurant • ΔΔ $$ ØØ

450 Marsh St. (Marsh freeway exit), San Luis Obispo; (805) 541-3474. American with seafood focus; dinners $10 to $25; wine and beer. Open daily; lunch 11:30 to 2, dinner 4:30 to 10. Informal to casual; reservations advised. Major credit cards. In a converted Victorian home; extensive fresh seafood menu, along with chicken, steaks and chops and assorted pastas. The place schedules occasional wine-tasters dinners.

Joshua's Restaurant and Vineyards • ΔΔΔ $$$ N

13th and Vine streets, Paso Robles; (805) 238-7515. American; dinner $9 to $25; full bar service. Lunch Monday-Saturday 11:30 to 2:30, dinner Monday-Friday from 5, Saturday-Sunday from 4., Sunday brunch 10 to 2. Informal to casual; reservations advised. MC/VISA, AMEX. Very appealing restaurant, fashioned into a century old Catholic church building; spacious, with some original stained glass. Menu focuses on steaks, sweetbreads, chicken, baby back ribs and seafood. Periodic "Meet the Winemaker Dinners," with five courses and five local wines.

The Loading Chute • ΔΔ $$

Fourth and Webster (Highway 229), Creston; (805) 238-5825. Western; dinner $8 to $16; wine and beer. Daily 10 a.m. to 9 p.m. Casual; no reservations. MC/VISA. Housed in a 19th century general store in the folksy rural village of Creston, northeast of Atascadero. The menu is as Western as the atmosphere—steaks, barbecued chicken and ribs and fire-breathing chili.

Old Harmony Pasta Factory • ΔΔ $$ ØØ

#2 Old Creamery Rd., Harmony; (805) 927-5882. Italian-Californian; dinners $10 to $16; wine and beer. Dinner nightly from 5 p.m. Informal to casual; reservations advised. MC/VISA, AMEX. Cute old place done in rural Americana, in the old Harmony creamery complex. Italian menu, with assorted home made pastas, pork and chicken dishes, plus seafood with California accents. Outdoor dining.

Olde Port Inn • ΔΔΔ $$$ Ø

On Port San Luis Pier; (805) 595-2515. American, mostly seafood; dinner $14 to $20; full bar service. Sunday-Thursday 5:30 to 9, Friday-Saturday 5:30 to 10. Informal to casual; reservations advised, essential on weekends. MC/VISA. Cheerfully rustic fish house perched on the Port San Luis Pier, with views of sand, sea and headlands. Daily seafood specials are fresh, often just off one of the restaurant's boats. The spicy *bouillabaisse* is excellent. Live 50s and 60s music on weekends.

Paso Robles Inn • ΔΔ $$ Ø

1103 Spring St. (Eleventh Street), Paso Robles; (805) 238-2660. American; dinners $7 to $16; full bar service. Daily 7 a.m. to 9 p.m. Informal to casual; reservations advised. Major credit cards. Turn-of-the-century dining room in Paso Robles' landmark multi-gabled inn. The menu fits the mood—steak, prime rib, chicken and chops, with a focus on local wines. Veranda dining; live music on weekends.

Rose Victorian Inn • ΔΔΔ $$$ Ø

789 Valley Rd., Arroyo Grande; (805) 481-5566. American-continental; dinner $13.50 to $18; wine and beer. Thursday-Sunday 5:30 to 9. Informal to casual; reservations advised. MC/VISA.Handsome restaurant with a short but innovative menu, such as roast Sonoma duck with mandarin Napoleon sauce, rack of lamb with Zinfandel mint sauce and seafood linguine. The decor is old world country inn.

This Old House • ΔΔΔ $$$ Ø

740 W. Foothill Blvd. (west on Los Osos from freeway), San Luis Obispo; (805) 543-2690. Western barbecue; dinners $13 to $21; full bar service. Monday-Friday from 5, Saturday-Sunday from 4. Casual; reservations advised. Major credit cards. Some folks say this 1917 house is haunted, that chairs move by themselves. Perhaps it's merely hungry diners reaching for another brace of ribs or a barbecued chicken wing. In a rural setting at the end of Foothill Boulevard, decorated with old photos, Indian sketches and Western regalia.

VINELAND LODGINGS

Santa Barbara County

The Ballard Inn • ΔΔΔΔ $$$$$ ØØ

2436 Baseline (Alamo Pintado Road), Ballard, CA 93463; (800) 638-BINN or (805) 688-7770. Rooms $145 to $185. MC/VISA. Elegant 15-room Victorian inn, furnished with antiques. Individually decorated rooms stocked with cheese, crackers and fruit; some rooms with fireplaces. Full cooked-to-order breakfast, afternoon wine tastings with *hors d'oeuvres*.

Danish Country Inn • ΔΔΔ $$$$ Ø

1455 Mission Dr., Solvang, CA 93463; (805) 688-2018. Doubles $79 to $109, singles $69 to $99, kitchenettes $135, suites $109 to $180. Major credit cards. Danish-style 82-room motel with TV and phones; some rooms with VCRs and refrigerators. Free buffet breakfast and afternoon wine and beer; swimming pool.

Meadowlark Motel • ΔΔ $$

2644 Mission Dr. (near Refugio Road), Solvang, CA 93463; (805) 688-4631. Doubles $42 to $54, singles $40 to $50, kitchenettes $55 to $68. MC/VISA, AMEX. A 19-room motel on two acres just east of Solvang; TV, pool. Pleasantly landscaped grounds.

Kronborg Inn • ΔΔΔ $$$ Ø

1440 Mission Dr., Solvang, CA 93463; (805) 688-2383. Doubles and singles $50 to $85, suites $60 to $120. Major credit cards. Danish-style motel with 39 rooms. TV movies, phones, balconies; free continental breakfast with morning paper; spa, pool.

Svendsgaard's Lodge • ΔΔ $$$ Ø

1711 Mission Dr. (Alisal Road), Solvang, CA 93463; (800) 733-8757 or (805) 688-3277. Doubles $50 to $80, singles $45 to $75, kitchenettes $90, suites $75 to $90. Major credit cards. Danish-style 48-room motel with remote TV, room phones; free continental breakfast, swimming pool.

Sheraton Royal Scandinavian Inn • ΔΔΔΔ $$$$ Ø

400 Alisal Rd. (P.O. Box 30), Solvang, CA 93464; (800) 624-5572 in California or (800) 325-3535 outside; locally (805) 688-8000. Doubles and singles $95 to $135, suites from $135. Major credit cards. A full-service hotel with 133 rooms; TV movies, room phones, Danish-American decor. Pool, spa, fireplace in lobby, dancing in Valhalla lounge. **Royal Scandia restaurant** serves from 7 a.m. to 9 p.m.; California-continental with Danish specialties; dinners $15 to $21.50; full bar service; non-smoking tables.

Tivoli Inn • ΔΔΔ $$$$

1564 Copenhagen Dr. (Atterdag Avenue), Solvang, CA 93463; (800) 266-1484 or (805) 688-0559. Doubles, singles and suites $85 to $190. Major credit cards. Nicely appointed Danish-style 29-room inn. TV, phones, fireplaces and mini-bars in rooms; swimming pool. **Pacific Coast Pub** serves "pub grub" 2 p.m. to midnight, $5 to $6; full bar service; California beach bar decor. Adjacent **Pacific Coast Cafe** serves seafood and California *nouveau.*

San Luis Obispo County

San Luis Obispo, Morro Bay and Pismo Beach have dozens of motels. Our list here covers only communities next door to the vineyards: Paso Robles, Arroyo Grande and Templeton.

Adelaide Motor Inn • ΔΔ $$ Ø

1215 Ysabel Ave. (Highway 46 exit), Paso Robles, CA 93446; (800) 549-PASO (California only) or (805) 238-2770. Doubles $46 to $50, singles $35 to $47, suites $72 to $81. Major credit cards. Nicely-appointed 67-unit motel; TV movies, video rentals, phones, radios and refrigerators. Heated pool; coin laundry.

Arroyo K Lodge • Δ $$

611 El Camino Real (Halcyon Road exit), Arroyo Grande, CA 93420; (805) 489-9300. Doubles $38 to $55, singles $32 to $40. Major credit cards. A 42-unit motel with TV, room phones; pool.

Arroyo Village Inn Bed and Breakfast • ΔΔΔ $$$$ ØØ

407 El Camino Real (Brisco or Halcyon exits), Arroyo Grande, CA 94320; (805) 489-5926. Doubles $95 to $110, singles $85 to $155, sites $125 to $165. Major credit cards. Seven rooms in a Victorian-style farmhouse, all with private baths; TV and VCRs available. Full breakfast, afternoon wines and *hors d'oeuvres*. Early American country decor; all rooms are smoke-free.

Best Western Black Oak Motor Lodge • ΔΔΔ $$$ Ø

1135 24th St. (Highway 46 exit), Paso Robles, CA 93446; (800) 528-1234 or (805) 238-4740. Doubles and singles $48 to $63. Major credit cards. A 110-unit motel with TV, radios, phones; some rooms with refrigerators. Swimming and wading pools, spa, sauna, coin laundry. **Black Oak Restaurant** serves 7 a.m. to 10:30 p.m.; American; dinners $10 to $18; full bar service; non-smoking tables.

Best Western Casa Grande Inn • ΔΔΔ $$$ Ø

850 Oak Park Rd. (Oak Park exit), Arroyo Grande, CA 93420; (800) 528-1234 or (805) 481-7398. Doubles $75 to $85, singles $58 to $72, kitchenettes $95 to $120, suites $90 to $110. Major credit cards. A 114-unit motel; TV movies, phones, some rooms with refrigerators, some efficiency units. Pool, spa, sauna, game room, small exercise room, coin laundry. Free continental breakfast, beer and wine. **Lyon's Restaurant** serves 7 a.m. to 11 p.m.; American; dinners $7 to $11; full bar service.

Country House Inn • ΔΔΔ $$$ Ø

91 Main St. (Vineyard Drive), Templeton, CA 93465; (805) 434-1598. Doubles $68 to $83, singles $68 to $78. MC/VISA. Bed and breakfast inn with six rooms; three with private baths. Full breakfast. An 1886 Victorian with country French furnishings and landscaped gardens.

Madonna Inn • ΔΔΔ $$$$

100 Madonna Rd. (just off freeway), San Luis Obispo, CA 93405; (800) 543-9666 or (805) 543-3000. Doubles and singles $82 to $170, suites $130 to $170. No credit cards. Legendary for its whimsical, gaudy architecture, the inn has 109 rooms, all decorated differently. Many travelers stop just to check out the architecture in the lobby, restaurant and even the restrooms. Rooms have TV, phones and flashy decor. **Dining room** serves from 5:30 to 9 (coffee shop from 7 to 9); American; dinners $16 to $30; full bar services. Dining areas are smoke-free.

Melody Ranch Motel • ΔΔ $$

939 Spring St. (just south of town), Paso Robles, CA 93446; (805) 238-3911. Doubles $38 to $44, singles $32 to $38. Major credit cards. Small 19-room motel with TV, radios and room phones; pool.

Paso Robles Travelodge • ΔΔ $$ Ø

2701 Spring St., Paso Robles, CA 93446; (800) 255-3050 or (805) 238-0078. Doubles $48 to $65, singles $38 to $45. Major credit cards. Thirty-one rooms; TV movies, room phones, refrigerators; pool.

Village Inn • ΔΔΔ $$$$ ØØ

407 El Camino Real (Grand Avenue exit), Arroyo Grande, CA 93420; (805) 489-5926. Doubles $85 to $110, singles $75 to $85. Major credit cards. Seven-room bed and breakfast inn. Rooms furnished with Victorian and American antiques; private baths; free breakfast. All rooms non-smoking.

South central coast information sources

Arroyo Grande Chamber of Commerce, 150 W. Branch St., Arroyo Grande, CA 93420; (805) 489-1488.

Paso Robles Chamber of Commerce, 1113 Spring St., Paso Robles, CA 93446; (805) 238-0506.

San Luis Obispo Chamber of Commerce, 1040 Chorro St., San Luis Obispo, CA 93401; (805) 541-8000.

Solvang Conference & Visitors Bureau, P.O. Box 70, Solvang, CA 93463; (805) 688-6144.

LEARNING ABOUT WINE

"It has flavors of blackberry-like fruit with hints of fresh plums, spice, cassis and beeswax with a cigar box quality."
—Description of a 1986 Santino Amador County Zinfandel

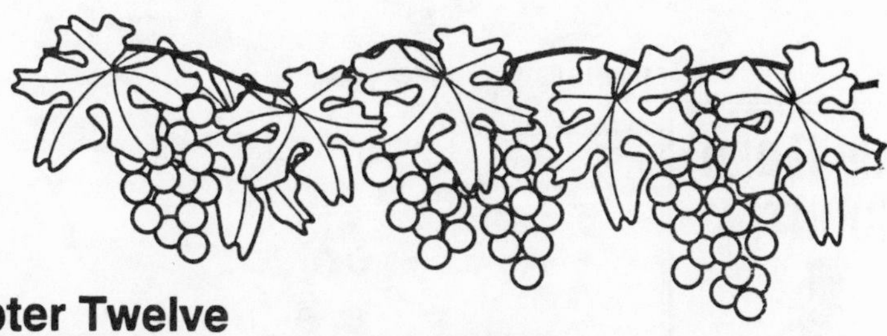

Chapter Twelve

THE GOLD COUNTRY

Bottled bullion from the Sierra foothills

No single region looms larger in California's history than the foothills of the Sierra Nevada. Here, the discovery of gold in 1848 catapulted a remote Mexican outpost into the most populous and prosperous state in the Union.

Surprisingly, this also was the one of the state's first major wine-producing areas. It is today one of California's most diverse and scenic winelands.

During the rush to riches, towns germinated overnight, then faded as the gold ran out. In the fading, they left a treasure trove of sturdy brick buildings, grand balconied hotels and Victorian homes. These now house antique and curio shops, museums and bed and breakfast inns. The area has more state historic parks than any other region of California.

All this yesterday lore is set in scenic foothills of oak clusters, pine forests and tawny meadows. Vineyards are draped over ridges, terraced up steep slopes and tucked into hidden canyons. They merge with woodlands, pastures and an occasional Christmas tree farm to create a rumpled green patchwork quilt.

Sierra foothills tasting rooms are inviting places, often in intriguing settings. Some are in log or rough stone cellars dating back to the gold rush. Others are in modern structures perched on high knolls, offering a panorama of the hilly countryside.

As further incentive to visit this region, the wines are excellent, winning a goodly share of medals, and they're remarkably inexpensive. It's primarily red wine territory. The area's Zinfandels are legendary, and account for more than half the total vineyard acreage. Sierra foothills reds are typically robust, spicy and full-flavored, without a lot of filtering and fining. They're straightforward and hearty, like the people who settled this land. Some excellent whites come from here as well, grown in the higher, cooler elevations.

There is no best season to tour the Gold Country's wine country. In winter, one can sip a bit of Zin after hitting the ski slopes a few miles above the vineyards. In spring, summer and fall, these mountains and their running

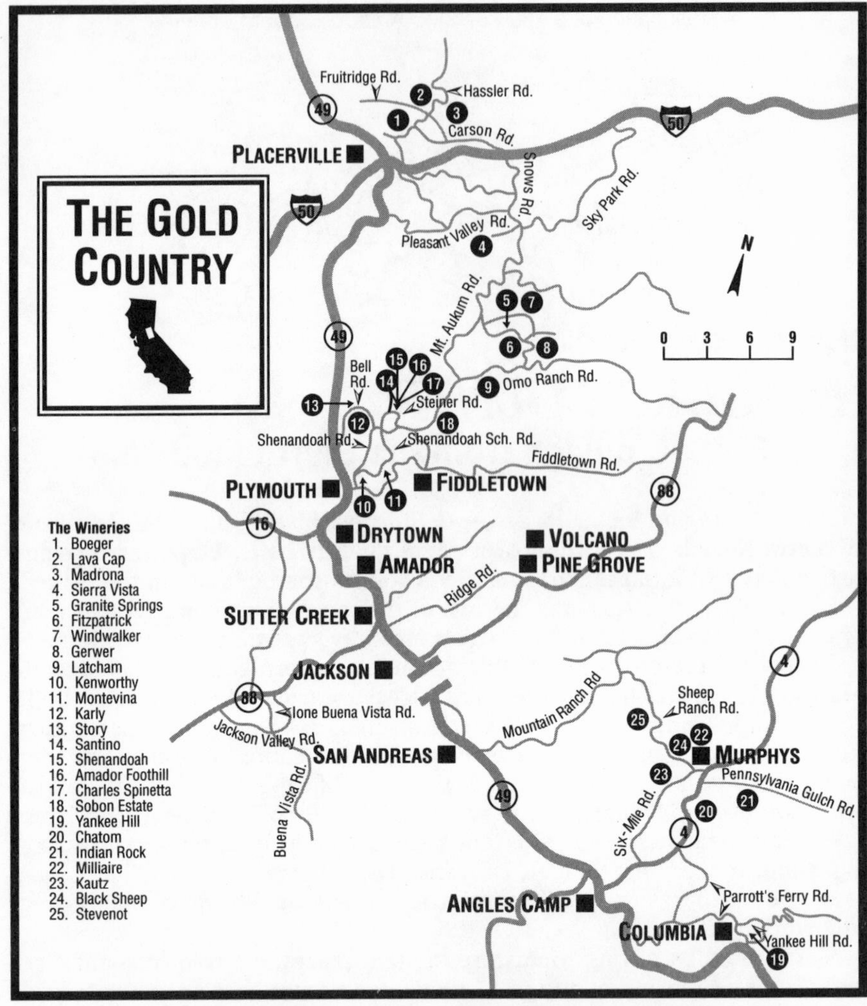

streams lure hikers, campers, white-water enthusiasts and fisherfolk. Dams, thrown across the rivers to feed thirsty flatlanders, form dozens of reservoirs that draw the boating set.

These streams ran unchecked for millions of years, leaching gold from the great granite *massif* of the Sierra Nevada—Spanish for snowy peaks. As they reached the foothills, the streams slowed their flow, depositing their valuable cargo.

On January 24, 1848, an itinerant carpenter named James Marshall had the dumb luck to find a bit of this gold in the tailrace of a sawmill. He'd been hired by John Sutter, a flamboyant Swiss entrepreneur, to build the mill on the American River. Sutter had conned 50,000 acres of land from officials of Mexican California, and he needed lumber to create a new empire. Checking his tail race one morning, Marshall saw something glitter. He bent down and picked up two tiny nuggets, about "half the size and of the shape of a pea." The rest is epic.

Most of the hundreds of thousands drawn by Marshall's discovery found nothing but frustration. Many moved down into the valley to start farms and to finish building the hastily-assembled cities of San Francisco, Stockton and Sacramento.

A few, mostly Italians, stayed in these sun-warmed hills and planted grapes. They figured their brethren still laboring in the mines would work up a mighty thirst. Soon, thousands of acres of vines thrived in the foothills of El Dorado, Amador and Calaveras counties. By the 1880s, a hundred wineries were operating.

They were never very large and all save one was closed, either by dwindling population as the gold ran out, by phylloxera or by Prohibition. Only D'Agostini Winery (now Sobon Estate) traces its roots to the gold rush. It was founded in 1856 by Adam Uhlinger who, like Sutter, was Swiss.

In the 1970s, U.C. Davis researchers found that the soil and terrain in some of the foothill areas provided ideal conditions for Zinfandel. Hot summer afternoons, cool alpine nights and tough granite soil produce high-sugar, high-acid grapes that ripen late, sometime between deer season and the first rains.

A few foothill growers had kept their vineyards after the earlier wineries closed. They found markets with flatlands vintners in Napa and Sonoma. Wine observers noted that many award-winning Zins bore curious names like Amador, Grandpère and Fiddletown. Soon, a new gold rush began in these hills—quieter this time, and from a different direction. Between 1970 and 1990, the number of wineries increased from one to more than 30.

Although Amador is the Sierra foothills's best known wine-producing area, El Dorado County just to the north is gaining in stature. Most of its vineyards are higher in elevation, offering suitable climate for Chardonnay, Sauvignon Blanc, Cabernet Sauvignon, Merlot and other cool-weather types. The county, in fact, likely has the world's highest vineyards, approaching 3,000 feet.

Just south of Amador, Calaveras County now boasts several hundred acres of grapes and seven functioning wineries. They're around Murphys, uphill from Angels Camp. South across the Stanislaus River in Tuolumne County, a single winery-tasting room functions near Columbia State Historic Park.

Frost is an ever-present danger in this high region, so vines often are located in pocket canyons, or on wind-graced ridges. Another problem, faced by few other California grape growers, is hungry deer. You'll note eight to ten-foot fences around many vineyards.

We'll divide our Gold Country winery tour into its three major areas. Assuming that you'll approach them one at a time, we'll suggest the most logical routes from the San Francisco Bay Area for each. Many wineries in this region are open only on weekends, so plan accordingly. Most of these, however, will offer tastings and informal tours on weekdays if you call ahead.

EL DORADO COUNTY WINERY TOUR • If you've ever been lured by the cool scenery and hot dice of south shore Lake Tahoe, you may have passed this way, driving eastward on U.S. Highway 50. Let the dice cool this time and get off in **Placerville,** where the dry Central Valley begins to rumple into the Sierra foothills.

The freeway ends here, resumes about a mile further up. You might like to detour through the old downtown area. Main Street, paralleling U.S. 50. It offers an interesting mix of brick front, cut stone, Art Deco and modern store fronts, sheltering assorted shops, boutiques cafes and antique stores. Check the beautifully restored **Cary House** hotel, on the right as you enter town.

Near the Greek federalist style **El Dorado County Courthouse,** turn left onto Bedford Avenue to re-join Highway 50 and continue north. After about a mile, exit on Schnell School Road, go left under the freeway, drive uphill a few blocks to Carson Road, and turn right. This takes you into **Apple Hill,** a high, rolling ridgeline area famous for orchards, Christmas tree farms—and now wineries.

During autumn, tens of thousands of visitors swarm over ribboned country lanes to buy apples, home-baked pies and other apple goodies from dozens of fruit stands, packing sheds and seasonal cafe/bake shops. Some operate the year-around. This is exceptionally pretty country. It's a patchwork of orchards, vineyards and evergreens—both Christmas tree farms and forests *au natural.* Clusters of cottonwoods and poplars provide dazzling bursts of yellow in autumn.

Incidentally, many of the area's weekend wineries are open daily from Labor Day through Thanksgiving, the peak Apple Hill season. Weekdays are best for an autumn visit, since the tasting rooms can be rather busy during weekends.

Climbing into the pine belt on Carson Road, you soon encounter your first winery, **Boeger,** down in a little hollow to your left. A mile and a half further along, look for Abel's Acres apple shed on your right, and turn left onto Union Ridge Road. Fork immediately to your right onto Hassler Road, take it a short distance to Fruitridge Road, turn left and you're at **Lava Cap Winery** on the right

Leaving Lava Cap, continue northward on Fruitridge, past the **U.S. Forest Service tree nursery** with its great swatches of tree seedlings, so small they look like coarse grass. Fruitridge soon bumps into North Canyon Road; go right and you'll return to Carson. Pressing northward for a mile, turn left into Visman's High Hill Ranch complex. This is more of an easement through an apple ranch than a road. Follow signs to **Madrona Vineyards**. (There may be a more direct route by the time you read this, so watch for the sign.)

Continue north on Carson Road a bit over two miles, then turn right under the freeway onto Snows Road (there's no interchange). A twisting, up and down four miles gets you to Newtown Road; go left and follow it to Pleasant Valley Road and go left again. Drive a bit over half a mile and turn right up Leisure Lane (between an Exxon station and a pink restaurant called Lillie Mae's Place). Two upward miles take you to **Sierra Vista Winery,** occupying a knoll with an impressive view of the Sierra Nevada. This is one of the few perches where you see the granite ridge itself, since lower mountains generally block your view.

Retreat from this perch, continue half a mile on Pleasant Valley Road and turn right onto Mount Aukum Road. You're headed for a cluster of wineries surrounding a wooded hamlet with a great name left over from the rush to riches, **Fairplay**.

Follow Mount Aukum about 6.5 miles, turn left onto Fairplay Road and drive 1.5 miles to **Granite Springs Winery,** up a narrow lane to your left. About a mile beyond, occupying a bluff with an awesome vineyard and mountain view is **Fitzpatrick Winery.** It's reached by a steep gravel road to your right. A short distance beyond Fitzpatrick, turn left onto Perry Creek Road at the tiny hamlet of Fairplay. Follow it two miles to **Windwalker Farm,** on an upslope to your right.

Now, retrace your route to Fairplay, turn left onto Fairplay Road and follow it briefly to **Gerwer Winery,** up a lane to your left. Just beyond, Fairplay bumps into Omo Ranch Road; turn right and within about three miles, **Latcham Vineyards** appears on your left.

This ends the El Dorado segment. If you continue west on Omo Ranch Road and follow it to Mount Aukum Road, you'll wind up in the Shenandoah Valley, home to **Amador County** wineries.

Boeger Winery • T CT ⌆

1709 Carson Rd., Placerville, CA 95667; (916) 622-8094. Daily 10 to 5; MC/VISA. All varieties tasted. Some wine logo gift items. Casual tours on request; attractive picnic facilities.

This rustic ranch style winery has two links to the past. Although the present facility dates from 1972, it was established on the site of the Fossati-Lombardo Winery, hearkening back to the 1870s. Further, founder Greg Boeger is the grandson of Anton Nichelini, who started the still-operating Nichelini Winery high above the Napa Valley in 1890. The Boegers and Nichelinis still share close ties, swapping grapes and probably stories of the old days. For a period, Greg served as the Nichelini winemaker.

The tasting room is in a rough-cut stone and log structure that housed the original Fossati-Lombardo facility. It's listed on the National Register of Historic Places as one of America's oldest winery structures. The family lived upstairs and stomped the grapes there; juice flowed down through wooden chutes to fermenting vats in the cellar. Those chutes are still in place, hanging above the tasting counter.

Pear trees, vines and flowers share the busy farmyard with winery buildings. Several picnic tables are tucked into assorted shady spots; some are on a shady terrace above a pond.

Tasting notes: Boeger produces a Chardonnay, Sauvignon Blanc, a couple of Zinfandels, Barbera, Merlot, Cabernet Sauvignon, Cabernet Franc and some proprietary wines. Our favorites were a nutty-fruity Chardonnay; El Dorado Zinfandel with a light nose but great peppery taste; and Hangtown Red, an excellent spicy jug wine with Cab, Barbera and Petite Sirah. Prices range from $7 to the mid-teens.

Vintners choice: Greg Boeger's wife Sue read them off: "Merlot, Cabernet Sauvignon, Barbera and Cabernet Franc. Our elevation, climate and soil are excellent for the reds."

WINERY CODES • T = tasting with no fee; **T$** = fee for tasting; **GT** = guided tours; **GTA** = appointment required for tour; **ST** = self-guiding tours; **CT** = casual tours or a peek into the winery; ⌆= picnic area; 🎁= separate gift shop or good giftware selection. Price ranges listed in tasting notes are for varietals; jug wines often are available for less. **DINING & LODGINGS •** ØØ = smoke-free establishment; Ø = non-smoking tables or rooms.

Lava Cap Winery • T GTA & CT ⛌

2221 Fruitridge Rd., Placerville, CA 95667; (800) 475-0175 or (916) 621-0175. Daily 11 to 5 Labor Day through Thanksgiving weekend, closed Tuesdays and Thursdays the rest of the year; MC/VISA. Most varieties tasted. Wine logo items. Picnic deck; casual peek into the winery or guided tours by appointment.

Lava Cap Winery, housed in a modern barn-like structure, sits among its own vineyards in the heart of Apple Hill. The curious name comes from the cap of volcanic ash and lava that once covered the area's gold-bearing quartz. David Jones, who opened the winery in 1987, teaches at U.C. Berkeley; not surprisingly, geology is a favorite subject. His and his wife Jeanne are primarily weekend vintners; their sons pretty much run things. Tom is the winemaker and Charlie tends the vineyards.

Tastings happen in a pleasant redwood paneled room. One set of windows opens into the winery and another looks over vineyards, orchards and the distant American River Canyon. That same view can be enjoyed from a picnic deck just off the tasting room.

Tasting notes: Wines are estate-bottled and the overall style is soft and lush, with lots of fruit. A Chardonnay Reserve was outstanding, full-flavored with subtle spice; the Sauvignon Blanc had a nice herbal nose that carried into the crisp, fruity flavor; a three-year-old Zinfandel exhibited nice berries, spice and a light finish. Fumè Blanc, Muscat Canelli, Cabernet Blanc and a white Zin and non-vintage red complete the list. Prices are $8 to $15.

Vintners choice: "Our Chardonnays are coming on strong and we've won lots of medals with our Sauvignon Blanc," said Dave.

Madrona Vineyards • T CT ⛌

High Hill Road (P.O. Box 454), Camino, CA 95709; (916) 644-5948. Daily 11 to 5 Memorial Day through December, weekends only the rest of the year; MC/VISA. Most varieties tasted. A few wine logo items. Informal tours by request. Picnic tables are placed about a surrounding glen.

Madrona occupies a shady retreat beneath the cinnamon-barked trees that inspire its name. Vineyards and orchards are just beyond. The neat wood-sided winery looks deceptively small from the front; it's a two-story affair occupying a two-story downslope behind the tasting room. Several picnic tables are tucked beneath the madrones, live oaks and pines.

Dick and Leslie Bush planted vines on the back side of High Hill apple ranch in 1973, then opened their winery seven years later. Like neighboring Lava Cap, their wines are all estate-bottled.

Tasting notes: Madrona produces two distinctive styles: light, dry whites and hearty, full-flavored reds. The wines include Chardonnay, Fumè Blanc, Gewürztraminer, Johannisberg Riesling, Zinfandel, Cabernet Franc, Merlot, Cabernet Sauvignon, plus late harvest Zinfandel and Riesling. We favored a peppery, spicy six-year-old Zin; an herbal, full-flavored Merlot; and a rich late harvest Zin that would be great for fireplace snuggling.

Vintners choice: "It depends on the year," says Dick, "although our Cabernet Franc, Gewürztraminer and late harvest Riesling are always among the tops."

Sierra Vista Winery • T GTA ⛌

4560 Cabernet Way, Placerville, CA 95667; (916) 622-7221. Weekends 11 to 5; most major credit cards. Most varieties tasted. Some wine logo gift items. Tours and weekday tasting by appointment. Picnic area with spectacular view.

Visitors here get twin views of the distant Crystal Range of the Sierra Nevada. The dramatic peaks are visible from the winery and picnic area, and they grace the wine labels. This lofty ridge—rimmed in vineyards—is one of California's most dramatic winery perches, and one of the loftiest, at 2,900 feet.

John and Barbara MacCready were among the first of El Dorado's modern-day vintners, buying their property in 1972 and starting the winery five years later. They've since shed their respective careers as a university professor and computer programmer to devote full time to vinting. They've built a simple, attractive wood-sided winery from their own pines, and increased their output from a handful of cases to 9,000 a year.

Tasting notes: Chardonnay, Fumè Blanc, Zinfandel, Cabernet Sauvignon and Syrah comprise the list, along with a white Zin, table red and a nice picnic style Sauvignon Blanc called Mother Lode Gold. Our wines of choice were a crisp, spicy, barrel-fermented Chardonnay; a Fumè with a great honeysuckle nose and fruit flavor; and a fine chili-pepper Cabernet. Prices range from $7.50 to the mid-teens.

Vintners choice: "We are a 'Rhône ranger' and produce a Chateauneuf-du-Pape style Syrah and Viognier (a Rhône Valley white)," says Barbara.

Granite Springs Winery • T CT ⩙

6060 Granite Springs Rd., Somerset, CA 95684; (916) 621-1933 or (209) 245-6395. Weekends 11 to 5. Most varieties tasted. Wine logo items; shaded picnic area near a pond. Informal tours on request.

The austere bungalow tasting room and simple, barnlike winery belie Granite Springs' success: It's one of America's top award-winning wineries. Not only have its wines been served in the White House, but its Chenin Blanc has been poured as the official reception wine for several years running.

Les and Lynne Russell planted their vines in a stubborn granite slope in 1980, then they blasted away additional granite to plant their winery against a hillside. They finished in time for their first crush in 1981. Since then, their wines have won more than a hundred medals. They hang by the cluster, like golden grapes, from the beams of the tasting room.

Tasting notes: Although we rarely comment on jug wines, we found one worthy of special note—the $5 Sierra Reserve Red, mostly Zinfandel, with a typical Gold Country spice overlaying a nice raspberry nose and flavor. Granite Springs' varietals range from $5.50 to $12. A three-year-old Zinfandel displayed a great peppery nose and herbal-berry flavor. Higgins Zinfandel, also age three, was even heartier, with more tannin. A three-year-old Petite Sirah was a classic black wine, bold in color, with a light nose yet big pepper-berry flavor. Also on the list are Chardonnay, that White House Chenin Blanc (crisp, touch of sweetness), Cabernet Sauvignon, Vintage Port and Black Muscat Port.

Vintners choice: "Our Petite Sirah is unusually rich and spicy; a winner of many golds," says Lynne. "And our Chenin Blanc, of course, that's being served in the White House."

Fitzpatrick Winery and Lodge • T CT ⚒ R

7740 Fairplay Road, Somerset, CA 95684; (209) 245-3248. Weekends 11 to 5; MC/VISA. Most varieties tasted. Picnic deck with valley view. Plowmans lunch served in the lodge on weekends. Rooms available; see listing under bed & breakfast inns, below. Casual winery tours on request.

A combined lodge and winery, Fitzpatrick occupies a high bluff with a stellar view of the surrounding hills. It's an imposing structure of heavy logs, with a rustic tasting room. A picnic deck offers vistas of vineyards and an occasional Christmas tree farm. Well-kept and tidy, with lawns and landscaping, it's among the more appealing of the Sierra foothill wineries.

Brian and Diane Fitzpatrick began their operation on Fairplay Road in 1980, near a nursery called Famine's End. Later, they moved two miles uphill to build, mostly by hand, their impressive tasting room and lodge, which looks like it was spirited away from Yosemite Valley. The rest of the winemaking operation is a few hundred feet away.

Tasting notes: The list is typical of hearty Gold Country wines: a fruity Chenin Blanc; a spicy and full-flavored Cabernet Sauvignon; a mellow and subtly peppery Cabernet Franc; a light Chardonnay; an herbal Sauvignon Blanc; and a spicy, raspberry-flavored Zinfandel. The Fitzgeralds also make a Zinfandel Port and a sparkling brut. Prices range from $6 to the early teens.

Vintners choice: "We specialize in wines made from organically grown grapes," says winemaker Brian, declining to pick a favorite child.

Windwalker Farm • T CT ⚒

7360 Perry Creek Rd., Somerset, CA 95684; (209) 245-4054. Weekends 11 to 5; MC/VISA. All varieties tasted. A few wine logo items. Informal tours on request. Shaded picnic deck.

Gaylene and Ken Bailey, late of Sacramento, offer an interesting combination for visitors, a winery and an Arabian horse ranch. This blend produced the romantic name, inspired by the Arabians great endurance as "drinkers of the wind." The Baileys are new to the winery, purchasing it in late 1990 from the L.W. Richards family. Like many foothills vintners, they come from different backgrounds; she's an administrator and he's an engineer. It's mostly a weekend project now, although they plan to retire here.

Windwalker produces about 1,500 cases. The modest winery and matching house are of Pennsylvania Dutch architecture, with double-pitched roofs. A picnic deck sits under sheltering oaks, featuring views of horse pastures and the valley below.

Tasting notes: Chardonnay, Chenin Blanc, Sauvignon Blanc, Johannisberg Riesling and Cabernet Sauvignon comprise the list. The Chard was soft yet buttery with a light finish; Chenin had a crisp flower nose, matched in the flavor; Johannesburg had a touch of sweet; and the Cab—made by the Baileys' predecessor—was medium bodied, with a nice peppery nose and taste. Prices range from $5.50 to $9.50.

Gerwer Winery • T GT ⚒

8221 Stoney Creek Rd., Somerset, CA 95684; (209) 245-3467. Weekends 11 to 5; MC/VISA. Most varieties tasted. Wine logo items and specialty foods (which are sampled). Large lawn picnic area under oaks; tours by request.

This small winery and its vineyards are off the highway, tucked into an upslope among oaks, blackberry vines, sheep pastures and other things rural. Expect to be greeted by an occasional squirrel and scolded by a Steller Jay as you prowl or picnic on its pleasantly wooded grounds. The tasting room is a simple, cozy wood-sided enclosure; planks laid across barrel heads serve as the counter.

Vernon and Marcia Gerwer started their small winery in 1981. They'd operated a dairy in the Sacramento area, so it was not a difficult agricultural transition, particularly after Vern took several courses at U.C. Davis. Active in local politics, he's also an El Dorado County supervisor.

Tasting notes: Chardonnay, Sauvignon Blanc, Semillon, white Cabernet, Petit Sirah, Ruby Cabernet and Cabernet Sauvignon comprise the list. Our choices were the Chard, with lots of fruit and a touch of oak; the nicely tart and fruity Sauvignon Blanc; a six-year-old Petit with good spice, herbs and tannin; and the six-year-old Cab, with nice spice and a rich, smooth flavor. Prices are modest, ranging from $6.50 to $8.75

Vintners choice: "Red wines, especially our Petite Sirah and Ruby Cabernet," says Vern.

Latcham Vineyards • T CT

2860 Omo Ranch Rd., Somerset; mailing address: P.O. Box 134, Mount Aukum, CA 95656; (209) 626-3697. Weekends 11 to 5; MC/VISA. Most varieties tasted. A few wine logo items. Informal tours; shaded picnic areas.

A courtliness in his manner and a primness to his dress tells you that 69-year-old Frank Latcham isn't an ordinary sodbuster. He's a retired San Francisco attorney, fulfilling an urge to get closer to the land. He and his wife Patty bought the land in 1980 and opened their winery ten years later.

A weathered old barn housing the winery operation is now matched by a new Midwestern style farm home. A small shed built off the barn serves as a snug, two-stool tasting room. Vineyards rim the neat, orderly complex.

Although he still does consulting with his old firm, Frank likes to roll up his white sleeves and get involved in the wine business. The Latchams' son and daughter-in-law, John and Joyce, complete the cast of this small family operation. Technical help comes from friendly neighbors, notably Boeger Winery's Greg Boeger, and Granite Springs' Les Russell, who serves as the Latcham winemaker.

Tasting notes: Chardonnay, Chenin Blanc, Sauvignon Blanc, Cabernet Sauvignon, Petit Sirah, Zinfandel and a couple of generics comprise the list. Good hearty, spicy flavors in the Sauvignon Blanc (with a touch of Chenin), Zinfandel, Cabernet and Petit are typical of these mountain-grown grapes. The two-year-old Zin was outstanding, and winner of a double gold. Son John, learning the business with courses at U.C. Davis, will continue the full-flavored spicy style that Russell is drawing from their El Dorado grapes. Prices are modest, ranging from $5.25 to $8.

AMADOR COUNTY WINERY TOUR • The Shenandoah Valley, home to most of Amador's wineries, is one of the few relatively level areas in the foothills. We did say "relatively;" it gently pitches and rolls like a green ocean of vineyards, pasturelands and oak groves. The attractive valley was settled in the 1850s by folks seeking farm and ranch land, not gold. Many Shenandoah settlers were "Downeasters" and Southerners (thus, the name).

There's still an eastern American air about its neat farms and occasional red barns.

If you continue westward from Frank Latcham's place, you'll wind up in the back end of this valley. However, after nine El Dorado tasting rooms, you've probably saved Amador for a different weekend. The logical access is from Highway 49, in the small hamlet of Plymouth.

Approaching on Highway 49 either from the north or south, turn eastward at a sign indicating the Shenandoah Valley, opposite Plymouth's main street. After a few hundred yards, fork left onto Shenandoah Road (sometimes identified as Plymouth-Shenandoah Road). The right hand fork would take you to Fiddletown, home to noted vineyards but no tasting rooms.

Your first winery, **Kenworthy Vineyards,** arrives quickly, on your right. A bit beyond, turn right onto Shenandoah School Road and follow it about a mile to **Montevina Winery**, on your right among the vines. Continue on Shenandoah School, which soon curves back into Shenandoah Road, and turn left—heading briefly back toward Plymouth.

After less than a mile, turn right onto Bell Road, which takes you to a pair of wineries. After about half a mile, watch for a sign directing you to the left to **Karly Winery.** Continue on Bell road, following it around a flat left turn. About the time it's running out of pavement, a sign on the right points you uphill to **Story Vineyard.**

Return to Shenandoah Road, turn left (east) and go about a mile before turning left again onto Steiner Road. Several wineries will appear in quick succession: **Santino Winery,** on the left at Steiner and Upton Road, and then **Shenandoah Vineyards** and **Amador Foothill Winery,** both uphill and above their own vineyards, to your right. Just beyond Amador Foothill, down in a hollow on the left is **Charles Spinetta Winery and Wildlife Gallery.**

Steiner Road curves back into Shenandoah Road, so stay with it. Then continue east about a mile and a half to **Sobon Estate,** on your right.

We didn't cover three wineries outside the Shenandoah Valley, but they're certainly worth a visit if you're in the area around Ione, below the Sutter Creek-Jackson area. **Greenstone Winery** (274-2238) is at Highway 88 and Jackson Valley Road; **Fiddle Farm** (274-4070) is on Jackson Valley Road in Buena Vista; and **Winterbrook Winery** (274-2466) is at 4851 Buena Vista Road in Ione. Get specifics from the Amador Vintners Association, listed under "Winery touring maps" below.

Kenworthy Vineyards • T GTA ⌆

10120 Shenandoah Rd. (P.O. Box 361), Plymouth, CA 95669; (209) 245-3198. Weekends 10 to 5; MC/VISA. Most varieties tasted. A few wine logo items. Small picnic area; guided tours by appointment.

John Kenworthy, looking unnecessarily stern behind his Mormon-style beard, started our meeting by insulting my line of work, suggesting that most guidebooks were probably a waste of good paper. Simultaneously, he maintained a cordial conversation with two visitors, leading one to speculate that he's a pleasant tasting room host when guidebook authors aren't on the premises.

Our brief chat did reach a higher footing. We talked about his winery, about government intervention, bureaucratic harassment of small businesses, warning labels, neo-prohibitionists, the history of Zinfandel and other subjects of substance to the industry.

Kenworthy's winery is a spotless, state-of-the-art facility—an anomaly within its skin of a weathered wooden barn. The tasting room is a small afterthought, tacked to one side. Requisite rusting farm machinery occupies key positions in the ranch yard, sustaining the rural Americana look. John and his wife started the winery in 1980, adding the tasting room in 1986.

Tasting notes: The list is short, uniformly excellent and modestly priced—from $6 to $8.50. Even older vintages don't go much beyond $10. A Granite Hill Vineyard Semillon was crisp with a subtly fruity flavor; Estate Bottled Zinfandel exhibited a nice dusky-berry taste with a light tannic nip; and Estate Cabernet Sauvignon was spicy with a nice berry flavor. A gentle and tasty everyday Zinfandel (a good buy at $5.50) was labeled Killer Red, proving that John harbors humor as well as disdain for guidebook authors.

Montevina Winery • T ⩙

20680 Shenandoah School Rd., Plymouth, CA 95669; (209) 245-6942. Daily 11 to 4; MC/VISA. Most varieties tasted. Good selection of wine logo items. Large, landscaped picnic area.

Bob Trinchero of Napa Valley's Sutter Home Winery was among the first to call attention to Sierra foothill grapes. He won scores of awards with his hearty Amador County Zinfandels in the 1970s. It seemed logical, then, to move closer to the source, so he bought Montevina Winery in 1988. He operates it as a separate entity.

Montevina was among the first of the post-Prohibition Gold Country facilities, established in 1970. It's a handsome complex—a Spanish-California structure rimmed by vineyards and landscaped grounds. Artworks and photos accent the spacious, cathedral ceiling tasting room. A picnic area occupies a paved courtyard beneath a shady arbor.

Tasting notes: The wines, displaying an overall light and fruity style, were fine. We're more curious about those to come, since Trinchero is planting Italian classics such as Sangiovese grosso, Nebbiolo, Refosco and Aleatico. Meanwhile, the short list consists of Chardonnay, Fumè Blanc, Zinfandel and Cabernet Sauvignon. The three-year-old Zin was soft for an Amador wine, with a nice raspberry nose and flavor, while a three-year-old Cab was pleasantly peppery with lush berries and a soft tannin finish. Prices range from $5.50 to $8.

Vintners choice: "Zinfandel," said general manager Jeffrey Meyers, uttering Trinchero's favorite word. "It's rich, with aromas and flavors of berries and cedar."

Karly Winery • T GTA ⩙

11076 Bell Rd., Plymouth, CA 95669; (209) 245-3922. Daily noon to 4; MC/VISA, AMEX. Most varieties tasted. Some wine logo gift items. Snacks served with wine samples. Small picnic area. Guided tours by appointment.

You may go to Karly for the wines, but you may return for *her* snacks. Lawrence (Buck) Cobb makes full-bodied wines, and his wife Karly serves oven-warm homemade bread and bits of cheese to weekend tasters. This happens in a neat tasting room that's also a kitchen, which is appropriate. A full set of appliances is installed behind the counter. The winery is a modern metal structure, bunkered unobtrusively into a slope, surrounded by vineyards. It's all in a small hollow, a short drive off Bell Road.

The Cobbs were drawn to this area to escape from the corporate rat race in 1980. Earlier, Buck served as an Air Force fighter pilot in Korea, and he now flies a high performance stunt plane.

Tasting notes: Buck likes a touch of oak in his wines; we found them to be quite tasty. Our picks were a silky Chardonnay with a bit of wood; a soft yet spicy and full-bodied three-year-old Zinfandel and a *big* two-year-old Zin that should be kept around for a bit. Others on the short list are Sauvignon Blanc, the requisite white Zinfandel and a tasty, sweet Orange Muscat. Prices range from $8 to the mid-teens; some library wines were available as well.

Story Vineyard • T GTA ⌆

10525 Bell Rd., Plymouth, CA 95669; (209) 245-6208. Weekends 11 to 5; no credit cards. Most varieties tasted. Picnic area with valley view; tours by appointment.

Following a narrow lane toward Story, you don't realize that you're approaching a crest with a striking view. The old farmyard winery sits on the rim of the Consumnes River Canyon, with a sweeping vista of vineyards, oak clusters and pine forests. The tasting room, in a wonderfully funky shack, perches on this knoll, beside a casually kept lawn. A few picnic tables entice one to linger for the view.

Founded early in the 1970s by the late Eugene Story and still run by his family, this is one of the foothills' oldest wineries. In classic Gold Country fashion, it focuses heavily on Zinfandel, since Eugene had the good fortune to find a ranch with some old vines still in place.

Tasting notes: A tasting here consists of a vertical sampling of Zins ranging from light fruity to big and boisterous. The youngest, a four-year-old, had a nice berry nose and flavor, with nippy acid. Older ones became progressively smoother and more complex; all displayed enough tannin to encourage keeping them around for a bit. The lone white was a Chenin Blanc, flowery and a bit on the sweet side, plus the usual white Zinfandel, which was pink, of course. Prices go from $5.50 to $8.50; a bit higher for some of the veteran Zins.

Santino Winery • T GTA ⌆

12225 Steiner Rd., Plymouth, CA 95669; (209) 245-6979. Daily noon to 4:30; MC/VISA. Most varieties tasted. A few wine logo items. Guided tours by appointment, for a fee. Shaded picnic areas.

Santino's tasting room is a comfortable blend of warm woods, soft light and print wallpaper. It's rather intimate, almost like a hideaway bar. Windows offer peeks into adjacent winery. The tile-roofed Spanish California facility sits below Steiner Road, rimmed by old Zin vines.

The winery's name comes from Matt and Nancy Santino, who established the operation in 1979 with Nancy's father, Joseph Schweitzer. He's a third-generation brewer from Alsace. The Santinos have departed, leaving only their name behind. Schweitzer remains, in partnership with his winemaker Scott Harvey, who owns the adjacent—and legendary—Grandpére Zinfandel vineyard, one of the oldest in the county.

Tasting notes: Zin's the name of the Santino game, and Scott Harvey's are excellent. His Grandpére was delicious, full of nice raspberry flavor with a tannic nip; his Amador Zin was a bit softer, but still brisk. Non-vintage Alfresco is a light, everyday Zinfandel, priced right at $6. White Harvest was one of the few white Zins we've liked, and it has won several golds. The list also includes a Sauvignon Blanc, Barbera, Merlot and several dessert wines, plus some interesting proprietary labels. Prices range from $7.25 to the mid-teens.

Vintners choice: "We are a Zinfandel house," said Scott, getting right to the point. "We're also known for our Barbera and dessert wines."

Shenandoah Vineyards • T ⌆

12300 Steiner Rd., Plymouth, CA 95669; (209) 245-3698. Daily 10 to 5; MC/VISA. Most varieties tasted. Some wine logo items; small picnic area.

Leon and Shirley Sobon claim to be risk-takers, although their timing appears to be good. When the aircraft industry slowed in 1977, Leon left his engineering job at Lockheed Sunnyvale, bought a piece of land with a handsome fieldstone house and started Shenandoah Vineyards. Three years later, they sold a chunk to Ben Zeitman (who started Amador Foothill Winery) at a tidy profit. Their wines have caught on quickly, winning numerous awards; their production has leaped from a few cases to 35,000.

In 1989, they bought the defunct D'Agostini Winery, one of California's oldest. Another timely risk?

Shenandoah is an appealing complex, with a modern fieldstone winery converted from a garage and fashioned to match the house. The tasting room is a delight: part rustic with log beam ceilings, and part art gallery, with rotating exhibits.

Tasting notes: The Shenandoah list is predominately red, typical for Amador, although the winery produces an excellent full-bodied Sauvignon Blanc. Our favorite reds included a rich yet dry Rhône style Serene (Petit Sirah, Grenache and Carignan); a tasty medium-bodied three-year-old Zinfandel Reserve and a two-year-old spicy, herbal Cabernet Franc. Cabernet Sauvignon, two vintage ports and two Muscats complete the list. Prices range from $7 to the mid-teens.

Amador Foothill Winery • T CT ⌆

12500 Steiner Rd., Plymouth, CA 95669; (209) 245-6307. Weekends and most holidays noon to 5; MC/VISA. Most varieties tasted. Casual tours of the winery, adjacent to the tasting room. Picnic area with valley and mountain views.

When we wrote ***The Best of the Gold Country*** several years ago, we conducted a blind tasting among knowledgeable friends to pick the Gold Country's best Zinfandel and white Zinfandel. To our surprise and Ben Zeitman's pleasure, his Amador Foothill wines won both. Ben and his wife Katie Quinn produce Zins that win in other arenas, as well. They've won awards in competitions much more prestigious than ours.

A former NASA chemist, Ben started the winery in 1980. Then in 1986, he had the good sense to marry Katie, who brought with her a master's degree in Enology from U.C. Davis. The winery is simple but on the leading edge of technology, a glossy white passive solar structure equipped with the best of the winemaking art and science. All this is visible from the tasting counter, on a gallery above the main part of the winery. Thus, a tour consists of looking over your shoulder, glass in hand. Ben or Katie will show you more if they aren't too tied up.

Tasting notes: Zinfandel, of course, dominates the list and it has won many of the awards decorating the walls. A three-year-old Grandpére Vineyards was herbal and full-bodied, one of the best we've tasted. A three-year-old Fiddletown displayed nice raspberries and a two-year old Ferraro exhibited lots of fruit and tannin; a fine candidate for aging. Ben and Katie's list also includes a nice complex and crisp Fumè Blanc and a very tasty version of the requisite white Zin. Prices range from $8.50 to a bit over $10.

Charles Spinetta Winery and Wildlife Gallery • T

12557 Steiner Rd., Plymouth, CA 95669; (209) 245-3384. Tuesday-Sunday 10 to 5; MC/VISA. All varieties tasted. Wine logo items and extensive wildlife art collection; frame shop. Large picnic area.

This square-shouldered masonry block building, rather austere from without, is a surprise package within. Visitors step into a huge, high-ceiling tasting room with an L-shaped counter. Wildlife scenes fill the redwood paneled walls and scores more occupy a mezzanine gallery above. Bronzes and other sculptures complete the collection. It's all for sale and generally affordable, since most are prints of works by leading artists.

The facility is an all-family affair. Charles, whose background is forestry management, bought the vineyards in 1979 and completed the winery-gallery about ten years later. Wife Laura runs a frame shop in the gallery and has framed the more than 250 prints on the walls. Son Jim manages the vineyards, Tony is into marketing and Michael, still in high school, likely will join the operation.

Each fall, the family hosts a harvest party that sounds like fun, crushing grapes with ancient equipment that has been in the family for generations. Call the winery for details.

Tasting notes: Wines are made by a nearby facility under the Spinettas' direction and cellared here, with prices ranging from $6 to $15. The Zins were our favorites, unfiltered and full-flavored. We tasted a mellow nine-year-old Eschen Vineyard entry from 80-year-old vines and a lighter five-year-old Amador Zin. Also on the list are sweet and dry Chenin Blancs from the Spinetta vineyards, Cabernet, Merlot, a sweet Muscat Canelli and a rich, ice-wine style Frost Chenin Blanc.

Sobon Estate • T ST

14430 Shenandoah Rd. (mailing address: 12300 Steiner Rd.), Plymouth, CA 95669; (209) 245-6554. Daily 10 to 5; MC/VISA. Most varieties tasted. Good giftware selection, deli and picnic fare. Self-guiding tour of Shenandoah Valley Museum. Shaded picnic area.

It's nice to know that the old D'Agostini winery is in good hands. Since buying the facility in 1989, Leon and Shirley Sobon have installed the Shenandoah Valley Museum in the main cellar, thus preserving this state historical landmark. Museum exhibits focus on the gold rush, Shenandoah Valley pioneers and early wine production. It also captures that wonderful musty-grapy-old library smell typical of ancient wineries.

The large tasting room, in another of the venerable buildings, fits the historic theme, with heavy ceiling beams and barnwood paneling. It offers the best selection of gift and specialty food items of the foothill wineries.

Tasting notes: Many Sobon Estate wines use grapes from the old

D'Agostini vineyards, although they're produced mostly at the family's Shenandoah facility. Selections include a Fumè Blanc with a spicy-herbal flavor; a complex and fresh young Chardonnay; a light, berry-filled Pinot Noir; a tasty herbal Zinfandel and a Cabernet Sauvignon with a big chili pepper nose and herbal-berry flavor. An Orange Muscat Canelli and Zinfandel Port complete the list. Prices range from $9 to the early teens.

CALAVERAS-TUOLUMNE WINERY TOUR • The southernmost wine country in the Gold Country also is the newest. Of Calaveras County's six tasting rooms, four opened in the decade of the Nineties. Neighboring Tuolumne County's only winery-connected tasting room is a newcomer as well. Thus, as you tour this south central area of the Mother Lode, you'll see new wineries a-building and new vines a-growing. You'll be rewarded with considerable variety as well, from funky tasting rooms to modern winery caves.

The direct route to Murphys, around which most of the wineries are focused, is via State Highway 4 from **Stockton**. You can pick it up from Interstate 5 or U.S. 99 and follow it through **Angels Camp**.

Another approach, used by many Bay Area visitors, is via I-580 to I-205 past **Tracy**, then State Highway 120 through **Manteca.** Follow signs to and through **Sonora** on Highway 49, drive north four miles and fork right onto Parrotts Ferry Road, headed for **Columbia State Historic Park**. Parrotts Ferry skims Columbia's edge, then spirals down to **New Melones**

Restored gold rush towns such as Sutter Creek compete with Zinfandel in luring visitors to California's Sierra Nevada foothills.

Reservoir of the Stanislaus River. You enter Calaveras County at that point, climb out of the canyon, pass **Moaning Cavern,** then hit a stop sign at Highway 4. Go right to reach Murphys 4.

Using either route, you'll encounter the stylish new winery and tasting room of **Chatom Vineyards** on your right, near the hamlet of **Douglas Flat**. Continue a couple of miles to Murphys and turn right onto Pennsylvania Gulch Road, opposite an Ace Hardware store. A one-mile drive into pleasant oak woodlands takes you to **Indian Rock Vineyard.** Return to Highway 4, continue east for a few hundred feet and follow signs (a left and a quick right) into the business district of **Murphys.** Driving along Main Street, watch on your right for **Milliaire** (*millie-AIR*) winery. It's easy to spot, for it's housed in a former service station.

Shaded by huge locust and elm trees, Murphys is one of the Gold Country's more charming towns. It offers a nice collection of old brick and false front stores. Take time to visit its boutiques, antique shops and the venerable **Murphys Hotel**.

Having done that, turn left at the hotel onto Algiers Street. You may not find a street sign (we didn't); just turn at the hotel corner. Algiers takes you past the neat little city park, then becomes Six Mile Road. After a mile and a half of oaks and pasturelands, you'll see the new **Kautz Vineyards**, on your right, just beyond Hay Station Ranch.

Return to Main Street and go left a short distance to **Black Sheep Winery.** It's in a weathered structure on your right, where Main dips down and splits into French Gulch Road and Murphys Grade. Retrace your prowl along Main and turn left onto Sheep Ranch Road at the **Old Timers Museum.** (Look for a black and orange Mercer Caverns sign.)

Sheep Ranch seems too narrow to be a serious road, but it quickly takes you out of town, into pine and oak woodlands. Considerable twisting and turning takes you to **Mercer Caverns**. The road then swings right and spirals down into a hideaway canyon, green with pines and vines, home to **Stevenot Winery.**

You'll certainly want to explore **Columbia State Historic Park** and visit Tuolumne County's lone tasting room, Yankee Hill Winery, which offers great hours—10 a.m. to sunset. Columbia is a restored mining town with timeworn but carefully preserved buildings housing boutiques, curio shops, restaurants and gold rush hotels. The only traffic on Main Street is an occasional stagecoach or pony, hauling grinning tourists. It was once the "gem of the Mother Lode" one of the largest and most prosperous of the foothills mining towns.

To reach **Yankee Hill Winery,** go east past the Columbia post office on Jackson Street. It becomes Yankee Hill Road and delivers you to the winery after less than a mile; it's up a lane to the right.

Chatom Vineyards • T ⌅

1969 E. Highway 4, Douglas Flat; mailing address: P.O. Box 2730, Murphys, CA 95247; (209) 736-6500. Daily 11 to 4:30; most major credit cards. All varieties tasted. A few wine-logo gift items. Landscaped picnic area under arbor.

Gay Callan, daughter of a long line of growers and ranchers, planted vineyards in a sheltered valley near Calaveras County's San Andreas in 1980.

She started making wines five years later. After winning a number of awards, she "went public," opening a striking new winery and tasting room on the highway to Murphys in mid-1991.

The structure, part masonry and part vertical wood slat, is something of a blend between French country and early American railroad station, which is more appealing than it sounds. The tasting room is light and cheerful, trimmed with oak and artwork. A picnic area is particularly inviting, with bentwood lounges as well as tables. It's sheltered by a sturdy arbor which, as the seasons pass, will become entwined with vines.

Tasting notes: Light, fruity and crisp are proper adjectives for the Chatom wine list. It includes a Calaveras Fumè, Cabernet Sauvignon, Semillon, Chardonnay, Merlot and Zinfandel. Our picks were a dry, subtly spicy Chardonnay; a full-flavored four-year-old Cab with a soft tannin finish; a full-flavored four-year-old Merlot and a four-year-old Zinfandel with a great raspberry nose and flavor. Prices range from $6.50 to $10.

Indian Rock Vineyard • T CT ⨯

1154 Pennsylvania Gulch Rd. (P.O. Box 1526), Murphys, CA 95247; (209) 728-2266. Weekends 10 to 5; no credit cards. All varieties tasted. Pleasant picnic area on lawn beside a lake. Casual tours on request.

Boyd Thompson and his son Scott have teamed up to become the newest members of the Calaveras County wine clan. Boyd, who was CEO of a major medical care group, longed to pursue a more bucolic life, so he bought an historic dairy ranch. Scott, who has been making wine since he was a kid, happily signed on as winemaker. They started planting in 1985, began producing wine three years later and opened the winery in 1991. They plan to burrow aging caverns in a nearby hillside.

Indian Rock occupies an idyllic glen among the pines and oaks just east of Murphys. Old pasturelands have become new vineyards and the tiny tasting room and winery are housed in an ancient whitewashed milk barn. Picnic tables are placed about a grassy lawn beside a pond. Sitting under a shady oak, sipping a bit of Chardonnay, listening to the birds and squirrels discussing important issues, one is reluctant to leave this spot.

Tasting notes: Scott had released only one wine when we visited, a classic buttery and spicy Chardonnay, which sells for $12. By the time you visit, selections will include Cabernet Sauvignon, Merlot and Charbono.

Milliaire Vineyard Selections • T

276 Main St. (P.O. Box 1554), Murphys, CA 95247; (209) 728-1658. Weekends 11 to 4:30; MC/VISA. Most varieties tasted. A few wine logo items.

"Fill 'er up" takes on a new meaning when you visit Milliaire. It may be America's only winery operating in a former service station. The overhang that sheltered the gas pumps is still in place, although the pumps themselves are gone. "Maybe we should find some of those old gravity feed ones for color," Liz Millier mused.

The ancient little building began as a carriage house, then served as a livery stable and service station before assuming its new role. The tasting room, with a simple plank over a barrel head, occupies the store portion of the station, where you once paid for your gas and picked out a new set of wiper blades. Wine ages in the garage portion, where grease racks once stood.

Steve and Liz Millier started their winery in 1983 and moved to their unique quarters in 1990. *Milliaire,* derived from Steve's family name, means "milestone" in French. A U.C. Davis grad, he was winemaker at Stevenot for several years. He currently makes wines for the new Kautz Vineyards, in addition to producing about 500 cases a year for Milliaire. Liz runs the business end and is active in local affairs. She was president of the Calaveras Wine Association when we visited.

Tasting notes: Milliaire reflects the big, spicy character of Gold Country wines. We liked all the varietals: a fruity and herbal Sauvignon Blanc; spicy and buttery Chardonnay; Zinfandel with a great herbal-berry flavor; a full-bodied, oak-finished Cabernet Sauvignon; and a spicy Merlot. Three dessert wines were rich but not yucky-sweet: a late harvest Zinfandel (Robert's Cuvee), Sauvignon Blanc (Cuvee du Soleil) and an orange Muscat (Catherine's Cuvee). Prices range from $7.50 to $12.

Kautz Vineyards and Winery • T ST

Six Mile Road (P.O. Box 2263), Murphys, CA 95247; (209) 728-1251; MC/VISA. Most varieties tasted. Some wine logo items. Tours of winery caverns; pleasant shaded picnic are beside a lake.

Quick! Visit Kautz before the tasting room is moved to a modern, state-of-the art winery/hospitality center. We like its original locale—tucked into cool manmade caverns in a steep cliff face. Hearkening back to the days of the Fortyniners, the underground portion of this brand-new winery was blasted eight feet at a time, through stubborn Calaveras schist and limestone. Although it has been gunnited, it still has the rough-hewn texture of an old hardrock mine.

An underground spring—discovered during the "mining"—trickles into a reflection pool at one end. This cool subterranean retreat is one of the nicest spots in the wine country, popular for underground dinners and other gatherings.

John Kautz, a successful Lodi grower and vintner, began planting vines near Murphys' historic Hay Station Ranch in 1988, then blasted tunnels as his first "buildings" in 1991. Although outbuildings and a new tasting room may be in place by the time you get there, self-guiding tours of the 600 feet of caverns will remain a part of the Kautz visitor experience.

Tasting notes: When we visited, the wines were mostly from Kautz' Lodi facility and mostly whites, with the typically crisp, dry and fruity valley style. The lists consists of a John Kautz Chardonnay; Kautz Vineyards Chardonnay, Cabernet Sauvignon and Cabernet Franc; plus a Chardonnay, Merlot, Symphony, Sauvignon Blanc and orange Muscat under the Angels Creek label. Our wines of choice were the soft barrel-fermented Kautz Vineyards Chardonnay, a nicely spicy three-year-old Kautz Vineyards Cabernet Sauvignon and a subtly peppery Angels Creek Merlot. Prices range from $6 to the mid-teens.

Black Sheep Vintners • T CT

Murphys Grade and Main St. (P.O. Box 1851), Murphys, CA 95247; (209) 728-2157. Weekends noon to 5 or by appointment; MC/VISA, AMEX. All varieties tasted. A few wine logo items. Informal tours.

Black Sheep *looks* like a Gold Country winery, occupying a weather-textured wooden building with a rusting corrugated roof, at the far end of Murphys' oldstyle Main Street. Inside, rough-cut logs hold up the ceiling; tasting occurs in a small space shared by tiers of sleeping wines. A collection of sheep figurines—given by friends to honor the winery name—clutters a shelf behind the rustic tasting bar.

Dave and Jan Olson bought the old Chispa Cellars in the mid-1980s. They'd been farming near the hamlet of Sheepranch in the hills above Murphys, so they decided to use a woolly reference for their winery name. They were the black sheep of the business, Jan recalled, when they decided to turn home winemaking into a profession. They weren't greenhorns, however, since Dave had worked for Stevenot earlier, and received some of his winemaking training from Steve Millier.

Tasting notes: Black Sheep Zinfandel has been one of our standards for years; typically spicy with big berry flavors. Other wines we sampled were equally tasty: a five-year-old Cabernet Sauvignon with lots of berries and a touch of oak and tannin at the end; a spicy, silky barrel-fermented Chardonnay; and a full-flavored Sauvignon Blanc with Semillon added for complexity. To honor nearby Angels Camp's annual frog-jumping celebration, the Olsons created "True Frogs." It's a light, fruity and dry Chenin Blanc with a great label—two grinning croakers enjoying a lily pad picnic. Prices range from $7 for the euphoric frogs to $12 for the top varietals.

Vintners choice: "Our Zinfandel—very fruity with nice berry flavors," says Jan. "It's our hallmark wine."

Stevenot Winery • T CT

2690 Santo Domingo Rd., Murphys, CA 95247; (209) 728-3436. Daily 10 to 5. Most varieties tasted. Good wine-related gift selection and picnic fare. Arbor picnic area; tours on request.

Sitting at the bottom of a deep draw, walled by pines and limestone slopes, Stevenot occupies one of prettiest settings in all the California wine country. This pastoral scene is further enhanced by the "Alaska House," a sod roofed log cabin that seems to have sprouted from the earth in centuries past. It serves as a warm and cozy tasting room and gift shop. A vine-entwined picnic arbor and lawn invite visitors to linger. Old ranch buildings sheltering modern winery equipment and several acres of vineyards complete this idyllic setting.

The first Stevenots came to the Sierra foothills seeking gold in 1849 and stayed on as ranchers and farmers. Fifth-generation Barden started planting vineyards at the historic Shaw Ranch in 1974 and converted the hay barn into a winery in 1977. Newer facilities have been added since. It's the oldest winery in the county and the largest in the Sierra foothills, producing about 50,000 cases a year.

Tasting notes: Stevenot wines have won many awards for their spicy, fruity foothills style. Typically, Zinfandel monopolizes the list. A three-year-old Grand Reserve aged in American oak was spicy-herbal with a nice tannic nip; and a two-year-old late harvest Zin displayed huge flavors and spices. Also on the list were a crispy and light Chenin Blanc; a medium-bodied and spicy Chardonnay; a bigger, more buttery Chardonnay Grand Reserve; an herbal, subtly tannic Merlot; and a complex, tasty Cabernet Sauvignon with an oak touch. Muscat Canelli dessert wines and the requisite white Zinfandel complete the list. Prices range from $6 to the mid-teens.

Vintners choice: "Reserve Chardonnay, Cabernet Sauvignon and Merlot," says the winery's Carrie Shinn.

Yankee Hill Winery • T CT ⌅

11755 Coarsegold Lane (P.O. Box 330), Columbia, CA 95310; (209) 533-2417. Daily 10 to sundown; MC/VISA. All varieties tasted. Some wine-related gift items and picnic fare. Shaded picnic area with barbecue; informal tours on request.

Ron and Gudrun Erickson's simple masonry block and wood winery is terraced into an oak-covered slope, reached by a graveled lane off Yankee Hill Road. Red-clothed picnic tables and a barbecue occupy a deck just off the small tasting room, inviting visitors to lounge in this pleasantly wooded setting. Although the Ericksons buy their grapes, usually from other Gold Country vineyards, a few rows of vines are being planted on a stairstep slope just below the winery.

Yankee Hill is old by foothills standards, dating back to 1970. Erickson, who has dabbled in an assortment of businesses and presently teaches courses at next-door Columbia College, bought it in 1977.

Tasting notes: The list is quite versatile for a small winery: Chardonnay, Chenin Blanc, several proprietary blends, Cabernet Sauvignon, Barbera, an Extra Dry sparkling wine, a Spumante, California Port and cream sherry and five fruit wines—apple, red currant, blackberry, loganberry and raspberry. We favored the buttery, crisp Chardonnay aged in toasted barrels, a fruity yet dry Rhine blend and the nutty cream sherry, made in the classic solera style. Fruit wines were very tasty, rich but not sticky-sweet. Erickson's prices are modest, ranging from $4.25 to $9.

THE BEST OF THE BUNCH

The best wine buys • Sierra foothills vintners consistently offer some of California's best premium wine buys. We found little price difference, winery-to-winery.

The most attractive wineries • Montevina Winery in El Dorado County; Santino Winery and Sobon Estate (with its museum) in Amador County; Chatom Vineyards and Stevenot Winery (setting) in Calaveras County.

The most interesting tasting rooms • Boeger Winery and Fitzpatrick Winery in El Dorado County; Santino Winery, Charles Spinetta Winery and Wildlife Gallery, Shenandoah Vineyards and Sobon Estate in Amador County; Kautz Vineyards and Stevenot Winery in Calaveras County.

The funkiest tasting rooms • Gerwer Winery in El Dorado County; Kenworthy Vineyards and Story Vineyard in Amador County; Milliaire Winery and Black Sheep Vintners in Calaveras County.

The best gift shops • Charles Spinetta Winery and Wildlife Gallery, and Sobon Estate in Amador County; Stevenot Winery in Calaveras County.

The nicest picnic areas • Boeger Winery, Madrona Vineyards, Sierra Vista Winery, Fitzpatrick Winery and Gerwer Winery in El Dorado County; Montevina Winery and Story Vineyard in Amador County; Yankee Hill Winery, Chatom Vineyards, Kautz Vineyards and Stevenot Winery in Calaveras-Tuolumne.

The best tours • Sobon Estate (self-guiding tour of winery museum) in Amador County; and Kautz Vineyards (self-guiding tour of wine caves) in Calaveras County.

BEYOND THE VINEYARDS

Like Monterey and Santa Cruz, the Sierra foothills are more famous for tourism than for wineries. We only touch on the highlights here. For more detail, pick up a copy of our other guide, ***The Best of the Gold Country*** available at better book stores everywhere.

The favored route for exploring the Sierra foothills is Highway 49, named in honor of the peak year of the gold rush. Call the "Golden Chain," it meanders for 310 miles through the full length of the Sierra Nevada mining area, from Vinton in the north to Oakhurst in the south. It's a popular vacationers' route; some folks spend days wandering its serpentine course. As we have noted, only its central area offers functioning wineries.

Using each of the three wine-producing areas as a base, we'll suggest some driving tours that take you past some of the other Sierra foothill attractions.

El Dorado County

Placerville was so rowdy in its early days that it was initially called Hangtown. Later, more sedate citizens changed the name. After exploring its lures, you can continue east to south shore **Lake Tahoe** with its alpine glitter. This was the route of the **Pony Express** and markers chart its progress through the Sierra Nevada.

If you follow the twisting course of State Highway 193 fifteen miles north of Placerville, you'll encounter **Georgetown,** one of the best-preserved of the old mining towns.

A short, winding drive northwest on Highway 49 will take you to **Marshall Gold Discovery State Historic Park** in **Coloma**, where James Marshall found his pea-sized nuggets that started all this business. Beyond, you travel through the ruggedly imposing **American River Canyon** and arrive in **Auburn,** which has a funkily attractive Old Town section.

Amador County

Little remains of Plymouth's glory days, although **Drytown, Amador City** and **Sutter Creek,** south on Highway 49, have preserved much of their yesterday charm. They're noted for boutiques and antique shops and they offer several bed and breakfast inns, handy stops for Shenandoah Valley wine country visitors.

Sutter Creek-Volcano Road heading northeast from Sutter Creek leads through one of the prettiest creek valleys in the foothills, ending at the rustic mining town of **Volcano.** Just above is **Daffodil Hill,** where acres of daffodils bloom every spring. And just below is **Indian Grinding Rock State Park,** preserving the history of the area's earliest residents.

Calaveras-Tuolumne counties

Several historic hamlets draw visitors to Calaveras County, most notably **San Andreas,** where stage coach bandit Black Bart was jailed, and **Angels Camp,** made famous by Mark Twain's frog-jumping yarn. Both have historic districts with the requisite boutiques and antique stores.

You already know that an uphill drive on Highway 4 takes you to the wine country around Murphys. Stay on the highway and you'll reach the high Sierra and the famous **Bear Valley** summer and winter resort. On the way, you'll pass **Calaveras Big Trees State Park,** whose giant sequoia groves are definitely worth a stop.

Neighboring Tuolumne County brims with gold rush lore, starting with **Columbia State Historic Park** and continuing south on Highway 49 to **Sonora** and **Jamestown** Both are treasure-troves of early California architecture and memorabilia. **Railtown 1897 State Historic Park** is "Jimtown's" premier attraction. A drive north from Sonora takes you to the piney hamlets of **Twain Harte** and **Pinecrest,** popular Sierra retreats.

Drive east from Jamestown on Highway 49, then Route 120, and you'll climb up to the neat old mining town of **Groveland** and then to the Sierra Nevada's most famous attraction, **Yosemite National Park.**

Gold Country activities & attractions

Apple Hill • Nearly 50 Apple Hill growers offer direct-to-consumer products—particularly apple goodies, between Labor Day and Thanksgiving. Contact Apple Hill Growers, Inc., 4123 Carson Rd., Camino, CA 95709; (916) 644-7692.

Cave tours • Three limestone caverns are located near Calaveras County's wine country: California Caverns at Cave City above San Andreas and Moaning Cavern near Murphys, both (209) 736-2708; and Mercer Caverns above Stevenot Winery, (209) 728-2101. Admission charge at each.

Farm products • For a map and guide to farms selling fresh and prepared fruits, vegetables and wines (including Apple Hill Growers), contact ***El Dorado Ranch Marketing,*** c/o El Dorado County Chamber of Commerce, 542 Main St., Placerville, CA 95667; (916) 621-5885.

Gold country tours • Mother Lode Tours, two to five-day excursion in the Gold Country, Murphys, (209) 728-1190; Hidden Treasure Mine, Columbia State Historic Park, tour of a working gold mine, (209) 532-9693.

Gold panning • Appropriate to the area, one can pan for gold at: Columbia State Historic Park, (209) 532-9693; Jensen's Pick & Shovel Ranch, Angels Camp, (209) 736-0287; and Gold Prospecting Expeditions, Jamestown, (209) 984-GOLD.

Historic museums and parks •

Amador County Museum, 225 Church St., Jackson; (209) 223-6386. Wednesday-Sunday 10 to 4; modest admission charge. Relics of early Amador County; mine exhibit and mining gear.

Angels Camp Museum, 753 S. Main St., Angels Camp; (209) 736-4444. Daily 10 to 3; modest admission charge. Historic relics and old farm and gold-mining equipment.

Chaw'se Indian Grinding Rock State Historic Park, 14881 Pine Grove-Volcano Rd., Pine Grove, CA 95665; (209) 296-7488. Museum open weekdays 11 to 3 and weekends 10 to 4; day use fee for park. Reconstructed Miwok village, museum and huge Indian grinding rock; campgrounds.

Calaveras County Museum and Archives, 30 N. Main St., San Andreas; (209) 754-4023. Daily 10 to 4; modest admission charge. Pioneer museum in old Hall of Records building; original jail cell out back where Black Bart was held.

Columbia State Historic Park, Parrotts Ferry Road (P.O. Box 151), Columbia, CA 95310; (209) 532-4301. Most museums and shops open 10 to 5 daily; free. Restored gold mining town that once was the gem of the Mother Lode. Stage coach rides, horseback rides, gold panning, mine tours, costumed docent tours, hotels, restaurants.

El Dorado County Historical Museum, 100 Placerville Dr., Placerville; (916) 621-5865. Wednesday-Saturday 10 to 4; donations requested. Artifacts of early-day Hangtown and El Dorado County.

Marshall Gold Discovery State Historic Park, P.O. Box 265, Coloma, CA 95613; (916) 622-3470. Museum open daily 10 to 4:30 Memorial Day through Labor Day, 11 to 5 the rest of the year; day use fee. Historical buildings and exhibits, reconstruction of Sutter's Mill gold discovery site.

Old Timers Museum, 470 Main Street at Sheep Ranch Road, Murphys; (209) 728-2607. Thursday-Sunday 11 to 4; small admission charge. Early-day mining relics and reconstructed blacksmith shop.

Railtown 1897 State Historic Park, Fifth Avenue, Jamestown; (209) 984-3953. Gift shop and roundhouse open daily 10 to 5 (shorter hours in off-season), free admission; train rides weekends 10:30 to 3; fee charged. Old time steam trains, roundhouse and rail memorabilia.

Tuolumne County Museum and History Center, 158 W. Bradford Ave., Sonora; (209) 532-1317. Daily 9 to 4:30; donations accepted. Gold rush and pioneer relics, old jail cells, gold nugget exhibit.

White-water rafting • Rivers that once carried gold from the Sierra Nevada now carry rafters splashing through their rapids. Among regional river-runners are:

Calaveras-Tuolumne County (all 209 area codes) — Ahwahnee Whitewater Expeditions, P.O. Box 1161, Columbia, CA 95310, (800) 359-9790 or (209) 533-4101; American River Touring Assn., 24000 Casa Loma Rd., Groveland, CA 95321, 962-7873; OARS, P.O. Box 67, Angels Camp, CA 95222, 736-4677; Sierra Mac River Trips, P.O. Box 366, Sonora, CA 95370, 532-1327; Zephyr River Expeditions, P.O. Box 510, Columbia, CA 95310, 532-6249.

Eldorado County (all 916 area codes) — A Whitewater Connection, 7170 Hwy. 49, Coloma, CA 95613, 622-6446; Adventure Connection, P.O. Box 475, Coloma, CA 95613, 626-7385; American River Recreation, 6770 Marshall Grade Rd., Coloma, CA 95613, 622-6802; California River Trips, P.O. Box 460, Lotus, CA 95651, 626-8006; Chili Bar Whitewater Tours, 1669 Chili Bar Ct., Placerville, CA 95667, 622-6632; Gold Country River Runners, 431 Coloma Heights Rd., Coloma, CA 95613, 626-7326; Mother Lode River Trips, P.O. Box 456, Coloma, CA 95613, 626-4187; Outdoors Unlimited, P.O. Box 854, Lotus, CA 95615, 626-7668; River Runners Inc., P.O. Box 433, Coloma, CA 95613, 622-5110; Wilderness Adventures, (800) 323-7238.

Wine country tour • Abacus Luxury Limousine, Amador County, (916) 756-0162.

Wineland events • Sierra Showcase of Wines, early May; (209) 274-4766; Shenandoah Valley Wine Festival, June, Amador County Fairgrounds in Plymouth, (209) 245-6314; Fairplay Wine Festival, June, (209) 245-3467;

Amador County Fair, Plymouth, late July; (209) 245-6921; El Dorado County Fair, August, (916) 621-5885; El Dorado County Harvest Faire, September, (916) 621-5885.

Winery touring maps • ***Discover Amador County Wine Country***, Amador Vintners Assn., c/o Amador County Chamber of Commerce, P.O. Box 596, Jackson, CA 95642; (209) 223-0350. ***Calaveras Wine Country***, Calaveras Wine Association, P.O. Box 1851, Murphys, CA 95247; (800) 999-9039. ***El Dorado Wine Country Tour,*** El Dorado Vintners Assn., P.O. Box 1614, Placerville, CA 95667; (916) 622-8094.

WINE COUNTRY DINING

El Dorado-Amador counties

Bellotti Inn • ΔΔ $$ Ø

53 Main St. (downtown), Sutter Creek; (209) 267-5211. Italian-American; dinners $13 to $16; full bar service. Sunday-Thursday 11:30 to 9, Friday-Saturday 11:30 to 10, closed Tuesday. Casual; reservations accepted. MC/VISA. Housed in a hotel dating back to the mining days. The menu features veal scaloppine, Parmesan, cacciatore and other Italian fare, plus such American standards as prime rib and fresh fish on weekends.

Carriage Room Restaurant • ΔΔΔΔ $$ Ø

At the historic Smith Flat House, 2021 Smith Flat Rd., Smith Flat; (916) 621-0667. American; dinners $9 to $17; full bar service. Lunch daily 11 to 2 daily, dinner Sunday-Thursday 5 to 9 and Friday-Saturday 5 to 10. Informal to casual; reservations accepted. MC/VISA, DIN. Generous portions of pioneer history come with the menu of steak, chicken or chops. The 1850 structure was a hotel, restaurant, wagon and stage stop, dance hall, Pony Express stop, post office and general store. A mine shaft leads from the old fashioned saloon to the Blue Lead Channel, which yielded $18 million in gold.

Imperial Hotel Restaurant • ΔΔΔ $$ Ø

14202 Highway 49, Amador City; (209) 267-9172. American-continental; dinners $10 to $18; full bar service. Daily 5 to 9 p.m. Informal to casual; reservations accepted. Major credit cards. High ceilings and period decor in a century old hotel. Small menu features seafood marinara pasta, chicken picatta and filet mignon with sauteèd mushrooms, plus innovative appetizers and desserts. Local wines highlighted.

La Casa Grande • ΔΔ $$

251 Main St. (at Spring, just off Highway 50), Placerville; (209) 626-5454. Mexican-American; dinners $6 to $13; full bar service. Casual; no reservations. MC/VISA. Family-style Mexican restaurant housed in a pair of 1896 storefronts in the historic area of Placerville; typical Mexican menu with children's specials.

Perlagonium Restaurant • ΔΔΔ $$$ ØØ

51 Hanford St. (Highway 49), Sutter Creek; (209) 267-5008. Contemporary American; dinners $13 to $23; wine and beer. Monday-Saturday 5:30 to 9. Informal to casual; reservations advised. No credit cards. Changing, innovating fare served in a romantic Victorian setting. Small, health-conscious menu with a poultry, meat, seafood and vegetarian entrèes; herb roasted leg of lamb is a specialty. Local wines featured.

Powell Brothers Steamer Company • ΔΔ $$

425 Main St., Placerville; (209) 626-1091. Seafood; dinner $10 to $12; full bar service. Daily 11 to 10. Informal to casual; no reservations. MC/VISA. Lively place with "wharf atmosphere" in one of old town Placerville's store fronts. Menu features oysters, *cioppino,* seafood stews and pastas. Extensive foothill wine list. Sunday afternoon jazz.

Sutter Creek Palace • ΔΔΔ $$$ $$ Y Ø

76 Main St., Sutter Creek; (209) 267-9852. American-continental; dinner $10 to $16; full bar service. Lunch 11:30 to 3, dinner 5 to 9 daily. Informal to casual; reservations accepted. MC/VISA. Gold rush ambiance with stained glass, polished woods and Victorian decor; the building dates from 1896. The menu is more contemporary, ranging from tournedos topped with artichoke bottoms to wine country scallops.

Calaveras-Tuolumne counties

City Hotel Restaurant • ΔΔΔΔ $$$$ Y ØØ

Main Street (Jackson), Columbia State Historic Park; (209) 532-1479. American regional; $28.50 for prix fixe dinner; full bar service. Lunch Thursday-Saturday 11:30 to 2, dinner Tuesday-Sunday from 5, Sunday brunch 11 to 2. Informal; reservations accepted, essential on weekends. MC/VISA, AMEX. Splendid Victorian dining room in restored gold rush hotel; considered by many as the Sierra foothills' finest restaurant. Four-course prix fixe dinners, featuring items such as grilled chicken breast with sweet potato gravy, *polenta* cakes and corn salsa. Lunches may be ordered from the menu.

Columbia House Restaurant • ΔΔ $$ ØØ

Main and State streets, Columbia State Historic Park; (209) 532-5134. American; dinners $9.50 to $14; wine and beer. Breakfast-lunch weekdays 8 to 3, dinner Thursday-Sunday 5 to 8 and Friday-Saturday 5 to 9. Casual; MC/VISA. Sturdy American fare, innovatively spiced, served in a gold rush cafe dating back to 1850 (although the original was in a tent). Country decor with wainscoting, print wallpaper and quilt panels. Charbroiled chicken, chops, steaks and pastas. Smoke-free.

El Sombrero • ΔΔ $ ØØ

11256 State Street (between Main and Columbia), Columbia State Historic Park; (209) 533-9123. Mexican; dinners $7 to $10; wine and beer. Sunday-Thursday 11 to 9, Friday-Saturday 11 to 10. Casual; MC/VISA. One of the Gold Country's better Mexican restaurants, in the heart of historic Columbia, housed in a turn-of-the-century cottage. Homey atmosphere; good food. Typical tacos, tamales, enchiladas and such, plus Mexican steak and a remarkably tasty Chili Colorado and Chile Verde. Smoke-free; outdoor tables.

Murphys Hotel Restaurant • ΔΔΔ $$$

457 Main Street (Algiers Street), Murphys; (209) 728-3444. American; dinners $9 to $15; full bar service. Sunday-Thursday 7 a.m. to 8, Friday-Saturday 7 to 9. Informal to casual; MC/VISA, AMEX. Oldstyle restaurant in 1856 hotel (listing below), featuring country American fare such as fried chicken, New York steak and home made soups. Elaborate period decor includes hurricane ceiling lamps, pioneer photos and relics.

Peppermint Stick • ΔΔ $

454 Main St. (downtown), Murphys; (209) 728-3570. American; meals $5.25 to $6; no alcohol. Monday-Saturday 11 to 9, Sunday 11 to 5. Casual; no credit cards. Cute oldstyle fountain in a century-old building; white wrought iron chairs, folk art decor. Light lunch and dinner fare, including unusual "miners chili" and "old timers beef stew" served in a hollowed-out bread loaf. Slurp the soup and eat the bowl.

VINELAND LODGINGS

El Dorado-Amador motels, historic hotels & inns

Best Western Placerville Inn • ΔΔΔ $$$ Ø

6850 Greenleaf Dr. (Highway 50 at Missouri Flat), Placerville, CA 95667; (800) 528-1234 or (916) 622-9100. Doubles $64 to $75, singles $59 to $69. Major credit cards. Attractive 105-room motel with Southwest decor. TV movies, phones, some fireplaces. Pool, spa. **Brawley's Restaurant** serves 5:30 a.m. to 11 p.m., 24 hours Friday and Saturday; American, dinners from $9; full bar service; non-smoking tables.

Gold Quartz Inn • ΔΔΔ $$$$ ØØ

15 Bryson Dr., Sutter Creek, CA 95685; (209) 267-9155. Doubles and singles $75 to $125, including full breakfast and afternoon tea. MC/VISA, AMEX. Nicely maintained 24-room Queen Anne style inn. Rooms furnished in period decor with American and Victorian antiques; TV, phones, sitting porches and private entrances. Free beverages; concierge services.

Gold Trail Motor Lodge • Δ $$ Ø

1970 Broadway (Point View), Placerville, CA 95667; (916) 662-2906. Doubles $41 to $58, singles $36 to $41. Major credit cards. A 32-room motel on landscaped grounds with picnic area, pool. TV, room phones, some room refrigerators and hair dryers.

Imperial Hotel • ΔΔΔ $$$$ Ø

14202 Highway 49 (P.O. Box 195), Amador City, CA 95601; (209) 267-9172. Doubles $60 to $90, singles $55 to $85, including continental breakfast. Major credit cards. Nicely restored brick 1879 hotel; six individually decorated rooms with period furnishings and modern private baths. **Restaurant** and bar; see listing above.

Mother Lode Motel • Δ $$ Ø

1940 Broadway (Point View), Placerville, CA 95667; (916) 622-0895. Doubles $48 to $53, singles $36 to $43. Major credit cards. A 21-unit motel with pool, lawn area. Rooms have TV movies, phones; some refrigerators.

Shenandoah Inn • ΔΔΔ $$$ Ø

17674 Village Dr., Plymouth, CA 95669; (800) 542-4549 or (209) 245-4491. Doubles $58 to $62 singles $50 to $55, suites $99 to $100; prices include continental breakfast. Major credit cards. New Spanish style inn with 47 rooms; TV movies, phones, refrigerators. Pool, spa, landscaped grounds.

Sutter Creek Inn • ΔΔΔ $$$ Ø

75 Main St. (P.O. Box 385), Sutter Creek, CA 95685; (209) 267-5606. Doubles $50 to $97, singles $42 to $92, including full breakfast. No credit *cards; checks accepted.* A 19-room inn fashioned from an 1850s Greek revival house; furnished with a blend of antique and contemporary. Some rooms with fireplaces, all with private baths. Landscaped grounds with hammocks; afternoon refreshments.

El Dorado-Amador bed & breakfast inns

Chichester House Bed & Breakfast • ΔΔ $$$$ ØØ

800 Spring St., Placerville, CA 95667; (916) 626-1882. Doubles $75 to $80, singles $70 to $75. Three rooms, all with half-baths; full breakfast. MC/VISA, DISC. Nicely furnished 1892 early American style home with Victorian, American and country antiques. Conservatory, landscaped garden, porch with old fashioned swing, fireplaces in parlor and lobby.

Culbert House Inn • ΔΔΔ $$$$ ØØ

10811 Water St., Amador City, CA 95601; (209) 267-0750. Doubles $80 to $105, singles $75 to $100. Three rooms, all with private baths; full breakfast. MC/VISA. A restored 19th century home, decorated in French country style. Rooms have private verandas; one with fireplace. Formal gardens with flower beds and mature trees. Evening snacks and wine tasting.

The Foxes • ΔΔΔΔ $$$$ ØØ

77 Main St. (P.O. Box 159), Sutter Creek, CA 95685; (209) 267-5882. Doubles $95 to $135, singles $90 to $130. Six rooms, all with private baths; full breakfast. MC/VISA, DISC. Beautifully-appointed inn fashioned from an early day merchant's home. Period furnishings with fox decorator theme; radio/tape players in rooms, some rooms with TV. Landscaped grounds, gardens and covered porches.

Fitzpatrick Lodge • ΔΔ $$$ Ø

7740 Fairplay Road, Somerset, CA 95684; (209) 245-3248. Doubles $79 to $99. Four rooms, all with private baths; full breakfast. MC/VISA. Handsome new log chalet with hilltop view of mountains and valleys; part of Fitzpatrick Winery. Comfortable country-style furnishings; all rooms with view decks. Chalet-style sitting room with fireplace; afternoon wine and snacks.

The Hanford House • ΔΔ $$$$ ØØ

61 Hanford St. (P.O. Box 1450), Sutter Creek, CA 95685; (209) 267-0747. Doubles $75 to $100, singles $65 to $100. Nine rooms, all with private baths; expanded continental breakfast. MC/VISA, DISC. A stylish brick inn fashioned from a 1920s home. Large rooms furnished with early California antiques; fireplace in honeymoon suite. Sun deck and patio.

The Heirloom Bed & Breakfast Inn • ΔΔΔ $$$$ Ø

214 Shakeley Lane (Preston Avenue), Ione, CA 95640; (209) 274-4468. Doubles $53 to $85, singles $48 to $80. Six rooms, four with private baths; full breakfast. No credit cards. An 1863 antebellum brick mansion listed as a Native Sons of the Golden West "Dedicated Historical Site." Rooms done in American and Victorian antiques and art works; all with fireplaces or wood burning stoves. Extensive grounds with swings, hammocks, croquet court and gazebo. Convenient to Ione-area wineries.

Indian Creek Bed & Breakfast • ΔΔ $$$ ØØ

21950 Highway 49 (three miles north), Plymouth, CA 95669; (800) 24-

CREEK or (209) 245-4648. Doubles $55 to $95, singles $45 to $85. Four rooms, two with private baths; full breakfast. MC/VISA, DISC. Restored log home on ten wooded acres; decks, lodge-style living room with fireplace. Furnished with a mix of antiques, pine and country crafts.

Mine House Inn • ΔΔ $$$ Ø

14125 Highway 49 (P.O. Box 245), Amador City, CA 95601; (209) 267-5900. Doubles $55 to $65, singles $50 to $60. Eight rooms, all with private baths; continental breakfast. No credit cards. Attractive inn fashioned from an 1880 mining office building. Rooms with Victorian antiques; sitting room, art gallery and swimming pool.

Calaveras-Tuolumne lodgings

City Hotel and Fallon House • ΔΔΔΔ $$$ ØØ

P.O. Box 1870, Columbia, CA 95310; City Hotel: (209) 532-1749, Fallon House: (209) 532-1470. Doubles $44 to $85, singles $50 to $80, one suite for $115; rates include continental breakfast. MC/VISA, AMEX. Impeccably restored gold rush hotels in the heart of Columbia State Historic Park. Furnished in the style of the 1860s and 1870s. Wainscoting, print wallpaper, Victorian and American antiques; service staff in period dress. Some half-baths and shared showers. **Restaurant** in City Hotel; see listing above.

Columbia Gem Motel • Δ $$

22131 Parrotts Ferry Rd. (P.O. Box 874), Columbia, CA 95310; (209) 532-4508. Doubles $35 to $65, singles $30 to $45. MC/VISA. Vintage "auto court" style motel with 12 rooms in individual cottages. TV, in-room coffee. Near state historic park.

Dunbar House, 1880 • ΔΔΔ $$$$ ØØ

271 Jones St. (P.O. Box 1375), Murphys, CA 95247; (209) 728-2897. Doubles $95, singles $90. Four rooms, all with private baths; full breakfast. MC/VISA. Imposing American style home furnished with country and Victorian antiques. Rooms have wood-burning stoves and refrigerators stocked with a bottle of local wine. Afternoon refreshments; country-style gardens.

Murphys Hotel • ΔΔΔ $$$

457 Main St. (P.O. 329), Murphys, CA 95247; (209) 728-3444. Doubles $50 to $60. MC/VISA, AMEX. National historic landmark hotel, handsomely refurbished in Victorian style. Presidential Suite where President Grant once slept, is particularly opulent. Nine rooms in 1856 hotel with share baths, 19 in conventional motel wing with private baths.

Gold/wine country information sources

Amador County Chamber of Commerce, P.O. Box 596, Jackson, CA 95642; (209) 223-0350.

Calaveras County Chamber of Commerce, 1301 S. Main St. (P.O. Box 111), Angels Camp, CA 95333; (209) 736-4444

El Dorado County Chamber of Commerce, 542 Main St., Placerville, CA 95667; (916) 621-5885.

Tuolumne County Visitors Bureau, 16 Stockton Rd. (at Washington St.), P.O. Box 4020, Sonora, CA 95370; (800) 446-1333 (California only) or (209) 533-4420.

"This lively, intense wine is light enough on its feet to let the grapefruit, nutmeg and vanilla flavors extend over a long finish."

—Description of a Markham Napa Valley Chardonnay

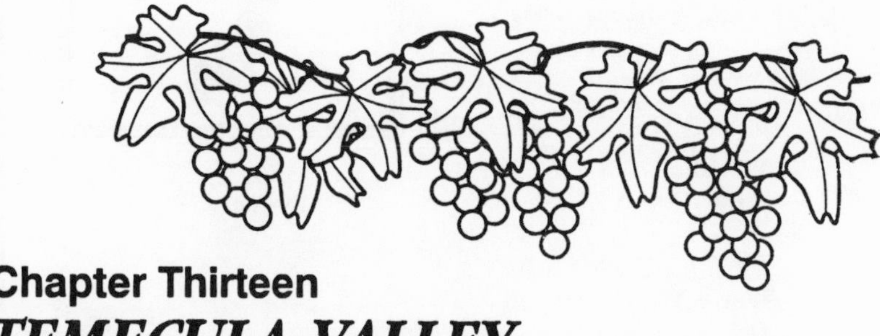

Chapter Thirteen
TEMECULA VALLEY
Chardonnay in a Southern California suburb

In the beginning, California's population was centered in the north central area and wine production was focused in the south. Now, of course, the roles are reversed.

Pioneer planters such as Jean-Louis Vignes and William Wolfskill made Los Angeles the center of the state's commercial wine industry in the 1830s. A utopian colony of Germans planted tens of thousands of vines in Anaheim, not far from the land now ruled by Mickey Mouse.

Urban growth pushed the vines eastward from Los Angeles and Anaheim toward Cucamonga, where a dozen or so wineries functioned from the 1930s until the 1960s. New population growth and the popularity of orange groves put the squeeze on the grapes again and they shifted southward.

In the 1970s, a new home was found for Southern California's wine country—the Temecula Valley between Los Angeles and San Diego. Although a few wineries are still scattered about the Southland, Temecula offers the only concentration of vineyards and vintners. It's in southern Riverside County, about 15 miles from the Pacific, close enough to benefit from ocean breezes.

Those cooling breezes, morning fogs and a 1,300-foot elevation provide suitable climate for premium whites. Chardonnay and Sauvignon Blanc are the most popular, and we found some excellent specimens here. Reds also do well, and growers are beginning to make room for Cabernet, Merlot and Petit Sirah.

Temecula's vineyards aren't exactly sheltered from the Southland's population sprawl. In 20 years, the town has rocketed from a quiet, cowboy hamlet into a semi-planned community of nearly 40,000. One sees a virtual explosion of subdivisions, shopping centers and business parks. According to the 1990 census, this area is one of California's fastest-growing regions.

However, the vines are in a protected agricultural zone, to the east of the mushrooming city. Here, they share dry, sandy hillocks with avocado groves,

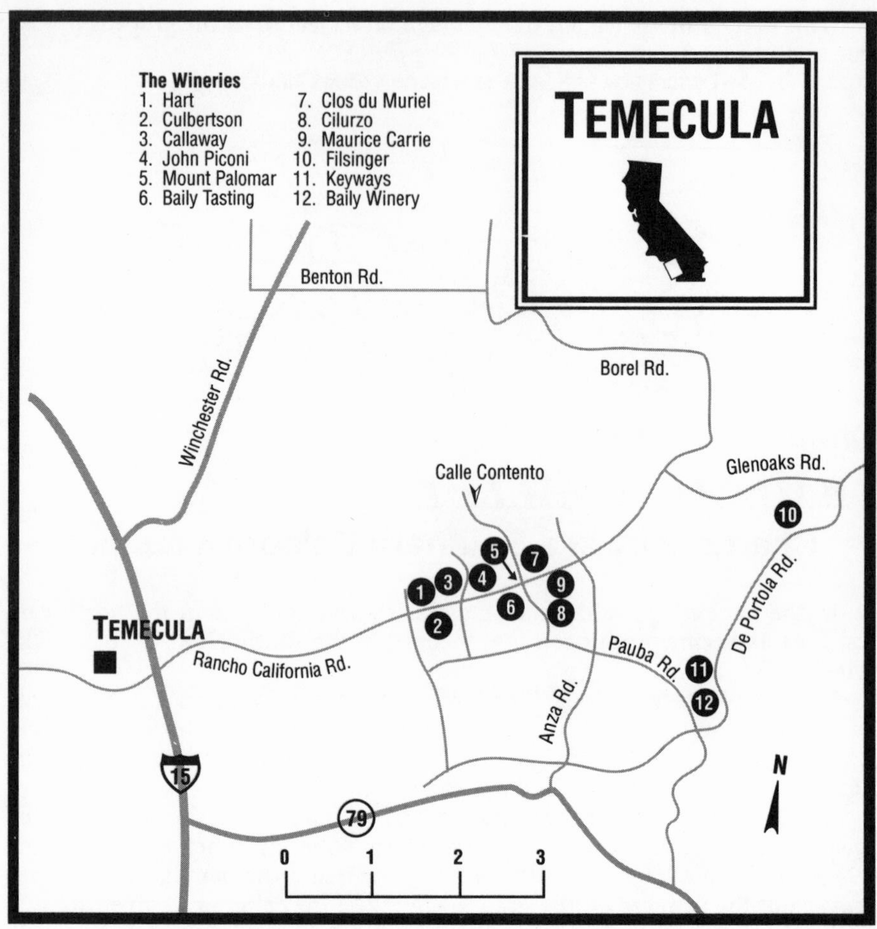

fancy horse ranches and a remarkable tally of luxurious country estates. The area's architectural look—apparently by some silent dictate—is Spanish Southwest. From business parks to ranch mansions to shopping centers to winery tasting rooms, the rule is beige stucco, pink tile and Spanish arches, with salmon and turquoise accents.

Temecula began as a genuine cowtown, laid out in 1884 to serve the commercial needs of the huge Vail Ranch, which filled most of the valley. The town consisted of the Longbranch Saloon, the Stables Bar, a folksy restaurant called the Swing Inn, and a couple of stores. Real cowboys and Indians, likely employed on the ranch, strolled about the streets. Passersby called the place quaint. The name is quaint, too. "Temecula" is an Indian word for "Valley of Joy."

In the late 1960s, it became just that, at least for land speculators. The ranch was sold to Kaiser Development Company, and the planned community of Rancho California began taking form. The die was cast for the pink tile and turquoise Temecula of tomorrow. Old Town sought refuge in boutiques and antiques. It survives today as a resolutely Western shopping and dining area.

Vineyard growth has nearly out-paced the spread of tile roofs. The entire Temecula wine industry has emerged in less time than it takes an infant to reach drinking age. A dozen vintners now exist where only one, Callaway, stood in 1974. The first vineyard was planted in 1967 by Vincenzo Cilurzo, who started his winery in 1978. More than 4,000 acres of vines now thrive in the shallow valley.

TEMECULA VALLEY WINERY TOUR • The area offers a pleasing assortment of wineries and tasting rooms, from family funky to corporate opulent. Most are clustered along Rancho California Road east of Temecula.

Winery touring is relatively simple. Approach Temecula on Interstate 15, take the Rancho California exit and head toward the sunrise. The first two miles will carry you through new shopping centers and monotonously attractive tile-roofed housing tracts. After one final subdivision—appropriately called Chardonnay Hills—you enter real Chardonnay country.

Small **Hart Winery** is on your left, up a narrow lane; the imposing new **John Culbertson Winery** is just beyond, on the right. Practically across the road from Culbertson is **Callaway Vineyard and Winery. John Piconi Winery** and **Mount Palomar Winery** are just beyond, on the left.

Baily Winery's tasting room is perched on a nearby knoll on the right, at Rancho California Road and Calle Contento. Turn left onto this unpaved but reasonably smooth road and you'll find **Clos du Muriel,** at the end of a country lane. Now, reverse yourself on Calle Contento, cross Rancho California and you encounter **Cilurzo Winery** (*chee-LURE-so*), about a third of a mile up, on your left. Return to Rancho California, turn right and you quickly see the fanciful **Maurice Carrie Winery,** on the right, just beyond Calle Contento.

The remaining wineries require a short drive, providing an excuse to admire some of the opulent estates perched on the knolls. From Carrie, continue a bit more than a mile on Rancho California and turn right onto Glenoaks Road (at the blue and white O'Neil Retreat sign), then follow Glenoaks 2.7 miles to De Portola and turn right. After two miles, you'll see the small Spanish-style tasting room of **Filsinger Vineyards and Winery**, on your right.

Another two miles takes you to **Keyways Vineyard,** also on the right and also Spanish style. A short distance beyond, turn right up unpaved Pauba Road and follow its sandy course about half a mile to **Baily Winery**. (This is winery that belongs to the tasting room we encountered earlier.)

To get back to Temecula, retreat down Pauba, turn right and continue on De Portola until it bumps into Anza Road. Go left and you soon encounter State Highway 79. A right turn will return you to I-15 and Temecula.

Hart Winery • T ⌆

41300 Avenida Biona (P.O. Box 956), Temecula, CA 92390; (714) 676-6300. Weekends 9 to 5; MC/VISA, AMEX. Most varieties tasted. A few wine-logo items. Small picnic area.

WINERY CODES • **T** = tasting with no fee; **T$** = fee for tasting; **GT** = guided tours; **GTA** = appointment required for tour; **ST** = self-guiding tours; **CT** = casual tours or a peek into the winery; ⌆= picnic area; 🎁= separate gift shop or good giftware selection. Price ranges listed in tasting notes are for varietals; jug wines often are available for less. **DINING & LODGINGS** • ØØ = smoke-free establishment; Ø = non-smoking tables or rooms.

This small barn-board winery started as a weekend venture by Travis (Joe) Hart, who taught school weekdays in Carlsbad, a coastal town west of here. He planted vineyards in 1974 and built his winery six years later. His son Bill now helps out, mostly in the business end. The winery is nearly a full-time activity now, although Joe and Bill still commute from the coast.

The tasting room is a small, cozy place where you'll be hosted by one Hart or the other while sipping their sturdy, tasty wines.

"Dad's a seat-of-the-pants winemaker, mostly self-taught," Bill said. "He started out making wine as a hobby, then took a few courses at Davis."

Tasting notes: The Harts among the few area winemakers focusing on reds as well as whites. Their three-year-old Cabernet Sauvignon was properly peppery, with medium tannin, and a Cabernet Blanc displayed good spicy varietal character. They also do a Merlot, but it was sold out when we visited. A light, crisp Sauvignon Blanc, mildly herbal and pleasantly tart Cabernet Sauvignon and a dry, nippy Chenin Blanc complete the list. Prices range from $7 to $9.75 for the whites; the Cab sells for $14.

Vintner's Choice: "Our Sauvignon Blanc is consistently good," said Bill. "And we we're happy with our Cabernet Sauvignon and Merlot."

Culbertson Winery • T$ GT R

32575 Rancho California Rd., Temecula, CA 92390; (714) 699-0099. Weekdays 11 to 3, weekends 11 to 6; MC/VISA. Three sparkling wines tasted for $6; wines also sold by the glass. Tours weekends only; hourly from 10 to 5 Saturday and 10 to 4 Sunday. Extensive giftware selection. ***Cafe Champagne*** *adjacent; see listing under "Wine country dining" below.*

The new Culbertson champagnery is one of the more opulent of the Temecula Valley wineries. It's a Mediterranean-style chateau done in textured stone brick, built around a courtyard and fountain. On weekends, you can join hourly tours, followed by a sit-down tasting of three sparkling wines for $6. During the week, tastings are conducted in the stylish Champagne Bar, which adjoins a large gift shop. You can by bubbly by the glass here, and adjourn to indoor or outdoor tables.

John and Martha Culbertson began making wine at their home in nearby Fallbrook in 1981, became intrigued with sparkling wine and opened their Temecula facility in 1988. All are made by *mèthode champenoise.*

Tasting notes: The three Culbertson sparklers we sampled exhibited good character and complexity. The non-vintage Brut had a nice herbal nose and taste with a soft yet crisp finish. Cuvee Rouge—a recent gold medal winner—has the ruby look of sparkling burgundy that was popular two decades ago, but it's much drier and more civilized. Cuvee de Frontignan is a dessert sparkler made from Muscat grapes, slightly sweet and quite pleasant for sipping. Blanc de Noir, Vintage Brut Rosè and Vintage Natural complete the list, with prices in the teens.

Vintner's Choice: "Our vintage line is comparable to the dry French Champagnes," says the winery's Fely Church.

Callaway Vineyard & Winery • T$ GT

32720 Rancho California Rd., Temecula, CA 92390; (714) 676-4001. Daily 10 to 5; MC/VISA, AMEX. Four varieties tasted for $2 fee (includes glass). Arbor picnic area. Extensive gift, wine logo, deli and specialty foods selection. Tours hourly from 11 to three weekdays and 11 to 4 weekends.

Callaway is the oldest and by far the largest of Temecula's wineries, with an output of 225,000 cases. Ely Callaway started the facility in 1974, expanded quickly and sold to the Hiram Walker combine in 1981.

Those hundreds of thousands of cases emerge from a facility that resembles a light industrial park, crowning one of the valley's sandy hillocks. The large tasting room and gift shop are more attractive, with vine-covered exterior walls and big windows offering pleasing valley views. Picnic tables are sheltered under vine-entwined arbors near the vineyards.

Tasting notes: Our four-wine ritual began with a "Calla-Lees" Chardonnay, aged on its yeast cells to give it a hearty flavor. Fumè Blanc, barrel fermented in French and American oak, had a hint of that wood with a complex, crisp taste. Our favorite was Sauvignon Blanc, with a nice pepper-herbal smell and taste and a soft finish. Morning Harvest Chenin Blanc had a light nose and flavor and light acid; suitable for picnics. White Riesling, Muscat Canelli and Cabernet Sauvignon complete the list. Prices range from $6 to $14.

John Piconi Winery • T$ CT ⌅

33410 Rancho California Rd., Temecula, CA 92390; (714) 676-5400. Daily 10 to 5; MC/VISA. Most varieties tasted for a $1 fee (applied toward wine purchase). Small picnic area. Informal tours. Wine logo and specialty food items.

Dr. John Piconi began the wine business in partnership with Vincenzo Cilurzo, then started his own operation in 1982. The tasting room was opened just recently. He picked a good spot for his Spanish style facility, on a high ridge with 360-degree views of the valley.

One gets a quickie tour en route to the tasting room, for the path follows a catwalk past the winery's stainless steel and wooden tanks. Windows in the small tasting room take advantage of the valley view. Outside, a single picnic table perches in the shade of the tile-roofed building.

Tasting notes: Chardonnay, Carmine (a Cab-Merlot hybrid), Petite Sirah and a couple of white blends comprise the list. Our choices were the Country Cuvee, a soft, rich blend of Chardonnay, Sauvignon Blanc and Riesling; a lush, full-flavored three-year-old Carmine; and a three-year-old Petit Sirah with a fine berry nose, big berry flavor and enough tannin to encourage aging. Prices range from $5.39 to $10.

Mount Palomar Winery • T ⌅

33820 Rancho California Rd., Temecula, CA 92390; (714) 676-5047. Daily 9 to 5; MC/VISA. Most varieties tasted. Good selection of giftwares, specialty foods, picnic fare and deli items. View picnic area.

One of Temecula's earliest wineries, Palomar was established by John Poole; it has won an impressive number of awards since its creation a decade ago.

It's an attractive place, on a ridge and tucked behind a hill, out of sight of the busy Rancho California corridor. A multi-gabled Spanish facade hides the business-like winery and picnic tables have been placed under just about every available tree. The tasting room is done up in white stucco and barn board—a nice effect.

Tasting notes: Whites dominate the list, and we found most to be full bodied with nice herbal undertones. Among our favorites were a Paloverde Dry Semillon, spicy with a hint of oak; and a soft and silky barrel-fermented

Chardonnay. A four-year-old Cabernet Sauvignon was peppery with good berries and a soft tannic finish. The solera-style cream sherry was rich and nutty, among the better we've tasted. Prices range from $6 to $10.

Baily Tasting Room • T & T$

33833 Rancho California Rd., Temecula, CA 92390; (714) 676-9463. Wednesday-Sunday 10 to 5; MC/VISA. Most varieties tasted free, 25 cents for some. A selection of wine logo items. View picnic area.

Housed in a hilltop bungalow, this tasting room was opened in late 1990 by Phil and Carol Baily. They wanted to spare visitors the bumpy drive to their winery on Pauba Road (see listing below). A small picnic area under a shady arbor takes advantage of the valley view.

Tasting notes: The brief Baily list consists of Chardonnay, a Sauvignon Blanc-Semillon Montage, Riesling, Cabernet Blanc and Carmine. We preferred the fruity, nutty Chardonnay with a nice crisp finish; the Montage, with its interesting herbal-dusky flavor; and a spicy, complex dry Mothers' Vineyard Riesling. Prices range from $6 to $10.

Vintners choice: "Our two styles of Riesling—dry and off-dry, and our Montage," says Carol Baily.

Clos du Muriel Winery & Vineyard • T$ GTA

40620 Calle Contento, Temecula, CA 92390; (714) 699-3199. Daily 10 to 5; MC/VISA, AMEX. Most varieties tasted for $1 fee. Good selection of wine logo and gift items. Picnic area; tours by appointment.

This is one of the valley's most appealing spaces, inside and out. Clos de Muriel is housed in a large designer barn, accented by bits of Bacchus in leaded glass windows. The interior is a great open space of massive laminated beams and winery paraphernalia. The tasting room and gift shop blend into one end, with no partitions to clutter the open feeling. Gift items are scattered about on barrel heads, drawing browsers into the winery. To shop is to tour.

The facility was assembled in the mid-1980s as Britton Cellars, then purchased in 1989 by Joshua Wines, Ltd. The Clos de Muriel label began appearing in 1990.

Tasting notes: The wines are uniformly excellent, with good body and complexity in both whites and reds. Moving down the list: Sauvignon Blanc was fruity and herbal; Chardonnay was lush, satiny and crisp, one of the better we've tasted in the state; a four-year-old Cabernet was peppery and mellow, with soft tannins; two-year-old Cabernet Franc exhibited lush berry flavor and a spicy finish. White Zin and white Cab complete the list. Prices range from $8.50 to the mid-teens.

Vintners choice: "The Chardonnay, with a creamy pineapple flavor and buttery finish. Also, the Sauvignon Blanc and Cabernet Franc," says winemaker Tom Di Bello.

Cilurzo Vineyard and Winery • T ST

41220 Calle Contento (P.O. Box 775), Temecula, CA 92390; (714) 676-5250. Daily 9 to 5; MC/VISA. Most varieties tasted. Giftwares and a good selection of specialty foods. Self-guiding tours. Picnic tables near winery.

Vincenzo and Audrey Cilurzo are the senior members of the young family of Temecula winemakers. They planted their vines in 1967 and have raised both grapes and children here. Daughter Chenin is a now bi-lingual tour guide for Domaine Chandon in the Napa Valley, while son Vinnie has remained at the home front, sharing winery chores with his parents.

This is a world apart from the glitter of Hollywood, where Vince has worked for decades as a highly respected lighting director. He has an Oscar to prove his skill, and the tasting room walls are papered with photos of stars who've been placed in his limelights. In true Hollywood fashion, he and Audrey met on the set of the Roy Rogers show.

The rambling winery, tasting room and gift shop run together in a pleasantly inviting scatter. Visitors are encouraged to follow a self-guiding tour for one-on-one encounters with filters, vats and barrels.

Tasting notes: Tastings are conducted in a sit-down classroom style, often by son Vinnie. The Cilurzos produce the best reds in the valley—unfiltered, with big body and complex flavors. We liked a lush, herbal Merlot with a soft finish; a peppery medium-bodied Cab with a nice tannic nip at the end; and an outstanding six-year-old Petit Sirah, a bold and black wine with enough tannin to carry it into the next century. Sauvignon Blanc, a nice barrel-fermented Chardonnay, Chenin Blanc, Muscat Canelli and a rich, late harvest Petit Sirah complete the list. Prices range from $6.50 to the mid-teens.

Vintners choice: "We're particularly noted for our full-bodied Petit Sirah," says Vinnie.

Maurice Carrie Winery • T ⌆ 🎁

34225 Rancho California Rd., Temecula, CA 92390; (714) 676-1711. Daily 10 to 5; most major credit cards. Selected wines tasted. Extensive giftware and specialty food selection. Picnic area and children's playground.

The Carrie complex is both imposing and cheerful, an intriguing mix of French country manor and upscale American farm architecture, with an old-fashioned windmill for good measure. Lawns, landscaping, picnic areas and even a kiddie land complete this inviting picture. The cheery tasting room is accented with beam ceilings, French windows and lace cafè curtains.

It's a safe bet that Gordon and Maurice Carrie Van Roekel are the only vintners who entered to this profession on roller skates. They retired to the valley in 1984 after successful careers as skating rink operators, then they soon became bored. They bought a vineyard in 1985, and completed their elaborate winery and hospitality center two years later.

Tasting notes: Following current trends toward light, crisp whites, Maurice Carrie has won a fair stack of awards for a young winery. The list is small: A crisply acidic Fumè Blanc, a semi-dry Sara Bella Cabernet Blanc, a fruity and clean Chenin Blanc, a light and tasty Zinfandel and a soft and herbal Cabernet Sauvignon. Prices are small as well, ranging from $7 to $9.

Filsinger Vineyards • T GTA ⌆

39050 De Portola Rd., Temecula, CA 92390; (714) 676-4594. Weekends 10:30 to 5; MC/VISA, AMEX. Most wines tasted free; $1 for sparkling wines. Wine logo gift items. Guided tours by appointment. Attractive picnic gazebo.

The Filsingers' cottage-style tasting room is one of the coziest in the Southland, an inviting Spanish colonial space with ceramic tile floors, a carved tasting counter and lazily-turning ceiling fans. A nearby picnic area is equally appealing, housed within a large gazebo. The plain, business-like winery is a discreet distance away.

This pleasant enclave is the handiwork of physician Bill Filsinger and his wife Kathy. In fact, they built much of it with their own hands. They planted vines in 1972 and started making wine eight years later. Son Eric now has a hand in things as well, as assistant winemaker.

Tasting notes: Dr. Filsinger's wines are full-flavored and complex, with the medals to prove it. He makes one of the few Gewürztraminers in the valley and it's properly herbal and rich. Others we liked were a piquant, fruity and crisp Chardonnay; a lush and complex Chenin Blanc; a spicy buttery Fumè Blanc; and a fine medium-bodied Cabernet Sauvignon, aged in American Oak. Three *mèthode champenoise* sparkling wines were tasty as well. The good doctor also produces a white Zinfandel that we actually liked. A blend of Gewürztraminer, Muscat and Cabernet give it a complexity rarely found in this infamous picnic wine. Prices are modest, ranging from $7 to the early teens.

Keyways Winery & Vineyard • T$ ⌶

37338 De Portola Rd., Temecula, CA 92390; (714) 676-1451. Weekends 10 to 5; MC/VISA, AMEX. All varieties tasted for $1 fee (applied toward wine purchase). Some wine-related gift items and picnic fare. Exhibit of Americana antiques; small picnic area.

This medium-sized Spanish-style facility is an interesting blend of winery, tasting room, art gallery and American folk museum. An impeccably restored Model-A Ford sits opposite the tasting counter; an electric train rustles overhead on a circular track. A pot-bellied stove, oldstyle kitchenware and a copper-topped tasting bar complete an American Gothic image. From an art gallery loft, one can peer into the winery, which is mostly a cellaring facility, since Keyways wines are made elsewhere.

Carl Key is one of those people who has a problem with retirement. After succeeding rather handsomely in the restaurant and liquor business, he built an elegant Spanish style mansion in this valley. Getting restless, be began growing grapes and producing wines in the 1980s, then he opened this facility in 1989.

"I keep retiring, but it never seems to work out," he grinned.

Tasting notes: Light and soft describes the Keyways style. Prices also are soft, from $7 to $9. The list includes a crisp, clean Chardonnay; a dry and fruity Sauvignon Blanc and a delicate, medium-acid Johannisberg Riesling. Misty Key is one of the more interesting wines, a dusky-fruity blend of Gewürztraminer and Emerald Riesling.

Baily Vineyard and Winery • T CT ⌶

36150 Pauba Rd., Temecula, CA 92390; (714) 676-WINE. Weekends 10 to 5. Most varieties tasted. Some wine-related gift items. Informal tours; picnic area.

This attractive little gray stucco facility is tucked into a hillside hollow above the Temecula Valley floor. A walk to the tasting room is a trip through the winery, since an open passageway leads past stainless steel vats and other vinting devices. Once in the small, inviting tasting room, you can take your selection to cafe-style and enjoy a valley view. Outside, a shaded picnic area also takes advantage of this Temecula Valley vista.

Most Baily patrons sample the wines at the new visitor center on Rancho California Road. However, we feel it's worth the additional drive, including half a mile of sandy bumps, to see where they're made.

Tasting notes and Vintners choice: See tasting room listing above.

THE BEST OF THE BUNCH

The best wine buys • John Piconi Winery, Mount Palomar Winery, Baily Winery, Maurice Carrie Winery, Filsinger Vineyards and Keyways Winery & Vineyard.

The most attractive wineries • Culbertson Winery, Maurice Carrie Winery and Clos du Muriel Winery & Vineyard.

The most interesting tasting rooms • Cilurzo Vineyard & Winery, Clos du Muriel Winery & Vineyard, Filsinger Vineyards and Keyways Winery & Vineyard.

The best gift shops • Culbertson Winery, Callaway Vineyard & Winery, Mount Palomar Winery, Maurice Carrie Winery and Clos du Muriel Winery & Vineyard.

The nicest picnic areas • Callaway Vineyard & Winery, Mount Palomar Winery, Maurice Carrie Winery and Filsinger Vineyards.

The best tours • Culbertson Winery (guided tour with sparkling wine tasting) and Cilurzo Vineyard & Winery (self-guided).

BEYOND THE VINEYARDS

What lies beyond Temecula's vineyards is the whole of Southern California, one of America's leading vacation destinations.

An hour's drive south on I-15 gets you to **San Diego,** where you can soak in the sun at the beaches, visit California's first mission, its oldest park and its finest zoo. An hour and a half north delivers you to the **Anaheim-Los Angeles** area, with multitudinous touristic offerings.

Temecula's immediate surrounds provide a few vineyard distractions as well. **Murietta Hot Springs** just to the north is a family resort offering mud and mineral baths. (It was closed at this writing, but scheduled to reopen.) **Lake Skinner** county park, immediately northeast of the vineyards, offers water sports, fishing and camping. **Lake Elsinore** to the northwest, off I-15, and **Lake Perris,** north off State Highway 215, are major water sports areas with shoreside resorts. Beyond Elsinore, State Route 74 wanders through the oaks, pines, campsites and hiking trails of **Cleveland National Forest.** It ends at the Pacific, just beyond **San Juan Capistrano,** home to the mission of the swallows.

A more direct route to *El Pacifico's* beaches is State Highway 76, reached via I-15 about 12 miles south of Temecula. The approach takes you through the wooded **San Luis River Valley,** past **Mission San Luis Rey** to the coastal towns of **Oceanside** and **Carlsbad.** Both have extensive public beaches and Carlsbad is home to the famed **La Costa** resort.

If you head inland on Highway 76, you'll encounter **San Antonio de Pala,** the only California mission still fulfilling its original role—serving Native Americans. It's on the Pala Indian reservation. Beyond is **Palomar Mountain State Park** and the famed **Palomar Observatory** with its giant 200-inch telescope.

Temecula area activities & attractions

Hot air ballooning • Dae Flights, P.O. Box 1671, Temecula, CA 92390, (714) 676-3902; Fantasy Balloon Flights, 83-701 Avenue 54, Thermal, CA 92274, (619) 568-0997; Rainbow Flights, P.O. Box 1150, Murietta, CA 92362, (800) 634-7174.

Museums and such •

Old Town Temecula Museum, 28670 Front St. Temecula; (714) 676-0021. Wednesday-Sunday 11 to 4; donations requested. Exhibits of Temecula's early Indian, Spanish and American ranching days.

Pala Mission, off Route 76 in Pala; (619) 742-3317. Tuesday-Sunday 10 to 3; mission free, small charge for museum. Mission-era relics and mineral exhibit.

Palomar Observatory museum and gallery, in Palomar Mountain State Park; (619) 742-3476; free. Astronomy museum open daily 9 to 4:30; Hale 200-inch telescope visitors gallery open 9 to 4.

Water sports • Lake Elsinore resorts, (714) 674-3171; Lake Perris resorts, (714) 657-0676; and Lake Skinner County Park, (714) 926-1541.

Wineland events • Temecula Valley Vintners Association Barrel Tasting, early February, (714) 699-3626; Temecula Valley Balloon and Wine Festival, mid-May, (714) 676-5090.

Winery touring map • ***Temecula Valley Wine Country***, available at area wineries or contact: Temecula Valley Vintners Association, P.O. Box 1601, Temecula, CA 92390; (714) 699-3626.

WINE COUNTRY DINING

The Bank • ΔΔ $

Front and Main streets, Temecula; (714) 676-6760. Mexican; dinners $6 to $11; wine and beer. Daily 11 to 9. Casual; MC/VISA. Basic smashed beans and rice place in an interesting setting—the 1912 Temecula Bank building, called "The Pawn Shop" by its rancher board of directors. High ceilings; large open space brightened by a few Mexican artifacts.

Cafe Champagne • ΔΔΔ $$$ Ø

At Culbertson Winery, 32575 Rancho California Rd., Temecula; (714) 699-0088. California nouveau; dinners $12 to $20; daily 11 to 9. Informal to casual; reservations accepted; essential for weekend lunches. MC/VISA. Stylishly modern restaurant with dishes designed to match Temecula Valley wines. Herbs plucked from a nearby garden to season the California *nouveau* fare. Dining indoors or on a patio with vineyard views.

The Silver Spoon • ΔΔ $

28690 Front St. (Third Street), Temecula; (714) 699-1015. Greek-American; dinners $7 to $10; wine and beer. Tuesday-Friday 11 to 9, Saturday 7 a.m. to 9 p.m., Sunday 7 to 3. Casual; MC/VISA. Greek specialties such as gyros in a Western-style cafe? Why not. It also serves American-style hamburgers and other homey fare, in a cute little pink dining room and on a patio.

Steak Ranch Restaurant • ΔΔΔ $$ Ø

28910 Rancho California Rd. (at I-15 interchange), Temecula; (714) 676-6788. American; dinners $8 to $15; full bar service. Daily 7 a.m. to 10 p.m.

Informal to casual; reservations accepted. MC/VISA. Attractive designer-Western restaurant with booths, ceiling fans and leaded glass. Prime rib, steak, seafood and an occasional pasta.

Swing Inn • ΔΔ $$

28676 Front St. (Third), Temecula; (714) 676-2321. Western American; dinners $7 to $12.50; wine and beer. Daily 5 a.m. to 10 p.m. Casual; MC/VISA. The sign says "World famous" and it is if Temecula's your world. Swing Inn has been getting up with the roosters and feeding folks breakfast, dinner and supper since 1927. An authentic slice of the Old West, updated with 1950s Formica. Steaks, chops, chickens and even chicken fried steak; generous portions.

VINELAND LODGINGS

Best Western Country Inn • ΔΔΔ $$$ Ø

27706 Jefferson Ave. (at I-15 Winchester exit), Temecula, CA 92390; (800) 528-1234 or (714) 676-7378. Doubles $60 to $70, singles $45 to $50, suites $85 to $115. Major credit cards. A 74-unit motel with TV movies, room phones and refrigerators; some in-room spas. Pool, outdoor spa, fireplace lounge.

Doubletree Suites Hotel • ΔΔΔΔ $$$$ Ø

29345 Rancho California Rd. (at I-15 exit), Temecula, CA 92390; (800) 528-0444 or (714) 676-5656. Doubles $69 to $109, singles $59 to $99. Major credit cards. Attractive resort complex with pool, spa and other amenities. All two-room suites; 136 units with TV movies, VCR, room phones, microwaves and refrigerators. **Harvest Cafe** serves from 6:30 a.m. to 2:30 p.m. and 5:30 to 9:30; American fare; dinners $6.25 to $17; full bar service; non-smoking areas.

Loma Vista Bed and Breakfast • ΔΔΔ $$$$ ØØ

33350 La Serena Way (off Rancho California), Temecula, CA 92390; (714) 676-7047. Doubles $85 to $115. Five rooms, all with private baths; champagne breakfast. MC/VISA. Handsome new Spanish mission-style inn on a bluff overlooking vineyards, between Callaway and Piconi wineries. Rooms nicely done in early American and California style; afternoon wine and cheese.

Temecula Creek Inn • ΔΔΔΔ $$$$$ Ø

44501 Rainbow Rd. (Highway 79), Temecula, CA 92390; (800) 962-7335 or (714) 676-5631. Doubles and singles $105 to $115, suites $135 to $150. Major credit cards. Opulent Southwest-theme resort with 27-hole golf course, tennis courts, pool and spa. Eighty-four rooms with TV, phones, safes, honor bars, refrigerators and balconies or patios. **Temet Grill** serves weekdays 6:30 a.m. to 10 p.m., weekends 6 to 10; continental-Southwest; dinners $16 to $25; full bar service; Southwestern decor; non-smoking areas.

Temecula area information source

Temecula Valley Chamber of Commerce, 40945 County Center Dr., Suite C, Temecula, CA 92390; (714) 676-5090. Send a stamped, self-addressed business size envelope for an information packet.

CONQUERING WINE LIST PANIC

You and your archrival, Watercooler Willie, are being considered for that vice presidency slot. Your boss invites you and your wife out to dinner; the bastard's testing your social graces. He's a wine aficionado but you wouldn't know a Cabernet from a cantaloupe. A guy with a spoon hanging from his vest hands your boss the wine list and—omygawd—he passes it over to you! It flashes through your mind that you have four choices:

1. Hand it back.

2. Smile stupidly at the waiter and say: "It's difficult to pick from such a wonderful selection. What would *you* suggest?"

3. Order White Zinfandel.

4. Go for it.

You didn't become manager of the Vertical Flange Department through timidity, so you decide to go for it.

Here are the five basic steps to bluffing your way through a wine list:

1. Thumb—casually—to the California wine section. It's easier to pronounce Zinfandel than *Côtes de Provence Sociéte Civile des Domaines Ott Fréres*.

2. Remember that—as a general rule—white wines are more suitable with subtly-flavored foods such as poached fish or mildly-seasoned fowl. The flavor of heartier reds will stand up to red meats, highly-spiced dishes and just about anything Italian, up to and including Gina Lolabrigida.

3. Poll your table to see what's been ordered. If it's a mix of fish and red meat, go for a light red such as a young Zinfandel, or for a more complex white like aged Chardonnay. Resist the temptation to order rosé. Make major points by suggesting that the Chardonnay shouldn't be *too* cold, lest it mask that wonderful spicy aroma. Or be Joe Cool and order a sparkling wine—to celebrate your coming promotion? (If it's from California, don't call it Champagne.)

4. When the wine arrives, the waiter or *sommelier* will unplug the thing and hand you the cork. F'gawdsake, don't sniff it! Check its little bottom to see if it's damp (meaning it was properly stored), then place it on the table.

5. Now, here's where you nail down that vice presidency. Swirl the wine vigorously, keeping the base of the glass on the table so you won't shower the boss. (If you ordered a sparkling wine, you ***don't*** swirl it, of course.) Then sniff the wine with one long, dramatic inhalation, purse your lips thoughtfully and—don't sip it!* Nod knowingly to the waiter and tell him it's fine.

**If it's a bad wine, you can tell by the smell—a pungent vinegary or sour aroma. Refuse a wine only if it's spoiled; not because you chose poorly and don't care for it.*

"The finish is long with the opening fruit tones looping back at the end to complete a rich cyclic experience."

—Description of a 1984 Beaulieu Private Reserve Cabernet

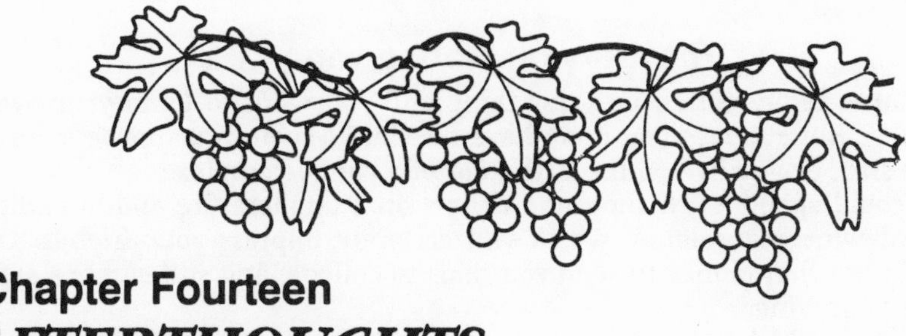

Chapter Fourteen

AFTERTHOUGHTS

Wine serving & storing tips; a winetalk lexicon

Now that you have completed your rich cyclic experience through this book, we shall loop back to the end with a few items of useful information. We begin with the basics: serving and storing wine.

Pulling the cork on food & wine rules

Wine is the only adult beverage created primarily to be consumed with food—with the exception of iced-down beer at a Texas chili cook-off. It is therefore helpful to determine which works with what. For many of us, wine *is* food, as much a part of the evening meal as the meat and veggies.

Unfortunately, some wine writers and winery brochures complicate a simple issue with a lot of specific rules about wine and food combinations. One suggestion, for instance, is that Zinfandel should be served with game. But Zinfandel can range from a light and soft young wine to bold, high-tannin, industrial strength stuff from century-old vines. A Chenin Blanc can be fruity and lush with a touch of sweetness, or dry and crisp. Do you really want sweet, fruity wine with filèt of sole?

So, you wonder as you wander through this wilderness of wines, what rules *does* one follow. The rules are simple. Both of them.

1. Match the wine to the strength of the food. Bold wines are best with highly-spiced meat and pasta dishes; delicate wines work well with mildly flavored dishes. The idea is to balance the two, so the flavor of one doesn't overwhelm the taste of the other.

2. If both spicy and subtly flavored dishes are being served (he ordered pepper steak, she 's having scallops), try a light yet lively wine. This is where rosès, sparkling wines and young reds are useful.

Serving temperatures

Here's a rule that may be *too* simple: Experts tell us to serve white wines chilled and reds at room temperature. But chilling can muffle the bouquet and flavor of a lush and spicy, barrel-fermented Chardonnay. At room temperature—particularly if it's August in Tucson—a delicate young red may lose its fresh berry taste.

Our rules? We serve crisp whites, rosès and sparkling wines at about 50 degrees, full-bodied whites and some young reds at 55 to 60, and heartier reds around 65 to 70.

The story on storing wine

So you've really gotten into this thing and you want to build your own wine cellar. But suppose you don't have a cellar? Maybe your house is on a concrete slab, or you live on the 12th floor of a condo complex.

You could spend a few thousand dollars on a temperature and humidity controlled wine mausoleum, which will certainly impress your friends. Or you could use that money to send your kids to college, and still create a safe place for your wines.

Bottles should be stored on their sides to keep the corks moist. They should be in a dark, cool place with little day-to-day temperature variation. Extreme changes cause expansion and contraction, pushing wine out through the cork and drawing in air. Remember, wine plus air equals expensive vinegar. A dark closet on the north side of the house will provide proper protection for your precious wine cachè. If your house is on a raised foundation with a crawl space, tuck those puppies down there. An old refrigerator or freezer can serve as a good, inexpensive wine vault. Don't plug it in! You just want to take advantage of its insulation.

It's wise to peel the lead foil caps off the bottles, so you can keep an eye on the corks. If you see discoloration—a sign of leakage—you'd better schedule that bottle for tonight's dinner.

What price wine?

Someone once said that a good bottle of wine shouldn't cost more than a good bottle of Scotch. Wine is less complicated to produce, and it's taxed at a much lower rate.

So why are $35 Chardonnays, $45 Cabernets and $125 *Louis Jadot Chevalier-Montrachet Les Demoiselles* on the market? Because people will pay for them. We don't question their motives, but guidebook authors—even clever ones—can't afford such extravagance.

If you follow wine-tasting results, you'll often note little similarity between quality and price. We regularly discover fine wines for under $15, and often for under $10. Only by sampling a variety can you determine which is best for you and your budget. That's one of the great advantages of wine country tasting.

Come to think of it, isn't that why you bought this book?

The great house wine heist

Do you often order house wine, because you're dining alone or your partner doesn't drink, and you don't want to tackle a full bottle?

Chances are you're not getting your money's worth, particularly if you desire two glasses to get through a meal. House wine is the single greatest profit item of many restaurants.

Let's say you order an August Sebastiani or Mondavi jug Cabernet. The restaurant probably paid $4 to $6 wholesale, and it's nicking you $3.50 a glass. A 1.5-liter bottle contains 52 ounces, from which the establishment can get 13 four-ounce servings. Multiply that by $3.50 and you've got $45.50. Not a bad return on the restaurant's investment, but a lousy bargain for you. And if you're getting Gallo Hearty Burgundy at $3.50 a pop—try not to think about it.

You're better served, literally, by ordering a half-bottle or half carafe if the place offers one. That gives you about two and a half glasses. If the place sells premium wines by the glass, they may be a better buy than the jug stuff.

In California and a few other civilized states, the law allows you to take unfinished wine home, so go for a regular bottle and ask for a brown paper doggie bag. Full bottles generally are marked up three to five times over wholesale. That's still rather steep, and we think restaurants in general charge too much for their wine. But it's better than the ten-fold mark-up on a jug. And you'll be getting a better quality wine.

A WINETALK LEXICON

As in most professions and avocations, wine world participants and enthusiasts have their own language. What follows is a glossary of general vintners' and wine enthusiasts' shoptalk.

Acid — The tartaric and malic acid in a grape that give a wine its crisp after-taste.

Appellation — The term describes a legally defined grape-growing area, under the American Viticultural Area (AVA) system. For a label to bear an appellation designation, 85 percent of its grapes must come from that area, and the wine must be "fermented, manufactured and finished" there. Dry Creek, Carneros, Chalk Hill and Shenandoah Valley are typical California appellations. France's version—much older than ours—is *Appellation d'Origine Controlee* (AOC), which dictates the types of grapes that can be grown in each area. Typically, French wines are named for their appellation, while American premiums are named for the grape varietal.

Aperitif (*a-PERI-teef*) — A drink taken before a meal as an appetizer; often a full-flavored but dry wine like Vermouth or dry sherry.

Aroma — The smell of the grape from which the wine was made.

Balance — A catch-all term describing a wine in which nothing is out of balance: not too acidic, not too sweet, not too high in tannin.

Berry — To a vineyardist, grapes are berries; berry-like describes the flavor of the fruit in wine.

Big — No, it's not a large bottle. "Big" in winetalk refers to a wine with strong, complex flavor, full-bodied and often high in alcohol. Tasters use the expression "big nose" to describe a wine with a strong aroma and bouquet.

Binning — Storing wine away, or "putting it down" for aging.

Blush — A term to describe a pink wine made from premium red grapes, usually Grenache, Zinfandel, Cabernet Sauvignon or Pinot Noir.

Body — The fullness of a wine, sometimes—but not always—referring to the viscosity or alcoholic content. A thin and watery wine lacks body.

Bordeaux (*bor-DOE*) — A large area of France that produces some of world's finest red wines, usually blends of Cabernet Sauvignon, Merlot, Cabernet Franc, Malbec, Petit Verdot and Carmenere.

Botrytis cinerea (*bo-TREET-is sin-AIR-e-ah*) — A mold that wrinkles ripening grapes, causing a concentration of sugar and flavor that produces a rich, full-bodied wine. Call "noble mold" by romantics and "noble rot" by cynical romantics.

Bottle sick — The condition of a wine immediately after bottling, when it has been filtered, shaken and other wise abused. The condition passes after the bottle has rested a few weeks.

Bouquet — The often complex smell of wine that comes from fermenting and aging, as opposed to aroma, which is the smell of the fruit.

Breathing — The practice of letting a wine stand open so it absorbs oxygen, supposedly to enhance its aroma and taste. Experts disagree on its usefulness, but it's a harmless gesture to let your wine catch its breath.

Brilliant — Not a measure of the winemaker's cleverness, but the clarity of the wine. All good wines should be brilliant. So should a good winemaker, for that matter.

Brix — The measure of sugar content in a grape, which will determine its alcoholic level upon fermentation.

Brut (*brute*) — One of the driest of champagnes.

Bulk process — Cheap method of making sparkling wine by fermenting it in large sealed tanks to capture the bubbles.

Cap — Layer of skins, pulp and other grape solids that floats to the top of a fermenting vat of grapes. The winemaker "punches it down" or pumps the wine over itself to keep it broken up.

Cave (*Kahv*) — French for cellar; "Cava" in Spanish.

Chai — French word for a small building, usually above ground, for aging wine in small oak barrels. Some California wineries now use the term.

Champagne — A term describing sparkling wine in the United States. In the rest of the civilized world, it's applied only to effervescent wine produced in France's Champagne district. Some American winemakers honor this tradition and call their product sparkling wine.

Character — Term used to describe the good qualities of a wine. A poor wine, like a poor citizen, "lacks character."

Charmat (*SHAR-mahn*) — French term for bulk process champagne-making.

Chateau — Not necessarily a house, "chateau" is commonly used in France to describe a particular vineyard.

Claret — Usually referring to a Bordeaux in England, but used to describe just about any red wine in the rest of the world.

Coarse — A full-bodied wine, but with ragged edges and perhaps a harsh aftertaste; no finesse.

Cooperage — Wooden wine containers—barrels, vats and such.

Corky — A wine that has been invaded by a disintegrating cork, giving it a bad flavor.

Crush — It's often used as a noun in winetalk, referring to the harvest and subsequent crushing of wine grapes. "We had a good crush this year," a winegrower might say.

Cuvee (*Coo-VAY*) — A specific blend of wine, as in the "cuvee" used for a particular champagne. Also refers to a vat or tank used for blending or fermenting wine.

Demijon — A large, squat wine bottle, sometimes covered with wicker.

Demi-sec — Sparkling wine with rather high residual sugar content; sweeter than sec.

Disgorging — Removing sediment that has settled in the neck of a bottle of sparkling wine; most of it is trapped in a small plastic *bidule*, placed there for that purpose

Dosage — The mix of sugar syrup, wine, brandy or other product added to champagne to make it less dry.

Dry — Crisp and not sweet or sour. In winetalk, it has nothing to do with lack of wetness.

Enology — Winemaking science; one who makes wine is an enologist. Classic spelling is *oenology*.

Estate bottled — A wine in which all the grapes came from the vintner's estate" or vineyards.

Fermentation — The reason for all this: the wine industry, winery touring, this book in your hand. It's the process of converting sugar in grape juice into alcohol and carbon dioxide by the addition of yeast.

Fining — Clarifying wine to remove the solids, usually by adding an agent such as egg white that collects them.

Finish — The aftertaste of a wine, created primarily by the acid. A crisp, properly balanced wine will have a "long, lingering finish"; a thin, watery one won't.

Flowery — The aroma of a wine more akin to blossoms than to the grapes.

Fortified — A wine whose alcoholic content has been increased by the addition of brandy or other high-alcohol beverage.

Fruity — The flavor of a wine that comes from the grape.

Generic — A wine of no particular pedigree, sometimes named for a wine-producing region of Europe, like Burgundy or Chablis.

Grapey — A wine that tastes too much like grape juice (think of Welsh's). The grape taste should be subtle and is often described—particularly in reds—as berry-like.

Grassy — A subtle grass-like flavor, sometimes found in reds; sort of herbal without the herbs. Not necessarily unpleasant.

Green — A wine not ready to drink; too young; harsh and raw- tasting.

Haut (*oh or auh*) — French for "high" or "upper", referring to wine-producing regions. Haut- Sauternes is a general term applied to a sweet white wine from upper Sauternes; the name has no bearing on quality.

Hock — Generic term for white wine, usually used in England.

Horizontal tasting — No, it doesn't mean you've sampled too many. It's a comparative tasting of the same variety of wines from different vineyards. Vertical tasting is sampling the same wine variety from different vintages.

Jerez (*hair-eth*) — A city and a wine-producing region of Spain; the birthplace of sherry.

Jeroboam — Oversized wine bottle holding the equivalent of six .750 liter bottles.

Late harvest — A wine made from grapes left on the vine until their sugar content was unusually high; produces a full-bodied high-alcohol wine, and sometimes a very sweet wine if the fermentation is interrupted to leave residual sugar.

Lees — Dead yeast cells and other sediment cast off by a young wine as it's being aged.

Light — Referring to a low-alcohol wine and currently, a low-alcohol beer.

Magnum — A container twice the size of a normal wine bottle.

Maceration — A method of softening red wines after fermentation by letting them sit with their skins and seeds in hermetically sealed tanks for up to four weeks.

Malolactic fermentation — A secondary fermentation that occurs in wine, converting malic acid into milder lactic acid and carbon dioxide. This action, often occurring in reds, helps reduce their youthful harshness to create a softer, more complex wine.

Marsala — Italian fortified wine.

May wine — Sweet white wine, sometimes flavored with leaves or herbs; of German origin.

Meritage — A term recently adopted by a group of California wineries to designate red or white premium wines blended from classic Bordeaux grape varieties. Red Merigage seems to be more common. A winery must join the Meritage Association to use the label, and must meet strict blending criteria. Fewer than 25 wineries qualify.

Mèthode champenoise (*me-thoad sham-pen-WAH*) — The classic French method of making sparkling wine, in which it is produced and aged in the same bottle.

Methusalem — King-sized glass wine container, holding the equivalent of eight ordinary bottles.

Micro-climate — Specific climatic conditions in a small area—a sheltered valley or exposed knoll—that make it ideally suited to a particular variety of grape.

Must — The liquid of crushed grapes, en route to becoming wine.

Nature — The driest of sparkling wines; in other words, one that is natural, with nothing added (although a small dosage usually is).

Noble grapes — The term—given somewhat arbitrarily—to the Cabernet Sauvignon of Bordeaux, Pinot Noir and Chardonnay of Burgundy and Riesling of Germany.

Nose — The aroma and bouquet of a wine.

Oakey — Wine—usually red—with a strong flavor of the wood in which it was aged.

Off — Slang taster's term; used to mean a wine is "off base"; not "on."

Off-dry — A wonderfully silly winetaster's redundancy for slightly sweet.

Ordinaire (*or-dee-nair*) — French for ordinary. *Vin ordinaire* is a jug wine.

Oxidized — A wine that has been exposed to air, and is starting to become vinegary.

Phylloxera (*fill-LOX-er-ah*) — Nasty little plant louse, 1/25th of an inch long, which destroys grapevines by attacking their roots. It raised havoc in America late in the last century and destroyed 75 percent of France's wine crop. The scourge was stemmed by grafting European varietals onto native American root stock, which is phylloxera-resistant.

Proof — Measurement of alcohol by volume, in which the proof number—for some odd reason—represents half the alcohol content. A hundred-proof whisky is half alcohol. Wines rarely use this figure; its measure is "percentage of alcohol"—by volume, not by weight.

Proprietary wines — Wines named by the winery owners, usually reflecting place names or some pet fetish. They're almost always blends. "Riverside Farms White" or "Workhorse Red" are examples.

Pulp — A grape's fleshy part.

Punch down — The process of breaking up the thick layer of solids that float to the top when a wine—particularly a red—is being fermented.

Racking — Clarifying a wine by drawing off the clear liquid from one cask or vat to another, leaving the lees and sediment that has settled to the bottom.

Residual sugar — The sugar that remains in a wine to give it sweetness, usually measured by percentage. In table wines, fermentation is stopped by lowering the temperature to kill the yeast cells, thus leaving residual sugar. In dessert wines, brandy is added, which pickles the yeast and stops fermentation.

Riddling — Periodically turning and gently bumping champagne bottles to work the sediments into the neck. Can be done by hand or with automatic riddling racks.

Rotten egg — The harmless but yucky flavor of hydrogen sulfide sometimes found in a carelessly made wine.

Sack — Elizabethan term for sherry; thus "Dry Sack."

Schloss "Castle" in Germany, synonymous with France's "chateau" in describing a winery.

Sec — French for dry (not sweet), yet it describes a sweeter style of champagne.

Secondary fermentation — Creating a sparkling wine by injecting sugar and yeast in a still wine and keeping it contained (in the bottle or other sealed container) so the carbon dioxide bubbles can't escape.

Sekt — German for sparkling wine.

Set — The appearance of berries after the grapevine has finished flowering.

Soft — A wine lacking harshness or rough edges.

Solera — The process of blending wines of different ages but the same type to achieve a consistency of style, commonly used to produce sherries. *Solera* refers not to the sun, but to *suelo*, Spanish for "floor," since the wines usually are blended from tiers of barrels, from top to bottom.

Sparkling burgundy — A sticky sweet wine made from nondenominational red wine. Once popular in the U.S., it has fortunately fallen from grace.

Stemmy — An unpleasant green flavor to wine, as if stems were left in during fermentation.

Still wine — Any wine that isn't sparkling wine.

Sulfuring — Sterilizing wine casks or barrels to eliminate harmful bacteria, and dusting vines with sulfur to eliminate fungus.

Sur lie aging — The technique of letting white wines rest on their yeast lees (and sometimes other solids) for several months, resulting in the release of amino acids, esters and other compounds. This adds to the wine's complexity.

Tannic — Wine with the acidic flavor of tannin.

Tannin — Organic acids found in most plant matter. In wines, it comes primarily from the skins of grapes. Reds are higher in tannin because they're usually fermented with their skins. Tannin adds complexity—and an acidic harshness—to wine. Aging mellows these tannins while leaving the full, complex flavor. Don't be alarmed, but tannic acid is used to treat leather, thus the word "tan."

Tartar — Those sparkly little crystals you may see on the underside of a cork are tartaric acid, which occurs naturally in wine and settles out during aging. If the wine is stored upside down—which it should be—the crystals settle onto the cork.

Tirage (*tee-RAJ*) — French word with three definitions: 1. the sugar-syrup yeast mixture added to still wine (*liqueur de tirage*) to begin secondary fermentation; 2. drawing off wine, usually from a barrel into a bottle; *en tirage* indicates bottles stacked for aging.

Topping — Topping off barrels of wine as it ages to replace that lost through seepage; otherwise oxygen would intrude and spoil the wine.

Varietal — A word you'll encounter thousands of times. It simply means "variety," describing a wine made from a specific grape. Cabernet Sauvignon is a varietal; rosè is not. In most of Europe, wines are blended and named for the region in which they are produced. In America, wines are named for the primary grape therein. To be a "varietal," a wine must contain 75 percent of a particular variety of grape.

Vermouth — Yes, that stuff that adds zing to your martini is a wine. Vermouth originated in Germany and is flavored with assorted herbs and spices. The word comes from *wermut* or wormwood, whose flowers are used to add aroma. Both sweet and dry Vermouths are produced in California. In Europe, sweet Vermouth is usually made in Italy and dry Vermouth is associated with France.

Vertical tasting — Sampling several wines of the same variety from different vintages, usually from the same winery. Horizontal tasting is sampling the same variety of wines from different wineries.

Viniculture — The science of growing grapes for wine production. Viticulture refers to grape-growing in general.

Vintage — The year in which grapes of a particular wine were harvested. A wine bottle can be "vintage dated" only if 95 percent of the grapes therein were harvested in that year. The harvest itself is sometimes called the "vintage."

Vineyard designated wine — A varietal named for the particular vineyard where the grapes are grown; 95 percent of the grapes must be from that area.

Vitis labrusca — The American grape, found growing wild and used unsuccessfully in early attempts at winemaking. Its root stock, however, proved resistant to deadly phylloxera, so it became the base for many premium grapes.

Vitis vinifera — The source of most premium grapes; the vine grew wild in Asia Minor and was cultivated throughout the Mediterranean.

INDEX